Praise from around the Northwe
regional gardening advice.

From Creston, British Columbia:

"Thanks to you, I had no trouble growing anything this year, which is gratifying since I am the family black thumb. Your good, practical, easy-to-understand information and wisdom . . . gave me one successful, enjoyable garden."

From Lebanon, Oregon:

"Thanks for a book that can be understood by someone who knows absolutely nothing about gardening. Thanks for a book that entertains while it teaches, and delivers what it promises. Thanks for a book that convinces readers that they really can do it. And thanks for a book that literally changed my life."

From Arcata, California:

"Steve Solomon's organic gardening book is like a bible to me. The man is an extremely talented writer. He is witty, knowledgeable, communicative, and right on track."

From Harbor, Oregon:

"After bumping our noses around the garden for four years, at last we are having great success after following your suggestions. Just wanted to say thank you."

From Scio, Oregon:

"This is our fourth year using your gardening direction, and we have nothing but the highest praise for the results. Any problems can be traced to failure to follow instructions, especially regarding planting times. In most cases, though, the problem is what to do with so many vegetables. I've cut down our garden size, but we still have an embarrassment of riches. Thank you—you have our support!"

From Snoqualmie, Washington:

"I must take a moment to thank you for what you have done for gardeners in this area. I hope it won't sound excessive if I say you have revolutionized my garden thinking. . . . Thanks to you, my family will be eating better every year."

From Lynnwood, Washington:

"I just wanted you to know what a wonderful thing you have done for me. Every day after work I go home to a gardener's paradise, where I renew my spirit, fill my tummy, and replace my smiles. I thank you for my sanity. You have made my garden a success, and secured another devoted fan."

GROWING VEGETABLES

WEST OF THE CASCADES

Steve Solomon's Complete
Guide to Natural Gardening

Sasquatch Books
Seattle

Library of Congress Cataloging-in-Publication Data

Solomon, Steve.
    Growing vegetables west of the Cascades.

    Rev. ed. of: Growing organic vegetables west of the
Cascades.
    Includes index.
    Bibliography: p.
    1. Vegetable gardening—Northwest Coast of North
America.   2. Organic gardening—Northwest Coast of
North America.   I. Solomon, Steve. Growing organic
vegetables west of the Cascades.   II. Title.
SB324.3.S67 1989   635'.0484'09795   89-4319
ISBN 0-912365-20-X   CIP

First edition published in 1981 as *The Complete Guide
to Organic Gardening West of the Cascades*; second
edition published in 1985 as *Growing Organic
Vegetables West of the Cascades*.

Edited by Maja Grip
Design by Fran Porter Milner
Cover art by Jean Emmons
Interior illustrations by Fran Porter Milner

Typeset in Caslon
by Weekly Typography & Graphic Design, Seattle

Sasquatch Books
1931 Second Avenue
Seattle, Washington 98101
(206) 441-5555

Other regional gardening titles from Sasquatch Books
    The Year in Bloom
    Three Years in Bloom
    Winter Gardening in the Maritime Northwest

Contents

contents

Introduction

*The cheapest experience
you can get is
second-hand experience.*
—My father's favorite saying

Introduction

This book is a hybrid, the consequence of crossing two or more horticultural trends. In the seed world, if I wanted to give you a rapid sketch of the hypothetical lettuce variety "Fastbowl," I might ask you to imagine a cross that combined the intense maroon color and rapid growth of Red Salad Bowl with the broad, frilly leaves of Slobolt. To quickly show you how my book approaches food gardening, I must say it combines organic gardening with the best of an "establishment" scientific outlook.

I was bitten by the gardening bug during a six-month sabbatical from my teaching job when I worked on an Israeli cooperative farm. Upon my return, I changed life-direction. I gave up elevating the young savages, started a small business in Los Angeles and subscribed to a "wish book"— Rodale's *Organic Gardening and Farming* magazine. The business flourished, and I soon bought an old suburban house on an acre of ground to indulge my new interest. Serious about gardening right from the first, I built a collection of old *OGF*'s going back five years, read every garden book in print (or in the public library, at least) and found myself mostly agreeing with agriphilosophers like Sir Albert Howard, the father of the organic farming movement, and the German metaphysician and founder of biodynamic farming, Rudolph Steiner.

After a few years, my huge garden was the talk of the neighborhood, and I found myself frequently giving advice over the fence. Too soon to develop much perspective, I wrote an embarrassingly naive garden guide called *California Vegetable Growing*, the start of what was to become my series of regional gardening books. Perhaps fortunately, it did not sell well.

My first book stated emphatically that the *only* way to grow healthy, bug- and disease-free vegetables was to till in loads and loads and loads of organic matter, a practice *OGF* repeatedly assured us would build up any old claypit or gravel pile into a veritable "garden of eatin'." Today, I don't think that's necessarily the truth. In *California Vegetable Growing*, I also speculated that our agricultural college research system might be in collusion with the chemical industry and perhaps the medical profession to destroy the very foundations of our society's health. These days I get along pretty well with the Extension Service folks (though still not with the croakers).

I might have remained a true believing, capital-O Organic garden writer, but the novelty of self-employment faded, and having a pocket unnecessarily full of money seemed pointless. So I cashed out and moved to a Lorane,

Oregon, homestead where I soon wrote a second, slightly less naive, regional garden book (the forerunner to this one) and started a mail-order garden-seed business. Both book and business were focused strictly on gardeners west of the Cascades. While writing organic gardening books tends to bring in occasional letters of praise from avid readers, it seems that founding a highly successful from-the-homestead mail-order business typifies one class of American dream. Consequently, the hamlet of Lorane, Territorial Seed Company and I all became somewhat famous in the maritime Northwest.

The business grew fast, and within a few years 100,000 mail-order catalogs and several thousand copies of my second book (revised and enlarged) were going out every year. Back in came several letters a day demanding an answer to this or that garden problem. To answer these queries responsibly, I had to learn a lot more than I already knew. The richest source of regional horticultural information was Oregon State University, but spending one long afternoon talking to Horticulture Department professors about beginning some formal study was enough! I was too old and had for too long been successfully in charge of figuring things out for myself to put up with college. But I did come home from OSU with the course outline and bibliography for a degree, and several armloads of texts. I started studying seriously and after about a year I awarded myself an informal B.Sc. Hort. This was the start of my own hybridization.

Back when I was a capital-O Organic gardener, I also believed that hybrid seeds were "of the devil" and that open-pollinated seeds were virtuous. I was convinced that hybrid varieties were less nutritious, wouldn't grow well without artificial fertilizers and were more susceptible to insect and disease predation if not sprayed with poisonous substances. I also thought the multinational corporations might be conspiring to monopolize the world's food supply by making everyone dependent on the hybrid varieties they controlled—thus eliminating people's ability to save their own seed. They might further, I thought, be plotting to breed hybrid varieties that would grow only when sprayed with patented chemicals produced by subsidiaries of those same corporations.

When I started selling seeds by mail, the first catalog forthrightly expressed these popular capital-O opinions, and virtuous Territorial Seed Company offered mainly open-pollinated varieties. But those tricky multinational seed companies that supply the entire garden-seed trade kept slipping small packets of their best hybrid varieties into the trial samples I requested; each year, I had the chance to grow hybrid and open-pollinated vegetables side by side. The differences were so remarkable that even my most firmly held prejudices crumbled against the evidence of hybrid superiority. Gradually Territorial's catalog listed more and more hybrid varieties, and its statements about the virtues of open-pollinated varieties became milder and then disappeared altogether. I also came to understand that raising seeds is not sufficiently capital-intensive and is far too international to become an oligopoly—and without a severe restriction on the number of players in an industry, no serious scheming is possible. Try as they might, the seed growers aren't going to be able to fix the game any more than the personal-computer makers are.

I like to be proud of what I do. Running a regional seed company responsibly meant sifting through the thousands of varieties available from a world-wide market to find the highest-quality, best-adapted ones most suitable to the garden, so I grew a serious trial ground. Varietal trials consist basically of comparison plots, where (under the influence of those ag. school texts I'd been studying) I started to experiment a bit with fertilizers and sprays as well. I confess I fell so far from grace as to painstakingly compare chemical fertilizers and pesticides to organic fertilizers and natural pesticides. I was quite surprised to discover that there were more similarities than differences between chemicals and organically acceptable amendments and sprays. I concluded that fertilizer was an inevitable necessity for growing vegetables, but that organic materials made better fertilizer than chemicals did. I also concluded that pesticides were rarely necessary in an intelligently run garden, and when they were, for the health of those eating the food, natural ones were far more desirable.

Knowing both sides of the story, I have remained an organic gardener. But I have become "small-o organic," with professional experience that has made me overcome serious limitations common to most capital-O Organic believers and to garden writers in general. Because of my time in the seed business, I now fully appreciate the importance of correct varietal selection and top-quality seed. Being Mr. Answerman with a hort background, I have discovered that the whole country is not like my back yard. I now know that climates cannot be separated from the soils they create, and that soils differ significantly from place to place. Each soil type in each climate demands different management. There is no easy answer like, "Incorporate lots of organic matter and everything will grow great." I know that every district has a different ecology where the pests will vary in kind, severity and handling. I have even transcended the traditional antagonism between the organic gardeners and extension Service experts and discovered that *much* of what is taught in ag. school is true. And I don't mind telling the extension agents so right off, which smooths down their feathers mighty fast once they find out I'm not only sympathetic but can also adroitly sidestep the ritual arguments they use to prove organic gardeners wrong. After all, we're both just trying to help folks grow food better.

In sum, my progression as a garden writer has gone from revealing the simple secrets of sure success—"You do exactly what I do in my back yard"—to attempting to help readers come to think intelligently about raising food at home, so they can solve their own unique problems as they occur.

Needless to say, some of my old capital-O "friends" are upset with me.

But I admit I'm a rather changeable fellow, which can be alienating to old friends. I become intensely excited about my current interests, but go from one thing to another every few years. Before I learned that I could create my own employment, I worked as a carpenter, warehouseman, paste-up artist and high-school history teacher; I was also a serious student of the martial arts and lived for extended periods abroad. I philosophize about life and then act on my conclusions. I like my own company better than most other people's; usually I'd rather meet the authors of fiction through reading their novels than visit with neighbors or friends. I don't enjoy tricky games, subtle dishonesty, office politics or using people as though they were production units.

This brings me to the other line or strain that runs through this book. This lifetime I've increasingly come to value simple virtues like self-sufficiency, independent living and natural hygiene. Like a farmer, I believe in producing the necessities for my family's economic survival at home and doing it outside the marketplace as much as possible. Since there's no way to homestead in the United States without being part of the cash economy to some extent—if only to pay county land taxes—I choose self-employment (like writing this book) as the lesser of two evils. But I don't enjoy many aspects of doing business on Earth.

At age 35, when I cashed out from Los Angeles to homestead in Oregon, I sold a very profitable small business. I was free and clear on five rural acres, had no great need for money and actually hoped to avoid business relationships as much as possible. Territorial Seed Company was conceived as merely a part-time affair—one that wouldn't require other employees and that would expand slowly to eventually serve at most 2,000 serious gardeners interested in obtaining exotic imported varieties for growing complete year-round gardens west of the Cascades. It did not work out that way. I had no idea how great the demand for a responsible regional garden-seed company would turn out to be—and I did not anticipate how much unpleasantness would be involved in trying to buy seed I could feel proud to sell.

In 1979, when I was first setting up Territorial, I asked Rob Johnston (the founder of Johnny's Selected Seeds) which suppliers of his could be *fully* trusted. After a moment's reflection, his laconic Maine answer was a slightly disappointed, "None of them." He also said that if I always complained loudly when shafted, I'd end up getting more good seed and fewer sweepings off the seedroom floor.

Buying seed frequently made me feel disappointed in humans. I can hardly conceive of another business where subtle frauds and deceits are more possible than the garden-seed trade. Even on the closest inspection, one bag of seed looks much like another. Without growing out a seed purchase to maturity, what can you know about its potential except its ability to sprout in a laboratory? Thus comes about one seed-trade term: the "race horse sample." That's the free packet sent for trial that just exploded from the ground and speedily grew perfect, uniform plants, *but*, when I decided to include that variety in my catalog, wrote some dynamite copy expressing my enthusiasm for it and ordered a big bag of seed, turned out to be not quite the same stuff. That wouldn't have been so bad but for the fact that I didn't find out I was fooled by a race-horse sample until after I'd already sold that seed to thousands of people—who trusted me. Fortunately, I discovered that some suppliers were reliable *most* of the time, and once I learned which ones I could pretty much depend on, most of my seed purchases grew what I had been led to expect. But no matter how skillful I became, the big boys always had a new wrinkle. (I'll tell you a lot more about how *you* can improve the odds of buying good seed in Chapter 5.)

As Territorial relentlessly expanded, some very aware merchants began to demand seed racks. At first, our racks were few in number and mainly in "natural" stores or co-ops where the management appreciated what the company was all about. But as the business grew, I increasingly came in contact with owners of garden centers. Some of these retail merchants were fine people, motivated by a desire to help others enjoy their gardens; they were happy to put up with the extra trouble and lower profit margins they had to accept to sell Territorial seed. But others only wanted to make as much profit as possible by taking every advantage of anyone they could—including me. Again, most disappointing!

Though I had originally intended the seed company to be tiny, it mushroomed into the largest employer in Lorane (no great shakes in a community of a few hundred), with local families depending on me to provide seasonal labor in the seedroom and about 20,000 regional gardeners depending on me, too. Not only was I unsure whether I wanted a big business, but it took too many years for the seed company to become tangibly profitable—a fast-growing business started on a shoestring requires the reinvestment of virtually every cent. (Fortunately, I had a trial ground full of food and believed in simple living.) After five years of hard work, I began to see some serious take-home money on the horizon and could afford to pay attention to my frustrations. Feeling "burnt out" by devious suppliers, unethical seed-rack holders and three years with virtually no discretionary money, I excused myself from growing variety trials one summer and took the family to the Fijian islands in the South Pacific for a five-month sabbatical. I thought I'd let the passage of time clear my head and see how I felt about the business when the journey was over.

Fiji changed us in surprising ways. The independent poverty of the Fijians was inspiring. These dignified people live as serenely and healthfully as one can on Earth—and with very little income. Fijians actually enjoy a far higher degree of economic security than most North Americans, because they fish and garden-up virtually all their own food, living on tax-free land they cannot lose or sell because their personal allotment is granted on the basis of need from extended-family or clan landtrusts. They can build their own tidy houses from materials available at hand, require few clothes in the mild islands' tropical climate and *need* little that cash buys. Consequently, the Fijians' profound economic security creates a pervasive atmosphere of generosity and benevolence rarely seen on Earth.

It felt very good to be in Fiji. The big, broad-shouldered men stride along confidently, though they might not have five dollars to their name. The women are strong and proud. When you meet adult Fijians of either sex on a quiet street in a town, they smile broadly and greet you with an emphatic *M'bula!*, which means more than hello. *M'bula* means something like "Health and well-being to you!" If you walk in the country, Fijian people sitting in front of their houses will almost invariably invite you in for a drink and conversation and are genuinely interested in meeting someone from abroad. Fiji is also a very safe place, with an accepting culture and little serious crime. Confronting Fiji, I had to wonder: why not live more that way myself? At that moment, I realized Territorial Seed Company had already grown large enough that I could sell it and our property and create a self-sufficient homestead in Fiji (or maybe Costa Rica or Oregon), very modestly financially independent. I jokingly called this proposed level of wealth "financially independently poor."

Introduction

We returned to Oregon primed for a major life change. After a few months back in harness, I still felt like going back to live like a Fijian, so we sold the business to Tom and Julie Johns, two fine young enterprising folks who had been customers of mine from the beginning. But we never made it back to Fiji. After traveling for about two years, looking for the ideal location to homestead in independent poverty, my wife, Isabelle, and I found ourselves back in Oregon, but this time convinced by experience that western Oregon is the best place on Earth for us— and not significantly more costly than Fiji. Today, I live right on the Umpqua River, in a county with low land taxes. We produce the greatest portion of our food year-round, fresh from a bottom-land garden; to live that way, we've intentionally adjusted our dietary habits to suit what the climate will produce. We have grown to have even less personal need for money and little interest in having most of the stuff Americans believe is necessary to live the good life. Most of what we do want cannot be bought with money.

Over the years I have come to believe in simple, independent living, and I think our world would be a much better place if more of us tended to our gardens instead of slaving in the marketplace for lucre's sake. So for my benefit and yours, I'd like to share with you some of the skills and attitudes it takes to live that way. Through three previous revisions going back 10 years, I've been working at creating a complete and honest guide to help you conveniently grow as much of your own garden food as possible, 12 months a year, naturally, simply, practically and effectively.

You don't have an ordinary garden book in your hands. It will ask you to think about gardening in what may be unsettling ways. If you'll but follow me through the subject, I think you'll end up with a much more profound understanding of growing your own food. I believe this book, like many hybrids—plants, animals and cultures—expresses the better traits of its parent philosophies. And it's still pretty much organic.

Botany 101

But he will survive,
in this world of competition.
—Bob Marley, "Natty Dread"

People seldom do anything without making a problem out of it. We bumble along, not quite succeeding at this, failing at that, constantly wondering if we should be doing something else, and always ready with justifications for our lack of success. When we encounter those rare individuals who don't create soap opera lives, their clarity shines. We can't help but admire the soulful singer, the runner who runs with heart and soul, or even the simple gardener who really and totally gardens for all he's worth. I have exactly the same admiration for my giant savoy cabbage, proudly showing off its September perfection.

I prefer plants to people. To me, plants outshine all but the top 5 percent of humans because they invariably put forth their very best effort to be the most they can possibly be. Even civilized garden vegetables can be counted on to be completely honest. And plants don't kid themselves about the state of the world, substituting fantasy for reality the way we humans do.

There's a strong theme in Anglo-Saxon culture that the world should become a place of sweetness and light. When world news reporting makes this illusion impossible for us to maintain, we say that at least our country is a civilized place. And when the media present the bare truth about our government, our politicians, our major corporations and poor inner cities, we fearfully retreat to our park-like suburban neighborhoods, to the illusion that everything is under control.

Well, beautiful though they appear, plants and gardens, even the ones growing in suburbia, are not full of sweetness and light. Part of Earth's highly competitive life system, each and every plant is fiercely struggling for survival. If gardeners do not referee that competition, they're not going to have much success. The garden changes from a scrawny weed patch into a thing of beauty only when the gardener directs the survival struggles going on in it.

Plants can be considered as all sorts of things depending on who's doing the considering: from cute little spirits each and every one, to individual manifestations of a great "cabbage" entity or "fir tree overmind," to life forms without consciousness. I think the most successful growers of plants will think of them as genetically programmed solar-powered chemical factories, each with a similar goal—which, if it could be stated by the plant, would be something like this: to take over as much of the entire planet as possible. That sounds more like a world conqueror than a cute little pixie, and definitely is not sweet.

Plant basics

Most plants—certainly all the ones we will be concerned with in the garden—organize their survival struggles similarly. Vegetables grow by exposing large surface areas (the leaves) to the sun to serve as sunlight-powered fuel factories and mining (with the roots) the soil below for water and mineral nutrients. The stems and stalks form a supporting structure and contain the vascular system, a network of tubes to transport fuel, nutrients and water throughout the plant, just like the blood circulation in an animal.

The green parts of plants are microscopic sugar factories, synthesizing the basic fuel plants run on. Sugar is made from water extracted from soil and carbon dioxide gas taken from the air. The plant uses "sugar fuel" for the immediate needs of staying alive and may convert surplus sugar into insoluble starch or oil for more efficient storage. Some plants store lots of reserves, others merely make present-time growth with any surplus food. (If you want to experience some stored sugar, chew on the pith of a corn stalk before the pollen drops.) Sugar can also be converted into cellulose and, with a little additional raw material, into lignin—both materials plants use to construct stems and other supporting tissues.

Plants need more than sunlight, water and carbon dioxide to live and grow. The entire plant, including the roots, must breathe oxygen, just like an animal. And like people, plants can't live on sugar alone—so the roots must pull in small quantities of various other elements required to perform other aspects of plant chemistry. Most gardeners learn early on about nitrogen, phosphorus and potassium—the NPK of fertilizer analyses—but plants also need numerous other nutrients. Scientists have isolated about 24 separate vital plant elements, including the big three, and sulfur, calcium, magnesium, manganese, molybdenum, boron, zinc and so on. There are probably others beyond the ability of Science to be certain of. The complex chemistry of plants can occur only at a certain range of temperatures, and as is true of most chemical reactions, as the temperature increases, so does the speed of reaction. All things being equal, plants grow faster when it is warmer, unless it gets too hot.

A plant's primary and immediate concern is gaining and maintaining access to light, air, water and nutrients. In nature, wherever these factors are present within the range of quantities and qualities plants can adapt to, there on exactly that spot will already be growing the most perfectly adapted wild plant uniquely suited to those conditions. In other words, if a particular species could be growing there, it will be there already.

Competition for space and resources spawns a multitude of survival strategies. Trees first grow tall and strong, building up huge food reserves over many years, delaying their reproduction until they gain height and capture light. Then they make jillions of seeds that can travel long distances as they fall to earth. Lettuce spreads broadly and thickly at first, quickly shading out competing seedlings; after its space is thoroughly under control, it stores up some reserves in a thick juicy stem, then uses its reserve food to suddenly bolt high above any remaining competitors and make seed—all in one year. Some vines grow thinly, interspersed with their neighbors; others climb all over the competition and shade it out. Some species root deeply and draw on resources below the reach of their competitors. Some biennials store up food and nutrients one summer and then spend them furiously the next spring as they shoot up a tall flower very early, completing their reproductive cycle before the competition can even begin.

Each competitive strategy has its own particular beauty. If there is a harmony in nature, it is to be found in the beauty of the battle, and is more likely to be fully appreciated by the martial artist than by the pacific spiritual seeker. The basic prize in this game of life for all plants and animals on Earth is continued possession of the token we call a body and continuation of the species to which we belong. Only *Homo sapiens*, of all life forms, *may* have the potential to transcend struggle and live harmoniously on Earth. But we haven't achieved that yet, and I'm not holding my breath until we do.

Under the stiffest possible competition, wild plants have acquired pro-survival traits that make most of them poor table fare. They tend to have thick, strong cell walls that give them tough stems and leaves. Bitter, unpalatable flavors discourage would-be consumers, as do assorted unpleasant chemical contents. Requiring fewer nutrients may permit a species to thrive in poor soil, but also force it to develop smaller plants with a woody composition. Large numbers of small, hard seeds widely broadcast are more likely to sprout before rotting or being eaten by animals than are a few fat tender ones. In the maritime Northwest, wild species best suited to our leached soils mainly consist of coniferous trees, with grasses and certain minor species here and there. Few of these native wild plants are much good for people to eat.

Improving on nature

Unless settlers from outer space brought some of their own plant species with them, the first human agriculturalists gradually developed vegetables from wild plants by breeding them for succulence, flavor, uniformity and nutritive value. American horticulturalist Luther Burbank observed that when he took a wild plant into his garden it immediately responded to cultivation by growing many times its wild size. He also noticed that wild plants seemed to "know" they were being taken care of, because within a few generations, the plants would cooperate with their grower by trying to become what the cultivator wanted them to become. Burbank's system of plant breeding involved first studying the wild species in all its many variants to see what potentials the species naturally had, and then visualizing—strongly, clearly and continuously—exactly what he wanted that species to become. If Burbank kept that visualization in mind as he worked with the species, and in each generation propagated only those individual plants that contained even more of the traits he wanted, the species would eventually be exactly what he envisioned.

Burbank's method sounds very primitive compared to the scientifically mathematical procedures developed by his contemporary, Austrian botanist Gregor Mendel. Interestingly, Burbank said he understood Mendelian genetics and that he believed it worked and was True, but that he personally did not prefer to be a statistician. Burbank bred an amazing assortment of new and improved varieties and even some new species with a more intuitive system that suited his genius.

Burbank noted that certain general changes inevitably occur when a wild plant is cultivated. Root systems become less extensive because crops are fertilized, perhaps watered, and certainly protected from competition by weeding and by thinning surrounding plants. A portion of the plant's energy can be then diverted away from root development and redirected by the breeder into thicker, juicier leaves, pods or stems, larger flowers, bigger, sweeter fruit, tastier seeds. Protected by the gardener, vegetables do not need the same degree of vigor required to compete in the wild. So vegetables can be inbred, which emphasizes desirable traits and makes the variety uniform at the expense of vigor.

Unfortunately, having become less competitive and less vigorous than wild plants, vegetables do not grow well untended by a gardener. *The successful gardener's unavoidable task then must be to create much better growing conditions than are found in natural wild fields.* The maritime gardener must increase the amount of water available to the vegetables during our warm and very dry summers. The entire subject is discussed in the chapter on irrigation. The gardener must increase the low nutrient levels naturally available in our leached-out soils, and should also increase the level of oxygen in clayey soils. This complex subject is explained in the next chapter. The gardener should also select vegetable species and varieties best adapted to our maritime climate, local pests and diseases. This is covered in the How to Grow It chapter.

To weed or not to weed?

Often new gardeners doubt that vegetables need all this pampering. They soon find out differently and either change their ways, or quit gardening. One common error new gardeners make is to permit weeds in their garden. They may have heard of some gardeners who deliberately leave a few weeds to confuse insects, and use that data as a justification to avoid what seems a tedious chore. But the key phrase here is *a few*. Their error is multiplied exponentially by the fact that new garden sites are unusually full of weed seeds and require much more thorough patrolling than established plots. In the porous, fertilized, watered universe of the garden, weeds respond like Burbank's wild plants, propelled into a rush of growth they never enjoy in nature. So intrinsically vigorous are weeds that they inevitably outgrow the relatively defenseless garden vegetables manyfold. Fortunately, the gardener does not have to remove every weed from the garden—only most of them. Here is a list of the most common garden weeds in the order of their priority for control.

Grasses. Grasses have highly invasive and dense root systems. Though low-growing grasses may not overtop vegetables and compete for light, their roots rob the soil of most available nutrients and much of the water, stunting nearby vegetables. Grasses have a strong ability to grow in weak light, even when heavily shaded, and multiply rapidly through underground runners. Since established grasses don't pull out easily and yanking out large clumps can damage neighboring root systems, grasses must be nipped in the bud (actually, pulled out roots and all) if they are to be controlled. Great thoroughness and persistence are needed when patrolling the garden for grass.

Pernicious weeds. Certain weeds are very hard to eradicate because they regrow quickly from their roots or very quickly make huge quantities of seeds. Included in this group are thistle, morning glory and nightshade. These weeds should not be permitted to make seed in or anywhere near the garden. It's wise to mow a swath 25 to 50 feet wide around country gardens to prevent seed from nearby wild plants blowing into the garden. Incidentally, thistle stalks store so much water and nutrients that they have the ability to develop mature, viable seed even after a blooming plant has been cut down. They also can regrow rapidly after being hoed. Consequently, thistles should be targeted for early and thorough hoeing.

Other weeds. Any weed that grows taller than neighboring vegetables begins to compete for light. Once it gets strong light, the weed will then outgrow and stunt the vegetables. Pull these when they emerge above the carpet of vegetable plants. Any weed that begins to flower should be pulled before it sets seed. Established gardens that have been well-patrolled for a few years reward the gardener with a greatly reduced weeding workload.

A *few* weeds left around the garden will produce strong aromas, which confuse destructive insects, as well as provide homes for many beneficial species. Many gardeners like to interplant strong-smelling herbs here and there in the garden for the same purpose.

Thinning for success

It doesn't do much good to pull the weeds if the vegetables themselves are forced to compete with each other. Radishes, if not thinned carefully and early, will not bulb at all. Unthinned carrots don't develop well, unless the seed stock is so highly variable that a few uniquely vigorous individuals crowd out their neighbors, producing some good roots. When crowded, bush beans set too many small, tough, hard-to-pick pods; sweet corn makes fewer well-developed ears; heading lettuce doesn't head; etc.

I wish I could provide novice gardeners with some absolute writ-in-stone plant spacing rules to guide them, but I can't. The experienced gardener will consider many trade-offs when deciding final plant density. The very dense stands recommended by trendy French Intensive authors, if combined with double digging and super fertilization, may produce the highest possible overall yields in terms of harvested pounds per square foot of growing bed for most crops. What these Authorities don't tell you is that the percentage of deformed, small or otherwise unappealing vegetables is also high. And the amount of time needed to pick and wash the crop increases as the size of the vegetables decreases. If the most attractive, largest, easiest to harvest and best-tasting food is desired, plants should be spaced far enough apart that they do not compete with each other for light, even when fully developed. Yet there is no absolute for this either, as final vegetable size depends on variety chosen, soil conditions and the weather that year. Spacing somewhere in between these two extremes results in the highest useful yield. I recommend that the inexperienced gardener start out following the middle-of-the-road spacing suggestions given in the How to Grow It chapter.

As a general rule, it's wise to sow a lot of extra seeds and thin in three or four gradual steps over three to five weeks. This ensures a stand even if germination is low or if bad weather slows early growth and you lose a lot of seedlings to insects or diseases. I sow three or four large seeds (corn, beans, squash, melons, cukes, radish) for every final plant wanted; I sow five to 10 small seeds for every plant wanted.

During the first week or so after sprouting, weaker seedlings will thin themselves by falling prey to damping-off diseases and insects. The better-established survivors should then be thinned just enough to prevent clusters of seedlings from overcompetition. At this stage, small seedlings should stand one-quarter to one-half inch apart; big ones, an inch apart. The more vigorous individual plants will begin to stand out about two weeks after sprouting. At this point, pull out the weakest individuals, to give the strong enough growing room. After another week, a few extremely vigorous plants will probably be showing themselves, standing head and shoulders above the others. Surprisingly, it is usually best to pull these out, as any off-type (outcrossed) plant is liable to be bursting with hybrid vigor and outgrow its neighbors. But what it finally becomes may be very disappointing.

Guiding all these thinning steps is the idea that seedlings should never ever be allowed to compete with each other for light, water and nutrients. Once small seedlings are four to six weeks old, they may be considered "established" and then thinned to the desired final spacing. Larger, more vigorous seedlings such as corn, beans, squash, radish, cucumber and melon are usually well established and may be finally thinned within two weeks or so of sprouting.

The facts of light

To coddle vegetables, the grower can improve soil fertility, provide more water, control competition and remove weeds. One growth factor the gardener can do little to improve is the level of light, yet a good understanding of how light affects growth potential is critical.

Though people in temperate climates appreciate that the days lengthen and shorten, and that the "force" of the sun increases and drops with changes in season, they may not realize how much this affects plant growth rates.

Depending on a year-round garden for the bulk of my family's food supply has made me as responsive to changes in solar energy as my plants

Botany 101

The relationship between solar energy and plant growth

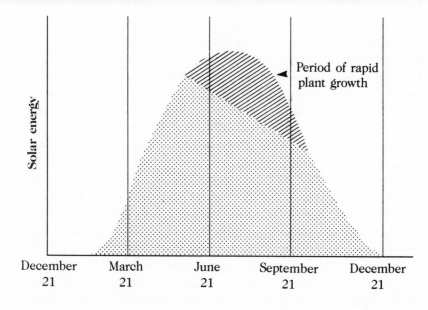

Period of rapid plant growth

| December 21 | March 21 | June 21 | September 21 | December 21 |

are. Every year about March, I begin to feel the strength of the sun again and know there's enough force in it to grow those species that can conduct their chemistry under cool conditions—and I sow peas, radishes and greens. By early April, the sun is forceful enough to permit root crops to accumulate sugars, so I plant beets, onions and carrots. A few more weeks pass and the sun feels strong—I can begin to grow the popular tropical species outdoors, crops like beans and tomatoes and corn. In mid-summer I sow for fall harvest, knowing there are still two or three months of rapid growth ahead. I start overwintered species in August, so they will gain some size before October's low light levels check their growth, but not become so big they tend to rot out in winter.

About early September I begin to mourn the loss of summer. That may seem a strange thing to do just when the summer garden is at its peak. But not only does it become difficult to get a suntan after August, the flavor of all our delicious garden fruit starts to go. Usually triggered by a short spell of unsettled weather, tomatoes suddenly lose their richness;

melons aren't as sweet anymore and the vines begin to look a little scruffy; leaves and fruit on peppers and eggplants start getting smaller. By the second week of October, plants can no longer mature fruit they've already set and root crops no longer are able to manufacture surplus sugar to store. Even if frost or rain haven't induced killing molds and mildews, fruiting plants begin to die.

Under winter light, only a very few species are able to grow new leaves. A few more barely maintain those leaves already grown. Thus winter gardens must of necessity consist largely of very hardy leafy greens. Even protected from frost in a greenhouse, summertime vegetables gradually lose leaves as the days shorten and deteriorate as their consumption of stored food exceeds their ability to make sugar under very low light levels. The only way to have producing tomatoes, peppers, zucchini, cucumbers and the like from November through March is to provide intense artificial light.

We gardeners addicted to vine-ripened tomatoes and fresh garden cucumbers might take a cue from the marijuana "addicts," and set up a legal indoor halide/sodium light system for ourselves. After a casual investigation, I think electricity cost and equipment depreciation for a 10' by 10' growing area would just about equal the supermarket price of all the tomatoes, peppers, cucumbers and a few other miscellaneous tropical species a serious summer-fruit junkie could consume. But the flavor and nutritional value of fully vine-ripened artificial light food could be much higher than supermarket fare. And you'd have the fun of growing it. The electricity might actually serve dual purposes in winter, as all the kilowatt hours driving a couple of halide/sodium lights turn into needed heat and could well lower one's heating cost significantly. And wouldn't it be amusing to have the police raid your tomatoes!

Rate of increase

Have you ever considered the speed at which plants grow? It seems on first look that most plants start out growing slowly and then pick up more and more speed as they age. They don't. What actually happens is that many plant species grow at a fairly uniform rate of speed, but the *amount* of growth increases geometrically. Not every species grows at the same uniform rate, though. And sometimes the growth rate slows or stops once the species starts fruiting or setting seed. The specific growth patterns of each vegetable family are discussed in Chapter 8, How to Grow It.

The typical pattern of growth is easiest to observe in a plant with

Botany 101

a rosette growth habit, such as lettuce. A tiny lettuce seedling seems like it will never grow, but is actually doubling in size frequently. A few days after emergence, the lettuce seedling is barely an eighth of an inch in diameter. After a time, the plant becomes twice that size. Let's call the amount of time it takes a plant to double in size the *rate of increase*. For most types of lettuce grown during the period of maximum light intensity in this part of the Northern Hemisphere (May/June/July), the time needed is about one week per doubling. The table shows how lettuce seedlings grow from one-eighth inch to a harvestable eight-inch size in about six weeks while not changing their growth rate a bit.

Growth rate of two different sowings of lettuce

Date	Doubling Rate	March 1 emergence	April 21 emergence
March 1	21 days	⅛ inch	
March 21	17 days	¼ inch	
April 7	14 days	½ inch	
April 21	10 days	1 inch	⅛ inch
May 1	9 days	2 inches	¼ inch
May 10	8 days	4 inches	½ inch
May 18	8 days	8 inches/harvest	1 inch
May 26	7 days		2 inches
June 2	7 days		4 inches
June 9	7 days		8 inches/harvest

Growth rates change with the seasons as the amount of available light energy changes. Sown in the short days of early spring, lettuce has a very low growth rate, taking two to three weeks per doubling. For this reason, early sowings don't result in equally early harvests. As the season advances, increasing light levels and longer days decrease the time needed to double. The table also shows how sowing lettuce seven weeks later in spring results in a harvest only three weeks later. Sowing later also means better germination and less slug trouble.

In September, the growth rate of all species slows; even the winter species that are hardy enough to survive frost and rain hardly grow at all. So crops for fall harvest have to be started in July to be full-sized by the end of September. Started too early, they'll mature too soon—and who wants an unharvested patch of kohlrabi rapidly turning woody when there are still tomatoes and zucchini? Started too late, the harvest will be disappointingly small.

The annual cycle of rapid and slow growth can work for the gardener. While it is critical to weed thoroughly during the months of rapid plant growth, it becomes decreasingly important as the season goes on. There is much less urgency to pull weeds that appear in established plantings after mid-August, as they are not capable of rapid growth and will not likely be able to compete effectively with large growing plants. The only time to worry about late weeds is when they are about to go to seed.

Keep the idea of "growth rate" in mind when the chapter on planning the garden comes around.

A word on tools

Weeding and thinning can be done by hand, but it's much easier and faster to do most of it with hoes. Many new gardeners don't have any idea how to use a hoe, exhaust themselves trying and decide that they need a rototiller. Tillers *are* very good for weeding between widely spaced rows over 100 feet in length, but depending on one of these noisy machines may make the gardener miss out on the singing birds and the ease and higher productivity of raised-bed gardening. (For more on raised beds, see Chapter 3, Planning the Garden.)

Actually, a properly used *sharp* hoe is efficient enough for almost any size of garden. Proof: for many years I personally hoed all the weeds in an immaculate three-quarter-acre trial ground—that's about 32,000 square feet! I worked less than an hour a day on the average, mostly during the peak period of light intensity when the weeds and vegetables were growing fastest. I think that if the garden's actual growing area (not including paths) is less than 5,000 square feet, planting in single rows and weeding with a tiller are unnecessary unless the gardener has some profound physical handicap (and if that is the case, the tiller itself may be too hard to manage).

So how *do* you use a hoe? Well, first understand that a weeding hoe is a knife-like slicing instrument, sometimes a scraping instrument—but almost never a chopping instrument. Yet most people go out and chop weeds! The chopping motion is exhausting and highly inefficient. If you examine the blade angle of a common weeding hoe, you'll find that it is set so the blade will lie flat on the ground when the handle is held comfortably, hands near your body. If it doesn't fit that way, it's because your body is not designed with the height or arm-length that the hoe-maker envisioned. The hoe blade is attached to the handle by a rod of fairly soft mild steel, which you can easily bend in a vise to correct the blade angle for your body.

Envision a common hoe. *If the blade were very sharp,* you could slice off weeds in long strokes by pulling the hoe toward you just beneath the surface of the ground—as long as the weeds were small and tender and the soil reasonably soft. If you hoed every week or 10 days, the weeds would be small and tender, and the soil's surface would remain reasonably soft. If the soil were very compacted, such as in a pathway, you could use the blade as a scraper by extending it far from you and pulling it across the soil while pushing down on the handle, cutting off the weeds at the surface. When you use a *sharp* hoe either of these ways, you develop strong wrists and hands, not a sore back and tired arms.

Ah, but there's the rub! How do you buy a sharp hoe? When the common hoe comes from the store it has the suggestion of a bevel ground into the front of the blade, but rarely is the bevel complete or sharp. Taking one of those "hoes" into the field makes the gardener think a hoe has to chop things to do any work. If I owned a garden center, I'd buy a big bench grinder and quickly sharpen every hoe and shovel that went out at the time of sale. That would make some happy customers—and would I make lots of money! I'd make a bit more by selling every hoe or shovel customer a brand-new file to keep the tool sharp.

But I'm reasonably sure you bought your tools from a garden center that did not bother to sharpen them for you. If you do not have an elec-

A word on tools

tric grinder available or don't know how to use a power grinder without burning the blade and ruining its temper, clamp the blade of a dull hoe in a vise and hand-sharpen it on the outside edge. If you don't have a vise, the hoe can be held on a porch step by standing on the handle; file while bending over it. Unlike a knife, a hoe is sharpened on only one side. The edge should be brought to a smooth 20-degree bevel—when finished, you should be barely able to cut your finger on the edge if you press hard. I suggest using a common eight- to 10-inch mill file with a good tight handle or a large and very coarse carborundum stone. I'm sorry to inform you that the first time you sharpen a new tool by hand-grinding it can take a lot of time and some sweat. And you have to really get into the motion of grinding and *concentrate* on every stroke to ensure a smooth bevel. Don't forget that old files get dull and stop cutting after a few years.

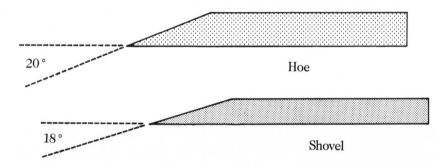

20° Hoe

18° Shovel

The steel of most inexpensive hoe blades is not highly tempered— perhaps so the blade doesn't chip on stones (the charitable view). And perhaps because home gardeners are not a "critical trade" and don't know a good hoe from a poor one (the cynical view). Soft steel will not hold a very acute angle or become knife-sharp no matter how long or carefully it is ground. When hoeing with a cheap tool, the place for your file or stone is in your hip pocket, because the edge will need touching up every hundred feet or so. A garden post is sturdy enough to prop the hoe against. Touch-up only takes a few strokes, but the time and effort taken to hone the edge is saved manyfold during the next 10 minutes of hoeing. Sharpening makes a nice break from hoeing.

Some tool manufacturers have realized that many people think edgeless hoes are to chop with, and so have responded to market demand— not as they should have, by providing sharp tools on the rack, but by making special "weeder hoes" that automatically make you lay a thin, sharp blade flat on the ground and slice off the plants at the root line. Weeding hoes that work on both the push and pull are best; two common trade names for this sort of tool are "action hoe" and "hula hoe." A few hoe-makers sell quality tools that come sharp from the factory, with well-tempered tool-steel blades that can hold a knife-sharp bevel for hours and hours of work.

Over the years I bought every new kind of hoe I saw, especially when I was in the seed business and looking for good merchandise to sell. Now I'm only a civilian, so my collection has been thinned to the best few. For general weeding in paths and between rows across raised beds, I like the Goserude "glide and groom," a push/pull with a thin seven- or eight-inch-wide tool-steel blade shaped like a propeller laid flat on the ground. Goserude also makes a very fine quality, light-weight "regular" sort of hoe with a delicate five- or six-inch blade. I've cut my finger on this one just taking it out of the factory box. For weeding onion rows and getting close to other delicate plants, I have two onion hoes, made of spring steel, three-eights of an inch wide, in a loop two inches in diameter attached to the end of a stick. Both edges of the loop are sharpened. One onion hoe is on a long stick that I work standing up; the other is on a 20-inch stick I use for close, delicate work. One of my favorites is a thinning hoe with a stiletto-like knife blade that lies flat on the ground. Both edges can be sharpened to an acute point. This blade will slice right along a row of tiny seedlings and remove only some of them, or hook out one seedling and leave another, which saves on hand-thinning. If any tool is going to contribute to the ruination of my once-flexible back, it'll be this hoe. I've also got one well-worn discount-store huge honker sort of a hoe, the kind that gets dull in a flash. What's left of this blade after so much sharpening is great for chopping off sunflower stalks or the occasional big thistle that got away from me, and sometimes for slicing out swaths of weeds between widely spaced rows. It's also good for chopping up big chunks of soil after I turn over a raised bed with a spade.

Many gardeners do not realize how much easier it is to dig with a sharp shovel. Except for the very cheap discount-store ones, the blades of shovels and spades are generally made of highly tempered springy steel, which will take and hold a much more acute edge than will common hoes. But, like hoes, they are inevitably unground when purchased. For my stoneless garden, I sharpen shovels as acutely as possible, because a really sharp edge will cut into earth like a hot knife into butter. With a sharp long-handled spade, I can loosen up a 100-square-foot raised bed 12 to 14 inches deep, use a hoe to finely chop the top four or five inches while incorporating compost, lime and fertilizer, and then rake it out to a fine seed bed—all in less than one pleasant hour. If more gardeners knew how to sharpen their tools, there'd be a lot fewer rototillers sold.

Further reading

The Secret Life of Plants, Peter Tompkins and Christopher Bird, revised edition (London: Lane, 1974).

What is a plant? What is the nature of the living system we are all part of? Those who think they already have the answer to these questions, or who would like to explore them further, are advised to read this most interesting book.

A Short Course in Soil Science

Ya got ta grow it to da max!
—Benny's favorite Grower's lore

A Short Course in Soil Science

 When I first moved to Lorane, Oregon, I did not know the town was in a small way like Willits, California—a center of marijuana profiteering. In fact, when I went out of L.A. looking for a place to homestead, I had rejected the redwoods along Highway 101 for that very reason and headed farther north. In the late seventies the strip from Willits to Eureka was a series of boom towns lazy-rich on drug profits—and though sparsely settled, it was still California, which to me means a poisoned paradise, pervasive with anxieties I can actually feel when I'm there. And I don't mean just an occasional whiff of fear, but overlapping intermeshed inescapable 24-hour-a-day anxieties simultaneously generated by millions of insecure strivers who have overcrowded the mellow climate, struggling like dogs at a medieval banquet for economic crumbs from the few truly wealthy who own virtually all of Babylon's really important means of production.

Oregon did not seem like California in either respect. I began to smile broadly as soon as I came away from California's mental field—which I can feel all the way up the Smith River and past Grants Pass. Once I was over the first big hill out of Merlin, something palpable vanished. California's pressure disappeared and I felt the real Oregon. Southern Oregon's overall emotion is one of calm, broad tolerance. I believe it comes from the general financial independence of Oregon's rural homesteaders, who create modest but secure livings harvesting timber, their family-sized logging companies successfully competing on equal terms with such economic giants as Boise and International Paper. Farther north in the Willamette Valley, Oregon's mildly prosperous farms tend to be family-size too, not like the corporate giants that dominate California agribusiness. People don't come to Oregon to get rich—just to *live*.

Lorane at first seemed yet another slice of Oregon, one where I was close enough to get to Eugene if I wanted "city" and where the land was not as costly. So I settled there, put in a big garden, learned to make homebrew, grew a winter garden, studied other money-saving self-sufficiency tricks, wrote another garden book and started a seed business. I didn't realize that in certain Oregon fringe hill communities like Williams, Deadwood and Lorane, perhaps 10 percent, in some places more than that, made a good portion of their living raising dope.

Benny was a local, hired for the day to help pour and finish the slab for my first little seed warehouse. He was small, quick, graceful and drank Bud steadily while he smoothed the concrete. There was something about him I liked, but I didn't get to find out what it was. Benny did his work and shyly left. Later, the carpenters told me Benny was a Vietnam vet—Special Forces, highly decorated, too much combat, perhaps a little psycho—and, as I could see, vaguely feared. I didn't know then that Benny belonged to one set of Growers, the carpenters to another.

Benny must have liked something in me, too. He stopped back a few months later with a cold six-pack "to inspect the slab for cracks." We became acquainted and, over the winter of 1980, drank up my homebrew as fast as I could make it. When Benny decided I could be trusted, he revealed his real business, named me Seedman and introduced me to some of the local growers. I began to discover that a lot of Lorane households containing folks under 40 grew pot.

They don't anymore. The government's war on West Coast drug production has driven all but the most incorrigible from the trade (while greatly enhancing profits for big drug importers at the expense of our trade balance). Today, isolated backcountry homesteads along 101 are bargain-priced, and many small town houses are for sale cheap without drug cash floating around to bolster the local economy.

From the first, what I liked about Benny was that he was still a warrior, still dangerous, and a profiteer, which is a sort of warrior/entrepreneur with a dash of the criminal who wants something for next to nothing, and who enjoys personal risk. I too have been a risk-taker and entrepreneur, though not one to take advantage of some legal quirk to make outrageous profits. But I like and feel safer around uncivilized, dangerous people like Benny. It's the meek fellow, the kind most ordinary people feel comfortable with, that you can't depend on when life gets hairy.

Capital-G Growing

I could tell you stories about Benny, his friends and enemies, and Lorane guerrilla farming culture. Perhaps I will someday. But I can see my editor picking up her red pencil, thinking, "Is this a garden book, or what?" All that's relevant here is that Benny taught me about capital-G Growing, which is what most successful marijuana growers did. Capital-G Growing, as opposed to merely growing, means doing everything possible to make a plant as large as possible as fast as possible while keeping it as healthy as possible. Not all marijuana growers bother to do this, because the species is really a weed with a wild plant's vigor, which means it will survive and produce even under very poor conditions. When they do Grow, it's done almost exactly the same way some gardeners Grow prize pumpkins over 100 pounds each.

In early spring, they dig huge holes on a south- or southwest-sloping hillside to get the best light; on flat ground, they pick a spot where the plant will not lose the hot afternoon sun until nearly sunset. The holes are at least four feet deep and five feet around—big enough for a fully developed root system. They tailor-make soil to go back into the hole, adding compost so it stays loose and holds air four feet down, permitting maximum root development. They blend in lime, bone meal and other natural fertilizers (chicken manure is popular) so the plant will have complete mineral nutrition. All this stuff is usually backpacked deep into publicly owned woodlands, load after load. Then as early as possible (late April to early May around Lorane), they transplant the biggest possible seedling from their greenhouse or cold frame into the hole. Started in February and grown to the max, these seedlings might already be as much as two feet tall in gallon pots.

At this point, the Organic controversy starts even among pot Growers. Capital-O Organic Growers (who are usually the hippies and counterculture folk) frequently spray their fast-growing plants with fish emulsion, seaweed concentrates and other natural hormones and witchy brews too secret to mention to the Seedman. Others, concentrating less on being good and pure and more on being practical (bikers and just plain working-class folk), foliar spray Rapid-Gro, or add it when they water. Rapid-Gro is the most expensive balanced chemical fertilizer available, with an NPK of about 20–20–20 and all known needed chelated trace minerals. Most of the Growers I knew used Rapid-Gro, bought economically in 25-pound sacks. The object of both classes of Grower is to produce the largest possible plant by providing every nutrient it can conceivably use, in the largest quantities it can handle.

Growers "get into" their plants, study the life cycle of the species and figure out how to help the plant become all it can be. They don't learn this from a book, but by a process L. Ron Hubbard called *obnosis*, which means observing the obvious. For example, Benny was unhappy because his little transplants started shortly after New Year's under fluorescent lights were spindly and had thin wobbly stems. He thought and watched and thought and finally figured out that the seedlings needed exercise to toughen up, just like they got outdoors when the wind blew. The obnosed solution: use a big window fan to jostle them around for an hour or so every day. That's real intelligence, the kind that probably kept Benny alive when 90 percent of his airborne unit failed to survive Vietnam.

Obnosis taught the Growers to change fertilizer later in the summer when flowering begins, from a rapid-growth mix to a low-nitrogen/high-phosphorus blend, because at this stage in the development of *Cannabis sativa* vegetative growth ceases and further nitrogen is not needed. To make the fattest, heaviest flowers, Organic Growers stop spraying nitrogen-rich fish emulsion and concentrate on kelp; those who supplement a good healthy organic soil with chemicals switch from Rapid-Gro to a 0–10–10 blend with trace elements.

The result of all this is a plant that in a single season grows 16 feet tall with a six- to eight-foot spread at the base, a magnificent female that after drying yields at least a pound of fragrant, seedless flowers. The flowers on such a plant will be denser, 50 percent bigger than those on a mere eight-foot plant and more potent. Of course, Growers have a powerful incentive to maximize their efforts, as the government's prohibitions have made a single 16-foot giant like the one described above worth more than $2,000, depending on the potency and flavor achieved. Despite the uselessness of their studied species or the evident lack of character exhibited when one profiteers, I must believe gardeners can learn from Benny and his Growing friends or I wouldn't have risked some readers' disapproval by even mentioning this aspect of my past.

What Benny and his friends were studying under the name Growing is the same thing crop scientists might call the "concept of limits"—the optimum management of crop species. The Growers were simply making as certain as they could that the only factors limiting the growth of their pot plants were those totally out of their control—the amount of light energy available, the atmospheric level of carbon dioxide gas and the weather.

There's not as much in it for a gardener who Grows a vegetable plant to the max. No one will pay even $20 for a 35-pound cabbage, nor could a family likely eat one that big before it lost its freshness. But with much less work than it would take to "max out" a vegetable, we can get one half as large, equally tasty and nutritious. I hope you'll be inspired by the vision of a 16-foot marijuana tree or a 35-pound cabbage or a 150-pound pumpkin, and some year get totally into at least one garden species, think about what it needs and how to help it, spare nothing and really Grow a plant to the max.

The concept of limits

The speed at which most simple life forms will grow is in direct proportion to the availability of needed growth components. If any one component is in short supply, growth will be reduced to the level of that component. Suppose plants need air, water and 15 soil nutrients; if 14 nutrients are available in abundance while one is in short supply, then the growth rate will be reduced to the level permitted by the fifteenth one. On our leached maritime soils, we can be certain that more than one nutrient is deficient. Increasing the level of scarce nutrients can cause amazing increases in growth—occasionally it takes only a few micrograms of a limiting nutrient to result in hundreds of grams of increased plant weight.

Plants are mostly water. When fully dried out, they lose 75 to 90 percent of their weight; the remainder is composed of various elements combined into complex organic substances. Carbon is the next-heaviest component. When plants combine carbon with hydrogen and oxygen, they form sugars, starches, cellulose and lignins—most of the basis of the plant. Carbon comes from carbon dioxide gas in the air, hydrogen and oxygen come from water. Rarely are these nutrients severely limited,

Factors that limit plant growth

Air | Water | Mechanical Support | Potassium | Nitrogen | Other Nutrients | Phosphorus | Organic Matter | Heat | Light

Air | Water | Mechanical Support | Potassium | Nitrogen | Other Nutrients | Phosphorus | Organic Matter | Heat | Light

The level of water in the barrels represents the level of plant growth. On the left, nitrogen is the most limited nutrient. Even though the other nutrients are present in more adequate amounts, plant growth can be no more than that allowed by the level of nitrogen. When more nitrogen is added, the level of plant growth is controlled by the next limited nutrient—potassium.

though under stress in dry soil, plants do become stunted. Conversely, in greenhouses where carbon dioxide levels can be artificially raised, growth rates can sometimes be increased dramatically. I've seen this effect in a small lean-to greenhouse near Lorane. The greenhouse, being warm, was also used to brew moonshine mash, which bubbled away in the corner in a plastic garbage can, giving off CO_2. The plants in that corner were twice the size of the rest.

Deduct carbon, oxygen and hydrogen and what remains is no less significant to the plant's health and growth, though it amounts to only a percent or two of the total dry weight. Nitrogen, phosphorus, potassium, calcium and magnesium compose the largest part of the balance and so are called the major or macronutrients. Traces of manganese, boron, copper, molybdenum, iron, sulfur, chlorine, cobalt and zinc (and in a few species, silicon, vanadium and sodium) make up the remainder of the plant's dry weight—these naturally are called micronutrients. Lack of any nutrient, macro or micro, can limit, stunt or cripple plant growth. For example, nitrogen is a major building block of proteins, but proteins can't form unless a tiny amount of molybdenum is also present. Phosphorus is the key factor in energy transfers within every plant cell. Potassium builds disease resistance, strengthens stalks, fattens seeds and greatly increases the yield of tubers such as potatoes. Magnesium is an essential ingredient in the production of chlorophyll, the substance that conducts photosynthesis and makes sugar. Iron is also essential for the formation of chlorophyll, but can't be used without some copper present. Zinc seems to be essential to the production of certain plant growth hormones.

All these nutrients are taken from soil through the interaction of the plant's root system with soil particles and soil organisms. But most of Earth's soils fail to provide an ideal nutrient balance. In fact, most are far from ideal. A few of the places where soils likely do (or did) provide extremely high and well-balanced nutrient supplies are: parts of the American and Canadian prairies; some spots in California's coastal valleys; alluvial soils along the Nile before the annual floods were controlled; alluvial soils on the Fijian island of Viti Levu along the Sigatoka River and the entire "garden island" of Taveuni, also in Fiji. Sigatoka river-bottom ground comes from a deposit of extraordinarily mineralized lava upstream; every few years a hurricane brings a flood and a new deposit of fertile river silt. Some Sigatoka farms have produced bounteous vegetable row crops for over 20 years without ever being fertilized and without rotation. The soil there is so rich that the very first time I ran my fingers through some, I felt a powerful lust to possess it, so strong I almost moved to Fiji. I suspect

Plant composition

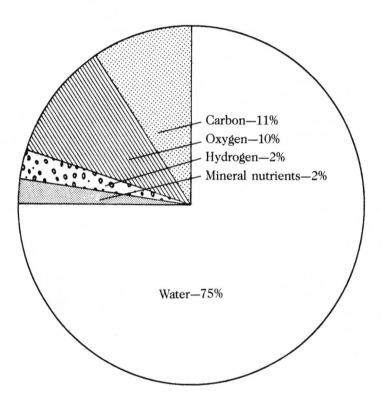

Carbon—11%
Oxygen—10%
Hydrogen—2%
Mineral nutrients—2%

Water—75%

Master Fukuoka, Japanese permaculture guru and author of *One Straw Revolution*, has also got some first-rate ground, judging by the fact that he can take two grain crops annually off his land year after year without fertilizing or rotating into pasture.

Nowhere in Hawaii are there really rich soils; most soils derived from the Appalachian mountains are low in nutrients; and virtually the entire eastern seaboard of the United States lacks really rich ground. And I can brashly state without any uncertainty whatsoever that no native soil west of the Cascades can continuously provide anywhere near the maximum possible useful mineral nutrition. Please glance ahead to page 63 and take a preliminary look at the table there. Note the wide range of possible soil fertilities.

Every year, a specific soil body releases certain predictable amounts of plant nutrients from reserves held in unweathered soil particles. Where the amounts prove insufficient for food crops, two basic approaches are used to increase them—soil management systems and fertilization. Both have their limitations.

Soil management

Slash-and-burn agriculture is an ancient soil management technique; if not overdone, it is a sustainable system on highly leached forest soils such as those in the maritime Northwest and other rain forests. Native Americans in the eastern U.S. used slash-and-burn plots before they lost their land to Europeans. The idea is to let forest growth accumulate nutrients for a while, then clear-cut a patch, burn all the nutrient-rich slash and return the mineralized ash to the soil. Leaves and other organic residues naturally deposited thickly on the site are then blended with soil, greatly accelerating decomposition. Essentially, the nutrients contained in organic matter built up by many years of forest growth are made available at one time.

Slash-and-burn fields can be extremely fertile for a few years, after which growth declines greatly. Eventually the patch must be allowed to grow forest again for a slow rebuilding of fertility and another cropping cycle. I observed how the Fijians grow magnificent gardens using this form of agriculture. Fijians have a complex and sophisticated soil-classification system, which names soils according to the number of years a patch can be used, the succession of crops it will support as the soil declines in fertility, the type of vegetation that takes over when the plot is abandoned and the number of years' regeneration required before the plot can be cleared again. Rich plots can be grown four years in seven; the poorer might only support one skimpy harvest of the least-demanding crop they know—tavioca (also known as manioc or cassava)—with over 15 years' rest in between crops.

Like slash-and-burn, rotations also increase fertility by building up what is there already. The field is put into grass, pasture or a cover crop for some seasons or years while plant nutrients accumulate. When the sod is thick enough or sufficient rotations of cover crops have been grown, the vegetation is plowed in, rapidly releasing a large nutrient accumulation. With rotations, a field too infertile to produce a high-yielding food crop at all might grow one every few years; a field not fertile enough to grow continuous food crops might grow them two years in three, or three years in five. On a field somewhat deficient in only one nutrient, sometimes all that is necessary is to one year grow a crop that has little demand for the scarce nutrient or that accumulates the scarce nutrient in a por- tion of the plant not removed from the field; the next year, grow a crop that needs the scarce nutrient. Rotations also serve to prevent build-up of disease organisms and control pest populations. Every field has its own optimum potential rotations to be discovered; many non-industrial cultures have traditional rotations that may not be scientifically optimum, but are satisfactory.

It is important for the gardener to keep in mind that fertility-building rotations are used to grow such field crops as corn, wheat, barley, oats, rice, millet, beans, peas, soybeans, clover—not most vegetables. When rota- tions are practiced in the garden, they're used to break up disease or in- sect cycles.

Fertilization

We can also bring in nutrients not already present in the soil. Tilled- in seaweed, manure or fish wastes will increase the level of soil nutrients for a time. So will leaves, dried blood, ground bones, brewery wastes, finely ground mineralized rocks, ground seashells and many other organic and inorganic substances that contain significant amounts of plant nutrients. Around 1840, a German chemist named Justus von Liebig analyzed plant ash and revealed that NPK (nitrogen, phosphorus and potassium) were the principle elements in plants. Thenceforth, farmers began producing marked growth responses by spreading water-soluble NPK. Fertilizing seems a lot more efficient than concentrating nutrients already in the soil, because there appears to be no limit to how much or how often fertilizer can be applied, allowing high-value crops to be grown every year.

Organic gardeners tend to think that manures, plant wastes, composts and other organic substances naturally contain sufficient amounts of all needed nutrients or increase the release of "hidden reserves," and that adding them to the garden inevitably results in high yields and excellent plant health. This belief is broadly correct. But if it's put into practice crudely without understanding, things often won't work out as the gardener believes they will.

Organic gardeners often go wrong when they confuse the nutrient needs of *field crops* with those of *vegetable crops*. Before Liebig, when farmers used manure and crop rotations to fertilize their fields, a few wagonloads of horse or cow manure per acre or a lush stand of clover turned into reasonably fertile soil were enough to grow good field crops: corn, wheat, barley, oats, sorghum, peas, beans, potatoes, carrots, beets or kale. But the more exacting vegetable crops, like cabbage, cauliflower, Brussels sprouts, celery, lettuce, melons, tomatoes, peppers and squash, require much higher nutrient levels: in olden days these crops were Grown by market gardeners located close to town where the freshest, purest, most potent stable and chicken manures were available. In those days, when they took a wagonload of produce to town, market gardeners never missed the chance to return with fragrant loads of choice hot manure.

Some garden writers call the vegetable crops in my second list "demanding" vegetables, while the field crops mentioned in the first list are called "undemanding" or "low demand" vegetables. No maritime Northwest soil can capital-G Grow the demanding vegetables without chicken manure, fertilizer or expertly made high-potency compost free of sawdust, straw and other carbonaceous fillers. Fortunately for organic gardeners, there are some readily available, very concentrated natural substances we consider acceptable fertilizers—such as seed meals and processed animal wastes.

Today, most market gardeners use chemical fertilizers. That's understandable: organic fertilizers are five times the price of chemicals these days; high quality fresh manures free of bedding are not easy to come by; and making potent compost is an art similar to baking fine bread. However, where bread may be attempted daily until the cook achieves mastery, compost takes months per heap, and mastering the art of composting may take many years. That is not to imply that making compost is unimportant—compost should be made from vegetation collected from the garden and the kitchen, but it should be considered organic matter that does not contain much in the way of plant nutrients. *Compost* should be used to replace the organic matter that is inevitably lost when fertilizers alone are applied to row crops; *fertilizer* should provide the nutrients.

I am certain that some dedicated and well-read Organic gardeners will resent my unproven assertion that ordinary manure or indifferently made composts will not grow demanding vegetables very successfully on most maritime Northwest soils. Such a statement seemingly contradicts Doctrine. So before I describe how to make and use natural fertilizers, let me offer a brief explanation of why I believe fertilizer is so important west of the Cascades.

Weathering and the action of soil bacteria and other soil organisms break down rock particles and release plant nutrients, most of which dissolve into the water present in the soil. When dissolved, nutrients become available to plants, which take them in as the roots absorb water. This provides most of the plants' mineral nutrition. Manure and compost contain nutrients that are released and made available to plants as soil bacteria digest the organic matter. Increasing the level of soil organic matter with manure or compost also increases the rate of weathering and nutrient release from soil particles by feeding soil organisms, as well as improving conditions for these organisms by increasing the amount of air and water in the soil. That's why manuring is broadly effective and has for millenia been a basic farming technique worldwide.

The above paragraph is so true that it has become this untruth: "All you need to make a garden grow is to incorporate lots of any sort of organic matter or compost, and eventually, steadily and gradually the soil will become a virtual garden of eatin'."

"Our garden was not too good this year, but we're building up the soil and next year should be a lot better." I've heard this statement from countless folks. Many of them have been "building" their soil for a number of years and will keep on building without getting the results they dream of.

The main support for this practice comes from eastern garden books. In Michigan, where I grew up and had my first radish garden at age nine, soils contain significant levels of nutrient reserves, summers are virtually tropical, summer nights are as warm and balmy as they are in Fiji or Hawaii and soil temperatures get extremely high. Since the rate of biological activity is a function of temperature, hot soils weather and break down organic matter very rapidly and release the nutrients contained within that organic matter in a flash. In Canoga Park, California, where I gardened in the seventies, I couldn't maintain a high level of organic matter in my soil no matter how much I added. Even horse manure containing a lot of sawdust—which normally ties up soil nutrients for ages while it very slowly breaks down—would grow good crops a few weeks after being tilled in if I didn't use too much. In California, many native soils have organic matter contents below 1 percent.

West of the Cascades, our cooler soils come naturally with high organic matter contents of around 4 or 5 percent. Later, I'm going to go on at length about the importance of maintaining this 4 or 5 percent organic matter level in some garden soils and greatly increasing it in certain others. But unlike in California, where humus seems to burn out faster than it can be put in, in the maritime Northwest three serious garden problems can be caused by too much organic matter. Here are two of them—another just as bad or worse is yet to come in Chapter 7, Diseases and Pests.

A Short Course in Soil Science

Slow to warm in spring, our maritime Northwest soils will not usually release enough nutrients from rotting organic matter and their own
reserves to suit demanding vegetables until midsummer's peak
temperatures arrive. Corn may not green up and really grow fast until
July, which means it won't grow enough to produce big ears before its
heat-accumulation clock puts up the tassle and stops vegetative growth;
brassicas may limp through June, barely making more growth than the
insects chew down and then, when they finally do get growing, their final
size is very disappointing; lettuce gets bitter when it grows slowly. I could
go on, explaining the consequences of a nutrient-starved June to squash,
melons, cucumbers, peppers and so on, but I'll spare you the gloomy recita-
tion. Essentially, our cool summers demand that crops must have more
help to grow as fast as possible.

The second problem is that the manure or "compost" usually available
these days is what the old market growers called "long manure," containing a lot of sawdust or straw. Soil bacteria going to work on it will initially
take plant nutrients, mainly nitrogen, right out of the soil and away from
the growing plants. Until the material is well broken down, the plants remain nutrient starved—a condition that can last for several months *after*
the soil warms. Even thoroughly composted long manures don't contain
much nitrogen.

Of course, there are exceptions to this rule. Coarse-textured, dark-
colored, relatively highly mineralized soils warm up faster, contain more
air and can rot less-potent forms of organic matter fast enough to grow
a decent garden. However, even successful Organic market gardeners
around Eugene using black Willamette River Valley alluvial loams—the
best soils we've got west of the Cascades—rely on chicken manure and
organic fertilizers.

Chemical versus organic fertilizers

Okay, at least tentatively granted, we've got to use strong stuff to Grow
demanding vegetables. Does it matter what kind of fertilizer we use,
chemical or organic? Yes and no. In one sense, fertilizer is fertilizer is
fertilizer. All contain concentrated amounts of nutrients and release these
nutrients rapidly. Any fertilizer that creates high levels of nitrogen in soil,
be it blood meal, seed meal, chicken manure, urea or ammonium sulfate,
has a similar harmful side effect: it not only feeds the plants, but it also
increases soil bacteria populations. Just like plants, soil microorganism
levels are limited by growth factors—usually nitrogen. Add nitrogen and
soil microbes will multiply rapidly. Since their energy supply comes from

breaking down organic matter, the consequence of adding nitrogen fertilizer is a rapid reduction of soil organic matter. That's the main reason growing heavily fertilized crops results in a rapid decline of humus. And that's why when you start fertilizing, you should begin paying attention to maintaining organic matter levels.

Chemical fertilizers have certain advantages, some only apparent, some actual. Many chemicals are made with oil or natural gas. Currently they're much cheaper than organics and will probably remain so unless oil prices go up four to six times what they are now. This may or may not happen in our lifetimes. Converting a limited resource like oil into food does not seem sensible to some ecologically minded folks. Then again, exhaustion of Earth's resources may or may not be a real issue to people in 50 years.

Many gardeners mistakenly believe that chemical fertilizers as a broad group poison microlife. In fact, the opposite is true: they encourage microbial activity by reducing limiting factors—the same thing they do for plants. Only if the gardener fails to replace organic matter consumed by the bacteria will the health of the entire soil suffer—microlife declines and becomes unbalanced; plant diseases may occur; harmful soil-dwelling insects may increase. Organic fertilizers will do exactly the same harmful thing! On the other hand, I am pretty sure that one popular chemical fertilizer, ammonium sulfate, is toxic to earthworms, and it should be avoided in the garden. Unfortunately, ammonium sulfate is an inexpensive form of chemical nitrogen and is widely used. It may well be part of any fertilizer blend without the bag being so labeled.

A plus for chemicals: they are concentrated soluble nutrient and dissolve readily into the soil, provoking rapid growth. There may be times when a rapid response is called for. Chemicals can be mixed up in various proportions to provide nutrient balances specifically tailored to different crops and different occasions. That's why those guerrilla farmers liked Rapid-Gro. Commercial growers have dozens of chemical mixtures available for different crops. You want a mix to make strong stems? Or more colorful flowers? They've got it.

For quick response, Organic growers prefer fish emulsion, seaweed extracts or manure teas, which are also water-soluble and instantly available. But nitrogen-rich fish emulsion is 7–1–1 and seaweed extracts analyze around 2–1–6; combine the two and you *might* get 9–2–7. Unfortunately, there is just no way to create a balanced level of phosphorus with pure organics. For those reasons, I've come to feel that water-soluble chemicals, used like vitamins in conjunction with rich, organically fertilized garden soil, may be a superior way to grow the healthiest bedding plants. One clever small fertilizer company recently came out with an "organic" liquid fertilizer made of kelp/fish emulsion, but rated 5–10–10—an excellent balance for bedding plants. They don't say on the bottle that it also contains liquid phosphoric acid, which is as chemical a substance as you can get.

On the minus side, it's dangerously easy to overuse chemicals. One tablespoonful of chemicals sprinkled around a big plant can induce maximum growth response for a few weeks. A tablespoonful is not much! A little more might put the plant into shock, burn the roots or wilt it. Less is not maximally effective. So small precise quantities are often *banded* beside or below the furrow at planting time. Banding concentrates fertilizer close to the root system. After a month or so, more fertilizer is applied, either by sprinkling it between the rows or mixing it into irrigation water. If a scheduled fertilization is missed, growth slows or stops. Another liability can be certain adverse reactions on overall soil pH from some chemical fertilizers. Most of them make the soil more acid and require the addition of lime to counteract that effect.

Yet another liability is that chemical fertilizers *are* pure nutrients and provide solely what is intentionally put into them. Almost all chemical fertilizers contain only nitrogen, phosphorus and potassium, with a bit of sulfur inadvertently present because sulfuric acid is used to make cheap nitrate sources and to make rock phosphate water-soluble. But plants need a whole slew of other nutrients, and may not grow as well without them. Our leached-out maritime soils are certain to be deficient in some micronutrients. Your own body also needs a wide assortment of nutrients and other substances; if you don't have it in your soil, how is it going to get into your food? Organic fertilizers can contain wide ranges of trace elements. Depending on a garden for a major portion of one's diet makes it all the more important to make sure it provides complete nutrition.

The one chemical fertilizer I feel most positive about using is synthetic urea, the most inexpensive form of chemical nitrogen when figured in terms of price per pound of nitrogen it contains. Converted by soil bacteria into nitrates, urea does not provoke an acid soil reaction, is not toxic to microlife and is simply a synthesized form of a substance commonly found in urine (naturally part of animal manures), much like synthetic vitamin C is virtually identical to natural C. However, synthetic urea is ferociously potent and must be used with the greatest moderation. The best garden use for urea is making compost piles out of sawdust or other dry materials too low in nitrogen to heat up. I've known some really serious Organic gardeners who save up their own urine for this purpose.

In some ways, dry organic fertilizers can be more effective than chemicals. Most organics release nutrients over a period of three to six months. They are not water-soluble (except for blood meal) and must be broken down by microbial activity before the nutrients they contain become available. Chemical fertilizers can be made to be "slow release" by special pelletizing processes, but long-lasting chemicals are very costly—as much or more than organics. A single application of organics can conveniently Grow a plant from June to November without danger of overfertilization. Slow-release organics can be simultaneously broadcast and banded beside or below seeds or transplants. Each seedling starts out with a concentration of nutrients from the banded fertilizer; then, as the plant grows, the broadcast fertilizer becomes accessible to the expanding root system. As summer comes on, increasing soil temperature makes organics break down faster and faster, harmoniously supplying increasing levels of nutrients as the growing plant needs more and more. As summer starts drawing to a close, organics continue to remain synergistic—light intensities drop, plant growth slows, the need for nutrients decreases, the soil cools, the rate of nutrient release automatically slows. Such precise matching of nutrient availability to plant needs can't be achieved nearly as easily with chemicals. Organics are worth the extra price.

Organic fertilizers aren't dangerously easy to overapply, either. They're banded a quarter-cup to a pint per plant; one-half to one cup per five to 10 feet of row. If a bit too much or too little is used, no serious damage will result. They're broadcast at around a gallon per 100 square feet. Chicken manure has about half the potency of seed meal-based fertilizers and is slower to break down. A shovelful will grow a big squash vine; five gallons of fresh chicken manure or well-made chicken manure compost worked in along a 100-foot row of corn can have an amazing effect.

To take effect, organics (including chicken manure) must be blended into soil so bacteria can break them down. It is not workable to pour organic fertilizer into a hole below a seedling or merely sprinkle it over the ground and water it in. Large clumps of organics will putrefy if located below transplants, often attracting maggots that may attack the plant's root system, while not releasing sufficient nutrients. Below transplants, stir the fertilizer up a bit before planting. Broadcast into a bed before planting, organic fertilizers should be tilled in. Sprinkled atop the ground as an afterthought, they must be worked in shallowly with hoe or rake so they can break down. Chemicals are easier in this respect, because simply watering them in will increase the level of soil nutrients immediately; however, if you overwater chemicals all the nutrients will be washed so deep into the soil that the plants can't reach them.

A Short Course in Soil Science

Some care should be taken to keep organic fertilizer (including fresh chicken manure) out of direct contact with sprouting seeds, because the fertilizer promotes a rush of biological soil activity that can induce too much damping off (a fatal wilt) and greatly lower germination. When sowing seeds in rows, make a deep furrow with a hoe or furrower and sprinkle organic fertilizer along the bottom. Partially fill in the furrow, then sow and cover the seeds. Or fill in the furrow completely and make another shallow one directly alongside to plant the seeds in. When setting out transplants, mix a half-cup or so of complete organic fertilizer into about a gallon of soil directly below the seedling. Fertilize big, fast-growing types of vegetables traditionally planted in hills, such as squash or melons, by mixing a pint of complete organic fertilizer or a shovelful of chicken manure into five to 10 gallons of soil raised into a small mound. Then sow the seeds on top.

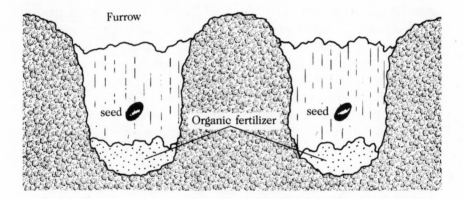

Well-balanced, pre-blended organic fertilizers are sold in sacks up to 40 pounds each for fairly stiff prices, especially compared to chemical fertilizers. But gardeners may easily mix their own complete organic fertilizer and save considerable money as well as tailor-make fertilizer blends to suit the plant and the season.

Seed meals

The basic constituent of a complete organic fertilizer is usually some variety of oilseed meal. After the oil has been extracted, seed residues are dried, sacked and sold primarily for animal food. Various seed meals are available in different parts of the country. In the maritime Northwest, California cottonseed meal is the most inexpensive and widely available. Canola meal is much easier to obtain in British Columbia right now due to an expanding canola oil business in Canada. Sometimes linseed or soybean meals are available. Over the past 10 years, cottonseed meal has fluctuated between $175 and $350 per ton depending on the volume of the cotton crop in California and Arizona. Other seed meals should sell for similar amounts—if faced with a choice, I'd buy the cheapest unless there were some other quality of the particular meal that might affect its use. Cottonseed meal, for example, is particularly easy to use: it is an odorless, dry-flowing granular material and blends easily with other fertilizers. Fish meal is also a good base for organic fertilizers and stronger than seed meals, but is unpleasantly smelly and attracts the interest of pets and rats. Leather dust and dried tankage or meat meal could also be used.

I am frequently asked if it's safe to use cottonseed meal, since cotton is heavily sprayed with herbicides and dangerously potent insecticides not approved for food crops. These chemicals tend to be oil-soluble and concentrate in the seed, so will not the seed itself carry large quantities of poisonous residues? It does. Fortunately for gardeners, before we buy the meal the seed is crushed and heated in a retort at high temperature with a most efficient solvent which dissolves *all* the oil. The dissolved oil is extracted from the seed mash, and the solvent is evaporated from the oil and recondensed for another use. The cottonseed oil thus obtained contains virtually all remaining pesticide and herbicide residues. Stripped of oil, the seed meal is now a fairly clean food, sold for animal food protein supplements and fertilizer; the oil is probably a fairly toxic food, sold to fast-food and Oriental restaurants for deep-frying and to salad-dressing makers. Think about that the next time you go out to dinner. And read the label on your favorite salad dressing, mayonnaise or tinned sardines.

Different seed meals contain different amounts of basic plant nutrients. Cottonseed meal, for example, varies from 5 to 7 percent nitrogen; the higher nitrogen lots are labeled as higher protein and sell for much more money. Most seed meals run from something like 4–2–1 (4 percent nitrogen, 2 percent phosphorus, 1 percent potassium) to 8–4–2. So seed meals are primarily nitrogen sources with significant amounts of phosphorus and a little potassium.

Pure seed meal alone will grow a passable garden, but the average garden plant does not Grow on a 4:2:1 nutrient ratio. Much better results come from a 1:2:1 ratio, so seed meal should be supplemented with phosphorus and potassium. I recommend either rock phosphate or bone meal to boost phosphorus. Bone meal is more expensive than phosphate rock, but breaks down much faster so less is needed. However, phosphate rock continues releasing for several years, giving long-term residual benefits that improve overall soil health. For potassium, the best source by far is kelp meal, which usually analzyes out at about 18 percent potassium and contains traces of just about every element and micronutrient a plant could use. Kelp also contains some plant growth hormones that may improve the overall vigor and stress resistance of plants. Certain potassium-rich ground rocks such as Jersey greensand and sometimes ground granite flours are also available.

Steve Solomon's not-so-secret fertilizer formula

This is the complete organic fertilizer mix I have recommended for years. All measures are by volume, not by weight.

4 parts seed meal or fish meal
1 part dolomite lime
1 part rock phosphate or ½ part bone meal
1 part kelp meal

Lime is included to offset the acidity of many seed meals. Dolomite lime contains both calcium and magnesium, which are essential plant nutrients. Even if the garden has been well limed, I'd still advise including dolomite in the mix. Such a blend will analyze about 1:1.5:1.

The fertilizer blend may be adjusted to suit various purposes; the ratios are not critical in any respect. For fertilizing legumes, which can manufacture their own nitrogen, the seed meal may be left out or greatly reduced. I use one part each when blending for beans or peas. In early spring when soils are very cold and seed meals release nutrients fairly slowly, one part seed meal may be replaced with blood meal. Blood meal, though expensive, is very high in nitrogen and is the only dry organic fertilizer that is water-soluble. It has an intense but relatively short-lasting effect.

Blood meal is the only organic fertilizer substance I know of that can easily burn plants if it sticks on leaves. It also contains health-producing plant growth regulators. British glasshouse growers, who raise lettuce on chemical fertilizers, apply blood meal for the last fertilization about three weeks before harvest. They say it gives lettuce a better "finish"; it comes out denser and can sit in the cooler longer without rotting or browning.

In midsummer, I lower the nitrogen percentage of the blend and increase the kelp percentage, changing the ratios to two parts seed meal, one part lime, one part phosphorus, one part kelp, because slower-growing plants handle winter better. Growth regulators in kelp meal make late fall or overwintered crops huskier and better able to handle freezing weather.

I mix my complete organic fertilizer in a big garden cart. It could also be done on a tarp spread on the lawn or on a concrete driveway. Simply dump out the stuff by the sack, and blend it by turning with a shovel until it's a uniform color, then shovel it into a large garbage can with a tight lid or back into the empty sacks for storage and use as needed. Lately, I've gotten so relaxed about proportions that I measure by the sack: for example, two 50-pound sacks cottonseed meal; one 50-pound sack of lime; one 40-pound sack of phosphate rock; one 55-pound sack of kelp meal. That's close enough.

The economics of organic fertilizer

Virtually all garden centers sell lime and most have dolomite lime in 50-pound sacks at reasonable prices. However, seed and bone meals often are sold only in small boxes of a few pounds each, at very high prices per pound. Phosphate rock can be hard to find in garden centers, too. Increasing numbers of suppliers are responding to consumer demand and offering organics in bulk or by the 50-pound sack, which is how the gardener interested in economy should buy them. The substances all store well. Seed, bone and kelp meals are almost always available by the sack, at prices barely above ton-lot rates, from farm-supply stores or feed and grain distributors. One other minor hint: there are two sorts of kelp meal on the market: expensive from Korea and twice as expensive from Norway. I think the difference has more to do with exchange rates and local wages than nutrient analysis.

Fertilizing a garden with organics is not expensive, even though it is much more costly than using chemicals. Suppose it takes 10 pounds of complete organic fertilizer to do 100 square feet and that the home-blended fertilizer costs 20 to 25 cents a pound. That's 2½ cents a square foot. With chemicals, the cost might only be half a cent a square foot. Big deal? To a commercial farmer, maybe yes. But Dick Raymond, a famous eastern garden writer who is closely associated with the nonprofit National Gardening Federation, carefully worked out the value of his garden a few years ago and discovered that each square foot yielded an average of 73 cents' worth of food if computed at the local wholesale price of the vegetable at the time of harvest, counting only unblemished, well-formed produce. That was in short-season Vermont. Based on my experience in the milder maritime Northwest, with our long growing season and ability to double up by following a spring crop with a winter one on the same ground, I figure we might get $1 per square foot. What's a few cents a square foot in fertilizer cost compared to that? But if manure and fertilizer are not used at all, yields might drop to 10 cents per square foot, while soil built up organically without using fertilizer "vitamins" might produce only 40 cents a square foot. And the gardener is going to use just as much seed and probably invest as much effort in either case. Why not use fertilizer and get the most for your efforts? And while you're at it, why not guard your own health and use the highest quality organics, which are much more likely to provide complete, balanced and steady plant nutrition?

Elementary soil science

If fertilizer is essential to success with most vegetables, it is only logical to wonder whether we could grow a garden using only fertilizer, like commercial truck farmers. Not as well, in my opinion. Highly successful gardening demands a soil management system, too.

Soil science is a complex subject. Gardeners don't need degrees in horticulture to understand how to grow plants expertly, though they should know a bit of high-school-level chemistry—and be willing to make a little mental effort. Few gardening books devote much space to the complexities of soil management; instead, they offer vague generalities or some specific instructions that can't possibly apply to all soils in every part of the country. But, as with other areas of understanding, if a person really comprehends the basics, apparent anomalies and mysterious events can eventually be grasped through that wonderful process of obnosis.

I hope my reader's patience is not unduly tested by what is to follow. In an attempt to present soil science within the space restrictions of a garden book but not overload anyone's interest level, I have carefully excerpted university-level information from Nyle Brady's *The Nature and Properties of Soils*, allowed for everything the reader may have ever been confused by in other garden books and magazines, filtered it all through my own soil management experience and then condensed the whole subject to a few thousand words.

The short story

But before I get deep into soil science, a word to the readers who are itching to get out in their garden *now*, or who think this is starting to sound suspiciously like school. Relax! You're excused. I've had a lot of experience figuring out "made simple" recommendations for the backs of seed envelopes and other types of garden writings. So for those of you who have already stifled a few yawns during this chapter or who are just not interested, I've put together a few workable yet simple rules that will help your garden succeed in almost any soil or circumstance west of the Cascades. Here is Steve Solomon's one-shot soil management system:

- Separate your garden into two equal sections, one part for growing summer crops, the other part for winter crops. I put a lot of consideration into that word *equal*; if you think you know better, look ahead to Chapter 3, Planning the Garden.
- In the fall before it gets too rainy and cold (October is best), spread a layer of leaves no more than two inches thick or a layer of horse manure no more than half an inch thick over what's left of the summer half of your garden. *No matter how tempting or what you have read elsewhere, do not spread any more organic matter.* If you're cursed with a heavy clay soil, this section does not apply to you—please persevere through the rest of this chapter.
- Spread 50 pounds of dolomite lime per 1,000 square feet.
- Spread cover-crop seed as evenly as possible: about two pounds of crimson clover *or* 10 pounds of winter-hardy small-seeded favas *or* 10 pounds of Austrian field peas per 1,000 square feet.
- Till it all in (vegetable stubble, manure, leaves, lime, seeds) *shallowly*, only two or three inches deep, so the seed isn't buried so far down it can't come up and so the organic matter can get enough oxygen to rot by spring.
- In the spring as early as the soil can be worked, spread approximately one gallon complete organic fertilizer per 100 square feet *or* five gallons of chicken manure *or* a cubic foot of ready-made chicken manure compost. Till or spade in fertilizer and green manure (the cover crops you planted last fall) together. Wait a week to 10 days and till again. (If it's too wet to till, hoe it all in shallowly after it hasn't rained for a few days, then wait another week to 10 days and hoe again.) Rake out a rough seed bed and plant your spring garden (peas, lettuce, radish, spinach). In June/July, when the spring crops are all done, spread and till in another dose of fertilizer and plant your fall/winter crops on this part. The year after this one, this section will rotate into your summer garden.
- On the other half of the garden, in mid- to late spring when your winter crops are done, spread reasonably well-rotted compost, a quarter-inch or so thick. A more expensive alternative would be 50 pounds of alfalfa meal (another product available

from a feed and grain store) per 100 square feet. No matter how tempting or what you have read, do not spread or till in any more organic matter. Do not use sawdusty manure at this time of year; it won't have enough time to break down before crops are planted. Better nothing, than that!

- Spread one gallon complete organic fertilizer per 100 square feet *or* five gallons of chicken manure *or* a cubic foot sack of ready-made chicken manure compost. Till in fertilizer and compost together, rake out a seed bed and plant your summer garden. In fall, prepare this section to be your spring garden next year.

And that's soil management west of the Cascades made as simple as I can make it.

Soil basics

Now, back to soil science. Soil is a complex mixture of particles, water, air and living things. Solid particles usually make up about half of the soil mass; the rest is water and air. Please think of soil as something active, something in a constant state of flux. Especially changeable is the balance of air to water. Periods of heavy rain fill pore spaces completely, driving out all air except for that dissolved within the water. As the water drains, soil air returns. Rock particles are slowly weathering and dissolving, releasing their mineral content to the benefit of the plants and soil organisms, which build their bodies from them. Organic matter may increase and decrease seasonally. Life forms change their ecology with the seasons, too.

In pastures and woodlots, organic matter is created and maintained by the plants that grow there. When they die, the tops fall over and rot into the earth; the roots decompose, breaking up the soil and permitting air to move deeper. Untilled soils arrive at a relatively stable level of organic matter, determined by the climate and native mineralization of the soil rock particles. The amount of organic matter produced each year is determined by the level of nutrients the soil mass holds in reserve, how much of that reserve is released each year, the amount of moisture present during the growing season, the length of the growing season, and the average temperatures through the year—all factors that control the rates of growth and decay. In different climates and in soils derived from different rock masses, organic matter contents vary quite profoundly. In the maritime Northwest, organic matter and soil organisms typically amount to 3 to

5 percent of the total weight in the furrow slice—the top six to eight inches of soil.

The importance of soil fungi

In healthy soil, many plants develop active symbiotic relationships with soil fungi that are essential to plant health. Called mycorrhizal association, this symbiosis is fully described in Sir Albert Howard's book *The Soil and Health*. What happens is that the threadlike structures of soil fungi, called hyphae, actively invade the plant's growing root tips and hairs by penetrating between individual cell walls. The hyphae rob the plant's internal food supply, but they return something even more valuable to the plant.

Soil fungi are able to aggressively break down mineral particles by releasing weak acids and then absorbing the dissolved nutrients. A plant can't perform this trick; it can only passively take up whatever is already dissolved in soil moisture and make the best of it. Fungi combine basic nutrients into complex organic chemicals, which move through the hyphae. When aging root hairs toughen, the invading hyphae are cut off and dissolve into the plant's vascular system. It seems that the fungal substances left in the plant act like essential vitamins. It has been well established that plants become diseased or grow poorly if mycorrhizal associations do not develop. However, not all plant species develop mycorrhizal associations; for example, cabbage family members do not.

Mycorrhizal fungi don't derive their main food supply from the invaded plant. If they did, they would probably kill rather than help their host. (There are other types of fungi that do parasitize their hosts and are considered soil-borne diseases.) Helpful fungi get most of their food by eating organic matter in soil. The plant only supplies that little bit of extra something the fungi need, which is exactly what the fungi symbiotically supply in return. As long as soil organic matter hasn't dropped below the 4 to 5 percent range—which west of the Cascades describes most soils that haven't recently been in commercial crops other than hay or pasture—there will be sufficient food to support mycorrhizal fungi. This is only one of many connections between the level of soil organic matter and the ability of many species of plants to grow.

Here's another! Most of a plant's root system is an inactive supporting structure and conductive tubes. All the action happens at the root tip, where the fine root hairs take in water and nutrients. The tip is constantly attempting to grow and new hairs are constantly being pushed out directly behind the tip. Root hairs remain absorptive only for a short time; then they become too tough and impervious to water, and drop off. So the root system is efficient only so long as it expands, and mycorrhizal associations work only when the roots are actively growing. Soil microlife breathe oxygen. Plant roots also breathe oxygen. Obviously, the development and health of the plant and the soil population can be limited by the level of soil air. Promoting a higher level of air in soil helps Grow the plants; maintaining a decent amount of organic matter does, too. It's symbiotic that the best way to aerate most soils is to somewhat increase the level of organic matter.

Organic matter in soil

Although organic matter comprises only a small percentage of native soils, it has a huge effect on soil texture, water and nutrient retention, and on the ratio of air to solids—which is called pore space. Pore space in some soils can be greatly improved by fairly large additions of organic matter; others are naturally well-structured and will grow fine crops with much lower organic matter content.

Organic matter starts out as complex materials that provide food for worms, insects, various other organisms and soil microlife. When it is thoroughly broken down and digested, it becomes a spongy black or brown material called humus, no longer recognizably leaves, manures and plant wastes. Humus is fairly stable and is consumed very slowly by microlife. While digesting organic matter, soil bacteria secrete large quantities of slimes and gums, which cement soil particles into larger clumps called aggregates. Some clay soils are naturally airless, restricting root development, so much so that heavy clays won't grow many types of vegetables. But when well aggregated, heavy clays develop large spherical particles called crumbs. These crumbs do not pack tightly, allowing much more air to penetrate deep into the earth. A well-aggregated soil is said to possess good crumb or good tilth.

Incorporating organic matter will help light soils retain water and will lighten up heavy ones, but the gardener must be cautious when adding manures, composts and other organic materials. As I mentioned earlier, one consequence of tilling in organic matter can be a total loss of available plant nutrients for a time. Soil bacteria construct their bodies of the same nutrients plants use, and their population explodes under the stimulus of a new food supply, robbing the soil of the very nutrients plants need to grow with.

This condition persists until the organic matter has been partially digested and is well on its way to becoming humus. The initial breakdown

Soil nutrient levels after addition of crude organic matter

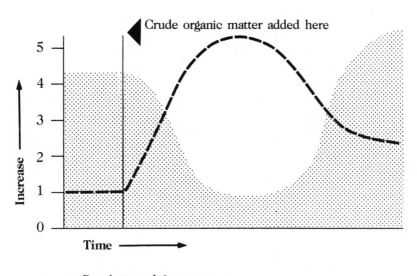

Crude organic matter added here

– – – – Population of decay organisms

Soil nutrient levels

When crude, undigested organic matter is added to soil, the population of decay organisms increases rapidly. These organisms construct their bodies from the same nutrients plants use to build cells. Consequently, the level of nutrients available to plants is lowered until the decay organisms have consumed about half the organic matter. Then their population begins to die off, the rate of decomposition slows, and as the bodies of the bacteria break down, the nutrients they contain are released for plants to use.

takes from a week to several months or even longer, depending on how much and what kind of organic matter was tilled in, and how fast it rots. Once the raw organic matter has been partially digested, soil bacteria die off and release nutrients back into the soil from their decaying bodies. The speed of rotting is determined by the amount of nitrogen in the organic matter, soil temperature, the amount of air in the soil, and the amount of nitrogen and other plant/bacteria nutrients already available in the soil. To get a practical idea of how this works, consider that tender spring vegetation or legumes like beans, peas and clover that have not set seed have high nitrogen levels and will rot in less than two weeks; an inch of sawdust, which is virtually all cellulose and a little potassium without any nitrogen or other mineral content, may create a three- to six-month bacterial bloom.

It is vital to maintain organic matter levels, but equally important to understand that different sorts of organic matter behave differently and must be applied in the right quantities at the right time of year. As a general rule, large quantities of organic matter, even those consisting mainly of cellulose like sawdust, rice hulls or straw, will be broken down by spring if tilled in during autumn. Well-composted materials have already largely been converted into humus and will not disrupt soil when tilled in. Fortunately, many soils do not require additions of much organic matter, and even those that need larger quantities do not need them tilled in more than once if smaller additions are made regularly thereafter.

Compost

Composting is accelerated bacterial digestion of organic matter, done above ground before it is incorporated into the soil. The subject is complex. To be understood intelligently, composting requires careful consideration of quite a bit of data, especially if the object is to make high-quality compost that can function as fertilizer. Rodale Press has published some very interesting (and very large) books on the subject that should be read by all serious gardeners, even if they then make the informed decision not to bother with making high-quality compost.

Every garden accumulates quite a bit of above-ground vegetable waste. There may also be the summer's grass clippings and fall leaves. The kitchen may have a compost bucket rather than waste all that organic matter down the garbage disposal or send it to a landfill. What I call the "corn and tomato" gardeners may choose to save up the grass clippings, spread them and the fall leaves on the garden in October, till them in along with the entire summer's growth of plant material and let it all rot in the soil over the winter. The technical name for this is "sheet composting." By spring, the soil microlife will have digested the material.

Year-round gardeners can't usually afford to use their growing space so wastefully. Fortunately, making low-grade compost in piles is very easy. City gardeners with tidy yards need to make at least two and likely three compost bins; country gardeners can simply use crude heaps. To retain heat and moisture, the heap should be five feet in diameter and about four or five feet tall when first built. Higher or wider piles don't allow enough air for the bacteria to breathe. The easiest tidy bin to make is a self-supporting ring of four-foot turkey wire (heavy 2 " by 4 " mesh) five

Compost

feet in diameter, held in a circle by hooking the wire back on itself.

As plant material becomes available, fill the ring or build the heap, layering in alternating materials a few inches thick at a time and thoroughly watering each layer. If it takes several weeks to several months to build, the ring should settle gradually as it is filled. By the time the ring is nearly full, it should be getting hot in the middle. A few weeks after the ring has been completely filled, unhook the wires and remove the supporting ring. Fork the material into a new ring (or turn the heap) in two- or three-inch layers, watering each layer thoroughly, starting with the outside of the old pile (which will not have rotted) and ending with the core (which should have partially rotted). If the core hasn't rotted or the pile did not heat, as the pile is turned sprinkle in a quart of complete organic fertilizer or a cup of urea on each new layer after it is watered.

After another month or two, the pile should have settled to about half its original height and the core will be rough compost. If you want finer, more crumbly compost, again remove the supporting ring and fork the rough outside materials to the bottom of a smaller new pile followed by the more finished core, watering each layer as you go. It shouldn't require any more fertilizer or urea. In another month or two, the compost

The country heap

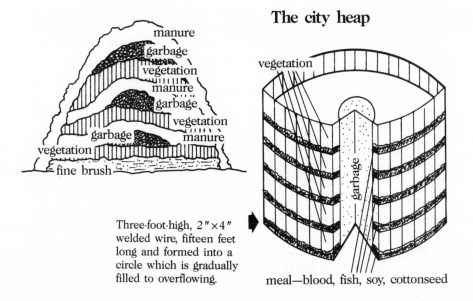

The city heap

manure
garbage
vegetation
manure
garbage
vegetation
manure
garbage
vegetation
fine brush

vegetation
garbage

Three-foot-high, 2″×4″ welded wire, fifteen feet long and formed into a circle which is gradually filled to overflowing.

meal—blood, fish, soy, cottonseed

will be crumbly and fine enough to pass easily through a quarter-inch sieve.

To retain water and to prevent leaching from heavy winter rains, it's not a bad idea to cover the pile with a sheet of heavy plastic. Two or three piles at different stages of decomposition will handle all the vegetable waste, kitchen garbage, grass clippings, leaves and so forth from an average household and kitchen garden. Once you start the process, the rest will come by itself, or you may become sufficiently interested to read up on it.

Soil classification

Scientists classify soils and work out management systems according to soil types. The first basic division is wet or dry. Wet soils, such as those found in the maritime Northwest, receive more rainfall each year than can evaporate. Dry soils receive less rainfall each year than can evaporate. Wet soils are usually forested and have high levels of organic matter if nutrient levels aren't too low. Dry soils usually grow grasses or scrub and may have high (prairie soils) or low (desert) levels of organic matter depending on how dry they are and on the average annual temperature (which determines how fast organic matter rots). Wet soils are usually relatively infertile because they are leached by water running through them. Unleached, dry soils tend to be much higher in reserve nutrients.

The next level of classification comes from the nature of the soil particles. Soil particles are weathered out of the solid rock below (upland soils), or are transported and deposited by water (alluvial soils), or are blown and deposited by wind (loess soils). Freezing and thawing, and the weak acids produced by microlife and by dissolved carbon dioxide gas, slowly reduce the size of the particles further while their mineral content is gradually dissolved, eventually leached into the ground water and transported to the sea. That's why the oceans are salty.

The largest sizes of soil particles are called sand; intermediate sizes are named silts; the finest are called clays. Under magnification, sand looks like small pieces of gravel or pebbles. The edges are usually rounded with few sharp angles. Because sands usually decompose slowly, their mineral reserve remains largely untapped. Silts are smaller and have not only weathered, but also have undergone some chemical decomposition. Under higher magnification, silts have less-angular corners and are more rounded than sands. Particle size is not merely of academic interest. The mineral content of silts is more available than that of sands because, being composed of smaller particles, they make a great deal more surface area available to the action of weathering agents.

Relative particle sizes for different soil types

Soil Type	Particle Size
sand	50 to 2,000 microns*
silt	2 to 50 microns
clay	under 2 microns

*Scientists describe soil particle size in a unit of measurement called the micron. A micron is a millionth of a meter or 1/1,000th of a millimeter, or about 1/25,000 of an inch. As a standard of comparison, grains of table salt or white granulated sugar are approximately 50 microns.

Clay particles have been fully broken down into individual mineral crystals, which have been chemically rearranged into substances altogether different from the original rocks they derived from. Clays are thin, flat crystals that layer themselves like pages in a book. Though clay crystals are so fine it takes the most powerful electron microscope to make a picture of them, it is easy to visualize the nature of clays if you remember that slate and mica are two minerals formed from subjecting clay to high heat and pressure. These layered rocks fracture into thin sheets much like the microscopic crystals that formed them. Being so fine, clay particles fit very tightly together, so clay soils tend to be heavy and airless. Clay particles are also negatively electrically charged, which causes clay to attract dissolved minerals, which themselves carry small positive charges when in solution. Calcium, potassium and other positively charged minerals are called cations (pronounced cat-ions) when in solution. Clays stick cations to themselves, holding them strongly between layers of clay crystals. (If this is getting over your head, you should take a breather and reflect on the folly of allowing high school students to pass science courses by rote memorization.)

Silt and sand will also hold a few cations, but through a different mechanism. Soil water, holding dissolved nutrients, forms a thin film that adheres to all soil particles, including clay. Sand and silt particles may be compared to books firmly closed, but clay is like that book with the pages fanned open. Being electrically charged and having more surface area, clay can hold a lot more water and dissolved nutrient molecules than can sand or silt. If sand's ability to hold water and cations were expressed numerically as one, silt would be three, clay 10 to 15 and, interestingly, humus 30.

Clay's ability to hold nutrients is very helpful, especially in our leached maritime soils, because without clay, winter rains would wash away almost all the dissolved nutrients built up every summer. This does happen every year in sandy ground. Even clayey soils are very badly leached on the wet slopes of the coastal mountain ranges, where winter rainfalls reach 100 inches a year and water virtually runs through the soil month after month. However, clay's ability to store nutrients may not help the gardener one bit. As heavy winter rains leach out more and more cations, the clay becomes increasingly negatively charged and so increasingly "hungry" for cations—and the soil pH tests increasingly acid. Under conditions of high soil acidity, any remaining cations are so strongly attached to clay particles that they are relatively unavailable to plants. Add fertilizer to highly

Effects of soil pH on the availability of plant nutrients

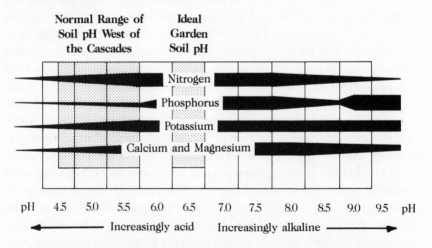

Width of the bar indicates the availability of some plant nutrients at various soil pHs. Increasing acidity below 6.5 makes nutrients more and more unavailable to plants. Simply by changing soil pH upward in the direction of 7.0, a far higher percentage of the soil's nutrients becomes available. If the soil is potentially rich, but acid, a healthy dose of agricultural lime will often turn it from an apparently poor soil to one that is quite good. In the same way, if you add nutrients to an acid soil, they only become immediately unavailable to the plants. The most basic, important step in soil improvement is adjusting the pH.

acid soil, and the clays grab the cations as fast as they're released, and hold them so strongly the plants get little. Under less acid conditions, clays act as little storage batteries, holding and releasing nutrients to plants on demand. If you are curious about how plants are able to "demand" cations or about the chemistry of clays, I refer you to a complete soils text. In fact, I hope many of my readers will be so intrigued by the data presented in this chapter that they'll get themselves a proper soils education.

Adjusting soil pH

Wet soils are typically acid, while dry soils tend to be alkaline. The remedy for high alkalinity is to spread and till gypsum, a common practice east of the Cascades and in California. The remedy for our overly acid soils is liming. Agricultural lime is made from finely ground calcium carbonate, very soft rock that dissolves rapidly into the soil, releasing huge quantities of cations. These calcium cations saturate clay, reducing its acidity, feeding clay's "hunger" and allowing a freer interchange of all types of cations.

It is impossible to make one exact statement of how much lime is needed to adjust a particular soil from one pH to another. There are several types of clays, each with different cation-holding capacities, and most soils are only part clay. I *can* state with pretty good accuracy that 40 inches of winter rain will remove about 500 pounds of calcium from each acre almost regardless of soil type—if the soil is not already so acid that cations can hardly be removed at all. Lime is about 50 percent calcium. As a general rule, even after a soil has been thoroughly limed, any soil can use another half a ton of lime per acre per year. If I were gardening without a soil test on soil that wasn't gumbo clay, I'd initially apply a ton per acre (50 pounds per 1,000 square feet), after which I'd drop it to half a ton per acre. Lime at about one ton per acre will increase the pH of an average clayey soil about half a step. This means that to move a clay soil from 5.5 to 6.0 takes about one ton per acre; from 5.5 to 6.5 takes about two tons per acre. Very clayey soils, which west of the Cascades usually have a native pH of 5.0 or less, may initially take up to four tons per acre.

Some gardeners believe that dolomite lime is superior to ordinary agricultural lime because it also contains magnesium carbonate, which is as vital a plant nutrient as calcium. Actually neither is "superior" if used alone. Plants do best when the ratio of available calcium to magnesium is in the range of 4:1 to 8:1. The mechanisms by which plants

A Short Course in Soil Science

Leached nutrient loss in pounds per acre

Soil Treatment	N	P	K	CA
bare soil	69	trace	86	557
grass	2	trace	74	364

This table is excerpted from the classic 1938 USDA Yearbook, *Soils and Men.* The field in question was at Ithaca, N.Y. Losses were computed by analyzing water flowing out of drain tiles installed below the field. Note that phosphorus doesn't leach, and that cover crops significantly reduce winter leaching losses.

"demand" calcium and magnesium are so similar that too much magnesium present in soil can induce an artificial calcium shortage; too much calcium can induce an artificial magnesium shortage. Since dolomite lime usually contains about 50 percent of each, to shoot for a safe 6:1 ratio, I'd suggest using dolomite every second or third liming or, even better, a mix of two parts agricultural lime to one part dolomite. What I do in my garden is broadcast regular lime and use dolomite in my complete organic fertilizer.

Don't worry too much about overliming. As pH gets closer to 7.0, it gets increasingly harder to change the pH further. So a bit too much won't hurt. However, in earlier editions of this book I told a story about how I experimentally brought a field at Lorane up well above 7.0 with 10 tons of lime per acre. Though things grew fairly well in this field, I did induce a severe magnesium deficiency by using cheap agricultural lime. Fortunately I discovered the deficiency from a thorough soil test and adjusted for it by adding epsom salts (water-soluble magnesium sulfate) to my fertilizer. The now-alkaline field also had less trouble with symphylans, though after four years in row crops, things have grown strangely and poorly. I'd not recommend this practice again.

Maritime Northwest phosphate problems

The fact of maritime rainfall makes for acid soils, something we have in common with other areas where rainfall exceeds evaporation. However, maritime Northwest soils have another significant nutrient problem not necessarily shared with other places that get 35 to 80 inches of rain a year. Soils west of the Cascades are almost uniformly low in phosphorus.

Once I had the opportunity to study a report from the OSU Soil Laboratory, which presented a year's compilation of soil analysis data county by county. Barely one percent of western Oregon soils tested high enough in phosphorus to grow fair crops. Eastern Oregon's dry unleached soils were better. These test results slanted towards better-than-average results because most of the tests were made for going commercial agricultural activities, so the poorer hillside and forest soils that gardeners often use were hardly included in the sampling at all.

The reason our soils test so phosphorus-poor is that the rocks that broke down to form our soils are not high in phosphorus. Possibly the richest are alluvial soils from the Cascades, including loams along the

Total mineral reserves in furrow slice of various loam soils*

Location	N	P	K	CA
Minnesota	1,200	3,600	8,400	70,000
Ohio	4,400	2,000	90,000	18,000
North Carolina	2,800	5,200	22,000	12,000
Georgia	2,000	800	2,400	14,000
Western Missouri	5,600	11,600	58,000	34,800
South Dakota	11,800	72,000	76,000	55,000
Nebraska	2,800	48,000	113,000	70,000
Arizona	800	68,000	106,000	91,000
Willamette Valley	2,300	2,200	48,000	15,000

*in pounds per acre

This chart shows the weight of various mineral nutrients held in reserve in the top eight inches of various Class I loam agricultural soils. When considering this chart, think about the climates of the various states. In every case shown, the nitrogen content is a direct reflection of the organic matter content. Please notice that the Arizona soil has a very high level of mineralization but a very low level of nitrogen because nitrogen is created only by growing organic matter. Though the dryness of Arizona's climate reduces leaching, contributing to the retention of mineral nutrients, it also prevents the growth of organic matter. The Minnesota and Georgia soils were derived from poorly mineralized rock; Ohio, North Carolina and Willamette Valley soils show leaching effects of high rainfalls on different starting mineralizations; the soils in Nebraska, South Dakota and western Missouri experience less leaching and were highly mineralized to begin with. What a range of difference!

A Short Course in Soil Science

Willamette, Umpqua, Santiam, McKenzie and Skagit rivers. These loams might contain total reserves of 2,500 to 3,500 pounds of phosphorus per acre in the furrow slice, with 15 to 20 pounds released and made available to plants each year. Upland Cascadian soils are not of the same quality, and they tend to be highly leached, clayey and acid. North of the Umpqua River to Washington State, soils derived from Oregon's Coast Range are broken-down sandstones, very low in many nutrients besides phosphorus. South of the Umpqua and into coastal Northern California lies a complex series of acidic metamorphic rocks, which also tend to be very low in nutrients, perhaps as bad or worse than Coast Range sandstones from an agricultural perspective.

Western Washington is very complex geologically. Areas of glacial soils brought down from B.C. are a mix of gravelly moraines and fertile flats. The bottomlands seem just about as rich as Cascades alluvium. Upland soils are too varied for comment. None of our soils came from rocks that held anything like the level of mineralization found in the soils of the Midwest's Corn Belt, the Canadian Prairies or in unleached desert soils, where reserves might run in excess of 50,000 pounds per acre in the furrow slice alone and where phosphorus release may exceed the needs of cereal crops.

Phosphorus deficiencies are frequently not readily identifiable from a vegetable's appearance, so many of this region's gardeners are unaware that phosphate fertilizer could make their plants grow a notch or three better. Phosphorus is involved in many aspects of plant growth: fruit formation, root development and flowering. With grain crops, high phosphorus levels give much larger seed yields. Where the Great Plains states and southern Alberta will grow 40 to 60 bushels of wheat per acre with a simple rotation, our best soils will probably only produce 20- to 30-bushel small grain crops without fertilizer or long fertility-building rotations climaxing in a small grain crop.

The most commonly available sources of phosphorus are chemical superphosphate and triple superphosphate, basic ingredients in all complete chemical fertilizer mixes. Superphosphate is merely phosphate rock (a naturally occurring mineral acceptable to organic gardeners) that has been treated with sulfuric acid. The more potent triple superphosphate is made of the same phosphate rock treated with phosphoric acid. The purpose of acid treatment is to make the virtually insoluble phosphate rock readily water-soluble. When incorporated into the soil, superphosphate granules dissolve completely in a few weeks. Compared to the much larger quantities of plain phosphate rock one would have to use to release the same amount of phosphorus, it's not expensive. Superphosphate is usually banded directly below seeds or seedlings. Phosphates released into acid soil may be available only for a short time before recombining into insoluble forms, but seedlings have the ability to absorb extra amounts of phosphorus without apparent damage and store it for later use. In many naturally infertile or acid farm soils, an initial feeding of chemical phosphorus is most of what the young plant gets to take it to maturity.

Liabilities of superphosphates are their short release period and the fact that the acids used to make phosphate rock soluble also acidify the soil and thus tend to reduce availability of the phosphorus itself. I think plants will be healthier if a steady supply of phosphorus is present throughout the growth cycle and throughout the entire soil mass. Phosphorus nutrition is so important that if phosphate rock or bone meal were unavailable, in spite of being an organic gardener I would use superphosphate, but I would apply it frequently throughout the growing season.

It's another tenet of the Organic movement that manuring and liming will significantly increase available phosphorus. In soils containing massive phosphorus reserves that is true, because phosphorus availability is pH-dependent and because manuring increases biological activity in the soil, which increases overall nutrient release. This technique does little good west of the Cascades. Additionally, most manures do not contain very much phosphorus, certainly not enough to balance the amounts of nitrogen and potassium they do contain. Only chicken manure (derived primarily from phosphorus-rich seeds) and shrimp wastes contain significant levels of phosphorus, though still far less than the ideal balance. Another organic practice is to grow deeply rooting phosphorus-concentrating cover crops, which pull nutrients up from the subsoil. This does work where the subsoil has something in it to concentrate, but not in the phosphorus-poor soils west of the Cascades.

Maritime Northwest organic gardeners can band natural phosphate sources with their other fertilizers and, preferably, also increase the total phosphate reserve of the soil, by spreading large amounts of phosphate rock in much the same way lime is used. With large quantities of relatively insoluble rock phosphate present, enough will be released steadily by natural processes to grow very healthy plants. When I start a new garden I spread phosphate rock at a rate of 50 pounds per 1,000 square feet, once a year for about four years, and thereafter maintain the high level of available phosphorus by including phosphate rock in my complete organic fertilizer mix. It's best to avoid spreading more than 225 pounds per 1,000 square feet in any seven- to 10-year period, to avoid the build-up of potentially phytotoxic (poisonous to plants) trace minerals present in certain types of rock phosphate. Survivalists, retirees and other serious-about-their-own-health gardeners might consider making a one-time application of about 200 pounds per 1,000 square feet (four tons per acre or an overall addition to the soil's phosphorus reserve of about 3,000 pounds per acre) as a sort of lifetime crop-insurance policy, guaranteeing that their growing plots will continue putting out sufficient phosphorus nutrition without further fertilization. Rock phosphate costs a lot more than lime—often nearly $300 a ton. Gardeners can afford to invest a few hundred dollars building phosphate reserves on small plots. Farmers could not possibly afford it by the tens and hundreds of acres and remain competitive, and so they use 100 pounds of superphosphate per acre per year, more or less.

The chemistry of phosphorus in soil is far too complex to discuss in a garden book, so suffice it to say that in soils containing even a moderate amount of clay, phosphorus will not likely leach out in one gardener's lifetime, though it can be removed by crops taken off the soil. Seed crops in particular remove large quantities of phosphorus because most plants concentrate the phosphorus they've collected into the seeds. A well-grown crop of wheat removes about 30 pounds of phosphorus per acre. A well-grown steer walks off to market with at least 50 pounds of phosphorus concentrated in his bones. When Master Fukuoka takes off two high-yielding cereal crops per year without fertilizing or rotating, obviously his very rich soil has to release over 60 pounds of phosphorus annually. If Fukuoka's soil has huge phosphate reserves, he could mine his field this way for a long, long time.

The story of my original homestead at Lorane can be viewed as a microcosm of the story of upland farming in the Oregon Territories—a tale of phosphorus depletion. In the latter half of the 19th century, when the woods were cleared and a slash-and-burn hillside field was first established, there were about 1,000 pounds of reserve phosphorus in the furrow slice and perhaps another 1,000 in the entire two or three feet of subsoil down to bedrock. The high initial level of organic matter released considerable nitrogen and potassium, and crops grew well at first. Growing continuous winter wheat and barley took away many pounds of phosphorus each year, while rapid winter erosion off that poorly covered hillside washed away much topsoil.

By the time the topsoil was mostly gone, the phosphorus release was no longer enough to grow even 20 bushels of wheat per acre. Soon, there was no topsoil and the field did not give back much more grain than it took to plant it. So the farmer gave up on small grains and put the field into pasture, cutting hay in June and grazing the stubble. But each hay crop got thinner as each grazing steer took phosphorus off to market. After a while the farmer no longer cut the thin hay, but merely grazed the field. The mineral-deficient cattle began to have trouble breeding and nursing their young unless they were given supplemental feedings. The grass got shorter, its seed heads lighter and lighter. And then a homesteading fool from the city came out and bought that pretty green hillside with the short thin grass that would barely set any seed at all, so deficient was the field in phosphorus.

However, that fool got smart fast. When he walked over to the old fence line where the forest started, he noticed the uneroded forest soil

Composition of some common manures and fertilizers

Type of Fertilizer*	Material	N%	P%	K%
1. Nitrogen plus humus	Steer manure	1–2.5	.4–.7	2–3
	Dairy manure	.6–2.5	.3–.5	2–3
	Horse manure	.7–1.5	.3–.6	2–3
	Compost	.4–4.0	.3–2.0	1–3
	Rabbit manure	2.5	1.5	0.5
	Goat manure	1.5	.25	1
2. Phosphorus	Rock phosphate	. . .	22–33	. . .
	Bone meal	3	20	. . .
3. Potassium	Kelp meal	1	. . .	12
	Wood ashes	. . .	. . .	10
	Granite/basalt	. . .	. . .	3–7
4. Humus	Sawdust	. . .	. . .	1–2
	Urea	42		. . .
5. Fertilizers (primarily to add nitrogen)	Urea	42	. . .	. . .
	Blood meal	12	. . .	. . .
	Hoof/horn meal	14	2	. . .
	Fish meal	10	6	. . .
	Cottonseed meal	4–8	2–3	1–2
	Chicken manure	2–4	1–2.5	1–2

went up in a sudden step about a foot high. And he noticed that in the old orchard at the bottom of the field, which probably had never been in wheat, the grass grew six feet tall in spring. So he chased the neighbor's cattle from the pasture, and except for a few acres around his house, permitted fir trees to re-seed themselves from the neighboring forest. The little fir trees grew very slowly at first, until their deep tap roots reached mineral reserves still in the soft crumbling rock below the subsoil; then they started growing 2½ feet a year. A few hundred years from now, when there is again a mature forest there (if that happens), the soil will be regenerated and capable of another slash-and-burn cycle. I hope people will be more sensible in the future and will have learned what J. Russell Smith, the author of *Tree Crops*, tried so hard to teach us—leave your hillside soils in tree crops and keep the plow away from them.

Incidentally, most maritime Northwest soils are reasonably well endowed with potassium. Many local gardeners, influenced by eastern gardening guides, written for a region where some soils are deficient in potassium, think they must build up soil potassium levels, and so needlessly spend money on greensand or granite dust. This is additionally foolish because common manures are rich in potassium.

Managing your own soil

Earlier, I brought up the subject of soil type and mentioned that soils are classified according to the size of their particles. But rarely is a soil pure sand, pure silt or pure clay. And how do you know what soil type you're dealing with? For garden purposes, it may be accurate enough to rub some dry soil between your fingers and feel it. Sandy soils feel gritty; silts have a talcum-like smoothness to them; clays can feel smooth too, but when dampened and kneaded, clayey soils get very gooey and sticky. Another solution for Americans is to pay a visit to the Soil Conservation Service office. The SCS is a branch of the U.S. Department of Agriculture, whose job it is to map and classify all soils and to make and administer programs to preserve the nation's soils. They have offices in most counties and are paid well to be very helpful. Take them a cup of dry soil and they'll be able to give you an immediate rough analysis of your soil type (not its pH or nutrient content). The SCS also has detailed air photo maps outlining soil types. It is very likely they'll be able to locate your land on their master map and give you a sheet containing general specifications of the exact soil you've got. (Canadian gardeners in need of professional soil analysis will have to go to private testing labs. Soil-testing has not been available through the British Columbia Department of Agriculture since 1986. Some provinces do offer this service; check with the provincial Department of Agriculture or Agriculture Canada.)

Soil types behave very differently and require tailor-made management strategies if the best gardening results are to be had. They till differently, hold moisture differently, and some grow various species better than other soils. Some soil types need large quantities of organic matter to be made into something that will grow vegetables; some are natural vegetable producers and only need reasonable maintenance to stay in shape.

Determining soil type by percentage composition of particle size

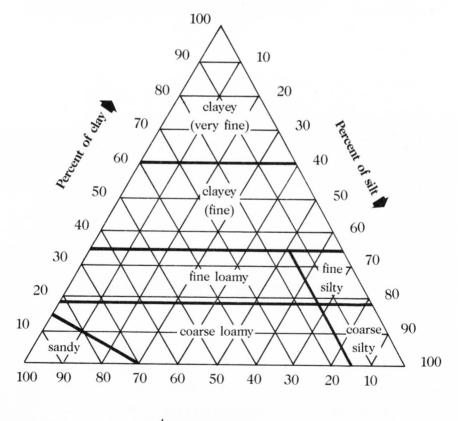

Percent of sand

Sandy soils

Over 70 percent sand, these soils are very easy to till even when very wet, do not form clods, drain extremely well and have very large air pores. Managed right, sands will grow great crops, especially roots and such heat-lovers as melons. But they don't hold much water and, without clay, don't hold cations well. Chemical fertilizers wash out very easily from sands; even with organics, great care must be taken not to overwater. Adding organic matter will improve this situation somewhat, but too much organic matter may encourage symphylans. I used to recommend large initial additions of organic matter (three to four inches tilled under in fall) followed by annual smaller ones of half an inch to an inch. Now, where symphs may be a problem, I think less is better. Instead, try to keep the soil in green manure over the winter; add minimal amounts of organic matter, but to enhance seed germination confine additions of manure or compost to the surface few inches; invest in very high-quality irrigation equipment that makes very frequent light watering easy and convenient. Because sandy soils have so little clay, not much lime is needed, and trying to build up reserve phosphorus may be an expensive waste. Assume just about everything you put in will wash out every winter. I suggest that you add lime (half agricultural, half dolomite) at 25 pounds per thousand square feet (1,000 pounds per acre), every year in spring before planting; use fast-releasing bone meal as the phosphate portion of your complete organic fertilizer to broadcast before planting, and include agricultural lime in your complete organic fertilizer.

Coarse loams

The most ideal stuff a gardener could dream of having, coarse loams are mostly large soil particles, unweathered and often fertile, with just enough clay to hold moisture and retain cations. These soils are so soft, they seem able to magnificently grow any seeds, whether they're planted with the greatest care or fired into the garden with a slingshot from the back porch. Drainage is excellent, pore spaces large, so that even asparagus beds don't usually die out, even in an extra-rainy winter. Coarse loam tills easily on the wet side without forming clods. It doesn't change size much wet or dry (shrink/swell) and it stays soft after tilling, so such roots as carrots and parsnips develop nicely. Crusts don't develop over emerging seeds.

Because coarse loams are fertile and growth-promoting, organic matter levels start out naturally high enough for good soil health, especially if your garden began as a pasture or lawn. Persistently following your summer garden with winter crops or growing overwintered green manures may keep those levels high enough for decent soil health. Jim Baggett at OSU runs his variety trials on this type of soil, and he maintains organic matter content by running a rotation of vegetables, then bush beans, then winter wheat. Growing row crops repetitively may drop organic matter content too low. If this is happening, it may reveal itself as soil that compacts or puddles during a hard rain or while being irrigated. I am currently having a lot of fun Growing on this sort of soil, and I seem to maintain maximum growth if I fertilize well and annually till in the lightest dusting of compost or one bale (100 pounds) of ground alfalfa hay per 250 square feet (four tons per acre). And even that little bit of organic matter may be quite unnecessary, but I'm afraid to find out. Each year I also till in half a ton of lime per acre, and I am building up my phosphate levels with a ton/acre of phosphate rock per year for a few years.

Fine loams and silts

These soils contain less sand, more silt and clay. The finer ones contain larger clay percentages and may be formally named silty clay loams, clay loams or clayey silt, though clay will still not be the major soil fraction. Loams are defined as soils predominantly composed of sand and silt; silt soils are mostly silt with minor fractions of sand and clay. The portion of unweathered soil particles in all loams and silts is high and these types tend to be fertile. However, clay crystals may fall between silt or sand particles, producing a soil of greater density with smaller pore spaces and slower drainage.

Cultural practices should be directed at increasing soil permeability through persistent additions of small amounts of organic matter, regular green manuring and reducing soil compaction through the use of raised beds. I'd guess that working in half an inch of compost or an inch of manure the first year would be more than enough, followed by half that in subsequent years. Because fine soils tend to form surface crusts, which interfere with germination and movement of air into the soil, additions of organic matter are best confined to the surface inch or so of soil, raked in rather than tilled. There's plenty of clay to hold nutrients, so building up reserve phosphorus is sensible; lime might be as much as two tons per acre (100 pounds per 1,000 square feet) the first time, with annual supplements of about a half-ton per acre. There's also enough clay to form clods fairly easily, so it's very important to wait until the soil has dried to the right point before tilling.

A Short Course in Soil Science

Clay soils

Clays have not yet weathered fully to the finest particle sizes. Clay possesses many of the same liabilities of fine clays but has reasonably good drainage, more fertility and thus a higher organic matter content, better aggregation and (usually) a somewhat higher pH. Sandy clays tend to dry out like concrete if not kept moist but are otherwise workable; silty clays are not bad to work at all *if* they're allowed to dry enough before tilling. I got reasonable results from silty clay for years at Lorane, though it demanded three times the work a coarse loam takes. Clay's workability may be a very fragile thing—it can fall apart and slump into an airless mass or become completely cloddy with the slightest mismanagement. I'd handle sandy and silty clays as though they were in the better silty soil category above with perhaps a bit more organic matter. Full-blown clays should be handled like fine clay soils.

Fine clays

Sometimes called gumbo by its unfortunate users, this is the most difficult of all types of soil to manage. It will absorb water only very slowly, becomes sticky when wet, takes forever to dry and then turns into concrete. Work clay when wet and it will form rock-hard clods; when dry, a shovel can't penetrate it. Fine clay can only be tilled to a good seed bed at exactly the right moisture, a condition tht might exist only a few days each season. Surface crusts form readily, preventing seedling emergence and shutting out air. Clay tends to shrink when drying, forming deep surface cracks. (The pattern of the cracks is similar to the shape of the clay crystals.)

Comprised of very thoroughly leached soil particles that have fully decomposed, fine clays tend to be mineral-deficient in rainy climates like ours. Being nutrient-poor and airless, these soils produce skimpy vegetation, and so are low in organic matter and support few microorganisms. Without the action of microlife, clays don't aggregate, which accentuates their bad tendencies. Even when heavily fertilized, plant growth can be very, very poor.

Fine clays can be temporarily improved by significantly upping organic matter content and thus encouraging soil aggregation, but doing this in western Oregon may increase the symphylan population to plague levels. The symphylan is only a minor problem in other climates and may not even cause much trouble in maritime Northwest gardens north of Olympia. So advice for handling clay soils must be divided into two: for those who have symphylans in their area and for those who don't. (Symphylans are discussed at great length in Chapter 7, Diseases and Pests.)

For those who don't have to worry about symphylans, cover the entire new garden area in late September with four or five inches of horse manure or the oldest, most rotten-looking sawdust you can find, plus three tons of agricultural lime per acre, one ton of dolomite lime per acre (50 pounds per 1,000 square feet equals one ton per acre) and two tons of phosphate rock per acre. Water well enough to soften up the rock-hard earth and till it all in. Don't worry about clods; they'll all break down by spring. If you used sawdust instead of manure, also broadcast about 25 pounds of urea per 1,000 square feet to make sure the sawdust is well-rotted by spring. Next year in late spring, when the soil has dried enough (pressed tightly into a ball it should break apart), you can till without forming too many clods. With a shovel, excavate the paths and make up permanent slightly raised beds, fertilize them and grow the garden as best you can.

In subsequent years, before planting, cover each bed with 25 pounds lime per 1,000 square feet and about half an inch of rotted horse manure or half that much compost; hoe all this in shallowly along with any weeds, green manure stubble or the remains of the last vegetable crop. Wait a few days for the vegetation to rot and then rake the surface into a seed bed. The many clods will fall off the top of the bed into the paths. Plant again. Never till or spade up the soil again. Handling the bed this way builds up the level of organic matter in the surface soil to over 10 percent, preventing severe crusting and cracking while allowing the soil to breathe. The extremely high organic matter content of the surface inch or so allows it to be worked fairly early in the season when deep tillage would be utterly impossible. The raised beds also drain better in winter. If the beds are *never* stepped on, they do not require tillage to remain soft enough to permit roots to penetrate and breathe. Worms and other soil life will gradually work the surface organic matter deeper into the bed, while the crops' roots (especially the dense root systems of over-wintered green manures) will rot into the bed, keeping it reasonably porous. A clay bed like this will not grow carrots or parsnips, but it will grow most vegetable crops acceptably well.

To grow carrots, or to create a permanent garden in symphylan country, forget about trying to improve fine clay soil. Instead, consider the native raw material a water-retentive subsoil and haul in good soil to put on top of it. When gravel companies sort out their products, they set aside something called "sandy loam," which is washed or sifted out of the coarse sand. Composed of the finest sand and silt particles, it is ready-made loam soil, lacking only in organic matter. It is for sale as cheap as sand or gravel, and can be hauled in for you 10 or 20 cubic yards at a time and dumped on your garden.

Do not mix sandy loam into clay! What a waste that would be. Instead, shovel it into raised beds 10 to 12 inches deep right on top of the clay. It should be treated just like a coarse loam, with the exception that in the first year it needs to have its organic matter content built up. Half an inch of compost or an inch of horse manure will be plenty to start things off. Surprisingly, even though it came from the bottom of a river or gravel pit, it may be quite weedy for a year or two.

If hauling in loam seems like a ridiculous amount of work or expense, compare the effort of working clay with how easy it is to work loam and multiply by the time you expect to garden on the site. I've had experience with both soils; I know how much work it is to haul pickup load after pickup load of manure in an attempt to fluff up clay. There is not only a huge difference in the amount of effort to get a crop—the crop you get on loam will be twice as large for the same amount of space, water and fertilizer. Vegetables will sort of grow on clay, but they Grow on loam. Your choice.

Further reading

I imagine some readers feel a bit overwhelmed at this point. Others (most, I hope) who have had a lot of gardening data floating around in their mental fact bins may suddenly find it much better aligned and organized in useful ways. For those who want to learn more about the soil and the health that comes from eating from it, I suggest the following:

The Albrecht Papers, William A. Albrecht. Edited by Charles Walters, Jr. 2 vol. (Kansas City: Halcyon House, 1982, 1983).

Acres, U. S. A. is a radical agricultural monthly paper. The group behind it also publishes books, among them this collection of shorter writings. William Albrecht was a vital force at the University of Missouri during the thirties, famous for his research on the interactions of soil fertility and plant nutrition on animal health. Time after time, Albrecht pointed out that livestock fed from well-fertilized, limed fields were healthy while those fed from acid, depleted fields were sick, and that given a choice, animals would invariably choose the most nourishing feed.

The Soil and Health: A Study of Organic Agriculture, Sir Albert Howard (New York: Schocken Books, 1972). Originally published as *Farm-*

ing and Gardening for Health or Disease (London: Faber and Faber, 1945).

The classic statement by the founder of the organic farming movement. The book describes Howard's odyssey as a young research scientist assigned to cure plant diseases on tropical plantations in the British Empire around the turn of this century. Invariably, Howard found connections between plant diseases and soil that had deteriorated from poor cultural practices. The diseases were frequently cured by increasing soil organic matter or improving plant nutrition.

Nutrition and Physical Degeneration, Weston A. Price (La Mesa, California: Price Pottenger Nutrition Foundation, 1977).

First published about 1937, taken through several illustrated editions including one self-published by Price himself, this big book full of dental photos is again available, for less than $30. Price was a Cleveland "society" dentist who in the 1920s wondered why his clientele—the richest, best-educated and best-fed people in the world—were losing all their teeth despite everything he did for them. Why did he wonder? Because he knew that archeologists had found many skulls of people who had lived under extremely poor conditions but nonetheless had died of very old age with all their teeth intact, showing no evidence of gum deterioration or caries. So before science even knew what a vitamin was, Price set out to travel the Earth, looking for people who still had good teeth. And he found them in many nations and of every race, but only in highly isolated places. In every case—Swiss, Scottish, Eskimo, Fijian, Hunzan, etc.—the diet was totally different, but comprised of only natural, simple, local foods, and in every case, there was no store, no white flour, no sugar, no canned food.

Price dispelled the myth that modern medicine makes people live longer. In a properly nourished society, people not only had good teeth, but the women had children easily without complication, infant mortality rates were much lower, there was virtually no degenerative disease and people were as likely to survive into their eighties as we are in our modern age of "medical progress"—and much more likely than we are to remain vigorous and active right to the end.

The Nature and Properties of Soils, Nyle C. Brady (New York: Macmillan, 1974).

Having gone through many editions without substantive change, this remains the standard agriculture school soils text. It is quite understandable and well worth a careful reading by anyone who wants to garden intelligently. A vague recollection of high school chemistry is helpful.

Tree Crops: A Permanent Agriculture, J. Russell Smith (New York: Harcourt, Brace and Company, 1929).

Smith campaigned much of his lifetime to save the world's hillside soils from destruction. He described in great detail admirable cases around the world where stable agricultural societies maintained hillside soil through permaculture—with tree/food crops and mixed grazing—and by doing so lived in health, relative prosperity and great ease. Another classic of the same magnitude as Price, Albrecht and Howard. Available in larger libraries.

One Straw Revolution, Masanobu Fukuoka (Emmaus: Rodale Press, 1978).

Fukuoka's mystical charm has made him today's leading permaculture guru. He describes his personal discovery process leading to a simplified agricultural system requiring no tilling, fertilizing or weeding. Fukuoka hopes that others will be inspired to work out similar no-till, no-fertilize, no-weed systems.

Botany, any recent university-level text.

A complete understanding of gardening is not possible without a thorough understanding of plants. I'd buy this text and the two that follow at a used-book store.

Geography, any university-level text.

Any introductory text will explain the world's weather and climate patterns, as well as variations in daylength and changes in solar energy.

Geology, any introductory university text.

Any first-year text will explain the formation of soils from rocks, widen one's appreciation for the variations in mineralization found in rocks and the soils derived from them and discuss the behavior patterns of rivers as they deposit alluvium.

Planning the
Maritime Garden

*It was about this time I
conceiv'd the bold and
arduous project of arriving
at moral perfection . . .
but I soon found I had
undertaken a task of more
difficulty than I had
imagined.*
—Benjamin Franklin's autobiography

Suppose I were to purchase 24 hybrid broccoli seedlings from the local garden center and set them out one May day. The result? During July, all 24 heads of broccoli would mature within a few days of each other, probably followed by only a few small side shoots. If a freezer full of broccoli wasn't what I wanted, my poor planning would have cost me a lot of effort and probably wasted usable food. If I had grown an old-fashioned, raggedy, open-pollinated variety or several different home-garden hybrids with varying maturities instead, I could have counted on a long harvest followed by lots of side shoots.

Here's another example of poor planning, all too frequently seen west of the Cascades. The typical garden is "put in" over one May weekend. Corn, beets, carrots, lettuce, radishes, squash and cucumbers are sown; tomatoes, cabbage, broccoli and cauliflower are transplanted. The result is so much food from July through early October that the vegetables can hardly be canned, frozen or given away fast enough. This glut is followed by eight months of famine as the empty garden's unprotected soil is pounded by winter rains.

North of the Sunbelt and east of the maritime Northwest, vegetable gardening ends with the coming of winter. With differing degrees of severity, the weather becomes increasingly frosty and the soil freezes solid for a time. In my native Michigan, soil is frozen from November to April; the frost line goes as deep as three feet in a severe winter. Farther south, the soil might freeze only a few inches down for several weeks during the most intense storms of mid-winter. In either case, freezing soil ends the life of most vegetables, though a very few types of onions and greens can survive in frozen soil to resume growth in early spring, especially if protected by a snow blanket. Sensibly, gardeners and farmers in Michigan plan on safely harvesting all food crops by November; no new fresh harvests are possible until early summer. Before refrigerated rail cars brought fresh California and Florida produce to the north, wintertime vegetables came out of root cellars or canning jars. "Fresh" root-cellar fare was limited to apples, pears, roots and coles, and their quality dropped lower the longer they were stored.

For someone who wants fresh food as much of the year as possible, the maritime Northwest can be a much better place to garden. Our mild winters almost never freeze the soil, and many hardy crops can grow outside until November's chill and low light levels check their development, and then stay alive until harvest, or resume growth in spring if not already mature. And since the ground is not frozen, our first sowings of the new gardening season can be made in February, as long as the rain-soaked ground can be worked up first. Twelve months of fresh vegetable harvest is possible most years in most maritime locations—if you know how.

Winter vegetable cropping techniques weren't known to the easterners who settled the Oregon Territory, so it was natural for them to expect a growing cycle beginning shortly before the last usual frost date and ending in fall. Ironically, most of the first Europeans in the United States had come from England, one of the few other temperate regions on Earth with a maritime climate, where growing wintertime vegetables is a tradition. But by the time the Oregon Territory was settled, Americans had long forgotten English food production systems. There was no Siletz Squanto here to teach Ohioans how to garden in this climate because the locals were hunter/gatherers. So for over a hundred years now, most Americans west of the Cascades have been planning gardens pretty much as though we still lived on the other side of the mountains. Canadians in the lower mainland of B.C., with their strong Commonwealth connection and prominent English community, have done better.

About 10 years ago, a few very aware gardeners who were connected with Seattle's P-Patch community garden and a regional alternative agricultural association called Tilth recognized our climatic similarity to England and "discovered" winter gardening. One of them, Binda Colebrook, wrote an enthusiastic book in the late seventies, *Winter Gardening in the Maritime Northwest*, which explained the possibilities of winter gardening in exacting detail and suggested techniques, varieties and seed sources. I was fortunate enough to arrive in Oregon just when *Winter Gardening* first came out. I now find the discovery of an exciting and new field of winter gardening to be ironic, because constant loss of pre-existing knowledge is typical of Earth—a place where we must continually relearn what we already once knew, thinking all the while that we're making progress.

Winter crops have such great value in the home garden that maritime Northwest residents should have rushed to take up the practice as strongly as the gardeners of England. But it's more than 11 years since *Winter Gardening* first came out and nine years since I started writing regional garden books and selling the seeds needed for year-round gardening—and most of us still don't garden over the winter.

One reason many maritime Northwest gardeners don't take to year-round gardening is that they don't care to eat a lot of strange vegetables. I call these folks "corn and tomato gardeners." There are few customs more resistant to change than people's eating habits. But finicky eaters who wouldn't dream of eating a rutabaga are missing something very important—a chance at much better health. Just about everyone these days would agree that a diet composed primarily of grains, nuts, fresh vegetables and ripe fruits produced on highly mineralized soil is healthful. The problem is that most people don't realize how actively unhealthy it is to depend instead on highly processed cooked food produced on demineralized, unbalanced soil. A diet of *apparently* fresh food actually picked unripe or held in long-term storage is also far from ideal. Unfortunately, the only way to solidly realize these truths is to first entirely change one's diet for a year or so without too much backsliding, and gradually find out firsthand how much better it feels to eat right.

Over the years, I have become more and more dependent on my garden, and my health and feeling of well-being actually have improved as I move into middle age. That's why I now prefer to eat fresh from my garden in the winter, even if that means living on Brussels sprouts, cabbage, carrots, beets, broccoli, endive, spinach, lettuce, sorrel, rocket, rutabagas, leeks, scallions, cauliflower, parsnips, parsley root, winter squash and potatoes. I prefer a winter of these vegetables, fresh and full of life force, to nutritional subsistence—even on organically grown canned green beans, frozen corn and homemade tomato sauce. Many types of fresh vegetables deteriorate so rapidly that within a day or two of harvest they lose whatever it was that set them apart from supermarket fare. This loss of quality is so marked that when I am traveling for more than a few days, eating supermarket produce and from restaurant salad bars, I find my body developing strange cravings for a "real meal" of meat and potatoes. Whatever it is that fresh organic garden food has, commercial produce lacks it.

I want the best possible health for myself and my family, and, like a sensible fellow, I know that my own family's happiness is best enhanced by the improved condition of all my neighbors. To that end, let me offer the reader some other thoughts about growing a year-round garden.

Some people prefer living in a self-sufficient manner. I wish more of us did. Our nation has a tradition of personal independence; most of us lived on subsistence farms when the Constitution was written. Our national government was created to protect the liberties of us independent rural folk, not to monitor and control hundreds of millions of dependent city dwellers. Americans are taught our liberties flow from the Constitution; actually, individual, independent self-sufficiency is the source.

Many people who admire the founders of the American republic and who think we would be better off to return to the values and institutions of our past consider themselves libertarians. I was first exposed to a libertarian viewpoint in 1961, when an old social radical named Scott Nearing came to address my high school about "living the good life." Even then, Scott was a gray patriarch who commanded respect, and he remained admirably active for the next 20 or so years (he died only recently, well into his nineties). Scott's message was that as individuals and families we could live much better, be more economically secure and have more free time and a higher quality of life if we independently produced our own goods on free and clear homesteads, living as much as possible outside the cash economy, free of tax. The members of his small Maine homesteading community lived like aristocrats and worked like peasants, but spent only four hours a day at "bread labor"—enough to provide virtually everything they needed. Scott contended that laboring eight hours a day was necessary only when there were layers of exploitative humans living off the actual producer.

Because there were some minor cash needs—land taxes to pay, an old truck to keep running and a few things to buy they couldn't make themselves—the community members had a cash industry, maple sugaring, that did demand considerable hours of labor, but only for about six weeks annually. The rest of the year, four hours of bread labor a day did it. Bread labor built all their own buildings of stone, rough-sawn or split lumber and home-quarried sand and gravel. The construction of storage or work buildings or homes for new community members required outside purchases only of cement, roofing tin, glass and a few nails. They grew virtually *all* their food, cut all their firewood by hand. Because they opposed exploitation of any life form, they neither ate meat nor kept work animals. Scott said that it was less work to spade a garden than it was to keep a plow horse fenced, fed and fitted out with harness and implements. (Since the 1930s when Scott started, our liberties have disappeared at the same rate that our self-sufficiency has declined! Try something similar in these days of building permits, septic approvals and the Uniform Building Code.)

Scott Nearing's quiet power and certainty made a deep impression on me. As the years passed and I experienced the disappointments of office politics, corporate opportunism, and all the other things an ordinary person has to put up with to earn a living, Scott's vision kept coming back. As soon as I could barely afford to be free and clear on my own homestead, I decided it was time to begin living the good life myself; I cashed in my California position and dropped out. I still dream of living a relatively cashless life, harvesting bitter-free acorns and other tree crops, growing a little grain by hand, raising a bit of wool to spin our own clothing and using sheep manure to grow a garden and home orchard. Year-round gardening is an essential part of that dream.

There are many people who garden to save a little money. These folks are trying to achieve a degree of self-sufficiency, even if they're not ready to abandon a regular job and really wing it. I support all honest efforts at independence and self-sufficiency. In winter, when supermarket produce is high-priced and of low quality, our own gardens can contain virtually free *fresh* food. *And I've found that it is much less work and takes much less time to grow a year-round garden than it does to can and freeze the summer garden.* I've done both.

What's a year-round garden worth to you? Hard to say. But it's not so hard to state what it *could* be worth. I've studied gardening techniques for many years, and I have a personality quirk my wife, Isabelle, labels "Mr. Efficiency"—I like to figure out the best, fastest and most direct way to do a job without waste motion or mistakes. So I am very fast at gardening. I figure my garden time is worth $10 to $15 an hour in terms of food produced, after deducting such expenses as fertilizer, seeds and electricity for the pump and accounting for depreciation on tools, deer fencing and irrigation systems. To be even more economical, I have intentionally and gradually changed my dietary habits to match what I can grow year-round.

The average American family of three-point-something persons spends about 20 percent of its income of $20,000 or so on food. That's over $4,000 a year. My family of three spends far less than half that much on food, and half of *that* half is on unnecessary indulgences such as prepared salad dressing we don't need to have at all and would in fact do better without. Year-round gardening is one reason we can live so inexpensively.

Winter gardening

Maritime winters can be tough on even the hardiest species and varieties. Low light levels and temperatures slow or stop growth while damage caused by repetitive frosts and pounding rain mounts up. Most plants that winter over have food reserves stored in stem or root, and they'll use some of these reserves to maintain health. However, a hard winter can gradually break down the plants' resistance, until they succumb to one of the many rots and molds that thrive under damp, cool conditions. Endive provides a good example of how weather can affect winter survival. When the winter is dry, or dry and cold, endive survives handily and tolerates frosts below 7°F without damage. However, when the winter is rainy and mild, moisture is constantly trapped in the dense rosette of thin leaves and the head slowly rots down to a nubbin, and the plant may die before growing conditions improve in spring. (This makes endive an excellent cold-frame candidate, because merely keeping off the pounding rain permits it to reliably overwinter.) Winter cabbage varieties, on the other hand, have thick waxy leaves that shed water like a duck's back, and the heads are wrapped in many protective outer layers that keep the rain away from the vital core. It doesn't really matter to the gardener or the cabbages if a few outer layers rot.

Plants deal with freezing by a combination of two tricks. One is that they increase the amount of sugars and other substances dissolved in the water contained in the cells. This acts like antifreeze. It also makes many species taste much sweeter after they've been well-frosted a few times. That's why kale and Brussels sprouts grown in California are pale imitations of the real thing. The second mechanism is to actually pump water out of the cell as the temperature approaches freezing, so that when the cell does freeze, the expanding water within won't burst the walls, killing the cell. Adjusting to freezing and thawing takes work and depletes food reserves. The ability to handle frost is also "learned": it improves each time the plant is exposed to freezing. And the ability varies from variety to variety. For example, most varieties of succulent cabbage contain too much moisture to be "antifreezed" or pumped in and out of the cells and, because they were bred for tenderness, their thin cell walls are weak. Tender varieties will die if they freeze solid. (It takes a short spell of very intense cold or an extended period of subfreezing weather to freeze a big cabbage head solid.) Freeze-hardy varieties have tough, dry leaves.

The winter tolerance of each vegetable species varies; the tolerance of each *variety* within each species may also be different and will fluctuate somewhat from year to year. For example, the December 1983 freeze suddenly dropped temperatures to 7°F at Lorane, after a long mild fall. Though conditions remained subfreezing for three and a half days, the very warm soil did not freeze. Yet varieties that in previous years had survived 3°F lows or had only 50 percent losses at 6°F were totally destroyed. Why? Because in that frostless and sunny 1983 autumn, the plants had grown lushly and were tender right up into December, not nearly as hardy as they would have been if they'd experienced a lot of rain and frequent lighter overnight frosts. Only a few individuals of one extremely tough cabbage variety survived, and we ate supermarket salads that winter. That same year, the Vegetable Crops Research Station at Agassiz, British Columbia experienced much frosty autumn weather and even a bit of snow during November. Most of its pre-toughened winter trials survived the December freeze, with somewhat colder temperatures than we had at Lorane.

There are a few maritime Northwest locations that don't encourage year-round gardening. For example, folks in the very northwestern corner of Washington State in Whatcom County can almost count on having blasts of Arctic air leak through the Cascades and wipe out much of their garden most winters. Similarly, people gardening at elevations much in excess of 1,000 feet may frequently experience low temperatures that will kill winter vegetables. At 900 feet, my Lorane garden was frozen out about once every three winters.

Averaging the odds, I suppose that Willamette Valley gardeners can count on likely winter survival five years in six; those from Drain and the Yoncalla Valley to the south can pretty much assume winter survival; in frosty Washington State, proximity to the sea is crucial—gardens close to the coast or to Puget Sound usually have mild winters, while farther inland or at a higher elevation winter survival can be dicey. Only a few miles south of frigid Whatcom County, the Skagit Valley offers such excellent winter gardening, combined with cool summers that don't degrade the seed vigor of certain species, that many international wholesale vegetable seed companies have flocked there. Col. Rex Applegate, the fellow who first surveyed Oregon and marked out the original Applegate Trail from Klamath Falls north to the Willamette, said that in his opinion the very finest places to homestead in the entire maritime Northwest were on the bottomland loams along the Umpqua River, with the best of the best being the stretch of river from Elkton to Scottsburg. In terms of winter weather, he was certainly right. If there's anywhere west of the Cascades where winters will be coastal-mild yet not any rainier than the interior, this banana belt is it.

Local soil conditions may also make year-round gardening difficult or impossible once the winter rains start up in earnest. When root systems remain waterlogged for days at a time, they are unable to take in oxygen. Plants then sicken and die. There are large areas in the Willamette with poor drainage, and I've noticed the same problem on the bottomlands between Monroe and Everett, Washington, and along the flood plains of various coastal rivers in both Oregon and Washington. In the Willamette, the cause is a thin layer of gooey fine clay two to three feet below the otherwise fertile topsoil. Geologists suppose the layer was deposited dur-

ing a huge flood some 15,000 years ago. When heavy winter rains fall
for days on end, the clay acts like the plug in a bathtub, and water fills
pore spaces until the soil goes underwater. Huge shallow lakes form, then
take a day or two to disappear after the rains stop. The only crop species
that can tolerate waterlogged roots for days at a time have been flax and
grass. The flax industry died with the onset of synthetic fibers after World
War II, and now farmers on these poorly drained soils grow grass seed
instead. If you're considering purchase of a rural homestead surrounded
by grass seed farms, or even a city house in west Eugene or other areas
where grass seed used to be produced, think twice if you're a serious year-
round gardener. (After they dry out in spring, though, grass seed soils do
grow good summer gardens.)

Poor winter drainage can sometimes be improved simply by making
raised beds, using paths as drainage ditches. Other situations may call
for deep ditching and drain tiles. Gardeners with problems can obtain
a free consultation with the Soil Conservation Service. Areas with high
winds can also be difficult spots for gardens, winter or summer. Fencing
and windbreaks can help; in fact, windbreaks aren't a bad idea for any
garden, especially in winter. Lowering the wind speed will raise the
temperature considerably and may permit plants to make a little more
growth, repairing the damage done by weeks of pounding rain and hard
frost.

Asset Location

The simple fact that light and plant growth go together means that
winter gardens must occupy as much space or more than summer gardens.
From June through September, relatively small plots will totally overwhelm
the kitchen: a 100-square-foot bed of summer squash fills a five-gallon
bucket every other day; a similar-sized bed of melons produces half a dozen
every other day while they're coming on; a bed half that size of mixed
lettuce varieties yields half a dozen nice heads every other day for three
weeks; and 100 square feet of bush beans picks five gallons every few
days. A dozen pole-trained tomato vines on less than 50 square feet will
keep a family supplied for months unless huge amounts of tomato sauce
are to be canned. In fact, unless a lot of summer food is to be preserved
or the family is extremely fond of winter squash or space-wasting sweet
corn, a few thousand square feet of well-grown, fertile summer garden
will likely yield more than enough for even a totally vegetarian kitchen.

But the winter garden is another matter. Since the vegetables don't
grow much from mid-October until early March, essentially what you've

got by winter is what you'll have—the vegetables are in cold storage out-side awaiting harvest. Each winter and the following spring, my family goes through a 100-square-foot bed of salad carrots (and could juice five times that amount if I were willing to grow that many) and equal amounts of parsnips, rutabagas, leeks, endive, lettuce, overwintered broccoli, over-wintered bulb onions and scallions, plus 200 square feet of kale, Brussels sprouts, fall and winter cabbage, overwintered cauliflower, and spinach. Add in enough space for miscellaneous items like rocket, sorrel, parsley, Chinese cabbage, fennel and so on, and it amounts to another 2,000 square feet of growing bed, not considering paths. My family does not eat sweet corn or much winter squash, so the total irrigated vegetable portion of my personal garden amounts to about 4,000 square feet of growing beds plus paths.

Green manuring

After all the work I've put into my garden soil, it now seems to me like a taxicab with its meter running: if I don't go somewhere, a lot of money is being wasted. Repeated applications of lime have increased the soil pH to nearly 7.0. This means that clay particles don't hold cations too tightly for the plants to take what they need, and—unfortunately— winter rains can more readily leach nutrients. Annual additions of manure or compost have increased organic matter levels a percent or two, great-ly upping available nitrogen. Even in spring when my soil is cold, available levels of nitrogen and phosphorus aren't too bad. The desirable conse-quence of all this is that plants will grow healthily almost any time of year, and even in early spring they don't show signs of nutrient deficien-cies. The undesirable consequence is that soil organisms are also perhaps overly abundant now, and they are busily consuming organic matter at a most rapid rate. Anything I can do to retard or prevent nutrient/organic matter loss is of benefit.

I use one simple technique to keep nutrients from washing out of soil *and* retard the loss of organic matter: I keep the garden green. A solid cover of lustily growing plants will pick up any available nutrients and make organic matter out of them. Later, this above-ground organic matter is dug in or returned to the soil after composting, releasing cap-tured nutrients and maintaining humus levels. The more I can keep my garden beds continuously green, the lower the nutrient losses. Green manuring might even increase organic matter somewhat. The most prof-itable way to accomplish this is to have food crop following food crop

Year-round planting calendar

February

Entire month	Transplant asparagus roots
15	Sow peas, favas, spinach

March

Entire month	Sow peas, favas, spinach, asparagus seed, mustard and related Oriental greens, radish, parsley, bulb onions, scallions
15	Transplant earliest broccoli and cabbage seedlings
17	St. Patrick's Day ritual—sow potatoes

April

Entire month	Sow peas, scallions, spinach (summer varieties), beets, turnips, radish, kohlrabi, chard, carrots, lettuce, broccoli, cabbage, parsley, sorrel, cauliflower, potatoes
1	Transplant earliest cauliflower
after 15	Transplant onion seedlings and early leeks Sow celery and celeriac

May

Entire month	Sow cauliflower, cabbage, beets, radish, chard, carrots, lettuce, broccoli, winter leek nursery bed, scallions, potatoes, lettuce
15	Sow snap beans, squash (summer and winter), basil, dill, dry beans, sweet corn Transplant tomato, celery and celeriac seedlings

June

Entire month	Sow cucumber, summer squash, melons, snap beans, beets, carrots, lettuce, broccoli, fall and winter cabbage, Brussels sprouts, cauliflower, scallions
15	Transplant peppers and eggplant

Year-round planting calendar (continued)

July

Entire month	Sow lettuce
	Transplant winter leeks
before 15	Sow parsnips, carrots, summer beets, fall cauliflower, bush snap beans, scallions
after 15	Sow rutabaga, kale, winter beets, spinach, overwintered broccoli

August

Entire month	Sow endive, spinach
before 15	Sow overwintered cauliflower, looseleaf lettuce
after 15	Sow overwintered bulb onions

September

before 15	Sow endive, corn salad, garlic and shallots, field turnips (as green manure)

October

Entire month	Sow green manures: favas, crimson clover, field peas

Note: This rough schedule is for the Willamette Valley garden. North of Longview, along the coast and at higher elevations, spring dates might be too early, fall dates a bit late. South of Drain, Oregon, spring dates might be a bit too late, fall dates a bit early. Starting dates for transplants are found in a similar schedule in Chapter 6.

through the seasons. Since more than half the weight of the crop is residue, either in the root system or in trim, food crops create a lot of compost and leave organic matter in the ground from their rotting root systems.

Having crop follow crop as much as possible also allows me to have a smaller garden—which means less manure, lime, phosphate rock, fertilizer, weeding, tillage, water and *work*. And if food crop cannot follow food crop, I grow what is called a green manure crop—some sort of fast-growing vegetation to produce quantities of mineral-rich organic matter.

So many crop successions are possible that it would be foolish to attempt a complete list. Variations in sowing date, microclimate and personal taste are too great. Instead, let me mention some of the successions I've used as illustrations. Earliest spring sowings of peas are usually harvested by mid-June and may be immediately followed by brassicas for fall or winter harvest. Later pea sowings can be followed by faster-growing brassicas such as kale and rutabagas, or by month-old transplants started in early June and ready to plop in behind the peas. Overwintered onions and spring sowings of spinach or other greens are harvested before the main heat of summer, and may be followed by beets, carrots, parsnips or chard. Overwintered broccoli and cauliflower are done by May, and their beds, after a dressing of compost and fertilizer, are perfect for let-tuce, beans, squash, melons, peppers or other hot-weather crops. Beds of peppers, melons and cucumber are all through in early October most years, though tomatoes and squash may hang on longer if there is no frost and a lot of sun. These beds may be put into overwintered green manures such as clover, field peas, fava beans, corn salad or high-grade varieties of field turnip, such as Tyfon. Corn salad and Tyfon have a bonus of being edible in winter.

Beds of fall- or winter-harvested coles are usually bare and somewhat weedy by early spring. This is a good time to add manure or compost, fertilize and then sow peas, favas or other spring crops. If the beds aren't actually needed for food production, peas and favas are still good spring-sown green manures to enrich the soil and make organic matter until you do want to plant a food crop. Early spring-sown brassicas, usually harvested by late June, can be followed by root crops, late sowings of let-tuce or other greens. Early sowings of potatoes may be dug by mid-July, leaving good spots for starting overwintered brassicas.

Once the garden becomes a year-round garden, crop flows harmonious-ly into crop. The garden can become almost self-sufficient in organic matter. To me, the beautiful garden is the all-green garden—I judge the skill of the gardener by the ratio of bare earth to vegetation.

Raised beds

American garden writers have hailed the raised bed as though it were a novel idea. Not new at all, permanent raised-bed culture has been used in the Orient for millenia and was a basic component of the European market garden before the age of machine cultivation. There are so many advantages to raised beds that they should be used whenever possible. Only a few vegetable crops are unsuited to raised-bed gardening: sweet corn, the more vigorous varieties of melons and vining squash.

Although the slick garden magazines tend to show raised beds as very tidy things neatly surrounded with planks or railroad ties, contained beds are not only expensive to construct but also are much more work to maintain. They're actually *too* permanent. Weeding container beds is a big chore—the hoe is constantly bumping against the retaining walls, while weeds, when rooted in cracks, become so strongly attached that they have to be painstakingly picked out in little pieces. And how can you rake clods out of a raised bed if they have to first be lifted over a wooden plank? One final objection: if the beds are virtually cast in concrete, how does the gardener rotate out of vegetable plots and relocate them?

For easiest maintenance, raised beds should be simply low mounds of earth with paths between them. The primary reason they are raised is to delineate them as beds—the bed being something nearly sacred that is never stepped on. If never compacted by feet *and* if kept busy growing vegetation, the bed seldom (if ever) needs to be deeply worked after it's first made. Additions of organic matter chopped into the top few inches of the bed with a sturdy hoe will keep the surface especially soft and friable, permitting amazingly easy weeding and successful seed germination. Vegetable and green manure roots densely penetrate the uncompacted soil 18 to 24 inches deep; as these roots rot, they loosen the soil further. The only time I feel I have to deeply work my raised beds is before I plant carrots or parsnips.

An additional benefit from raised-bed gardening is improved winter drainage. After only a few rainless days, the humusy top two or three inches of soil will be dry enough to work gently with a hoe and rake, permitting sowing or transplanting during short breaks in what can seem like perpetual spring rain. I get several beds planted during March and can easily sow very early spring green manures on beds that have been harvested bare during the winter. Solid masses of garden peas make excellent edible green manures for this purpose. Peas are especially good because they leave the soil particularly fluffy after they're cut and the stubble is hoed in, while the following vegetable crop will grow fast on the nitrogen the peas leave behind.

It's very easy to take a green manure crop off a raised bed without using a rear-end rototiller. Pull the vegetation by hand or cut it close to the ground with a scythe, hand sickle or lawnmower. Gather and compost it. Then rebuild the bed with compost, manure and complete organic fertilizer, chop in the fertilizer and stubble with a hoe, wait a few days or a week for the stubble to break down, hoe the bed one more time and then rake out a seed bed. If the bed isn't surrounded by boards, any clods on the surface can be effortlessly raked off into the paths, where foot traffic will break them up.

When you plant a green manure, the roughness of the seed bed is of little consequence, so it's okay to go over the paths with a shovel and return an inch of compacted soil to the bed's surface. Then broadcast the green manure seed and hoe it all in shallowly. In early spring, over-wintering green manures will be only a few inches tall and very tender. To sow very early crops, hoe the green manure into the soil, where it will rot in less than two weeks. This nearly effortless handling of green manures won't work when the vegetation is very tough, which is why I don't recommend using rye or other grasses as cover crops. Instead, grow tender succulent vegetation, which is easily handled with hand tools.

It is much easier to work up an entire empty bed at one time, so gardens are best planned with a single bed carrying one type of plant or a group of vegetables that will be both sown and out of the ground more or less at the same time. My beds are about 20 feet long. A raised bed should be as wide as possible to minimize wasteful path space, but narrow enough that the center can be reached from the path without stepping on the bed. So the length of the weeder's arm will determine the width. Most of mine are about four feet wide.

John Jeavons, author of the currently trendy bible of Biodynamic/French Intensive gardening, *How to Grow More Vegetables Than You Ever Thought Possible on Less Land Than You Can Imagine*, believes in sowing seeds by scattering them thinly over raised beds. He illustrates this with diagrams showing that more plants can be sown using hexagonal centers than by sowing in rows. I believe he's both right and wrong. He's right, in that there are more possible locations for plants; but wrong, because plants don't merely grow in perfect circles. Even in rows, plants will fill in any opening until the bed is a solid mass of leaves competing for every bit of available light. I've found that sowing in short four-foot rows across a raised bed allows me to keep the bed thinned and free of weeds using tools other than my fingers, which saves a lot of time and labor.

Jeavons and others of the same school also recommend double-digging raised beds. This is a laborious procedure designed to maximize production as quickly as possible by pulverizing the soil and blending in organic matter and rock minerals 24 inches deep. Jeavons's research was done in sunny Palo Alto, California, where light availability and intensity are much higher than they are west of the Cascades. I've found light is the factor limiting plant density on raised beds—not soil air, nutrients or water. Perhaps without double-digging I don't get all the vegetables I ever thought possible from less land than I ever imagined, but I am quite sure I do get almost as many with *much* less work.

I recommend making up raised beds initially by spreading the appropriate soil amendments for the type of soil being worked, and then rototilling the whole plot six to seven inches deep. Beds are then formed by shoveling a few inches of soil up from what are to be paths onto what are to be beds. This makes well-fertilized, airy raised beds nine inches deep—a good beginning and rich enough to grow two-thirds the amount of vegetables a double-dug bed might produce the first year with less than 20 percent of the work. Even if your soil is heavy and tends to compact, if you never step on the bed, and if you religiously grow cover crops and regularly apply fertilizer and organic matter to the bed's surface, yields will gradually increase over a few years as the soft bed gradually deepens. Eventually the soil will be easily penetrated by plant roots to a depth of 18 to 24 inches—without ever being tilled again.

Some of my readers may think I am against tilling or owning a tiller. In fact, I own a very good one. It gets most of its service tilling along raspberry rows, weeding paths between the beds and working the half of my garden that is in field crops. I will use it to make up a bed if it's already in the garden and handy. Rototilling is much easier and faster than hoeing and raking, but on a soft raised bed, not by *that* much.

Cloches and cold frames

There are lots of books on the subject of expanding the gardening season through the use of cloches and cold frames. Most of them were written for the eastern gardener and do not take into account the facts of light and growth in the maritime Northwest. One little book that did, called *Gardening Under Cover* (Eugene: Amity Foundation, 1984), was as regional a book as this one is, but unfortunately, it is no longer in print and is hard to find in libraries. The subject itself is so simple that if you're equipped with a few growing basics, you won't need to study an entire book on it. So here are the basics of gardening under cover in only a few pages. (People who are not intimate with a hammer and saw may wish to look over some library books for details on how the many different kinds of frames and cloches are actually built.)

Let's first consider and dismiss solar greenhouses designed for the east. There, cold frames and greenhouses demand maximum insulation; sometimes thermal masses are used to store heat. Because the winter sun shines so frequently in the east, heat loss can be minimized by reducing the area of glass and insulating the opaque north, east and west walls and part of the roof. Add black-painted barrels or cans of water to the north wall to soak up extra heat when the sun shines and reradiate it at night or on cloudy days, and you've got the classic solar greenhouse.

Solar greenhouses are not workable in the maritime Northwest. I know people who enthusiastically built one and then found the greenhouse a better place to store stuff than to grow plants. To understand why, first consider this: when the sun shines, most light comes directly from the sun, and so a south-facing window allows virtually all available light to enter. In a snowy climate with an average of 20 or more sunny winter days a month, it's reasonable to sacrifice a little bit of light accumulation

Year-round cloche/frame calendar

Planting Date		Harvest Period
September	Looseleaf lettuce, mustard greens, spinach, endive	Nov.–Jan.
October	Looseleaf lettuce, mustard greens, spinach, endive	Feb.–Apr.
February	Looseleaf lettuce, mustard greens, spinach, peas	Mid-Apr., May
March	Lettuce, mustard greens, kohlrabi, spinach, broccoli, cauliflower, cabbage, beets, chard, carrots	Mid-May, June
April 15– May 15	Tomato transplants, bush beans, squash	June–summer
Late May	Pepper and eggplant transplants, melons, cucumbers	July–summer

Note: This rough schedule is for the Willamette Valley garden. North of Longview, along the coast and at higher Oregon elevations, spring dates may be too early, fall dates a bit late. South of Drain, Oregon, spring dates might be a bit too late, fall dates a bit early.

on cloudy days for insulation and heat retention. In the same way, where the sun shines regularly, bedding plants can be grown in a south or west window. Here in the maritime Northwest, we're lucky to see the winter sun a few days each month. To keep greenhouse plants alive during *our* winters, we need to let in every available bit of light—*our* greenhouses need to be all "glass." And we can't grow stocky bedding plants on the windowsill.

If I were to attempt a simplified description of our climate in terms of light, I'd say that we usually see the sun five days in December, January and February, 10 in March, 15 in April, 20 in May, 25 in June, 30 in July, 25 in August, 20 in September, 15 in October and 10 in November. When it's overcast, light comes to earth with equal intensity from every direction at once, but the overall intensity of the light that does filter through the cloud cover is not nearly as strong as direct sunlight. So west of the Cascades, a greenhouse that allows in only light from direct sun fails to accumulate enough light to grow plants at all during the crucial winter and early spring months. In our mild rainy region, we need a greenhouse that captures every bit of available light, not one that preserves heat at any cost.

Such a dream greenhouse is a wonderful luxury, and some day when I'm rich I'm going to own one 100 feet long and 12 feet wide, with a solar-heated competition lap pool for my athlete-wife, Isabelle, down one side of it and a gorgeous salad garden full of radishes and the most delicate lettuces, spinaches and other cool-season greens down the other for me. And in the summer, I'll use that humid tropical environment to grow okra and peppers and other. . .well, back to reality. Greenhouses, though desirable, are expensive to build. Cloches and cold frames are compromise greenhouses, too low for a person to walk in but very inexpensive to build.

Though pleasant, greenhouses have one serious liability that can make them more expensive if you try to correct it with electricity: they don't retain much heat at night. Much more stable nighttime temperatures can be had by simply shortening the greenhouse from eight feet high to a cold frame one foot high and walking around the outside instead of working inside it. With only one foot of air to heat instead of eight, the soil becomes an effective heat sink. My garden cold frames are constructed of Cuprinol-treated 2x10 fir planks with 4x4 corner braces and are about 10 feet long by four feet wide, covered with recycled glass windows in wooden sashes. (Warning: some wood preservatives are toxic to plants, so use only a copper naphthenate-based treatment on cold frames and compost boxes.) If these frames ever wore out, I'd make new ones out of 1x10 boards with

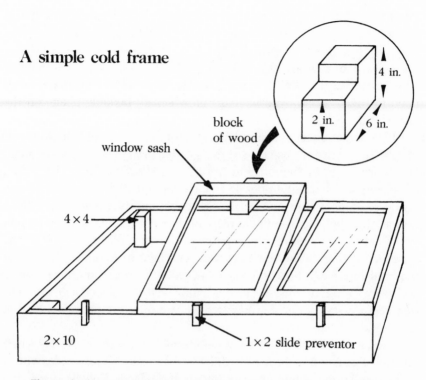

A simple cold frame

block of wood

window sash

4 in.

2 in.

6 in.

4 × 4

2 × 10

1 × 2 slide preventor

This is the best design for the wood blocks that will hold the cold frame windows open.

2x4 corners, because it takes two people to move my current frames. Like almost all carpenters, I tend to overbuild.

Ten inches is sufficient height for most winter greens. The frames should be sloped to allow rainwater to run off the "lights," but I'm a poor carpenter, so instead of sloping the boxes by cutting the side boards on a diagonal and doubling up two eight-inch boards on the back side (which would have to become the north wall), I slope the entire bed by raking the south side two inches lower than the north side. Opened sashes are prevented from sliding off by nailed-on pieces of 1x2 that stick up a few inches. The lights are held open by a block of 4x4 inserted opposite the "slide preventer." There is no weather stripping, no crosspiece to rest the windows on, no attempt to seal the big cracks. But the frames work, permitting maximum light entry while keeping off the rain and raising temperatures a few degrees at night. When the sun shines, I prop the windows wide open. On nights when frost threatens, I close them. During long rainy spells, I leave one light cracked open an inch to ventilate the box and prevent excess humidity and rot. Almost anyone could design unnecessarily better frames.

I have four such frames for salad greens—two are sown in September, and the other two in October. The September-sown frames are harvested from December through January, and the October frames are cut February and March. When the September frames are empty around the end of January, they are resown with more greens that are ready to harvest in late April and last into May. By April, when the October frame is through, greens may be sown outside without protection. It's that simple—occasional quality lettuce, spinach and endive salads all winter, instead of an entire season exercising my jaw muscles chewing tough cabbage and kale.

In spring, the gardener can figure that the season has been advanced by about six weeks inside a crude frame or cloche. What could be safely planted outside June 1 can be planted into a cloche April 15. This little bit of effort can make a huge difference in how long one gets those hot-weather vegetables that make gardening *gardening*. For example, at frosty Lorane I've had cloche-protected tomatoes, transplanted in mid-April, begin ripening heavily by early July. At Elkton, where tomatoes may be set out without protection mid-April, I've transplanted into a cloche March 10 and had my first ripe tomatoes in early June. Summer squash, direct-seeded into a cloche April 15, started yielding zucchini mid-June.

Melon and cucumber seeds may be sown in low cold frames like the ones I use in winter, but for forcing tomatoes and summer squash in spring, I switch to a different design. Low box frames have two liabilities. Though they do hold a more stable nighttime temperature the lower to the ground they are, they also heat up too much when the sun shines strongly and have to be opened wide. On very warm sunny days, the sashes may have to be removed entirely to avoid frying the plants. Also, the species I want to protect in spring need more head room. So I make tunnel cloches.

The tunnel cloche is, if anything, simpler than a wooden box, though in certain ways it's less convenient to use. Basically it's a sheet of clear polythene stretched over supporting hoops to make a plastic film tube. The edges of the plastic are held down with soil; to regulate the temperature, the ends may be open or closed. Tunnel cloches range from little tubes a foot high and a foot wide, supported by stout wire hoops stuck in the ground, to the kind I use, which are supported with 10-foot lengths of half-inch galvanized thinwall conduit purchased from an electrical supply company, bent into giant croquet hoops with a borrowed pipe bender right in the parking lot of that same electrical supply company. The resulting arch is about 3½ feet tall in the center and four feet wide at the bottom. Similar but shorter-lived supports can be made by twisting hoops of half-inch or three-quarter-inch plastic pipe and sticking the ends in the ground; I prefer the greater initial expense but long-term economy of metal conduit, because galvanized steel pipe will last as many years as I'm willing to keep the ends painted once the galvanizing rusts off after the first five or six years of use.

Every few years I buy a 100-foot roll of 10-foot-wide clear poly sheeting to skin the cloches. I make up a cloche by pushing both ends of each supporting arch about a foot into the ground, with arches every 3½ or four feet down a four-foot-wide raised bed. If your beds are wider or narrower, bend the hoops accordingly. Since the conduit comes in 10-foot lengths, a 10-foot-wide sheet of plastic leaves about a foot along each side to anchor thoroughly with slabs of compacted earth shoveled up from the paths. I allow some plastic sheeting to drape over the ends and anchor it with soil or a section of 4x4; it can be folded back over the top and anchored at the sides to keep the tube open. Early in the season when frost threatens, I close the ends in late afternoon. Otherwise, I leave them open all night. Even with both ends open, daytime temperatures inside the tunnel run 10 to 15 degrees higher than outside; nighttime temperatures hold two to three degrees higher. I leave the tunnel over the plants as long as possible— right up to the first harvest if I can. To keep the tunnel free of weeds or to thin, you'll either have to crawl through on hands and knees a couple of times before the plants get too big, or pull up the plastic on one side, work the bed and then reanchor the plastic. To water the tunnel, spray with hose and nozzle every few days or install a line of microsprinklers in the cloche when it's first set up (more about microsprinklers in Chapter 4).

It's easy to grow vegetables in frames and cloches. Prepare the bed and fertilize as usual; if the soil gets too dry in winter, take off the sashes on a mild, drizzly day. And enjoy autumn salads all winter, enjoy spring crops a lot earlier, enjoy summer vegetables four or five weeks longer each year.

Further reading

Winter Gardening in the Maritime Northwest, Binda Colebrook (Seattle: Sasquatch Books, 1989).

A major revelation when first published. The original was issued in 1977 and revised in 1984. Discusses the potentials and problems of winter gardening in detail. The latest edition includes updated source lists for winter varieties.

On Living the Good Life, Scott and Helen Nearing (New York: Schocken Books, 1954).

The Nearings anticipated our recent back-to-the-land movement by 40 years. In the 1930s they decided the world economic and social system was heading into violent convulsions that would not contribute to their health or serenity. So they packed up and moved to a worn-out Vermont farm and learned to subsist. Helen and Scott lived according to a humane and consistent ethical philosophy—one that required efforts on their parts to improve society as a whole, to deal amicably with their neighbors and to avoid any exploitative relationship or profit motive. In Vermont they constructed a novel social order, attracting much interest and a small community of followers. The Nearings are just about the only socialists I know of (except the more radical kibbutzniks in Israel) who, like libertarians, spent their lives living their philosophy rather than trying to figure out how to make everyone else live it, like authoritarians. Scott may be familiar to some left-wing readers as a major contributor to *The Monthly Review*, a magazine of socialist thought. See also their second book, *Continuing the Good Life* (New York: Schocken Books, 1979).

Textbook of
Sprinkler Irrigation

*Whatcha gonna do
when the well runs dry,
honey?*
—American folksong

Imagine there was no electricity to make the pump work, no uphill spring to conveniently provide gravity-flow water, no wind-filled water tank on a tower above your garden, no pressurized city water system, no pipes, hoses or bicycle-powered pumps. Imagine that your household water came from rain collected from the roof and stored in a cistern, or hauled bucket by bucket from a shallow well. Imagine that it was the year 1855, or 2055 after the holocaust, or perhaps 2155 and space-living humans had classified the entire home planet as a technology-free wilderness preserve. Imagine that you had some decent agricultural land and wanted to produce your own garden under those circumstances. What would you do?

If you lived east of a line drawn from eastern Texas up the center of Minnesota, gardening wouldn't be too much different from what it is today with irrigation. Summer rainfall would take care of basic moisture needs; occasional bucket watering could help along transplants, grow seedlings or nurse moisture-sensitive plants through a dry spell; mulching would help preserve soil moisture. Some droughty years might be difficult, but most years the garden would do fine.

If you lived west of the Cascade Mountains, gardening would not be so easy, especially if you lived south of Puget Sound. In summer, the jet stream moves north, taking weather systems over British Columbia, leaving Oregon and southwest Washington State as dry as California. This gives the maritime Northwest what I consider the finest summertime climate on Earth in terms of outdoor enjoyment—but perhaps not the finest weather from a gardener's viewpoint.

Gardening without irrigation

What kind of food supply might a really self-sufficient dryland homesteader produce west of the Cascades? Let's make a quick survey, starting with what the region's farmers already grow. Today, large acreages of small grains are produced commercially, sown in late September or early October after fall rains moisten the soil. Overwintered cereals grow vigorously in spring, use up all available soil moisture as they mature seed in June and are harvested in July when farmers can rely on blue skies and low humidity to dry down the seed. So we could grow our own wheat, rye, oats and barley.

In the Skagit Valley, some 20,000 acres of magnificent loam soil currently grow spring-sown freezer peas—soup varieties could be raised just as well throughout the entire maritime Northwest *on light soils that per-mit early tillage*. We could similarly grow lentils and garbanzo beans (which are relatives of peas). Unfortunately, most homesteaders don't have light soils—the problem to solve is dryland legume production on second-rate fields. This self-sufficiency puzzle has interested me since 1979, when I found myself dealing with clay soil for the first time. In the early eighties, I discovered that English farmers commonly grow very hardy strains of overwintered fava beans—like small grains, sown in fall and harvested in July.

What about corn/squash/beans agriculture, which the first European settlers learned from native Americans in the east? West of the Cascades, field corn can be grown without irrigation by sowing at the earliest pos-sible moment, spacing corn plants three feet apart each way and keep-ing the field absolutely free of weeds. But unirrigated corn makes extremely low yields compared to overwintered small grains and harvest doesn't oc-cur until September, when the return of fall rains makes drying down dicey. As self-sufficient homesteaders, we might want to produce a bit for cornmeal or popcorn; it certainly would not be our grain staple.

Phaseolus vulgaris, which includes such dry-bean varieties as navy, pinto, kidney and marrow, is the bean species most familiar to North Americans. These beans can be grown without irrigation, but yields will be one-quarter to one-third of those achieved with irrigation. Like field corn, they are dryland-grown by sowing early and spacing widely so each plant controls enough soil moisture to set and mature some seed before the soil becomes too dry. Some of the earliest pods can be harvested as snap beans, but the plants quickly get into moisture stress, stop making new pods and concentrate on maturing the seed already set.

Low yields of unirrigated winter squash can also be obtained by spacing the hills on eight- or 10-foot centers and growing only one plant per hill, keeping the ground well weeded and perhaps mulching. Winter squash might be worth Growing—digging big holes and hand-carrying 10 gallons of irrigation per hole per week from July through early September—about 850 pounds of water. That might yield 75 to 100 pounds of squash per hill compared to the unirrigated yield of perhaps 20 or 30 pounds. Then again, it might be easier to work up more ground and hoe more weeds than to carry that much water. It would depend on the distance.

Choosing between a low-yielding corn/*P. vulgaris*/squash diet and a high-yielding wheat, rye, oat, barley/fava bean, pea, lentil, garbanzo diet would really be no choice at all, though the latter diet would require more changes in cultural eating habits. There are also some other staple crops

Gardening without irrigation

Feeder root depth of various crops

Crop	Depth of Feeder Roots
Alfalfa	6 feet
Beans	2 feet
Beets	3 to 4 feet
Cabbage	2 feet
Carrots	3 to 4 feet
Corn	2½ feet
Cucumbers	2 feet
Lettuce	1 foot
Melons	3 feet
Onions	1½ feet
Peas	2½ feet
Potatoes	2 feet
Tomatoes	2 feet

that show promise for unirrigated fields west of the Cascades. Quinoa, a drought-resistant cereal relative of lamb's-quarters, comes from South America and is well adapted to our region (especially strains from southern Chile). Yields are as high as other small grains, and quinoa is most nutritious, tasty and easy to grow. Sunflowers will also produce fair yields of oily seeds if sown early and spaced on four-foot centers. Their slightly frost-hardy seedlings must be started as early as possible so there is enough soil moisture to mature seed. Far better for oilseed are annual poppies (*Papaver somniferum, P. rhoeas*). Sown at summer's end like winter grains, the plants flower in June and mature seed in July. Poppies are quite similar to thistles and make high yields on droughty, infertile soil. Poppy seed contains 40 to 50 percent vegetable oil; like sunflower seeds, ground poppy seed makes a good salad dressing. Unfortunately, there is some confusion at this time about the legality of growing *P. somniferum*— opium poppies—in the United States.

The dryland homesteader could also enjoy various perennial fruits and nuts. Many species will grow and produce well without further watering, if competing grasses are removed from around trees or shrubs each spring. This could be accomplished by growing overwintered green manures to till in each spring, or by permanent mulching. And thus we could have apples, pears, plums, perhaps persimmons, figs, filberts, walnuts, chestnuts and various small fruits—though probably not strawberries. Not a bad diet, and certainly a healthy one.

Holding capacity of various soils

Soil Type	Total Holding Capacity	Amount Held at Permanent Wilting Point
Sandy	1.25 inches per foot	.25 inch per foot
Medium	2.25 inches per foot	.60 inch per foot
Clayey	3.75 inches per foot	1.3 inches per foot

But what about all those other vegetable crops that make a garden a garden, you're wondering? What about cauliflower and carrots and peppers and beets and melons and tomatoes? Well, some of these species can also be grown without irrigation, though yields will be low and in some cases the quality may be a little poorer. Best adapted to irrigationless gardening are the root crops and species that are normally spring-sown. Since soil moisture is naturally adequate until June, the entire spring garden is no problem. Plants that mature in July can be helped by increased spacing and a bit of mulching. Early potatoes grown in rows about four feet apart will mature by July and hold in the soil all summer, to be dug as needed; the remainder can be dug in early October and put into storage. Some potato varieties do tend to sprout in the ground during the summer; others hold entirely dormant. Root crops especially lend themselves to dry gardening because the root systems of carrots, beets, parsnips and Hamburg parsley are, by nature, scavengers of water. Sown early on deep loamy soil and spaced six to 12 inches apart in rows four feet apart, they'll grow throughout the summer on moisture reserves three to five feet down. The final size and ultimate yield may be huge. I've produced carrots, beets and parsley root this way. Each one was five to six inches in diameter at the top and weighed several pounds. They can be dug from July through March.

Yes, yes, but what about cauliflower, tomatoes, peppers, melons and...? Sorry, but these crops simply have to be irrigated.

Gardening with irrigation

Most modern vegetables originated from wild plants much less hardy than those that became field crops, and, unlike cereals, they have been bred for centuries to grow in moist, manured soils. Consequently, slight nutrient deficiencies or short periods of moisture stress will greatly reduce vegetable quality. Lettuce turns bitter; cauliflower "buttons up" and if it makes a curd at all, it's the size of a silver dollar; summer squash may become dry and fibrous, winter squash doesn't set many fruits.

The most obvious example of moisture stress is when soil gets so dry that plants wilt and die. Slightly less damaging is temporary wilting, caused when hot sun temporarily evaporates more moisture from plants' leaves than the dryish soil will yield up to the roots. Although the plants may recover in the evening and look healthy the next morning, temporary wilting is a severe shock to most vegetables—one they won't fully recover from for many days or even weeks, if at all. Water-stressed root crops may not show any signs of wilting because the leaves can draw on water stored in the root, but the harvested roots may be poorly developed or woody. (Note that squash may droop its leaves under hot sun without damage, no matter how much water it receives. This is a prosurvival trait of the Cucurbitaceae family, limiting moisture loss by reducing the leaf area exposed to the sun.)

Gardeners quickly learn the consequences of water stress and so have watering equipment handy. However, very few have scientifically designed irrigation systems, nor do they water systematically. They should be scientific about maintaining soil moisture. Underwatering may be subtle and go unnoticed, with serious consequences, and overwatering may be equally harmful.

Many gardeners go out almost every day with hose and nozzle and wet down their garden. John Jeavons recommends this as a way to make sure intensive beds hold abundant moisture all the time. But even if the garden is watered daily, plants can become severely water-stressed. The consequence of frequent light watering is often that the surface soil (the top five to eight inches) becomes quite wet, while deeper soil remains bone-dry. Under these conditions, vegetables will not show signs of moisture stress, though they'll be stunted from lack of root development. Dense plantings of root crops, which form a deep taproot that naturally draws on subsoil moisture, are particularly badly affected. Recognizing this possibility, Jeavons recommends watering a bed with a fan nozzle until the entire surface becomes "shiny wet." This "shiny" layer results from water that has not yet flowed into the bed. It only lasts a second or so initially, but as the soil becomes increasingly saturated, the shiny lasts longer and longer. When it lasts one-half to 15 seconds, Jeavons says, the bed has been given enough water.

One-half to 15 seconds is quite a range of time. I suppose if one experimented and combined trying different shiny times with digging some holes in the bed to see how deeply it had become saturated, Jeavons's method could be workable. But without this check, gross overwatering or underwatering could result. Many clayey soils are slow to absorb moisture and could be deceptively shiny yet quite dry a few inches down; sandy soils take in water very rapidly and might be difficult to get shiny at all, no matter how much the gardener overwatered or how fast the water was put down, resulting in considerable overwatering. Jeavons did the research leading to his books on a clayey site outside San Francisco and, like many garden writers, he tends to generalize and blithely give advice from limited personal experience.

A wet-to-dry scale

Totally Dry	0%
Permanent Wilting Point	20 to 33%
Temporary Wilting Point	50%
Minimum Moisture for Good Vegetable Growth	75%
Field Capacity	100%

When soil is irrigated, each soil particle attracts to itself all the water it can hold against the force of gravity before it can flow deeper into the ground. Thus, the surface inches of soil can quickly become saturated, while deeper layers may still be dry. A layer of soil that has absorbed all the water it can hold is said to be at *field capacity.* The opposite of field capacity is totally dry soil. Rarely if ever do we find totally dry soil in nature, even in deserts. As soil particles dry down they hold moisture more and more tightly, until water clings harder to soil particles than vegetable roots or even evaporation at normal temperatures can extract it. The point on a wet-to-dry scale where vegetables can no longer extract soil moisture is called the *permanent wilting point.* Before the permanent wilting point is reached, plants experience temporary wilting when hot sun increases their need for water.

To maximize yields and eating quality in this age of handy irrigation, modern plant breeding has sculpted most vegetables so they produce even larger edible portions ever more quickly, at the expense of vigorous root system development. With much more inefficient root systems than they had even a century ago, vegetables can become badly stressed long before the temporary wilting point of cereals or other field crops would be reached. So, to avoid stress and encourage maximum growth, scientific irrigation attempts to keep vegetable soil not far from field capacity to the depth of the vegetables' root development (about two feet, on the average). Roughly speaking, when garden soil has dried down to about 70 percent of capacity to the depth of a foot, it should be watered up to capacity again. Tougher and more deeply rooting crops such as cereals may produce very acceptable yields even when available soil moisture in the top few feet of soil drops to near the temporary wilting point. (One of my current "hobbies" is either reverse-breeding vegetable varieties back to or finding an earlier, lower-yielding condition when they had better-developed root systems and grew more like field crops.)

Before you decide to avoid the dangers of moisture stress by frequently watering your garden even more thoroughly than you have been, consider the consequence of overdoing it. Overwatering rapidly reduces soil fertility. The gardener goes to a lot of trouble and expense increasing the level of available nutrients dissolved in the *soil solution*, the water film clinging to soil particles or trapped inside clay crystal lattices. As irrigation water flows into soil, it carries dissolved nutrients deeper. This action of water is called *leaching*. Leached soil has been lowered in nutrients while the deeper layers of soil have been enriched. When water penetration exceeds the depth of feeder roots, available plant nutrients are beyond reach, *where they remain*. West of the Cascades, irrigation-leached nutrients remain in the subsoil until heavy winter rains take them even deeper—into the water table and eventually out to sea.

Amount of water needed to bring two feet of soil from 70 percent to capacity

Soil Type	Irrigation in Inches
Sandy	½ to ¾
Improved sandy (much humus added)	1
Medium (loam)	1
Clayey	1½

This brings to mind another plus for organic fertilizers. If water-soluble chemical fertilizers are used, a single leaching strips the root zone of most nutrients and more fertilizer must be applied. If organic fertilizers are used, the root zone is only temporarily leached until the nutrient level builds back up from further fertilizer breakdown and gradual release of potentially available nutrients. But either way, growth slows or stops. Judging by watering recommendations in garden books and magazines, and by the equipment most gardeners use for irrigation, I suspect most gardeners grossly overwater more often than they underwater.

Intelligent irrigation means applying the right amount of water—and to the right places. The lawn sprinklers most gardeners use on their vegetables put out an enormous amount of water in a short time. Although most lawn sprinklers don't come with performance specifications as precise as those provided with agricultural crop sprinklers, it is easy to test them for precipitation rate. Simply set out some empty tin cans or other cylindrical containers: one near the sprinkler, one near the outer limit of its reach and a couple in between. Run the sprinkler for one hour, measure the depth of water in each can and average those amounts to calculate your sprinkler's precipitation rate per hour. Most lawn sprinklers lay down over two inches per hour. Oscillating sprinklers, which water in rectangular patterns, put down two to four inches per hour, depending on where the pattern adjustment knob is set. Soaker hoses and sprinklers designed to water small areas usually put out more than that. How much leaching do you suppose the average gardener causes by using one of these sprinklers?

Speaking of leaching, I recall reading with horror an *Organic Gardening* article by a woman from California's Salinas Valley, who wrote about how pleased she was with her new high-output irrigation system. If she ran her new sprinkler long enough (six hours or so), she could actually get puddles to form on her sandy ground. All her previous sprinklers had allowed the water to soak in as fast as she applied it. I imagine that in her subsoil, six to eight feet down, there was a clay hardpan or some other less-permeable layer of soil that blocked the rapid percolation of the sand above. After enough hours of watering, she filled the pore space of her sand all the way from this impervious layer to the surface. What an accomplishment! All her available nutrients were well on their way to the Pacific Ocean. Actually, any sprinkler that wets the ground fairly uniformly, even the super high-volume output one just mentioned, can water a garden effectively without leaching *if the gardener knows and allows for its rate of precipitation.*

The state of soil moisture is best determined five or six inches under the surface. Once evaporation has dropped soil moisture from capacity, where soil will feel very wet, to 70 percent of capacity, where soil will feel only damp, the amount of water recommended in the table (page 109) is applied. A more accurate method for determining what constitutes about 70 percent of capacity is to take some soil from five to six inches down and squeeze it hard into a ball—the classic "ready to till" test. If the ball feels gooey or sticks together solidly, the soil moisture is above 70 percent (unless the soil is fine clay that has to drop as low as 60 percent to pass the ready-to-till test). If the ball sticks together but breaks apart fairly easily, the soil moisture is around 70 percent. If the soil won't form a ball no matter how hard it is squeezed, it is severely in need of watering.

Peak soil moisture loss in various climates

Type of Climate	Inches per Day
Cool climate	0.2
Moderate climate	0.25
Hot climate	0.3
High Desert	0.35
Low Desert	0.45

July and August moisture loss in the warmer areas of the maritime Northwest runs from 0.2 to 0.3 inches per sunny day.

Another way to approach watering is to gauge the amount of water being lost from soil and periodically replace it in small quantities before the soil dries down too much. West of the Cascades, soils are kept wet to capacity by rain much of the year, and actively leached in winter. Usually, our soils begin to dry down during April but the surface layers of most soils don't reach that critical 60 to 70 percent of capacity (right to till for most soil types) until some time in May. Sensitive vegetable crops have to be irrigated from May until the late summer rains begin unless cooler temperatures have slowed water losses greatly. The rate at which sun, wind and heat dry out soil varies with the season and the amount of vegetation the soil supports, but not with the type of soil. In June, usually about one inch of water is lost per week. During the intense light and heat of July and early August, water loss will be around 1½ inches per week; during spells of really high heat, it can increase to slightly more than two inches per week. By September, losses are back to an inch a week, and by October, hardly any moisture is being lost, even if it does not rain.

In areas where extensive commercial irrigation is done, farmers are guided by timely government reports on soil moisture losses in their district. Gardeners can go by estimates, adjusting for cloudy days (when less evaporation will occur) and for any rain received. Remember that sandy soils should not be given more than half an inch of water at one time to avoid leaching and so must be watered much more frequently than clayey ones, which can easily accept 1½ inches without danger of leaching. More frequent light irrigations may be needed when sprouting seed, nursing small seedlings or growing certain species with unusually high moisture requirements, such as lettuce, radishes and celery.

The wide range of sprinklers on the market gives informed gardeners a wide choice of precipitation rates and droplet sizes. These factors can make quite a difference. Though it takes more low-application sprinkler heads to cover a given area, it is intelligent to use these sprinklers because they put out small, light droplets. High-application sprinklers usually put out large heavy droplets from big nozzles, which causes soil compaction (making cultivation and weeding more difficult) and reduces soil pore space (and thus plant root development). Large droplets pounding on the surface mechanically separate the finer silt and clay soil particles from the coarse sand particles, creating a concrete-like crust of silt/clay on the soil surface with the sand particles slightly below, in much the same way that a cement finisher brings the fines to the surface to make a smooth finish. Because crusts don't form on sod, most lawn sprinklers issue big droplets and produce precipitation rates in excess of two inches per hour— apparently a time-saving convenience to busy homeowners—even though sod leaches as easily as vegetable plots, with the same consequences. Think what can happen in the vegetable garden if one of these monster sprinklers is forgotten and runs a few hours too long.

Agricultural crop sprinklers are available with tiny nozzles, resulting in application rates as low one-tenth of an inch per hour. This is great for avoiding compaction and crusting, but sprinklers applying less than a half-inch per hour do have drawbacks. At midday, sun, wind and high air temperatures can combine to break up the stream of fine droplets and evaporate almost as much water as a small sprinkler can put out. This is not a serious liability, because at precipitation rates below two-tenths of an inch per hour, it is possible to water heavy soils all night from bedtime to breakfast without leaching; on light soils, provide a half-inch of water in the morning before the sun gets strong and the wind comes up. For rural homesteaders with limited water supplies, night is also the time when there is no competition from showers, dishwashing, and so on. Sprinkler systems with application rates from one-quarter to one inch per hour are best used before 11 a.m. to reduce evaporation loss.

Contrary to much gardening lore, night watering is not harmful to

Comparison of high- versus low- application-rate sprinklers

Nozzle Size	Operating Pressure	Discharge GPM	Radius in Feet	Spacing in Feet	Precipitation Rate in Inches per Hour
.0039	15	0.15	13	13 × 13	0.10
.0039	45	0.28	18	13 × 13	0.16
1/16	30	.45	33	20 × 20	0.11
1/16	60	.79	36	20 × 20	0.19
7/64	30	1.94	33	20 × 20	0.47
7/64	60	2.66	36	20 × 20	0.64
13/64	30	6.78	40	25 × 25	1.05
13/64	60	9.53	45	25 × 25	1.46
5/16	40	17.7	59	40 × 60	0.71
5/16	80	25.7	75	40 × 60	1.03

One-sixteenth-inch nozzles are about the smallest effective low-application-rate nozzles available. They also permit covering the maximum amount of ground at one time with the least amount of water. With application rates in the vicinity of .15 inch per hour, a ten-hour overnight watering will add 1.5 inches—perfect for bringing a heavy soil from 75 percent to capacity. Smaller nozzles can't spray far enough to achieve low application rates. Larger nozzles increasingly incur the liability of large droplet sizes. Nozzles emitting over about 5 gallons per minute (GPM) are too massive for the vegetable garden, though they might be excellent for pastures, golf courses, or corn fields.

plants. It may even be the best time to water. Plants are naturally dampened by dew almost every night. What *can* harm plants is being watered in early evening and then left damp all night—ideal conditions for the multiplication of disease organisms. Watering all night continuously washes bacteria and fungus spores off the plants before they can do any damage. Then, when the sun comes up, irrigation is stopped and the plants dry off quickly. This principle is well understood by nurseries, which propagate healthy plants by rooting cuttings under a continuous fine mist.

Sprinklers

Designing an economical sprinkler seems like an impossible puzzle—how can one sprinkler water a circle or a square uniformly from the

Textbook of Sprinkler Irrigation

center? This problem is easy to illustrate by doing an irrigation rate test on any sprinkler—whether lawn, garden, agricultural or commercial. Not only can no single sprinkler I know of accomplish uniform coverage, but most fail miserably. The reason: a circular sprinkler must cover much more area in the outer part of its pattern than in the center, while a single noz-zle cannot deposit nearly 10 times the amount of water on the perimeter that it does in the center.

A one-sprinkler garden

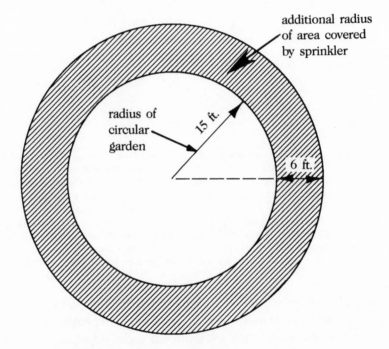

Circular sprinklers are usually spaced about 60–70 percent of their maximum throw. The illustration shows how I would design a garden if I planned to have only one sprinkler in a fixed position.

Many design tricks are used with agricultural sprinklers to approach the ideal of equal water distribution, but even the best only approximate it. Surprisingly, the one design that seems naturally to overcome this prob-lem, the oscillating sprinkler, is usually the worst of all. The cam arrange-ment that moves the oscillating spray arm always seems to pause too long at the turnaround point, so this type of sprinkler errs by putting too much water at the ends of its rectangular pattern and too little near the sprinkler itself.

Achieving uniform water application from a single sprinkler

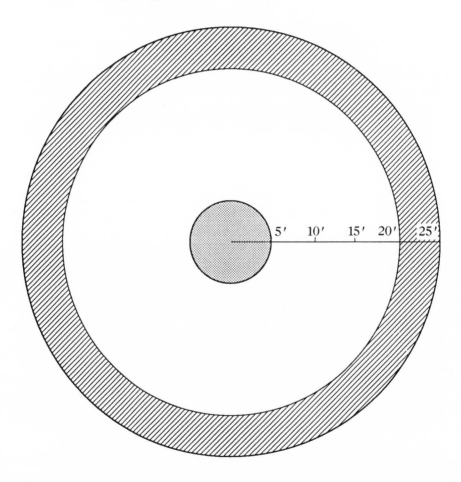

The formula for the area of a circle is $A = (pi)\ r^2$. Imagine a sprinkler with a 25-foot radius. The inner five feet of the sprinkler pattern covers 78.5 square feet (3.14×5^2). The area in the outer five feet of the pattern is 706.5 square feet ($[3.14 \times 25^2] - [3.14 \times 20^2]$). Thus the nozzle must deposit nearly 10 times as much water in the outer five feet to end up with the same application rate as the inner five feet.

The impact sprinkler has the opposite problem. It puts down too much water near the sprinkler, left there by the spraying action of the rocker arm that rotates the sprinkler head, and too little at the extremes of the pattern. Most consumer-quality impact sprinklers come with a diffuser arm or adjustable needle of some sort to shorten the radius and diffuse the spray. *More than the slightest amount of diffusion increases the tendency to overwater the center while leaving the fringes too dry.* The more the radius is shortened by breaking up the nozzle stream, the worse this effect becomes. Agricultural-quality impulse sprinklers do not use diffusers: instead, they have scientifically designed nozzles that, if used at the correct pressure, diffuse or "spray" properly all by themselves and give fairly uniform coverage, putting only about twice as much water near the center as they do on the fringes.

The only way I know of to have a fairly uniformly watered garden with a single fixed-position sprinkler is to make the garden circular, with a high-quality impact agricultural sprinkler in the center, and with the radius of the sprinkler at least one-third bigger than the radius of the garden, allowing the dryish fringe to grow grass or other drought-resistant vegetation like raspberries. However, circular patterns are hard to rototill and lay out, so most gardens are sensibly square or rectangular. To compensate for the inherent limitations of sprinkler design, farmers set out crop sprinklers in overlapping patterns so that one sprinkler's heavily watered area is included in another's deficiently watered one, and the differences cancel each other out. Any multiple sprinkler pattern still leaves a dryish fringe area where fewer overlaps occur. On the farm, these fringes are of no consequence; in the back yard, it may be essential to keep overspray out of neighbors' yards or off windows.

Sometimes sprinkler patterns are laid out in squares, sometimes in triangles. The triangular pattern covers slightly more uniformly within the pattern, but the square pattern may lend itself better to the back-yard situation. Agricultural crop sprinklers range from those that will cover a 13-foot circle to firehose-nozzle monsters that will water several acres at a time. The closer the spacing and the shorter the designed radius of the sprinkler, the smaller the fringe area will be, making short-radius sprinklers best for back-yard gardens. Probably the best quality all-brass impulse sprinklers are made by the Rain Bird Company. Its catalog is very informative and covers much of the same information found in this chapter. The smallest Rain Bird sprinkler emits three-quarters of a gallon per minute (gpm) and has about a 25-foot radius. Territorial Seed Company sells a uniquely designed and inexpensive line of low-output ABS plastic impulse

Sprinkler patterns

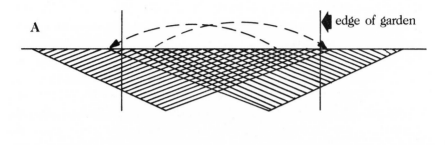

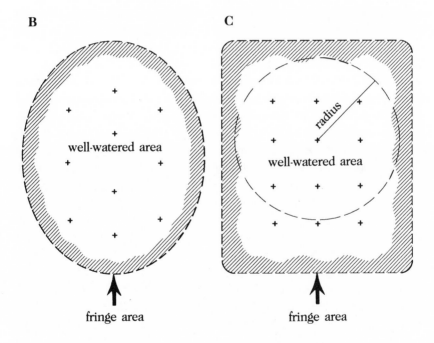

Using several sprinklers permits an overlap in watering patterns that will create an evenly watered garden area. The optimal spacing of these sprinklers is at about 60 percent of the sprinkling radius. (A) A side view of correct sprinkler overlap. The shaded area shows the relative amount of water applied to different parts of the covered radius by an average impact sprinkler; (B) sprinklers laid out in triangular pattern; and (C) sprinklers laid out in square pattern.

sprinklers from Israel that have emission rates down to ⅓ gpm and radii down to 13 feet.

Some gardeners use impact sprinklers with part-circle attachments to eliminate fringe areas, putting the sprinkler at the edge of the area to be watered and reducing the sprinkler's arc to 180° or 90°. Keep in mind that, with the usual impulse sprinkler, cutting the arc in half doubles the rate of application; cutting it to 90° quadruples the rate of application. This can cause leaching. A simple way to prevent full-circle sprinklers from spraying where they will cause trouble is to make a shield from a cut-out tin can attached directly behind the sprinkler. This is effective, though it does waste water by dumping the blocked spray at the sprinkler's base.

The design problem from using an impulse arm to rotate the sprinkler head is that it repeatedly breaks up the water stream and dumps too much water on the center one-third of the circle. One of the best alternatives has been developed by the Toro Company. Toro's Ag-1 and #300 series use an internal water-powered turbine to rotate the sprinkler head instead of an impulse arm. The #300 series also has similar turbine-driven multiple nozzle heads, which provide the most uniform coverage possible and, most interestingly, the ability to cover reduced arcs without increasing the application rate. Intended for the farmer, Ag-1 sprinklers have emission rates starting at one gpm and cost little more than an inexpensive impulse sprinkler. The more costly #300 series was designed for watering lawns and ornamentals in institutional situations where sprinklers have to be located close to buildings and windows and precise coverages must be adjusted to avoid sidewalks and so forth. Gardeners who are really interested in optimum irrigation design should also study Toro's catalog before making any major decisions.

Agricultural-grade sprinkler nozzles are designed with different angles of throw. High-angle nozzles allow the stream of water to go its maximum distance, covering the largest area with the fewest number of sprinkler heads while drawing the least number of gallons per minute. However, high-angle sprinklers are badly affected by wind, which can disperse the water stream, blow it off course and cause high evaporation losses, especially if the sun is shining. The smaller sizes of high-angle sprinklers can be a wonderful solution for homesteaders with very limited water supplies who want large gardens—if they avoid the sun and wind by watering at night. Low-angle sprinklers are best for windy situations. Throwing water at about six degrees above level, their radius is shortened up and the stream is kept close to the ground, out of the strongest wind gusts. More low-

Precipitation rate in inches per hour

Rectangular	GPM from Each Full-Circle Sprinkler							
Spacing (feet)	1	2	3	4	5	6	8	10
20×20	.24	.48	.72	.96	1.2	1.4	1.9	
20×30	.16	.32	.48	.64	.80	.96	1.3	1.6
20×40		.24	.36	.48	.60	.72	.96	1.3
25×25	.15	.30	.45	.60	.75	.90	1.2	1.5
30×30		.21	.32	.43	.54	.64	.86	1.0
30×40			.24	.32	.40	.48	.64	.80
40×40			.18	.24	.30	.36	.48	.60

This table gives some representative precipitation rates for different nozzle sizes and spacings. However, it doesn't cover every possibility, nor do nozzles usually emit water in even GPM increments. When sprinkler spacing and emission rate are known, a simple formula allows the precipitation rate per hour to be calculated for any situation.

$$\text{Rate of precipitation} = \frac{\text{GPM (nozzle gallons per minute)} \times 96.3}{\text{sprinkler in-row spacing} \times \text{sprinkler between-row spacing}}$$

---

angle sprinklers are needed to cover a given area, resulting in somewhat higher precipitation rates.

Designing an irrigation system

When gardeners go into an irrigation supply store for the first time and read over a commercial irrigation catalog, they sometimes leave confused. Sprinkler catalogs assume that buyers have sufficient understanding to lay out a proper system. Here are a few hints to make using them a little more successful. Agricultural sprinklers come with manufacturer's recommendations for spacing and operating pressure. These specifications should be more or less followed, because operating sprinklers too far outside their designed limits results in poor performance. With crop-sprinkler nozzles, the shape and smoothness of the bore are especially important. If the water stream jets from the nozzle at too low a pressure, the stream doesn't break up and "spray" properly. The impulse arm then causes too much water to be laid down near the sprinkler, the tight stream carries water to the fringes and very little water is laid down in the middle of the pattern. A "doughnut" pattern results. Run at excessively high pressure, the stream mists and breaks up too much coming out of the nozzle, shortening the radius and greatly increasing the rate of application near the sprinkler, making the fringes much too dry. Different nozzles are designed to operate at pressures from 10 to 100 pounds per square inch, with most ranging from 30 to 60 psi. City household water supplies are usually between 30 and 45 psi. High-angle sprinklers should not be spaced at more than about 65 percent of their radius. This compensates for overlaps in the pattern and for wind blowing the spray a little without leaving areas dry. Low-angle sprinklers are usually spaced 80 to 90 percent of their radius.

The best place to buy crop sprinklers is a farm irrigation company or large plumbing-supply store. Big plumbing suppliers generally have Rain Bird and Toro catalogs on hand, though the sprinklers themselves may be special-order items. Also available from these suppliers are tables showing pipe sizes required for amount of water being carried. The better ones gladly offer lots of good advice on how to assemble such a system.

Where there's a will, there's a way. If a complete, permanent, multi-headed sprinkler system that turns on from a single valve is beyond a gardener's interest or budget, uniform scientific irrigation can still be accomplished with only one good sprinkler that is moved around the garden and run for equal periods in semi-fixed positions, like those in a multi-sprinkler pattern. For several years I watered a half-acre trial ground with an ordinary garden hose connected to a single sprinkler head rated at 2½ gallons per minute—which was all the water my well could produce on a continuous basis. I moved that one sprinkler from spot to spot, irrigating six nights a week from 8 p.m. to 8 a.m. If I'd had a big well, I could have run many lower-emission sprinklers simultaneously, covering the entire trial ground at one time, watering all night every five to seven days. Then I discovered drip irrigation and greatly simplified my life.

However, I do not recommend drip systems to the home gardener. I used drip tubes on my trial grounds from 1982 until 1987 simply because drip was the only way to water extensive plots during daylight hours with low water consumption, and my disappointing well definitely had a low water output. Drip tubes are expensive, short-lived and troublesome, but at that time I did not care what it cost in money or effort to produce my trial grounds—I was growing information, not food. Drip tubes are easily cut with sharp hoes or shovels and, despite filters, tend to become plugged up at times. This means the entire system has to be carefully inspected every time it is turned on to make sure all the tiny holes are open and that no gushing leaks were created the last time the garden was hoed. Drip lines also move around a great deal from expansion and contraction, so they won't stay "spot-on" a new transplant and won't keep a row of germinating seeds wet without a lot of fiddling. Drip systems are not suitable for light soils because the water goes straight down through sand without spreading out horizontally, leaving large areas of totally dry soil that the plants can't root into. If the soil contains more clay, the water spreads out horizontally as well as vertically. High-quality, durable drip lines might be very workable for permanent plantings, such as rows of raspberries in heavier soils, but given any choice between drip systems and sprinklers, I'd always choose sprinklers.

Lately, new advances in plastics manufacture have created a sort of hybrid between drip and sprinkling, called micro-irrigation. These systems use inexpensive plastic tubing to carry water, cheap quick-disconnect fittings for corners and tees, cheap plastic spikes to hold sprinklers and little short-radius sprinkler heads with emission rates so low they are measured in gallons per hour, not per minute. Micro-irrigation systems provide an inexpensive and durable alternative for under-tree applications in orchards. They are also being used more and more by homeowners to water ornamental beds around houses and are very useful in spring cloches to keep plants watered for a few weeks until the cloche is removed. Micro-irrigation equipment is sold pre-packaged for the consumer in bigger garden center/discount stores, but is quite expensive purchased that way. Commercial irrigation suppliers have a much wider selection at a much lower cost.

Further reading

Small-Scale Grain Raising, Gene Logsdon (Emmaus: Rodale Press, 1977).

Gene was an active contributor to Rodale Press during the seventies, focused primarily on self-sufficient homesteading and small-scale organic cash farming. Here, in a nutshell, is how to grow grains on small plots of only a few thousand square feet.

Water, USDA Yearbook of Agriculture, 1955.

A huge survey covering all relationships of water and agriculture: erosion, irrigation, weather, forestry, dryland pasture management and drainage.

Seeds

*With all thy getting,
get understanding.*
—Advice to the
businessperson from
Malcolm Forbes

*Caveat emptor.
[Let the buyer beware.]*
—Ancient Roman advice
about dealing with the
businessperson

*The gardener gets
the sweepings off
the seedroom floor.*
—An agribusiness
executive to Steve Solomon

Seed basics

 From the time I was a green novice in the garden-seed business I made my intention clear: I would buy only high-quality seeds for my customers. Early on, this foolish young fellow was taken under the wing of a kindly old supplier to the garden-seed trade who patiently explained that his extensive list of low-quality seeds would be more than adequate for the home gardener—and far more profitable for me. I took his words to heart—and thereafter avoided buying most of the cheap items his company sold.

Other major seed-trade players tried to set me straight about the difference between commercial vegetable seed and home-garden seed. I was repeatedly told, "The gardener is not a critical trade." What they meant by "not a critical trade" was that the garden-seed buyer does not know why one packet sprouts, grows rapidly and produces uniform, attractive produce, while another packet of seed grows badly from the start, or ends up with a hodgepodge of variations, some of which are not very good eating. Why, then, should any sensible supplier of garden seed pay $100 for a pound of the best commercial-quality vegetable seed, when home-garden quality can be purchased for $2.50 a pound? Indeed! Why would any practical businessperson be more ethical or honest than the circumstances require?

Learning how to buy good-quality seeds sure taught me things: things about subtle levels of business dishonesty I had never before knowingly encountered, and interesting technical knowledge about using seeds—data I've never read in any book available to the gardener. This has greatly increased my success with seeds, and I plan to share this knowledge with you.

Seed basics

Let's start your seed education by going over some basics. A seed is a small food-filled container that holds an embryonic plant within. The embryo is dormant but alive—breathing and eating at a very low rate. It possesses genetic instructions to grow and develop into a mature plant. The seed is activated by moisture, and once sprouting starts it must be completed or the embryo will die.

Vigor

The most important and completely practical aspect of seeds is whether they sprout and start to grow vigorously or they don't. Everything else about seeds is irrelevant if they fail to germinate. The name for this ability to come up and grow is *vigor*. Vigor is easy to see, but it's far harder to precisely measure and assign a scientific number to. Vigor expresses itself as rapidity of sprouting and a husky initial appearance of the seedlings.

In a germination test lab, 10 different varieties of red cabbage started at the same time will show differences in vigor. A few will sprout in three days, most in four or five, a few in six or seven. The earlier sprouters will look sturdier and grow faster. That's vigor. Various years' harvests or one year's production grown in different lots on different fields—all these lots will vary in vigor. (The word *lot* is trade jargon for seed from a particular year and specific field. Each lot is assigned a number that stays with every bag and shipment, so in case of disease or other trouble, every bit of that seed may be traced.)

Highly vigorous lots come up in the shortest possible amount of time for that type of seed. The quicker-sprouting, more vigorous lots have thicker stems and bigger leaves and immediately begin rapid growth. Vigorous lots usually germinate at a very high percentage in lab tests. In the field, vigorous seedlings rarely succumb to damping-off disease during the first week of growth and quickly establish themselves, developing into large, healthy plants as rapidly as conditions permit. Less vigorous lots take longer to emerge. Slow-sprouting, non-vigorous seeds have thin stems and small leaves and grow slowly after emergence. Non-vigorous seeds usually germinate at a low percentage in the laboratory. Grown in the field, non-vigorous seeds sprout *much* more poorly than they do in the laboratory, and often will neither develop rapidly nor achieve the same size or yield as a vigorous lot.

When healthy parent plants receive complete nutrition and enjoy good weather, they are able to form vigorous seed—fat, dense and equipped with large reserves of complete nutrition for the embryo within. Vigorous seeds have a long shelf life, too. So seed growers do their darnedest to ensure maximum seed vigor. They fertilize and irrigate carefully, spray pesticides to defeat any insects that might reduce seed yield or parent plant vigor, and apply fungicides to eliminate any disease that could attack the forming seed or the next generation of sprouts. Sometimes, critical and valuable varieties are grown in a greenhouse with a resident beehive, to prevent even ordinary stressors like dew from lowering seed vigor.

In their quest for the best, seed growers flock to the most ideal production districts on the planet, places where weather conditions are perfect for a particular species to produce the most-vigorous seed possible. Consequently, 85 percent of the entire world's cabbage seed (and a great portion of its beet seed) is produced in the Skagit Valley around Mount Vernon, Washington; growers in California's central valley north of Sacramento and around Rocky Ford, Colorado, are used to seeing Dutch and Japanese fieldmen supervising squash seed fields; French bush bean and pea seed is grown in Idaho; English onion seed is produced on the Oregon/Idaho border; Italian hybrid broccoli seed from Japanese seed companies is grown in California's Imperial Valley; Dutch seedsmen grow their world-famous hybrid Brussels sprout seed in Italy. It is not unusual to find fieldmen from all over the world poking about these prime growing districts, competing to sign up yet another farmer. With all this accumulated knowledge and technology, seed productions come out reasonably vigorous most years. In fact, the seed grown today is generally a lot more vigorous than that used 50 years ago.

Still, many efforts at growing seed do not turn out successfully. Weather conditions during the growing season are outside the growers' control. Sometimes the parent plants just aren't as healthy as they might be. And though good vigor may be there when the seeds mature, it may be lost long before they arrive at the warehouse. To preserve maximum vigor, seeds must dry down at temperatures that cause neither degradation of the food reserves nor damage to the embryo—not too hot, not too cold; not too fast, not too slow; not too wet, not too dry. If seeds do dry down at the correct rate to the correct moisture range, and are harvested, threshed, cleaned and stored under proper conditions that avoid other types of damage or deterioration, the vigor is preserved. But bad weather at harvest time, mechanical damage from threshing (especially possible when seed is threshed at the wrong moisture content), improper storage temperature or humidity levels, damage caused by having to artificially dry seed during a wet harvest season—all can reduce seed vigor.

And even though vigorous seed may arrive at the warehouse all sacked up at the right moisture content, vigor is not a static condition—it goes down and down relentlessly. Because the embryo *is* a living thing, slowly breathing and consuming its food reserve, it can age and die like all life forms more complex than a single cell. Exposure to oxygen and the simple passage of time make the food supply slowly deteriorate and weaken the embryo. Eventually vigor will decline to such a point that the seed will no longer sprout successfully. How many years and months this may take depends on the storage potential of the species and the variety itself, the original degree of vigor and the conditions under which the seed is held. To slow the inevitable decline in vigor, a whole technology of seed storage has evolved. Later in this chapter, I'll show how understanding

Seeds

seed storage can save the gardener a lot of money.

To put it much too mildly, it is disappointing to sow low-vigor seed. Sowings that fail to come up, or spindly seedlings that grow very slowly or disappear shortly after sprouting, may be the result of low-vigor seed (especially if the soil is otherwise fertile and if sowings of similar species or other varieties made at the same time do germinate and grow well). In the field, getting anything but the strongest seeds to sprout can be a frustrating experience.

Sprouting is exhausting, hard and dangerous work. With the clock ticking fast from the moment the seed imbibes enough soil moisture to be activated, the embryo must build an entire functional plant before its limited food reserves run out. Even after emergence, the seedling must still draw on its food reserves, because its ability to manufacture food is insufficient for its needs. Only after the first true leaf has fully developed can the average seedling photosynthesize enough food to grow. If cold soil delays sprouting or soil compaction resists the seed's effort to move root and shoot through it, the seedling may emerge with overly depleted reserves and be unable to complete enough additional leaf to take off and grow. Seedlings weakened during sprouting often succumb to various environmental menaces shortly after emergence, or grow very slowly, reeling from every insect and disease that comes along. Exhausted seedlings seldom overcome their initial handicap; unless growth conditions improve dramatically immediately after emergence, they're unlikely to become big, healthy, productive plants. Vigorous seed has enough reserves to overcome a considerable number of environmental obstacles and still make a true leaf.

Germination rate

The fact of vigor is indisputable. Vigor is widely recognized and discussed by commercial buyers and sellers of vegetable seed. But until very recently it has been impossible to give a numerical value to vigor, and so the industry has powerfully resisted evaluating seed lots on the basis of vigor. The last thing a seed company wants to do is to claim that any particular lot of seed possesses any vigor at all. There are just too many potential variables to guarantee that even the most vigorous seed will actually come up—in the field. So seeds are bought and sold on the basis of laboratory germination percentage instead of by vigor. Germination rate is a characteristic of any bag of seed that can be given an absolute and repeatably testable number. There is enough of a connection between vigor and percentage of laboratory germination that if the users can be sure that they are sowing "high germ" seed, they can also be reasonably sure that it will be vigorous enough to survive sprouting and grow. So farmers and seed companies pay a lot of attention to seed germination percentage.

Seed-trade custom is that the seed company's responsibility is limited to providing seed that has a certain honestly stated ability to germinate in the laboratory. What happens in the field is the buyer's problem. Federal and state seed laws prescribe minimum germination standards; the buyer and seller may set higher standards. By law, every commercial bag of seed sold must be labeled with the results of a germination test performed within the past six months. The law allows seed to be sold when its germination falls below minimum standard germination, but only if the package is prominently labeled "below standard germination." (As is true of almost all government regulation, though those regulated "complain" about government interference in their business, the rules were written by and for the industry being regulated, and help rather than hinder that industry.)

The unfortunate thing about seed law from the gardener's viewpoint is that seed sold in packets of less than one pound—meaning garden-seed packets—does not have to show recent germination test results *as long as the results were above the minimum standards*. This sounds reasonable—avoiding great and unnecessary packaging expense that would be passed on to the consumer. It seems like it still protects the home gardener—but it doesn't. Actually, the legally mandated levels for standard germination are so low that no commercial grower would ever buy seed with germination anywhere near the minimum level. You'll understand this perfectly when you see how laboratory germination percentage relates to field performance.

Minimum standard germination for cabbage seed is 75 percent. Under very, very good field conditions—virtually ideal germination conditions almost never found outdoors—cabbage seed that tested at 75 percent germ in the lab might yield a 30 percent field emergence of sickly seedlings. Under ordinary good conditions, field emergence would drop to below 10 percent; under poor field conditions, 75 percent germ cabbage seed probably would not come up at all—not one single seedling. However, 85 percent germ cabbage seed might sprout at 50 percent under good conditions, 20 percent under poor ones. At 95 percent germ, cabbage seed might sprout at 75 percent under good field conditions and a few seedlings might emerge even under very poor field conditions.

Farmers are professional growers who understand that laboratory germination test results do not exactly correspond to what happens in the

How field conditions affect germination percentage

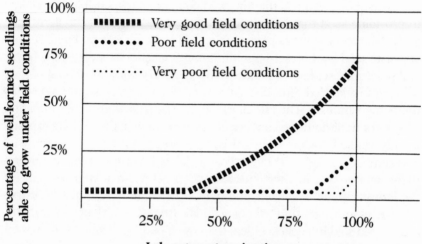

Percentage of well-formed seedlings able to grow under field conditions

Laboratory germination percentage

- ▪▪▪▪▪▪▪▪ Very good field conditions
- •••••••• Poor field conditions
- ·········· Very poor field conditions

field. It is difficult to sell a knowledgeable farmer a cabbage seed lot that has tests below 85 percent. (The farmer smiles when he is offered a 90 percent lot.) The farmer is a critical trade. The uncritical gardener, on the other hand, is offered a packet of cabbage seed usually not stamped "below standard germination," which was anywhere from 75 to 99 percent germ up to six months before it was packaged, and could possess anything from extremely low to extremely high vigor. What's a gardener to do?

Many people have a low failure tolerance. After a few bad experiences, some gardeners come to feel relying on picture-packet garden-store seeds is a very chancy thing. They decide they are better off to use transplants when they can. Most learn to sow seed thickly because it's easier to thin out extra seedlings than to make up for lost time when the packet fails to sprout well enough. (Some garden-seed suppliers turn this around to justify selling cheap seed, saying that gardeners sow too thickly anyway, so there's no harm in selling them low-germ seed—enough will still come up.) Some serious gardeners discover that there are a few *commercial quality* mail-order seed companies, such as Stokes and Harris, that do not depend on the gardener for the bulk of their business and sell the

Seed germination standards

Vegetable species	Federal Seed Act minimum standard germination percentage	Approximate minimum acceptable germination percentage	Approximate maximum germination percentage
Bean, fava	75	not commercial	95
Bean, garden	70	80	95+
Beet	65	80	90
Broccoli	75	85	99
Brussels sprouts	70	82	99
Cabbage	75	85	99
Cantaloupe	75	85	99
Carrot	55	80	85–90
Cauliflower	75	85	99
Celery/celeriac	55	75	85–90
Chard	65	not commercial	90
Chinese cabbage	75	85	99
Corn, sweet	75	85	98
Corn salad	70	not commercial	85
Cucumber	80	85	95
Eggplant	60	80	90
Endive	70	80	90
Kale	75	85	99
Kohlrabi	75	85	99
Leek	60	75	85–90
Lettuce	80	85	95
Mustards	75	85	99
Onion	70	80	92
Parsley	60	80	90
Parsnip	60	70	80
Pea	75	85	98
Pepper	75	80	90–92
Radish	75	85	99
Rutabaga	75	85	99
Spinach	60	75	82–85
Squash/pumpkin	75	85	95–98
Tomato	75	85	95
Watermelon	70	85	95

same quality seed in their little packets that they offer to the farmer in large bags. After all, the company never knows when the order is coming in from a knowledgeable farmer who is not only buying seed for the home garden but also a few trial packets to evaluate a new variety under consideration for extensive commercial planting.

Buying garden seed as opposed to commercial-quality seed means that a significant portion of the seed packets will contain a product of low-germination and vigor, instead of only an occasional one. Sometimes, weak seed must be sold even by a commercial seed company, because growing seed is not like making screws and bolts—you get only one chance every year, and the weather doesn't always cooperate. Sometimes even highly ethical seed companies are faced with the unpleasant choice of selling lower-germination seed or no seed at all.

Improving germination

Thus, even with the best suppliers the gardener cannot count on every packet containing seeds so vigorous that some will sprout even under poor field conditions. The most successful gardeners create sprouting conditions good enough that seeds of only average vigor and germination ability will come up and grow. I wish it weren't this way; I wish every seed packet were bursting with the highest vigor, and that every sowing would explode into life and grow fast, ending up as uniform as peas in a pod. But this is Earth and we have to make do as long as we're here, including getting the most out of every seed packet.

In the laboratory, seeds are sprouted under the most perfect conditions that can be created. By understanding what those ideal conditions are and how they improve germination, the gardener can try to create something similar in the field. In the germ lab, seeds are sprouted in an ideal medium, held at a specific optimum moisture level and at precisely controlled temperatures ideal for the species being tested. Those are the key factors: medium, moisture and temperature. They control the rate of sprouting and its success or failure.

The right moisture

Perhaps surprisingly, seed does not sprout well when wet. Soggy soils are cold and full of damping-off disease organisms, which can kill seedlings even before they emerge into the light and continue to pick them off in the first two or three weeks after emergence. The seedling will suddenly wilt or the stem will form a scaly collar at ground level, pinch off at that point and die. Damping-off organisms don't thrive under dryish conditions. Seed can absorb moisture from surprisingly dry soil—though not, of course, from soil that has totally dried out. Most testing labs get the highest possible percentage of germination by placing seed between sheets of damp (not soaking wet) blotting paper, all sealed into a small clear-plastic container. This way there is no risk of letting the seeds dry out or of accidentally adding too much moisture during sprouting. The very highest possible germination percentage being the goal, blotting paper, jar and water are all sterile.

When soil is occasionally used in a seed lab, it is sterilized, too. In preparation for a lab test, powdered dry loamy earth is slowly moistened until a handful squeezed very hard into a ball will just barely stick together and will easily break apart into fine particles. (Note that this is similar to the test used to determine optimum tilling moisture.) To prevent dehydration, soil sprouting tests, like blotting-paper tests, are done in airtight containers. In my own testing work, I found that soils in closed containers with low but adequate moisture levels could sprout twice the number of seedlings as soil that was exposed to open air and that had to be watered every day or two. Consider the implications of that fact if you're in the habit of sprinkling your newly sown seeds every day. "But what do I do when it's hot and sunny?" you experienced gardeners ask. "I don't want my seeds to dry out and die!" There are ways to prevent this, and we'll get to them shortly.

The right medium

But first, consider that the composition of the sprouting medium also has a big effect on germination. Emerging seedlings are capable of exerting only a small amount of force against surrounding soil particles as they push out roots and send up a shoot towards the light. In the laboratory, the testing medium provides no obstacle at all. Lab soil mixes are composed of fine, light, moisture-retentive particles similar to those used in greenhouse mixes. In finely sieved, compost-rich vermiculite/perlite/sand mixes, even the most delicate seedling can develop. In fact, in the laboratory, a fair percentage of otherwise very weak and non-vigorous seeds—seeds that would not likely germinate in the field—are capable of sprouting. The delicacy of most sprouts is why soil must be tilled before seeds are sown. Very few kinds of vegetable sprouts can get through compacted soil.

In the field, small seeds near the surface must be kept moist until they've got a root moving deeper into damp earth, or they die. However, frequent watering jeopardizes sprouting seeds: it increases damping off, makes the soil slump, settle and compact and also creates crusts on many soil types that can block emergence. By knowing that sprouting seeds prefer damp rather than wet soil, we can avoid unnecessarily watering the seeds on cloudy days. The gardener can also enhance germination in ways a farmer could never consider. Covering small, weakly sprouting seed with a prepared medium similar to that used in greenhouse mixes can greatly enhance sprouting of low-vigor seeds, and it's not much trouble on a home-garden scale. Finely sifted compost, sifted rotted horse manure, well-rotted sawdust or a mixture of half garden soil/half sphagnum moss are all materials that hold a lot of water, resist drying out quickly, act as a mulch to conserve soil moisture and *do not form a crust.* Five gallons of this sort of mix will cover well over 100 feet of furrow. I have found that during warm sunny weather, seeds covered with sifted compost need watering only every two days (except in the very hottest weather), while seed covered with soil has to be watered daily. I usually don't bother with a seed cover mix in spring or late summer when moist soil tends to stay damp by itself, except when field-sprouting very delicate seeds normally started indoors, such as celery and small-seeded herbs like oregano and basil.

The rule is to plant seed about three times the depth of its largest dimension. I generally sow very fine seed (celery, basil) about one-quarter inch deep; small seed (cabbage, carrot) about one-half inch deep; huskier seed (spinach, radish, beet, Chinese cabbage) about five-eighths to three-quarters of an inch deep; large seed (squash, cucumber, melon, beans, peas) about 1½ inches deep.

The right temperature

The other vital factor in successful germination is soil temperature, which determines the speed of cellular chemistry (growth). Cold seed sprouts slowly, if at all, and all the while, the weak and delicate emerging seedlings are prey to diseases and insects in the soil. Most vegetable seeds sprout between 60°F and 105°F, best at 75°F to 85°F. Below 60°F, sprouting stops; over 100°F, the seedling may die. Some tropical species like peppers, eggplants and melons won't sprout at all if soil temperatures fall below 70°F for very long. A few types of seed sprout better at slightly cooler temperatures. Spinach, for example, will sprout from 45°F to 85°F, best at about 55°F to 60°F; it seldom sprouts well over 70°F, so it's hard to get spinach going in July. In the lab, the germination cabinet is set at the optimum temperature. *In the field, 60°F is the critical minimum germination temperature for most summer crops.*

The relationship between soil temperature and laboratory germination percentage on two different lots of cabbage seed

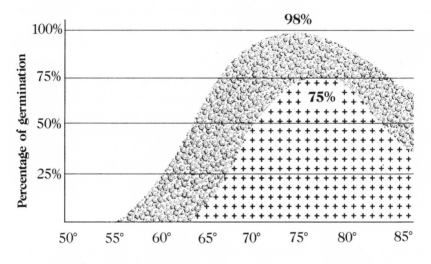

Soil Temperature

Note that the weaker lot of seed (75 percent lot) is much less able to tolerate adverse temperature conditions than the 98 percent lot.

The relationship between soil temperature and sprouting time

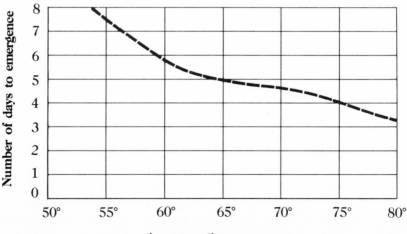

Average soil temperature

Planting by soil temperature usually works out better than planting by the calendar. In February, when spring soil warm-up begins, soil temperatures may be below 40°F. Different soils proceed to warm up at different rates. Dark-colored, well-drained, light-textured loams heat faster than clayey soils. Southern exposures warm up much more rapidly than eastern or northern ones. Many of our region's soils don't reach a stable 60°F until May or even early June. At Lorane, I worked a northeast-sloping, light-brown, MacAlpine silty clay at an elevation of 900 feet, and it wouldn't sprout bean seed until late May at best. Now I garden on rich, black, Malabon bottomland loam alongside the Umpqua River, less than 100 feet above sea level, and beans will sprout easily in early April most springs. Novices will have to pay close attention to their garden's soil temperature and find out for themselves when it is time to plant which species. Having a good soil thermometer helps gardeners intuitively connect weather with soil temperature. (A soil thermometer can also help you track how cloches and cold frames respond to changes in weather and season.) Experienced gardeners often tune into nature's own soil thermometer—the procession of bloom and the appearance of new plants each spring. For example, at Elkton when the crocus comes up, it's time to fertilize overwintered onions; when Japanese plums bloom, it's time to sow radishes; apple blossoms signify the beginning of lettuce season; and when the cow parsnips are in full bloom, it's safe to transplant tomatoes without protection. You'll have to observe the indicators around your own garden.

Weather changes will rapidly affect soil temperature several inches down. In spring when the sun shines strongly, soils heat up fast and can reach 80°F or more near the surface. At night, these same soils can drop to 60°F or less an inch below the surface but will warm again quickly the next morning if the sun comes out. However, if the weather changes and becomes cloudy or rainy, soils can drop into the mid- to low 50s in a flash and stay that way until the weather improves. Watering the seeds has exactly the same effect on soil temperature, so I try hard to avoid it. When watering is essential, I try to sprinkle my seeds in midmorning, just before the sun starts heating up the soil. That way, the soil will be hot enough by midafternoon to stay reasonably warm all night.

Planting during spring's unstable weather is an invitation to either a germination failure or the retarded emergence of a bunch of badly weakened seedlings on their way to becoming permanently stunted by further chilly, cloudy conditions. But *not* planting early can result in a late harvest. I highly recommend becoming psychic enough to successfully control and/or outguess the weather so that you can plan to sow just before the onset of a long sunny spell. If that fails, or if the weather escapes your control and turns poor, then replant as soon as conditions improve, even before you know the fate of the first sowing. If both come up, choose the group of seedlings that does best over the next three to six weeks. In cabbage years I'll cheerfully make three subsequent sowings if necessary.

There are so many obstacles to successful field sprouting! Soil-living insects eat the seed and especially enjoy the tender root tip and emerging shoot. If soil texture is not uniformly fine, it becomes difficult for the seed to pick up moisture and hard for the sprout to force its way to the light. Hard crusts, hot sunny weather that dries out soil before the seedling can send a root in search of moisture, chilly weather, overwatering, damping-off diseases—the contrast between germination rates in the field and the lab reflects how far from ideal field conditions can be. It's no wonder that wild plants strew about jillions of seeds in an effort to get even a few survivors to mature another generation. In the garden, you have to really get in there and root for your seeds from the time you sow them until they are established.

The lowdown on the seed business

I am about to give you an insider's look at specific seed companies, name names, offer criticisms and make recommendations. I feel I have always been objective about this subject in previous editions of my book, even though I still owned and operated Territorial Seed Company, one of the companies I will be discussing. But that apparent conflict of interest made me go out of my way to be more than fair to my competitors and to the seed trade itself. I also had good reason not to offend my suppliers. Readers who know the earlier books will note that so far in this edition I have been far franker about the seed business. I am going to continue to be frank.

I think it is only fair to reveal that I may yet have a conflict of interest. Though I sold Territorial Seed Company in 1985, I am still deeply concerned about its future development, for three reasons. One, I have some pride in my creation. After all, I started Territorial to provide a needed regional service and set the company on an ethical course. I am pleased to say that the present owners, Tom and Julie Johns, are continuing the business with little change, so Territorial will be praised in what is to come. Two, I retain a financial interest in my old business, which could cloud my objectivity but I believe does not. I receive a royalty from Territorial on its gross business, which will continue until 1995 if the company continues until then. Each year, that fee is enough to let my family live in what Scott Nearing might call "independent poverty" for one year and save enough for one or two more, and naturally I hope the royalty will increase with Territorial's growth. But that's not why Territorial Seed Company ranks highly in the coming evaluations. Three, I am a serious year-round gardener who intends to continue living west of the Cascades, and I personally need a company like Territorial to provide a vital service for *me*. With those facts in mind, I leave it to the reader to judge what I have to say about the garden-seed trade.

The seed-rack racket

Consider first the seed-rack business. Picture packets are readily available at everything from supermarkets to discount stores; the larger seed racks even offer a wide range of choices. So I wish I could wholeheartedly recommend picture-packet seed-rack seed. But I have a lot of misgivings about rack jobbers to share with you.

Lilly Miller, our most successful local rack jobber, feels it must serve a larger territory than the maritime Northwest. Only about six million people live west of the Cascades—not a big enough market to satisfy ambitious entrepreneurs. But supplying gardeners east of the Cascades as well means compromises in varietal choice—compromises that make money but often work to the disadvantage of the maritime gardener. Ferry Morse, Burpee and Northrup King, which have seed racks covering the entire nation, make a gesture at regionalizing the varieties found on their displays, but the varieties offered are often even less well adapted to our peculiar climate. When I see a Willamette Valley rack selling okra or Hale's Best Jumbo melons, I am saddened. Though both may do very well in warmer areas east of the Cascades, in our climate they rarely grow well.

Often rack seed is not fresh and vigorous—not always, but too often. This complaint is directed at all the abovementioned suppliers and also Ed Hume, Island Seed and Canadian rack companies supplying British Columbia's lower mainland gardener (who proudly proclaim their seed is all Canada #1 or better—but Canada #1 standards are similar to those set by the Federal Seed Act). Here's why rack seed is almost certain to be stale and often approaches minimum standard germination levels.

Picture-packet rack companies are in a highly competitive business with severe profit restrictions. After sharing 50 to 70 percent of the gross sales with the store the rack sits in, and then deducting their own overhead and distribution costs, there is not much left to cover the large number of unsold dated packets that must be returned, counted, and then discarded every year. Credit collections are frequently a big and expensive problem because the usual accepted terms of the trade force the rack jobber to consign racks in January and render no billing until the end of summer. Many garden-center owners with dollar signs for hearts take every possible advantage and will not pay for last year's seed until threatened with the refusal of next year's rack—and some won't pay even then.

Tight profit margins in this cutthroat business "force" rack jobbers to save every possible penny. They cannot afford the overtime labor and the extra machinery that would be required to packet mostly new crop seed and make up displays in the short time between the fall harvest of new crop seed and December, when the new displays must be sent out. For maximum economy, automatic seed-filling machines run steadily summer and fall, filling shiny packets with seed that was harvested the previous year or even earlier, and not necessarily stored under climate-controlled conditions to preserve vigor. The bright new packets are required by law to be stamped "packed for next year." To be fair, some packets that were made up after the end of September could be "new crop" seed. But who outside the company itself could know? The State Agriculture departments of Oregon and Washington do actively enforce minimum germination standards prescribed in the Federal Seed Act, but the seed often does not have sufficient vigor to really please.

Those narrow profit margins also mean that a high percentage of rack packets are filled with the most inexpensive seed obtainable, or with small quantities of more-costly stuff. The U.S. retail garden-seed market supports a few major producers of ultra-cheap vegetable seed, supplying a very large assortment of poorly maintained varieties. When grown out, these varieties are generally pretty ragged and contain numerous "off" types because little effort has been put into maintaining the purity of the variety. Minimally roguing the field (hoeing-out off types before they can release pollen or set seed) and careful stock-seed maintenance could more than double the price per pound. (Stock seed is the seed used to plant the seed field. Better producers grow special stock-seed fields that are meticulously rogued by the breeding staff; cheaper producers either use the last harvest as "stock seed" or buy a few pounds of some other company's commercial seed for stock seed.)

Critical commercial growers would promptly find a new supplier and might even sue if cheap garden seed were represented to them as being of commercial grade, no matter how vigorous the seed turned out to be (and sometimes these third-rate varieties are extremely high germ and have excellent vigor). But uncritical home gardeners do not realize why

25 percent of their cabbages have volcanic holes running down the center of the head, or why a third of their kohlrabies aren't round but taper to a point like a Cambodian temple, or the side shoots on their broccoli are larger than the central heads, why their mustard bolts much too soon, or their radishes come in several colors, shapes and textures—some not particularly tender or tasty. They blame their fertilizing, or their watering, or the weather that season. But it's the seed that's really at fault.

Not many of the companies that sell seed to the home gardener grow very much of their seed at all. Most vegetable seed is produced by several dozen high-quality international "primary" growers whose names are well known to large vegetable farmers. Only a few primary growers concentrate on cheap garden seed. Some of the big boys in the seed-rack trade—major international corporations like Ferry Morse and Northrup King—are also major commercial seed growers. Their racks contain a mixture of qualities: some packets are "home garden only" varieties probably purchased from wholesale seed growers who produce on the cheap for the garden-seed trade, and some packets contain the same premium varieties sold to the commercial trade.

How good is that commercial-grade seed likely to be? I don't know how those companies make decisions, but I do know what kinds of decisions have to be made, and I can speculate on the nature of the person making them. I suppose if I were the kind of person who was comfortable working for a big corporation, and if I had become successful and risen in my company because I had learned as my primary ethical lesson in life that "the way to get along is to go along" (that's often how big-corporation people rise to executive positions), and if I were in charge of allocating seed from my company's warehouse, and if I had a large quantity of aging seed in the back of my warehouse with germination below acceptable commercial levels, or if I had received a new lot that after a winter grow-out in Chile proved to be "suspect" because it produced too large a percentage of off-type plants—if I were that person (and I'm not saying that any particular company or individual would be this unethical), I'd be tempted to turn that suspect or lower germination lot over to my picture-packet division. Or I might want to recover some of the company's loss by selling it to one of those "on the cheap" primary producers for resale to a seed-packet company.

Mail-order seed companies

Buying mail-order garden seed doesn't guarantee getting top-quality or better-adapted varieties, either. Even more than rack jobbers, almost every mail-order garden-seed company is trying to serve the whole of North America through a single catalog. They do not tell the reader which variety is adapted to which location, if they even know. Instead, the more responsible companies describe how the variety grows on their own trial ground, or perhaps how the variety grows where it is raised commercially.

Mail-order companies range widely in quality and business ethics. The gardener sometimes has no certain way to know if the company actually has much of a trial ground, or what its in-house germination standards are like. Perhaps the company merely sends out an attractive catalog filled with old-fashioned, well-known varieties (most of them grown by those cheap producers for the home-garden trade), spiced with a few recent All America Selections promoted in gardening magazines, which are certain to be top-quality selections that will grow reasonably well almost anywhere in the U.S. (except the maritime Northwest, judging by the results I had in trials of heat-loving AAS varieties at Lorane).

Here's the story, as I see it, on a number of prominent mail-order companies. As with your favorite variety, there are other companies I don't mention because their catalog offerings have little relevance to the maritime garden, or I'm simply not personally acquainted with the company's product—no slight is intended.

Abundant Life Seed Foundation, Inc.

If I were to try to pigeonhole this non-profit corporation, I'd use words like alternative, counterculture, hippie survivalist, new age. The founder and director of ALS, Forest Shomer (*shomer* means "guardian" in Hebrew), considers it his mission on Earth to protect our regional gene pool. His guardianship includes the eastern side of the Cascade Mountains and goes into Idaho. So some of his vegetable varieties are not as good for gardens west of the Cascades as one might want. Others are uniquely adapted to cool maritime conditions. Recent germination test results are plainly stated in the catalog and tend to be unbelievably and uniformly high.

ALS is pointedly concerned with the issue of hybrid versus open-pollinated seeds, and you'll not find any hybrids in its catalog. Though Forest buys a portion of his heritage or old-fashioned varieties from the very same primary growers used by most of the garden-seed trade, a goodly percentage of his offering is seed uniquely home-grown by individual homesteaders who are "preserving" open-pollinated varieties. These supporters refer to themselves as a "network of seed people." Some of this home-grown seed is not up to professional standards in terms of uniformity, but I don't think it's supposed to be. The idea is to have collections of genes, not an identical bunch of peas in a pod that all get the same disease or simultaneously fall to an identical stressor. What I especially like about ALS's catalog are the survivalist crops—field corns, garbanzo beans, favas, quinoas, amaranths and poppies. There are also flowers, herbs, tree and shrub seeds, books, crystals (very big these days with the spiritually inclined in this new age of ours) and lots of trendy permaculture. *Contact Abundant Life Seed Foundation, P.O. Box 772, Port Townsend, WA 98368.*

W. Atlee Burpee Company

Until recently, Burpee was a family-owned and -managed company. It offered a pretty good mix: very little of the ordinary and cheap, many unique Burpee-bred and -raised selections, and some high-quality seed from other primary growers. Burpee quality was good enough that it supplied its own vegetable-seed productions and many flower varieties to the entire garden-seed industry at prices much higher than those charged by the cheapie producers. (It's an incestuous business—when you buy flower seed from Stokes, the seed may well have been actually grown by Burpee, while both Burpee and Stokes buy Miracle hybrid sweet corn from the same primary grower—Rogers Brothers in Idaho. And Rogers Bros. is owned by Sandoz, a Swiss chemical/pharmaceutical corporation.) Burpee's breeding and trials are carried out in California and Pennsylvania, so many of its varieties do not fit our climate.

In 1979, when I first began to find out about the inner workings of the trade, the Burpee folks had good morale and were proud of their high-germ, quality seed. Since then, I have watched as Burpee was purchased by one multinational conglomerate, spun off in a restructuring and bought by another. The result has been a demoralization of the long-time employees, and I think the ethics and products of Burpee bear close watching. *Contact W. Atlee Burpee Co., Warminster, PA 18974.*

Harris Seeds

The Jos. Harris Company was once a rapidly growing family vegetable-seed business headquartered in upstate New York. Because it grew fast in the fifties, Harris became more and more involved in producing its own seed in the bountiful Pacific Northwest, home to some of the world's most ideal production districts.

Companies that produce seed away from the home office usually contract with a local farmer, whom they supply with a few pounds of stock seed to plant. The company field man oversees the growth and harvest of the crop. If there's enough action in the district, there may be a number of field men and perhaps a small office there. So, back in the early sixties, Harris did the reasonable thing and acquired Gill Brothers Seed Company, a small, regional vegetable-seed business headquartered in Gresham, Oregon. Gill Bros. had a local office, a thriving Pacific Northwest commercial and mail-order garden-seed business, and—most important to Harris—a strong set of contacts with local production resources from the Skagit Valley to Idaho. Gill Bros. even had a mob of loyal gardeners who came to Gresham every spring to buy their seeds direct from the source— which they kept doing until recently, when the Gresham office was closed, probably as a consequence of Harris's merger several years ago with the Moran Seed Company of Salinas, California.

This little company had been our ethical regional seedhouse. Gill Bros. bred such local specialties as the Sweet Meat squash and supplied a fairly hardy variety of overwintered "pearl" cauliflower primarily used by the Salinas growers (now out of favor in Salinas and no longer available). Naturally, Harris found that most of the special Gill Bros. items it had acquired had little or no national relevance, and most disappeared from the Harris catalog. And there went one of the maritime Northwest's best quality regional suppliers! (When I started Territorial some 10 years later, I did not even know about Gill Bros. or the powerful vacuum left by the company's disappearance. I only knew that I got a lot more business than I had anticipated.)

Harris does its breeding work in upstate New York, in a climate that does not have the extremely hot summers found on Burpee's breeding plots. So before Harris became Harris/Moran, I used to recommend it more highly than Burpee. Harris's active breeding program produces, among other things, its own unique sweet corn and tomato varieties. A good many Harris varieties perform very well in the Willamette, as is proved year after year by Dr. Baggett's variety trials at Corvallis. And because Harris was a commercial company, the quality of most of the seed sold through its special garden-seed catalog was the same as that it sold to farmers. (The garden catalog also had a number of "junk" varieties in it not found in the commercial catalog.)

In 1985, Harris merged with the Moran Seed Company. Moran was a strictly commercial seed grower focused on supplying the vegetable-seed market in Salinas Valley—where the bulk of the nation's lettuce, cauliflower, broccoli and other vegetables is produced. Moran had its own breeding and seed production programs for Salinas specialties and Moran seeds did not trial as well in the Willamette as Harris's seeds. Trade gossip says Harris/Moran no longer had any use for its garden-seed trade, and sold off the home-garden business to a few old Harris employees who will continue to use the Harris name but run a separate company. The "consumer" Harris will buy the majority of its seed from Harris/Moran. This arrangement could result in a solid garden-seed company. How it applies to us in the maritime Northwest may depend on how much of the new gardeners' catalog is Harris, how much is Moran and how much is something else. *Contact Harris Seeds, Moreton Farm, 3670 Buffalo Road, Rochester, NY 14624.*

Johnny's Selected Seeds

Johnny's started up on a shoestring in the early seventies, about seven years before I went into the seed business. Founder Robert Johnston, Jr., set out to focus his business on the organic gardener in a specific territory, serving only the northernmost tier of states, high elevation sites and southern Canada where summers are cooler, seasons are short and winter is severe—just like on his Albion, Maine, trial ground. Rob believes in ethical business, so he tended to seek out smaller, quality, European primary growers rather than sell the junk seed common in the U.S. garden-seed industry. He also started out with an aversion to hybrids, believing that gardeners should be able to grow their own seeds if they wanted to. Johnny's has at least doubled in size since 1980, is developing a large commercial trade and is now beginning to breed a few of its own varieties. During the years I've followed the company's progress, Johnny's catalog has increasingly included hybrids. In the beginning, Rob also was Mr. Organic—but as his business and his knowledge grew, his statements about various tenets of the true faith have understandably become increasingly qualified.

Johnny's runs a very thorough trial ground on a 15-acre Maine farm. Rob realized early on that the federally prescribed minimum germination standards were too low for a person of conscience, and so the company maintained somewhat higher in-house minimums (though not quite up to top commercial standards), which were published in the catalog. Guided by these principles, Johnny's Selected Seeds made all the right moves in a unique market niche. Naturally the business grew rapidly.

By the late seventies, Johnny's Selected Seeds had become a major focus of attention. Rob was employing over a dozen people, doing close to a million dollars in sales a year from a rundown farm, and beginning to get into commercial seed sales. Articles about his company appeared in everything from garden journals to business magazines. Johnny's served as a model to my own efforts when I organized Territorial. I liked Rob's honest, forthright way of describing the pros and cons of his varieties and how his plain black-and-white catalog showed intelligent, youngish people intensely interested in his trial grounds, instead of the usual idealized full-color vegetable pictures printed from color separations supplied free to the catalog trade by the bigger primary growers. Rob was generous enough to be very helpful to an eager but ignorant young fellow named Steve Solomon, who pestered him on the phone for hours about starting up a similar shoestring regional seed company for the maritime Northwest, a small region for which Johnny's could not discover what was needed without setting up another trial ground on our side of the mountains.

Johnny's catalog is very informative. It shows soil temperature/germination response curves for each species. Cultural information is quite complete and truly without overstatement or sales puffs. The catalog describes precisely how each vegetable grows at Albion, Maine, and nowhere else. Maritime Northwest gardeners will have problems with some of Johnny's varieties. The tomatoes, for instance, seem to require warmer nights than are found west of the Cascades, and so are later and less prolific here than they are in Maine. (For some peculiar reason, Harris's tomato varieties, bred at a slightly more southern and warmer location, do better.) Crops for fall harvest, typical of what is needed in the east, tend to mature quickly and don't withstand maritime winter weather, though some are good here. If Territorial Seed Company did not exist, I'd be a happy but selective customer. *Contact Johnny's Selected Seeds, 299 Foss Hill Road, Albion, ME 04910.*

Nichols Garden Nursery

This is a local company, but not a regional one. Nichols operates out of Albany, Oregon, selling seeds all over the United States. The company does not produce more than a few of the seeds listed in its extensive mimeographed catalog of the gourmet and the unique. Nichols doesn't have a significant trial grounds of its own, but it takes advantage of the fact that Dr. Jim Baggett's OSU Vegetable Crops Research Farm is only a few miles away. More than once, I've met the folks from Nichols there. Dr. Baggett is a very kindly and helpful man, and he probably serves as their informal varietal consultant. Dr. Baggett's only remuneration is that Nichols offers a few of the many fine varieties he has bred with the home garden in mind, contracting for the seed through primary growers with Dr. Baggett's guidance. Based on various conversations I've had with

Nichols's management and the local State Ag. Dept. seed cops, about five years ago the company increased its effort to keep germination standards at or above federal minimums.

Nichols is highly secretive about the suppliers of many of its "rare European gourmet specialties." When you tour most seed companies, you'll see bags in the warehouse labeled with the names of many different suppliers from around the world. At Nichols, all I saw were big plastic tubs marked only with the catalog number and the variety name Nichols uses. Perhaps that secretiveness comes about because Nichols buys seeds from exotic and rare little French and Italian companies it doesn't want others in the trade to find out about. (How Nichols could prevent those rare and unusual companies from finding out about all those potential customers in North America like Territorial, I don't know.) And perhaps it's because some of their seed comes from ordinary, garden-seed-quality suppliers who list some of the same exotic variety names Nichols says are rare and special. *Contact Nichols Garden Nursery, 1190 North Pacific Highway, Albany, OR 97371.*

Park Seed Company

Here's a great company that makes every effort to buy the highest possible quality of seed for resale to its customers—a group that includes both gardeners and bedding-plant nurseries. But beware of the company's catalog, much of which is written from the perspective of its own South Carolina trial grounds. Many of Park's bulb onions are right for overwintering in the latitudes found in South Carolina and won't work in the maritime Northwest. Once I grew Park's Truckers' Favorite White sweet corn in my trials, listed in the catalog as growing about six feet tall and requiring 67 days to mature—which I'm sure it does in South Carolina. Started at Lorane on June 1, Truckers' was 16 feet tall with stalks two to three inches in diameter at the base 105 days later in mid-September, and just beginning to tassle out! Without frost, it might have matured by the end of November. If I lived in the southeast or in California, I'd be Park's customer for sure. *Contact Park Seed Company, Cokesbury Road, Greenwood, SC 29647.*

Stokes Seeds

Before I went into the business myself, I used to buy a lot of my seed from Stokes. Located on the Niagara River at St. Catherines, Ontario, near Harris Seeds, Stokes has a northern location that tends to select for varieties that adapt well to maritime summers. The company is also a big supplier to the commercial vegetable grower in southern Canada and the northern U.S. Most of the catalog is commercial seed of the highest standards. Stokes has a wonderful collection of Dutch cauliflower, pages of cabbages, dozens of unique onion varieties and some special garden varieties of its own (more on these in Chapter 8, How to Grow It). The catalog also contains detailed cultural information and makes great wintertime reading. I've never been disappointed by Stokes. *Americans: Stokes maintains a U.S. warehouse to avoid customs hassles. Contact Stokes Seeds, Inc., Box 548, Buffalo, NY 14240. Canadians: contact Stokes Seeds Ltd., 39 James St., Box 10, St. Catharines, Ont. L2R 6R6.*

Territorial Seed Company

I started Territorial in 1979 to be a Johnny's for the gardener west of the Cascades. The response to the first catalog in 1980 was three times what I expected. Territorial doubled in size every year for three years in a row; by 1982, it had mushroomed into the biggest employer in Lorane (no great achievement in a town of 150) and made the town's name familiar to tens of thousands of people. After my life-changing sabbatical in Fiji, I sold the business to Tom and Julie Johns. As the founder (and given my continuing financial interest), I am privy to a lot of insider information about the company.

Territorial, like most companies in the garden-seed trade, is basically a seed merchant. Tom Johns makes every effort to purchase seed at germination levels well above acceptable commercial levels. The seed is warehoused under climate-controlled storage to slow the otherwise rapid deterioration that occurs when seed is held at high humidity—which is what we have in this temperate rainforest for half the year. Unsold seed is tested twice a year and discarded if it falls below commercial standards.

To find the best varieties available for the maritime Northwest and to keep its suppliers honest, Territorial runs serious grow-outs and variety trials evaluated strictly on the potential for success in the home garden. The catalog offers a complete assortment of vegetable varieties, all of which will grow well in the maritime Northwest garden. There is also a modest assortment of herbs and flowers. Territorial custom-grows about a dozen "local" vegetable varieties itself and will probably do more of this in the future. The hat of trial-grounds master is now worn by a uniquely talented plant breeder, self-sufficiency gardener and vegetarian named Tim Peters, who is passionate about breeding plants and growing seed. Tim's varieties are beginning to appear in the catalog.

Territorial also has about a hundred seed-rack locations throughout the maritime Northwest, offering the very same seed sold through the catalog; locations are listed in the catalog. *Americans: contact Territorial Seed Company, P.O. Box 27, Lorane, OR 97451. Canadians: contact Territorial Seeds Canada, P.O. Box 46225, Stn. G, Vancouver, BC V6R 4G5.*

Thompson & Morgan

Some of the varieties most crucial to successful year-round gardening west of the Cascades are big commercial crops in England and Holland. That's why Territorial imports many thousands of dollars' worth of European Brussels sprouts, kale, cauliflower, overwintered broccoli, late-maturing cabbage, extra-hardy endive and slow-bolting spring leeks. Thompson & Morgan is a major English garden seed company whose colorful catalog is filled with many interesting items that are common in the British garden, as well as unusual European gourmet specialties such as chicory and sea-kale. Where Territorial offers two fava varieties, T&M may have a dozen. T&M also has an amazing selection of flower seed. Maritime Northwest gardeners will find the catalog most interesting. Unlike other British mail-order companies such as Suttons Seeds Ltd., Thompson and Morgan accepts U.S. dollars and ships to American customers from a New Jersey warehouse, so gardeners get fast, reliable service.

In Europe, the formation of cartels and industry-wide noncompetition agreements are not considered bad form, as they are in the United States, but merely ways for less-than-optimumly productive industries to guarantee themselves reasonable profits (in the same manner that European labor unions similarly guarantee their less-than-optimumly productive workers good salaries). Thus, European seed companies have used their respective governments to establish rules and conditions that limit or prevent price competition. When you see T&M's prices, you'll understand how stiff competition has made domestic seed inexpensive. *Contact Thompson & Morgan, Inc., P.O. Box 1308, Jackson, NJ 08527.*

Saving on seed purchases

Most gardeners are fearful of saving leftover seed, so they purchase new packets each year. Except in the case of a few species whose seed has a very short shelf life, this is a false economy. Most of the expense of a small packet is not the seed itself, but the handling—the envelope may well cost as much or more than its contents. Seed racks carry only small packets, though "bulk packs" are available on Lilly racks for a few fast-moving items. Most mail-order companies offer several packet sizes.

For example, a half-gram packet of open-pollinated cabbage seed may sell for 80 cents, four grams for $1.10, and 28 grams (just under one ounce) for $1.75. On a unit-cost basis, the seed in the half-gram packet costs more than 25 times as much per gram as the seed in the ounce packet. Obviously a gram of cheap seed doesn't cost more than a cent or two wholesale. The only time a much better volume/cost relationship does not hold true is with very expensive hybrid varieties, where wholesale seed by the pound might cost from 25 cents to $1 a gram.

Shelf life

Seed for most species usually has a vigorous shelf life of three to four years after harvest, while many species will last five to seven years under decent storage conditions. For example, an ounce of rutabaga seed I bought from Harris in 1973 still sprouted vigorously when I went into the seed business for myself in 1979. That one ounce grew all my rutabaga patches for six years for the price of two tiny packets—which by themselves would not have been enough for one year.

I wish I could give you a believable chart of anticipated seed life by species, but I know too much about seed at this point. Much sad and costly experience buying seed for Territorial has taught me that there is simply no way for a gardener to determine how intrinsically vigorous any seed lot was at the time it was purchased, how much it has already deteriorated and how much longer it might last. *But despite the uncertainty, it still pays to buy in bulk.* You won't throw out nearly the value you'll save. Besides, the seed you buy "new" this year might turn out to be older or less vigorous than the seed you threw away last year. With the exception of very expensive hybrids, the only species I'd hesitate to stock up on would be the alliums (onion, leek, scallions), parsnip, spinach and hybrid sweet corn, because they're known for very short shelf life.

Testing vigor

To prevent the disappointment of a germination failure with old seed, check the vigor of your seed supply each year. To make a fair evaluation, try to always plant more than one variety of the same species. (This is a wise practice in any event, because you're ensured against a total crop failure should one variety have trouble with a particular year's weather or soil conditions, or fail to sprout well.) Allowing for the weather and for soil temperatures, if the seed sprouts fast and produces husky seedlings, then figure that it will retain sufficient vigor for another year. If it does not seem vigorous, discard it that season. Each year you might also mark on the packet the number of days it takes to sprout. Then next year, if the time increases by several days *and* the weather has not been highly unfavorable, take that as a cue to discard the packet.

Storing seed

The gardener can also greatly retard the normal aging of seed through careful storage, easily making seed last four times as long as it would keep otherwise. For the purposes of this book, I'm going to define "normal storage" as a cardboard box on a shelf in a closet away from the woodstove, where humidity won't be excessively high and the air temperature will tend to be stable. More precisely, let's call normal storage 70°F and 70 percent relative humidity. The rule of thumb used in the seed trade is that for every 10-degree drop in temperature from normal combined with a corresponding reduction in humidity that lowers the seed's moisture content by 1 percent, the life of the seed doubles. It takes roughly a 10 percent drop in relative humidity to lower seed moisture about 1 percent. So at 60°/RH60%—60°F and 60 percent relative humidity—the seed life more or less doubles compared to normal. At 50°/RH50%, it doubles again, to four times normal.

Creating something like 50°/RH50% at home is a piece of cake. Just get a couple of big, freshly recharged silica-gel dessicant packets and seal them with your seed in a tight-lidded gallon jar. The dessicant lowers the humidity. If silica gel is not available, an inch of fresh dry powdered milk on the bottom of the jar will do almost as well. To create the cool part, store the jar under the house or in the cellar, bury it a few feet deep or keep it in a spare refrigerator. Even storage in a cool closet along a north wall is better than a shelf in the furnace room or a damp cardboard box outdoors in the shed picking up a lot of moisture. (Silica-gel packets can be purchased from chemical supply companies or home food-preservation stores. They come free with new electronic equipment to keep the circuits dry during shipping. To recharge old silica gel, put it in the oven at 250°F for a few hours.)

Seed-life response to temperature and humidity works the other way, too. Temperatures above 70°F and relative humidity above 70 percent age seed faster than normal. Seed at 80°/RH80% lasts half as long as normal; seed at 90°/RH90% lasts one-fourth as long. Keeping your seed in a damp place where it can get hot is sure to lead to germination failures.

Home-grown seed

In Chapter 8, I discuss growing your own seed for each vegetable.

The biggest problem facing the gardener who wants to produce vigorous seed is how to avoid sprinkling the drying seed when irrigating the rest of the garden. Accomplishing that is mostly a matter of careful layout to establish a special seed-growing area. Only fully mature seed will be vigorous, so the home seed-grower should take great care to allow the seed to dry down fully before harvest and threshing, but remember that seed needs to be harvested as soon as it dries down. Repeated dampening by dews or early rains greatly lowers seed vigor and germination percentage; if let stand too long, many species tend to shatter and lose a lot of seed on the ground. (If the weather doesn't cooperate, dry the nearly mature seed under cover before threshing.)

Although raising seeds of high vigor and purity is a specialist's art, seed of acceptable vigor and purity can be grown for most vegetable species in the maritime Northwest, while a few species easily produce vigorous pure seed in the garden. I do a lot of it in my own garden and find it's fun—and I'm really proud to use my own. I hope all my readers will, at least once, transplant a few surviving overwintered kale, endive, lettuce or beet plants in early spring to the dry fringe of their garden and let them have at it. Six kale plants will easily grow you a pound of seed!

The hybrid question

There is considerable controversy right now about hybrid versus open-pollinated seeds. A lot of Organic gardeners feel it is more ethical to avoid hybrids. I used to feel that way myself until I grew a professional trial ground where I compared hundreds of open-pollinated and hybrid varieties. Though reluctantly at first, I have come to believe that hybrid seeds are a lot better for the home garden than most open-pollinated types still available. I did not wish to discover this and, in fact, it took several years of variety trials before the disappointing condition of many open-pollinated varieties fully penetrated my prejudices.

My primary reaction to the hybrid versus open-pollinated question is to avoid it. The problem is more complex and the "sides" are less definitively opposed than most antagonists realize, while the big international seed companies (who have the resources to do something about it, if anyone does) are themselves becoming genuinely worried about the worldwide loss of genetic diversity. Besides, the real issue does not concern vegetables much—it's the cereals that the world lives on.

With an increasing number of vegetable species, the only quality varieties available are hybrids. There are good, non-conspiratorial reasons behind the hybrid takeover. Almost all customers like the fact that hybrids are usually perfectly uniform. In the small garden where every single plant counts, if you're growing only three cabbages, and one of them is an off-type with a worthless head, that's a big loss. With open-pollinated types, that sort of occurrence is common; with hybrids, it's rare. Farmers also appreciate knowing they'll harvest a higher percentage of marketable, uniform vegetables. Hybridization undeniably produces much more vigorous seeds and plants, and generally much higher yields, which more than compensate for the additional seed cost.

Seed companies like hybrids because the parent lines needed to grow hybrid seed can be kept secret by the breeder—something that was not possible with open-pollinated varieties—so that the developer of a popular hybrid variety can charge enough to recoup the considerable expenses of breeding. When a seed company releases a new open-pollinated variety, all its competitors have to do is to buy a few pounds from the originator, plant a seed field and cheaply increase it themselves—all without the cost of development. If they use a few pounds of the breeder's original seeds every year as stock seed, they can sell something nearly as good for much less. Even if the older open-pollinated varieties were maintained, even if patent laws permitted seed companies to protect their new open-pollinated varieties from imitation and exploitation in the same way drug and chemical patents encourage research and development in those industries, hybrids, with their greater yield and vigor, would still supplant them in the commercial trade, despite their greater cost.

Saving seed from hybrids

Many gardeners mistakenly believe that it is not possible to grow good seed from hybrid plants. They fear that hybrids will make them "slaves" of multinational food conspiracies. Their argument is that once hybrids have completely replaced open-pollinated varieties, seed companies will be able to charge any amount for the seed, or to breed varieties that can only be grown using special chemical sprays—often produced by that same seed company. Once gardeners realize that changing a hybrid variety back into an open-pollinated one only takes a few years, their fear of being controlled by multinational food monopolies diminishes.

It is not true that hybrids don't make seed. They do, though some hybrids are created by having one of the parent lines become self-sterile; when self-sterile hybrids are grown for seed, the first year's set is very light, but in subsequent generations, the seed sets normally. The first few generations from hybrid parents can be highly variable, producing many undesirable plants. But by selecting desirable plants and destroying the rest before they can pollinate others, in a few generations the home breeder can create a reasonably uniform open-pollinated variety similar to (though not as vigorous as) the original hybrid.

Where hybrid seeds can be produced economically, the old open-pollinated sorts rapidly decline in two ways. One, the open-pollinated varieties continue to be grown only for the home gardener who remembers the older variety names, and for the small Third World grower who cannot afford better seed—with all that that implies in terms of lack of breeder's attentions and stock seed maintenance. Two, the commercial trade uses many times more seed than the garden trade; when the open-pollinated sales volume drops significantly, the old varieties are no longer produced every year or two. This means that fresh, vigorous seed is harder to come by.

Where good open-pollinated varieties still exist, it's because hybridization of these species is not economically feasible *at this time.* Thus there are no hybrid lettuces, beans, leeks or peas. However, hybrid cabbage, Brussels sprouts, broccoli, onions, cucumbers, melons, summer squash, spinach and carrots have supplanted the open-pollinated varieties. In a few species such as beets, winter squash, cauliflower, tomatoes and peppers, good quality hybrids and open-pollinated varieties exist side by side. Remarkably superior hybrid corn took over the market 30 years ago, and today's open-pollinated corn varieties yield at best half as well as hybrids.

Future "seeds"

I am sure that the use of hybrids will spread through additional species as plant breeders figure out new tricks. Once I saw a dozen hybrid iceberg lettuce plants growing on Dr. Baggett's trial ground. He must have produced the seed by exacting hand-pollination—an act requiring virtual microsurgery to produce five or six seeds from each lettuce flower. I'm sure if hybrid lettuce seed were to be attempted with today's technology it would have to be grown in Guatemala, where labor costs a dollar a day, and would still sell for 10 cents a seed. But each of Dr. Baggett's identical hybrid lettuces was an attractive head the size of a big cabbage, twice the size of either parent line.

Two new technologies promise to eliminate the use of actual seeds altogether on vegetable crops that can be raised as seedlings and transplanted. The first, modular transplanting, is used a little in the U.S., much more widely in Europe. Transplanting can be accelerated and made much more efficient by using large growing trays containing small individual cells similar to those that six-pack garden-center seedlings come in. Field survival rates of transplanted modularized seedlings are very high, and high-speed transplanting can be done mechanically. Many European vegetable growers no longer even raise their own seedlings, but instead buy modularized transplants from professional seedling raisers. In some cases, the transplant growers contract to set the seedlings out with their own customized transplanting machines at so much per hectare.

The European seed industry has responded to this development by producing special seed lots of amazing vigor and germination ability, high uniformity and especially high price, so the modular trays can be direct-seeded by machine, one seed per cell, with a certainty of at least 95 percent survival from a tray full of seedlings exactly the same size growing at the same rate.

Another recent advance is micropropagation, or tissue culture. In a laboratory, plants are divided into microscopic cuttings containing only a few cells each. Each slice is grown under controlled conditions in special nutrient baths in tiny test tubes. Within a short time, the new seedlings are ready to transplant into modular growing trays. Literally hundreds of thousands of plantlets can be developed from one parent plant. This means it may soon be possible to produce unlimited numbers of transplants from a single mother plant forever, without ever using seed. Imagine the consequences of economical seedling trays of Dr. Baggett's hybrid lettuce.

Plant breeders frequently and easily produce amazing individual plants by experimental hybridization or find a *sport*, or mutant, with highly desirable traits. It's rarely possible, though, to turn that monster into true breeding seed stock that retains the same vigor. With micropropagation and modular transplanting systems, it may soon be possible to cheaply maintain any unique plant in a greenhouse and sell super seedlings indefinitely. Because the technology behind these tricks is not that expensive (and getting cheaper every year), micropropagated varieties promise to become competitive with the vegetable-seed industry, probably to the great detriment of the big international seed-houses.

And there's another new development on the horizon. Imagine taking one of those test-tube seedlings whizzed up from Dr. Baggett's hybrid mother lettuce, treating it with hormones to make it go into dormancy similar to the embryo in a seed and encapsulating it in a little nutrient packet—an artificial "seed" you can plant right in the field. Well, that has been done. Soon I expect it will be done cost-efficiently.

The future of seeds and their likely substitutes, combined with the technology of DNA manipulation, makes for mind-boggling possibilities. Perhaps the future of food plants on Earth is not one of genetic loss and things to fear. Whatever lies ahead is sure to be exciting!

Further reading

The Garden Seed Inventory, Kent Whealy (Decorah, Iowa: Seed Saver Publications, 1986).

A computerized inventory of 240 seed catalogs, listing all open-pollinated vegetable seeds still available.

Vegetable and Herb Seed Growing, Douglas Miller (Available from Abundant Life: 1977).

A 46-page guide for the gardener and small farmer. Features a section on hand-pollination.

Growing Garden Seeds, Robert Johnston, Jr. (Albion, Maine: Johnny's Selected Seeds, 1983).

Virtually everything the gardener needs to know in only 32 pages. Written by the founder of Johnny's Selected Seeds. Available from Johnny's.

Buying and Raising Transplants

*My well-beloved had a
    vineyard in a very fruitful hill,
And he digged it, and
    cleared it of stones,
And planted it with the
    choicest of vine,
And he looked that it
    should bring forth grapes,
And it brought forth
    wild grapes.*
—5 Isaiah, The Holy
Scriptures (Masoretic Text)

In May, vegetable transplants are available almost everywhere. Supermarkets, drugstores, garden centers—even bookstores have displays of bright bedding plants and eager-looking vegetable seedlings. Some of these are nearly as good as the best home-grown transplants; others are weak specimens, almost certain to die when set out in the garden. How do you tell them apart?

A good transplant looks sturdy, thick-stemmed and stocky rather than tall, spindly or soft. The seedlings should have at least three completely developed true leaves, be dark green (unless the variety is naturally purple or some other color) and be well rooted but not pot-bound. It's easy to see whether a transplant is stocky and strong and dark green, but to inspect the root system, you must carefully invert the pot and shake out the soil ball (this can be done discreetly).

Support the soil by placing two fingers on each side of the stem, fingertips facing the soil; gently tap the inverted pot until the seedling, roots and soil slide out and into your waiting hand. If roots have not yet filled the pot, few will be visible and the soil will tend to crumble and fall apart. Carefully pack that seedling back into its pot and put it down for someone else to buy. It is nearly impossible to avoid severely damaging an undeveloped root system when transplanting, so this seedling is almost sure to wilt when set out. If a poorly rooted seedling seems as large as it should be for the pot it is in, it probably was grown too warm and too fast with excessive nitrogen, which overstimulates top growth.

If instead the roots are wrapped around the outside of the soil ball in a thick mass, the plant is pot-bound. In the greenhouse, watered every day and fed with liquid fertilizer, a badly pot-bound seedling can continue to grow and look good for several weeks. But the seedling will probably wilt when set out unless severely pruned back or watered daily for about a week; it will certainly take a week or more for the tangled root system to push out into new soil. With some types of seedlings, especially cauliflower, cabbage and broccoli, becoming pot-bound can be a disaster. Once their root development is checked, these brassicas become irreversibly stunted and head-out or bolt long before they can develop into full-size plants. The result, predetermined from the time the seedlings were six weeks old, is a very small and poor-quality yield.

One way to have more success transplanting pot-bound seedlings is to clip off half the lower leaves. This simple action accomplishes several things: it reduces the amount of water that the roots have to supply while allowing you to bury the root ball as deeply as possible, which eliminates the need for daily watering, and it avoids exposing the seedling to moisture stress. Even though you have removed half the food-manufacturing ability of the seedling, it will resume growth much sooner and ultimately grow bigger than if you had not pruned the leaves.

If the plant is fully and properly rooted, many of its root tips will be visible but only a few will have begun to wrap around the outside. This seedling is just right for transplanting. When it's set out, the soil ball will probably hold together; not having been damaged, the root system will begin expanding into the new soil immediately. This seedling is unlikely to wilt if the root ball is buried fairly deeply, below where the soil dries out rapidly, and will take off and grow fast. This is why transplanting instructions specify burying seedlings up to the first true leaves.

A transplant can go from being insufficiently rooted to being pot-bound in a week to 10 days. Nurseries often move seedlings from the greenhouse to the point of retail sale several days before they are fully rooted and may not discard them until two weeks or more on the shelf. The gardener is best off buying transplants that are not quite fully rooted, holding them in the pots for one week while hardening them off and then transplanting when the root systems are ready.

Hard vs. soft seedlings

Though it is easy to see the root system's readiness for transplanting, the *hardness* of the seedling will have an equal effect on its likelihood to perform well. Hardness is a real thing just like seed vigor, but it's not so easy to gauge.

Plants respond to luxurious conditions with "soft" growth. When soil fertility is optimum, water abundant, days and nights pleasantly warm, winds gentle or non-existent, plants "relax" and grow very rapidly. Under ideal conditions, plants make larger cells with thinner cell walls that contain more water. Their leaves become luxuriant and broad, the stems longer and thinner and more delicate. If, on the other hand, the environment is not fully to the plants' liking, they grow "hard": smaller, tougher leaves, shorter, stockier stems and a stronger root system. Hard growth produces tough material with smaller cells and thicker cell walls, less likely to be damaged by handling, winds and insects. In this respect, plants and people are very similar.

A soft plant is likely to be shocked when exposed to stresses it has not yet experienced. Shocks can so weaken a soft seedling that it falls prey to disease and insect attacks, or, at the very least, stops growing until it can adjust to the more severe conditions. For example, a soft hothouse-grown pepper seedling that has always been held above 60°F at night and is then exposed to a single nighttime low of 50°F will be shocked so much that it may not grow for a week. Exposed repeatedly to temperatures below 50°F, it may not grow properly again all season. However, a hard-grown pepper seedling that has already experienced many nights in the mid- to low 50s might not be severely shocked until the nights fall to about 45°F. Cold rains with large, heavy droplets and the battering of wind can also be severe shocks to a hothouse plant. A light frost can stun even a frost-hardy brassica seedling, if that seedling has never experienced temperatures below 50°F before. Loss of root hairs, which is inevitable when transplanting, is a shock. Take a greenhouse seedling that has known only ideal growing conditions and relentlessly expose it to wind, rain, root damage, strong direct sunlight, low temperatures, soil diseases and predatory insects, and it is easy to see why transplanting is so often fatal.

The difference between hard and soft seedlings was powerfully impressed on me one year when I grew a tomato trial for Territorial Seed Company. At an elevation of 900 feet, surprising late frosts are almost to be expected. So when I set out frost-sensitive seedlings, I'd hold back a few "insurance" plants in four-inch individual pots in my cold frame for another 10 days or so, just in case. That year, a particularly disappointing frost on June 13 wiped out my tomato trial. Unfortunately, some varieties had not grown as well as I had hoped, so even with reserves I was short a few seedlings. Rather than waste the trial-ground space already allocated to tomatoes, I went into town and bought tomato seedlings from the local garden center. The difference in appearance between my cold-frame seedlings and the commercial greenhouse ones was amazing. Where mine looked stocky, thick-stemmed and tough, the garden-center ones were spindly, light-colored and delicate. Mine started growing as soon as they were set out; the commercial ones went into shock. Mine were untroubled by insects; the others were badly chewed by flea beetles and I had to dust them with rotenone twice. Though the garden center seedlings did eventually get growing, my home-grown seedlings ended up much larger, bore more heavily and generally ripened earlier.

When this is such an obvious truth, why do commercial growers not grow harder seedlings? Well, greenhouse space is valuable, so there is a natural inclination on the part of some commercial growers to rush transplants from seed to sellable seedlings as fast as possible. The way to do this is to raise them under warm, fertile conditions so that they go from seed to the sales bench in four to five weeks. More responsible companies transfer seedlings from the hothouse to an unheated greenhouse after two or three weeks, so their growth rate slows and they become harder. This can add a week or two to the total production time. I know of one highly ethical transplant grower who moves his seedlings after two weeks in a cold house to a windy, open-air cold frame consisting of little more than a plastic roof without sides, to further toughen the seedlings up for their last week before putting them out for sale. The less protection offered by the cold house, the harder the transplant is, the slower it grows and the more costly it becomes to produce.

As a home gardener, you can't be certain how hard a commercially raised seedling is at the time of purchase, though you can make an educated guess based on its appearance. If you've raised tough transplants of your own, you have a much better chance of making an accurate guess.

It's safest to assume that garden-store seedlings have not been hardened off, and then to check that they're not pot-bound. Bring them home a week before setting out in the garden and harden them off somewhat yourself. Hardening off consists of *gradually* introducing seedlings to environmental shocks. The first day, put new seedlings outside in bright shade to become accustomed to wind and light that is unfiltered by glass or plastic and put them indoors before sunset. The next day introduce the seedlings to direct morning and/or late-afternoon sun, and bring them in at night. Give them full sun all the third day and at night bring them in again. Then let them spend all night outside, unless the temperature will be shockingly cold—below 45°F or 50°F for tender species, or if frost threatens hardier species. After a few nights outdoors, they'll be tough enough to transfer to the garden, with a much higher likelihood of surviving the shocks that delay growth and retard maturity. If you're a working gardener who can't hover over seedlings, you might transplant each seedling into a three- or four-inch pot before hardening off so they don't have to be watered twice a day.

Growing garden-center transplants can be very disappointing for other reasons as well. Varieties popular with the bedding-plant raiser are often bred especially for the needs of the bedding-plant trade, primarily to create handsome five-week-old seedlings. The transplant raiser cares intensely that stems grow straight, that seedlings *appear* to be husky even if they're soft, that they size out at only four weeks old instead of five or six, that the marigold seedlings already have blooming flowers on them when put out for sale. That's profitable.

Commercial seedling varieties may be better adapted to more populous regions where seed distributors specializing in the bedding-plant trade have a larger market. As long as the seedlings look good, who cares if the broccoli is a variety that reacts to cool nights (common west of the Cascades but rare back east) by bursting apart in yellow flowers before sizing up? Well, maybe it'll be a warm spring, or maybe most of the customers will plant later in the season when the variety does better. Who cares if all the tasteless cabbages split two days after getting hard? Who cares if the marigolds quit blooming in midsummer? The gardener is not a critical trade.

Raising your own

The way to maximize garden success is to become very choosy about the varieties you grow, and, when transplants must be used, to raise your own. This may sound glib to working families that don't think they have the luxury of keeping one potential wage-earner at home or to those less dedicated to eating from their gardens than I am. I know that when I'm raising seedlings, I sometimes feel a little like a slave to my cold frame. During May and early June, it's often hard to allow even for daytime trips that take me away from the house for more than a few hours, especially around midday when the sun is strong and the seedlings need watching. To reduce the need to hover over a cold frame, try direct-seeding more of the species you may have been taught could only be started as transplants. Chapters 5 and 8 explain how to successfully direct-seed broccoli, cabbage, Brussels sprouts, cauliflower, celery, onions, cucumbers, leeks, lettuce, parsley, squash and cucumber—species that gardeners commonly start from purchased transplants.

Raising transplants *is* more difficult than growing a garden from seed. In the garden, many growth factors are left to nature, but while raising seedlings, the gardener must take responsibility for light and temperature as well as moisture, soil quality and fertility. Success will only come to the degree that each of these factors is understood and controlled.

Temperature

In Chapter 5, I discussed at length how temperature-sensitive the sprouting process is. As a general rule, most vegetable seeds will sprout above 60°F but sprout best when constantly held between 75°F and 82°F. Some tropical varieties such as melons, peppers and eggplants will not sprout at all below 70°F. On the other hand, celery and celeriac won't sprout well at all above 70°F; they do best in the low to mid-60s and will tolerate soil in the mid-50s.

The growth of seedlings is also greatly affected by temperature. Tropical vegetables, which only grow outside during the warmest parts of the maritime Northwest summer, thrive at daytime temperatures ranging from 75°F to 85°F, with night lows around 60°F. For melons, cucumbers, peppers and eggplants, anything below 65°F in the daytime will produce little or no growth, while temperatures below 50°F will shock the seedlings and prevent further growth for a while. "Hard" tropical seedlings are grown at about 72°F daytime; higher temperatures make lush but soft growth. At daytime temperatures below 65°F, they grow too slowly. Cool-weather seedlings—the coles, celery, parsley and lettuce—become very spindly and weak when grown at temperatures peppers would find ideal. These types do best with daytime temperatures of 60°F to 70°F and nighttime lows above 40°F. Ideal conditions for producing hard cool-weather species would be 65°F daytime, and 45°F to 55°F at night. Tomatoes do best at 70°F days, 55°F to 60°F nights, but most varieties can learn to tolerate lows down to 45°F without shock and make adequate growth if days are in the mid-60s. Tomatoes become very soft and spindly at temperatures suitable for eggplant.

Ideal growing temperatures

	Tropical Vegetables	Tomatoes	Cool-Weather Vegetables	Best All-Type Compromise Temperature Range
Day	75 to 80	65 to 70	60 to 70	68 to 70
Night	60 to 65	50 to 60	45 to 56	52 to 60

If you were only producing a single type of seedling, it would be feasible to set up and maintain one range of ideal temperatures. But a compromise is needed if you wish to grow many species at once. Probably the best single temperature range to permit most types of vegetables to thrive and grow fairly close to their best is 68°F to 70°F daytime, 52°F to 60°F at night. These temperatures are easiest to achieve in a house, often on a porch or area away from the woodstove or other heat source.

Soils for transplants

Transplants often have delicate root systems, particularly in the seedling stage. To promote rapid growth and good overall development, soil should stay light and loose while the seedlings are in the pots or trays, usually a period of five to eight weeks. If good root system development is prevented by compacted soil, the weakened seedlings may not transplant successfully. Soil in small containers also has a disturbing tendency to dry out rapidly, and if seedlings wilt, even once, they may not recover properly. Commercial growers monitor their seedlings every minute the sun is shining. Home growers are well advised to make sure their soil mixes are highly moisture-retentive and to use slightly larger containers than the commercial grower does, to maintain a bigger moisture reserve for the seedlings.

Commercial greenhouses raise seedlings in artificial soil mixes, which are usually sterilized. The basic ingredients are not soil at all, but moss, vermiculite, perlite, sand and compost. Greenhouses sometimes purchase pre-mixed and pre-fertilized potting soil; sometimes the nursery makes its own. It's important to understand that the commercial mixes sold in small sacks in garden centers, even if "fertilized," contain only enough nutrients to grow plants for a few weeks at most. Here are two sample commercial formulations:

Cornell "Peat-Lite" mix

11 bushels sphagnum moss
11 bushels horticultural-grade vermiculite or perlite
5 pounds dolomite lime
1 pound superphosphate
12 pounds 5–10–5 chemical fertilizer

University of California mix

75 percent coarse sand
25 percent sphagnum moss
Add to each cubic yard of mix:
    7½ pounds dolomite lime
    2½ pounds agricultural lime
    3 pounds 10–20–10 chemical fertilizer

Sphagnum moss is the dried remains of bog plants. It is usually sterile and has the capacity to absorb 10 to 20 times its own weight in water. Moss provides almost no nutrients itself and has a pH of about 3.5. It also contains some natural fungicidal substances that tend to inhibit damping-off diseases. Sphagnum moss usually comes finely ground and completely dehydrated, though it is often clumpy when it is broken out of compressed bales and can be improved by sifting through a quarter-inch mesh screen. Slow to take up water when completely dry, it should be thoroughly moistened before use.

Vermiculite is a naturally occurring rock, derived from compressed clay deposits, that expands greatly when heated until it pops like popcorn. When expanded, it weighs only six to 10 pounds per cubic foot (a cubic foot of solid rock might weigh 150 pounds), has a pH of about 7.0 and is able to absorb three to five times its own weight in water. Like clay, vermiculite has a strong ability to attract and hold positively charged nutrient ions such as potassium and nitrogen (cations). But unlike clay, vermiculite remains loose after becoming wet and then drying down again, unless it's compressed when wet. Vermiculite's cation-exchange capacity is useful when raising transplants because it tends to reduce the amount of fertilizer lost when water passes through the pots. Vermiculite is graded into four horticultural sizes: No. 1 is a bit coarse for bedding plants; No. 2 is the regular horticultural grade; the very fine No. 3 and No. 4 are used in commercial greenhouses as germinating media for extremely small seeds such as petunia or certain herbs. Vermiculite is usually sterile.

Perlite is a gray-white, pumice-like material mined from lava flows. The rock is crushed and heated so it pops like vermiculite, expanding the particles to small spongy bits that are very light, weighing five to eight pounds per cubic foot. Perlite will hold three to four times its own weight in water. It has no ability to hold cations, has a pH of about 7.0 and is usually used to lighten and aerate soil mixes.

Compost is a highly variable material available from many garden centers by the sack, from specialized recyclers by the yard and "unit," and often made at home by gardeners. It consists of well-rotted organic matter, often laced with large quantities of partially digested straw, sawdust or bark, and may range in pH from 4.0 to 7.0. Compost has the ability to hold many times its weight in water and loosens soil. Sometimes compost is nutrient-rich, sometimes not; using compost in soil mixes does not ensure adequate fertilization. Composts are not usually sterile, though they can be (odoriferously) baked into sterility.

Gardeners can obtain a better product and save money by mixing their own. Here is a formula I've used for many years. It is not sterilized.

Watering transplants

Seedlings grown in small containers need frequent attention. Bedding-

Steve Solomon's Seedling Mix

2 parts by volume sieved garden soil
1 part by volume sieved sphagnum moss
Add to each cubic foot (5 gallons) of mix
    1 cup agricultural lime or dolomite lime
    1 cup cottonseed meal
    1 pint soft rock phosphate or 1 cup steamed bone meal
    1 cup kelp meal

plant trays and pots, being shallow, usually have to be watered daily; in cold frames exposed to full sun, they may need watering late morning and midafternoon. This makes it essential to grow seedlings in soil that will repeatedly dry out and reabsorb water without shrinking, compacting or crusting over, because once soil is compacted or strongly crusted, it may not easily absorb more water. If the soil shrinks away from the sides of the pot, water may run down the sides and out the bottom without really wetting the soil. If the surface crusts over, water uptake may slow so much that the soil looks saturated when it actually is very dry. This is why bedding plant mixes use sphagnum moss, perlite and vermiculite. All these materials can take up and release water without compacting. However, a strange anomaly occurs with sphagnum moss. When allowed to dry out fully, moss is very difficult to remoisten and may actually inhibit water uptake. For that reason, I find that about one-third moss is the maximum safe level.

Tiny seedlings growing in light, loose soil can be disturbed easily; their root systems may be exposed or damaged if not watered gently. No one system or device is ideal for this purpose. For the home gardener, the gentlest and easiest system to use is a siphon. Made from a gallon jar, plastic milk container or bucket and a three-eighths-inch internal diameter plastic or rubber tube, the siphon gently pours water into the plant pot or tray. Water pressure may be adjusted easily by changing the height of the container; one to two feet of drop provides plenty of pressure. If the jar is allowed to stand at room temperature for a few hours before irrigating, the water can reach room temperature. This avoids any risk of shocking tropical seedlings with cold water. Because thin tubing is very flexible and light, the water supply can be conveniently located several feet away from the seedlings if necessary. Outdoors, I water my cold frame with a five-gallon bucket for a water supply, tie one end of the tubing to an old broom handle and, to provide pressure, rest the water bucket atop an inverted bucket behind the frame. The broom handle allows me to conveniently move the hose around in my cold frame.

Seedling containers

Rapidly growing seedlings require geometrically increasing amounts of root room. When cramped, they increase the density of their root systems and become pot-bound. The most convenient container is one large enough to accommodate a seedling from sprouting to transplanting size without repotting. This method is not used commercially because growing for profit places priority on the most efficient possible use of greenhouse space. Commercial seedlings are started thousands at a time in one big tray, "pricked out" when they have one true leaf and transplanted into the tray they will be sold from. The exacting practice of pricking-out is actually far more space-efficient than starting seedlings in individual pots or plant cells because it leaves the greenhouse benches free for bigger plants while the seeds sprout and develop their first true leaf. One additional efficiency is that by the time seedlings are pricked out, most losses from damping-off and damaged seedlings have already occurred. For the gardener it is much more convenient to sow several seeds per pot or cell and then gradually thin out the extra seedlings.

I can't glibly recommend any particular pot or cell size. Many factors can influence the growth rate and ratio of top to root, including light levels, temperatures, species, varieties and soil mixes. What is most important is to transplant before the seedling becomes pot-bound. If conditions outdoors are not welcoming at that point, the seedling may be repotted into a larger container. Generally, about four cubic inches of soil will provide minimal room for most species from sowing to transplanting. Certain tropical plants such as peppers, eggplant, tomatoes, melons and cucumbers and very large, fast-growing species such as squash and beans do better in slightly larger individual pots or cells.

Home transplant raisers are often very innovative about adapting ordinary household items into bedding-plant pots. Plastic or foam cups, egg cartons, milk carton bottoms and disposable aluminum cake tins have all been used. But none of these containers comes with drainage holes, and if water is allowed to stand in the pot, seedlings will become sickly or die, so several quarter-inch holes should be punched in the bottom to allow excess water to run out. When liquid fertilizers are used to promote seedling growth, it is helpful to wash out the soil periodically by running enough water through the pot to prevent fertilizer build-up.

I'm a garden nut who prefers raising the earliest possible garden to spending my time earning more money, so in spring I raise a lot of seedlings. I use plastic multicell trays, like the commercial seedling growers. Every three or four years, I buy a box of 100 insert sheets for about $40. These sheets come in all sorts of sizes and layouts. I personally prefer a husky, oversized seedling, so I use sheets containing only 32 cells, each cell 2⅜ inches square by 2¼ inches deep. Most garden centers sell much smaller seedlings, grown on a sheet with 72 cells. Each fragile insert sheet is supported in a 10- by 20-inch reusable tray. Tight-fitting, clear plastic covers turn these trays into moisture-tight germination chambers that won't need watering until the seeds germinate. (Before I got so professional, I used to put the trays into big plastic bags to seal in the moisture, and before that, I laid very thin sheets of clear plastic film over the trays, and before that, I used to water the trays frequently and experienced erratic germination.) With 2⅜-inch-square cells, I can raise brassicas, tomatoes and peppers to a very husky, four-true-leaf size without them becoming pot-bound, and even squash seedlings will hold for nearly a week without overcrowding. I also keep an assortment of sturdy pots on hand, ranging in size from two inches to one gallon.

Light and growth

East of the Cascades, the sun shines brightly more days than it is cloudy, so home gardeners often grow transplants in a sunny, south-facing window. However, in the maritime Northwest, windowsill-grown plants do not receive enough light to make proper growth during the months of February, March and April (some years, even May is frequently overcast), and consequently they become spindly and weak. This inescapable fact of light means that the maritime Northwest gardener must invest a bit more money and effort to raise healthy, strong transplants.

There are two solutions to our low light levels: indoor grow lights, and protected outdoor spaces such as cold frames, hot frames and greenhouses. By far the most manageable garden solution is the fluorescent indoor grow light. However, since light is every bit as essential a growth factor as nutrients or water, growing healthy plants under artificial light requires some careful consideration.

Here are some examples of how light quality and intensity have profound immediate effects on plant growth. Under low light, many kinds of fruiting plants make only vegetative growth; if fruit does set, it will not develop or ripen. Under very low light, many plants become spindly and long-stemmed. The name for this phenomenon is *etiolation*. Etiolation can be demonstrated easily by putting a potted vining plant in a dark closet for a few weeks. In extremes like this, the vinelike stems become 10 or more times as long as usual, and the leaves barely develop. In greenhouse experiments with several different artificial sources of intense light, such as halide, sodium and mercury lamps, great distortions in plant growth can be induced by using lamp combinations that differ in spectral composition from natural sunlight. For example, certain plants flower best under reddish light, a spectral quality that occurs naturally in late summer and early autumn; under bluish lights, their flowers are looser, smaller and less fragrant.

No one source of artificial light matches the sun. For plants to perform optimally and grow to maturity, a mixture of different light sources is required. This sophistication is not practical in the home, especially since some lights cost upward of $200 per lamp and are capable of illuminating more than 50 square feet at an intensity nearly equal to noon at the equator. Fortunately, one common and fairly inexpensive light source, the "cool white" fluorescent, promotes very good vegetative growth in seedlings.

Because fluorescent lights are of low intensity, they're impractical for growing large plants; however, they are sufficiently bright to sustain vegetable seedlings for a few weeks. They're commonly available in four- or eight-foot lengths, and the four-foot tube is the usual at-home choice. Two to six parallel four-foot cool-white tubes suspended over the growing area can produce stocky seedlings indoors at low cost. The highest possible light intensity is required for best growth, so the tubes should be placed as close together as possible and very close to the leaves to prevent etiolation. But the distance between the lights and the plant trays must be increased as the seedlings grow, so the lamps must be suspended in such a way that they can be raised and lowered on pulleys, or the shelf holding the seedlings must be movable, or individual containers must be gradual-

Using grow lights

Number of Tubes	Maximum Height above Top of Seedlings	Width of Strongly Illuminated Area	Period of Growth with Sufficient Light
2	2 inches	6 inches	4 weeks
4	3 inches	9 inches	6 weeks
6	4 inches	12 inches	8 weeks

ly lowered as the seedlings grow. Fluorescents produce a lot of heat; setting up the growing area on a porch or in a cool room will probably create the right temperature ranges.

To grow best, almost all kinds of plants need a period of darkness. In most cases, this period need not be longer than four hours per day. If maximum growth rate is desired, lights can be run for 20 hours a day. I suggest at least a 14-hour illumination. However, some kinds of vegetables are photoperiodic, which means they respond to changes in the length of dark versus light by switching from vegetative growth to flowering or bulbing. Included in this group are onions, mustards and spinach. Plants seem to alter their growth unfavorably when the light/dark periods are irregular, so I highly recommend buying an inexpensive 24-hour timer.

Fertilizers

No matter how carefully I make up potting soil, I have had to resort to liquid fertilizer. Really potent soil mixes made with lots of organic fertilizers tend to overfeed seedlings or reduce seed germination. On the other hand, when the pots are watered, nutrients leach out, greatly slowing growth. After many years of trying different approaches, I decided to consider potting soil primarily as a medium to enhance root development and hold moisture. Though the soil provides background nutrition, I regulate the growth of my seedlings with feedings of liquid fertilizer.

Unfortunately, even this approach is not foolproof. Liquid organic fertilizers are unbalanced; fish emulsion is usually 7–2–2 or thereabouts, while seaweed or kelp concentrates are 0.5–1–1, more or less. The best organic combination would be four or five parts liquid seaweed and one part liquid fish, diluted to half the recommended strength. Surprisingly, I've gotten far better results using Rapid-Gro, diluted to one-half or even one-quarter the recommended strength. This specific use is the only time I find chemical fertilizer to be superior.

I recommend using below-strength fertilizer because the home grower can incorporate enough slow-release organic fertilizer in the soil mix to produce a steady growth rate without risking overfertilization. Cautiously supplemented with liquid feedings, the result is controlled growth without overstimulation. Too much fertilizer, particularly too much nitrogen fertilizer, tends to result in lush, soft growth and spindly stems, especially when combined with higher growing temperatures. If one feeding of below-strength fertilizer does not result in rapid growth, a second feeding a few days later can be tried without danger of burning the plant or triggering wild growth. Plants should be fed every 10 days to two weeks, or when growth slows. Fertilizer can be supplied with every watering if it's diluted to about one-eighth normal strength. I do this when watering my cold frame, putting a scant tablespoonful of Rapid-Gro in every five-gallon bucket of water. I think the practice is synergistic, in that the more the sun shines, the faster the seedlings grow, and the more they need water and fertilizer.

Cold-frame climate

Cold frames for growing seedlings are often put together of recycled planks and used window sashes or plastic, fiberglass or polyethylene sheeting. A well-built frame with thick walls and well-fitted windows, caulked and sealed, can hold nighttime temperatures 12 to 15 degrees warmer than outside air. Even a hastily constructed, drafty frame is capable of holding nighttime temperatures five to 10 degrees warmer than outside, especially if a blanket is thrown over the frame when frosts threaten. The gardener who intends to raise only a minimum number of seedlings will need a cold frame no larger than three feet wide by five or six feet long, 18 inches tall at the back and six inches high at the front, built very much like the one described in Chapter 3.

Having both a cold frame and grow lights is highly advantageous. By mid-March, light levels in the frame will probably be higher than those inside under the fluorescents. Daytime temperatures, regulated by opening or closing the sashes, can be kept cooler than indoors (advantageous for cool-season transplants), and nighttime lows will not reach the freezing point. This makes the cold frame a fine place to transfer one- to two-week-old early brassica seedlings; after a few weeks of slow, hard growth in the frame, they'll be stocky and strong. By mid-April the frame will grow celery and tomato seedlings quite nicely. If four- or five-week-old tomato seedlings started under fluorescent lights are transplanted into individual three- or four-inch pots and put out in the frame at that time, they'll be hard and quite large by the time it's warm enough to put them in the garden. About the time no more frosts are expected and the frame is emptied of tomato seedlings, it becomes a suitable environment for hardening peppers, eggplants, melons and cucumbers, which should be held in the frame until really warm, summery weather settles in.

A hot frame is simply a cold frame with heat below. In the old days, these were called hot beds, made by setting cold frames over pits filled with fresh strong manure. Now most people use thermostatically controlled electric cables. Hot frames are interesting luxury items that permit a gardener to grow tropical plants such as peppers outside after March 1, to germinate cold-sensitive seeds, and to eliminate the need for fluorescent lights inside, removing gardening clutter from the house. Hot frames are not necessary for successful gardening; however, any serious transplant raiser will want a cold frame eventually.

Transplanting calendar

Sow under lights	Species	Move to cold frame	Transplant in garden
Feb 1	Autumn leeks	April 1	May 1–31
Feb. 1	Bulb onions	March 5–15	April 1–15
Feb. 15	Early cabbage, broccoli	March 5	April 1
Feb. 15	Celery, celeriac	April 15	May 15
March 1	Cauliflower	March 20	April 10
March 1	Earliest looseleaf lettuce	March 20	April 10
March 15	Tomatoes	April 15	May 1–15
April 1	Peppers, eggplant	May 5	June 1–15
April 15	Summer squash	April 25	May 1
May 20	Cucumbers, melons	June 1	June 5–10

Note: Dates in this table are for Willamette Valley gardeners. South of Drain, Oregon, these dates may be a week or two too late. North of Longview, Washington, at higher elevations in western Oregon and along the coast, these dates may be a week or two too early.

Enhancing germination

In commercial greenhouse operations, fungicide-treated seeds are sown in vermiculite. Germination trays are sealed with clear airtight lids, placed on electrically heated benches and kept at optimum temperatures until the seeds sprout. Sterile sprouting media and fungicide-treated seeds prevent damping-off diseases from killing seedlings. This convenient system is commercially profitable and efficient.

If garden soil and untreated seed are used instead, germination will drop from over 90 percent to somewhere around 50 percent at best. Unprotected by fungicide, even more seedlings will die from damping-off diseases during their first week. Perhaps only two-thirds of those that do sprout will survive this dangerous period. If the variety is open-pollinated, many of these surviving seedlings will not be particularly vigorous or desirable. The home gardener, then, should plant three to five seeds for every seedling ultimately desired, and cull out the weaker ones. With this approach, damping-off diseases are an easy way to allow nature to do some thinning of more disease-susceptible specimens.

To sow seed, punch a small hole to the proper depth with the blunt end of a pencil, and place a pinch of seeds in the hole (fewer seeds if cucurbits or beans are being started). Cover the container and wait for them to sprout. After germination, thin to about three plants per spot within the first week, and continue to thin as the tray becomes crowded. Don't let plants shade each other or force each other's stems very far off vertical as they compete for light. Thinning is best done with a sharp small scissors, snipping the stem near the soil line. By the time the seedlings have fully developed one true leaf and started the second one, the tray should be completely thinned to one plant per spot.

For most species, germinating trays are best set on a shelf on top of the fluorescent light bank, where the heat generated by the lamps and ballasts creates ideal germination conditions. The mantle over a fireplace insert or a shelf near the woodstove is also a good spot. Maintain the proper moisture level in germinating trays by covering each with a very thin sheet of clear plastic or seal it in a large, clear plastic bag until the seedlings emerge. When sprouting seeds in fiber pots or trays, which tend to lose moisture through their sides, seal the pots within clear poly bags until emergence.

How to grow transplants

Planting dates in this section are for the Willamette Valley. Gardeners to the south might start seedlings a little earlier; gardeners to the north of Longview might start seedlings a little later. Further tips and information about each species are given in Chapter 8, How to Grow It.

Beans

About three weeks before the last frost date, sow 1½ inches deep, two seeds per individual two-inch pot. Sprout at 75–85°F. Thin promptly to one plant per pot. Grow under lights about one week, and then move to cold frame until one pair of true leaves is fully developed. Transplant out at the same time bean seeds would be sown outdoors. An early start like this is almost essential to obtain any yield of lima beans. Snap beans will mature abundantly when direct-seeded, but may start producing beans two weeks sooner if transplanted.

Beets

Grow for transplanting only to have the earliest possible harvest. By mid-April, beets are much easier to direct-seed outdoors. Individual beet seeds usually produce clusters of seedlings. In March, sow two seeds per individual two-inch pot or cell, ½ inch deep. Sprout at 75–85°F. Grow three to four weeks at 60–70°F under lights, and then transfer to a cold frame if available. Do not thin. Hold in cold frame until seedlings have well-developed true leaves two to four inches tall. *Do not allow seedlings to become pot-bound.* Transplant clusters of seedlings 8 to 12 inches apart in rows 18 to 24 inches apart; each cluster will produce four to six nice roots at maturity. Use a slow-bolting variety like Early Wonder.

Broccoli

By April, broccoli is *much* easier to direct-seed, so start only early broccoli indoors. Earliest broccoli is always a big gamble: seedlings whose growth is checked by cold conditions at transplanting may not head out well, and the earliest seedlings start sizing up just when root maggots peak. During February or March, sow seeds ½ inch deep in clumps of three to five seeds per individual cell or two-inch pot. Broccoli sprouts fastest at 70–85°F. Grow two to three weeks under lights at 60–70°F daytime, above 40°F at night. Indoor growing temperatures over 70°F may cause spindly growth. Thin gradually so seedlings don't compete for light, ending up with one plant per pot by the time the first true leaf is totally developed. Transfer at the two-leaf stage to a cold frame if available. When seedlings have three true leaves (five to six weeks after sowing), they should be well rooted and ready to set out. In March, consider using hot caps or transplanting into a cloche.

Brussels sprouts

If transplants are desired, grow like broccoli; however, Brussels sprouts are much better if sown late and grown for fall harvest. I strongly recommend direct-seeding about June 1. See Chapter 8.

Cabbage

For earliest heads, grow exactly like broccoli. Start seeds during February or March. By April, cabbage can be direct-seeded outdoors. In this season, I recommend only Golden Acre or similar extra-early hybrids.

Cauliflower

Cauliflower is a little more sensitive to chilly conditions than cabbage or broccoli. Grow like broccoli, but do not start seeds before February 20. By April 1, cauliflower is better direct-seeded. For earliest sowings, I recommend Snow Crown Hybrid or "Alpha" types from Holland.

Celery/celeriac

Between February 15 and March 15, sow clumps of five to 10 seeds, ¼ inch deep in individual two-inch pots or cells. Seeds will sprout best at 55–70°F, but slowly, sometimes taking over two weeks. Thin gradually without permitting competition. Grow at 65–75°F day, 50–60°F night. Slow-growing celery requires high moisture and fertility levels and eight to 12 weeks to attain transplanting size. Move to cold frame for the last two or four weeks, but not before nighttime temperatures in the frame are generally above 50°F. Though celery is somewhat frost-hardy, too many hours' exposure to temperatures below 50°F will make seedlings bolt prematurely. Celery may also be direct-seeded in April.

Sweet corn

Handle the fast-growing seedlings like beans, if earliest possible production is desired. Sow four to six seeds per two-inch pot. Thin to three plants per pot. Transplant clumps of seedlings every 30 inches in rows 30 inches apart.

Cucumbers

Because the species is difficult to transplant, especially when large seedlings are grown, cucumbers should be started indoors roughly when the tomato seedlings are set out. Transplanting gives the gardener only a slight advantage; cucumbers direct-seeded about two weeks after the tomato seedlings are set out ripen fruit just a few days later than transplants started several weeks earlier. Raising cucumber transplants may have greater advantages farther north than I am used to gardening.

Sprouting cucumber seed (and other members of the cucurbit family such as squash and melons) requires warm, slightly damp conditions to avoid seedling diseases. Test potting soil carefully. It should barely form a ball when squeezed hard and should break up easily. Cucurbit seed will absorb water and germinate in surprisingly dry soil. *If the soil's too damp, allow it to dry out before using.* About the time tomato seedlings are transplanted outside, sow clumps of three to five seeds, one inch deep in individual two- to three-inch pots. To keep moisture even, place pots in sealed, lightweight poly bags such as those found in supermarket produce departments. Hold pots over 70°F until germination; the best temperature is about 80°F. When seedlings emerge, remove the bags. Grow under lights for about one week at 70–80°F daytime, over 55°F nighttime. Thin to the best two plants per pot by the time they have developed one true leaf. Transfer to a cold frame for a final week of *slight* hardening off; it is impossible to make cucumbers (or melons) very hard. *Transplant very carefully to avoid root damage.*

Eggplant

Handle like peppers (see below), but note that eggplant seedlings are even more sensitive to temperatures below 50°F. See Chapter 8 for more tips about this difficult species.

Kale

Like broccoli, but so vigorous that direct-seeding is easy. Kale is also so much better for fall than summer harvest that raising transplants to obtain earlier production seems pointless to me. And why fight root maggots for kale? I strongly recommend direct-seeding kale in early summer.

Kohlrabi

Like broccoli. There may be some reason to raise transplants if earliest spring production is desired, but I always direct-seed about April 1 and have all I want. For fall harvest, direct-seed about August 1.

Leeks

If late-summer harvest is desired, raise transplants like onion seedlings and use "fall" leek varieties. If fall/winter harvest is desired, direct-seed leeks during May and use "winter" varieties. See onions, below.

Lettuce

Raise transplants only for earliest harvest and grow like broccoli; otherwise, direct-seed.

Melons

Grow like cucumbers, but note that melons are even more sensitive to low temperatures and damp conditions in the seedling stage. See Chapter 8. In the Willamette, it may be necessary to raise transplants to ensure that melons ripen in time. South of Drain, direct-seeding may be sufficient. Seedlings need to be set out in a black plastic mulch or under cloches.

Onions

For the largest bulbs and earliest scallions, raise transplants. In February or early March, sow seeds ½ inch deep, eight to 12 seeds per inch in rows 2½ to three inches apart on a two-inch-deep flat; if using cellular trays, sow eight seeds per two-inch cell. Sprout seed between 60°F and 75°F. Grow at 50–70°F day; 40–50°F night. Do not thin. With sharp scissors, cut the tops back to about three inches every few weeks to promote thicker stems and better-developed root systems. Indoors, grow onions with at least a 14-hour daylength to prevent premature bulbing. Harden off in a cold frame, if available, starting mid-April. (Remember, daylength outdoors on March 21 is 12 hours exactly, rapidly increasing to about 16 or 17 hours on June 21.) Prune the tops again just before transplanting to reduce stress on the root systems. Transplant when stems are about 3/16 inch in diameter or by May 1 at the latest. Onions transplant very easily bare-rooted, so the individual seedlings may be separated by shaking them apart.

Parsley

Slow to germinate, parsley is often transplanted, though it is very easily direct-seeded if sown before things begin to warm up and dry out in the garden. Otherwise, grow like broccoli, but note that germination can take 14 to 17 days at 70°F.

Peppers

Peppers, being tropical plants, don't readily adapt to climatic conditions north of the Yoncalla Valley. If grown soft, they are often irreversibly shocked by temperatures below 55°F after being transplanted; if grown as hard as a tender pepper can be grown—which is not very hard, if stunting them permanently is to be avoided—peppers can learn to tolerate exposure to an overnight temperature slightly below 50°F without shock. Many gardeners make the mistake of setting peppers out at the same time as tomatoes—right after there is no frost danger. But this will almost certainly expose them to overnight temperatures of 45°F or even lower. Because their season is short, and because any surprisingly cool night during June can shock peppers sufficiently to stop their growth for a time, it is far better to wait two or three weeks more and set out the largest pepper seedlings possible to ensure a substantial yield.

Start slow-growing pepper seedlings about six to eight weeks before the last expected frost. In two- to three-inch individual pots or two-inch cells, sow a small pinch of four to six seeds, ½ inch deep. Sprout this heat-demanding seed over 70°F (best at 75–85°F). Grow at 65–80°F day; above 50°F night. Thin gradually to one plant per pot. When tomatoes are planted outside, pepper seedlings may be transferred to a cold frame and repotted in slightly larger containers if they are becoming pot-bound.

Grow in the frame for another two or three weeks, or until summer is really on. If given ample root room, peppers will make much more growth in a tight frame that stays above 50°F when nights drop into the 40s than they would if unprotected or even in a cloche.

Squash

Like cucumbers, and equally hard to transplant. Since squash seedlings are so large and make such rapid growth, very large pots are needed if seedlings are to be held more than a week after sprouting. I suggest germinating squash seeds at 75–85°F about 10 days to two weeks before the last anticipated frost, three seeds per individual two-inch pot or cell, thus avoiding the dangers of chilly, damp spring soil. Once they are up, thin to two plants per pot and move immediately to the cold frame if available. Grow in pots only four to seven days, until the seedlings are sufficiently rooted to hold the soil ball together, and then transplant. Squash is much more tolerant of cool conditions than its relatives, melons and cucumbers, and makes a good candidate for direct-seeding in a cloche. If big cloches are available, seedlings may be started indoors about five weeks before the last expected frost date and moved into a cloche about three weeks before the last expected frost date. Most years the cloche will provide enough frost protection to get the seedlings through unscathed while enhancing early seedling growth, so harvesting will start three or four weeks earlier than if squash were direct-seeded. To our family, an extra month of summer squash is worth quite a bit of trouble.

Tomatoes

For the earliest possible harvest, grow the largest possible seedlings. I start home garden tomatoes about March 1, move them to a cold frame by April 1, and transplant a few weeks later under a large tunnel cloche. Some years I've held the tomatoes in gallon pots in the cold frame until late May, setting out 18-inch-tall seedlings already bearing fruit. Either way, I start eating ripe tomatoes from my earliest varieties by the end of June. Tomato seedlings may be started as late as April 15. Sow four to six seeds in each two-inch pot or cell, ½ inch deep. Sprout at 70–85°F. Grow under lights at 65–75°F day; 50–60°F night. Thin gradually to one plant per pot. Move to cold frame, if available, after three or four weeks indoors. Try to keep nighttime lows in frame above 40°F.

Further reading

Teufel Nursery, Inc. Catalog. Oregon: 12345 N.W. Barnes Rd., Portland, OR 97229; (503) 646-1111. Washington: 666 134th St. S.W., Everett, WA 98204; (206) 743-4444.

Teufel is a well-regarded supplier to the horticultural trade. The catalog is full of items not available in garden centers, such as a complete line of bedding-plant trays and containers, fertilizers for the greenhouse, tools, agricultural chemicals, sprayers and greenhouse equipment. Note that with many items the company deals only in case-lots (dozens and hundreds)— amounts that may be too large for most gardeners (though not if you combine an order with friends or a club); the catalog indicates the minimum orders for these items. Teufel has no minimum charge and will ship promptly via United Parcel Service (since UPS also serves British Columbia, Canadians may order without difficulty).

J.M. McConkey & Co. Catalog. P.O. Box 309, Sumner, WA 98390 (800) 863-8111, (800) 826-4023 [Washington only], (206) 863-8111.

Teufel's competition, and every bit as good, with an even wider line of greenhouse supplies and professional greenhouses. McConkey is also the regional distributor of Agrinet, perhaps the most durable floating row cover, used for cloches and insect protection (see Chapter 7), and offers 6-foot-wide, 300-foot-long trial rolls for $50. Canadians may order without difficulty; for Agrinet, they will be referred to a Canadian distributor.

How to Grow More Vegetables Than You Ever Thought Possible on Less Land Than You Can Imagine, John Jeavons (Berkeley: Ten Speed Press, 1982).

For the postage-stamp gardener, a look at transplant raising as a way to get six weeks' more usage out of garden beds in much the same way greenhouse bedding-plant raisers sow flats and transplant week-old seedlings to get two extra weeks out of greenhouse benches with each crop cycle.

Diseases and Pests

*If I keep a green bough
  in my heart,
the singing bird will come.*
—Chinese proverb

*Stupidity is the
unknownness of
consideration.*
—L. Ron Hubbard

Oh, if only more gardeners truly understood Sir Albert Howard's maxim about the cause of plant disease and insect damage. Howard believed that before a plant has noticeable trouble, it is *already* an unhealthy plant in some respect. Conversely, a vigorous, healthy plant will either escape attack or outgrow insect damage and will not succumb to disease. I've witnessed this time and time again. In a bed of several dozen lusty Brussels sprouts, only one particular plant will be seriously damaged by aphids, while the other plants remain untouched; or some disease will pick off a single tomato plant, while others of the same variety surrounding and even touching the diseased one will not be affected.

I remember another good example of how this works. It happened when I first started gardening at Lorane on that awful clay hillside. I arrived on the property late in May, rushed to spread a little manure, fertilizer and lime, tilled it in, planted it all as best I could in a few days and put up my first deer fence. Not yet understanding all the benefits of direct-seeding, I bought cabbage seedlings. When the garden was all planted, there remained three little cabbages. Rather than waste them, I dug up a bit of space by hand on the untilled fringe of the garden and planted them there, blending in only a little fertilizer but no manure or lime. As the season went on, the difference between the cabbages in the garden and those on the fringe was astonishing. The garden cabbages grew big and healthy without problems. The ones on the fringe grew slowly, and were attacked first by flea beetles and then by cabbage worms, both of which I sprayed; I gave them extra fertilizer, but the roots were attacked by maggots and one wilted. When it was all over, the cabbages in the garden were eight to 10 pounds each and very fine-tasting; the two survivors on the fringe were one to two pounds at best, tough and bitter.

However, sometimes faith in Howard's maxim isn't enough. Unfavorable weather conditions can weaken plants and make them susceptible to disease despite the best soil and nutrition. When this happens, the organic gardener is going to lose a crop, while the grower who is willing to spray chemical fungicides may have a chance to fight the disease. And insect populations become highly unbalanced—usually, though not always, because of human interference with nature—and sometimes reach plague levels that no plant, no matter how healthy, can simply outgrow. An example of unnatural pest levels is found in Washington's Skagit Valley, where too many acres are devoted to insecticide-protected cole family crops. The poisons kill not only the cabbage fly and its maggots, but its predators as well. Consequently, the cabbage fly has become so numerous that effective controls must be used or cole crops cannot be grown in the Skagit district.

Another serious pest in the maritime Northwest garden can be the carrot rust fly, whose maggots riddle carrots and leave them inedible. I had little rust fly trouble at Lorane and it's the same at Elkton, where less than 1 percent of my carrots have maggots in them. I believe that's because both are marginal agricultural districts where the surrounding pastures are full of wild carrot. In some parts of the Lorane valley, where fields grew little wild carrot, gardeners did complain of rust fly problems. Gardeners also have problems in Eugene and in prime agricultural areas of the Willamette Valley where fields are too valuable to grow only low-quality pasture or hayfields full of wild carrot. Large, stable populations of wild carrot mean stable populations of both carrot rust fly and its predators. Wherever there are garden carrots but few wild carrots, the fly can quickly breed into a serious plague unchecked by predation. In the same way, the poorer hayfields and extensive waste areas around my Lorane and Elkton gardens contain lots of wild cabbage and wild radish, which tends to limit the cabbage fly population. Urban gardeners and those living in prosperous agricultural districts are probably going to have much more serious problems with pests than will rural homesteaders on infertile hillsides and in small upland valleys where a wide variety of plants supports balanced ecologies of insect pests and their predators.

Spray vs. fertilizer

Here's some very good advice. Before you rush to spray even organic poisons, first wonder if the plant is simply not growing fast enough to overcome the predation. Slow growth is the actual "cause" of most insect problems. Sometimes infertile soil is the real culprit; sometimes bad weather or sowing too early retard growth and lower the health of the plant. Often the first action to be taken is not an application of pesticide, but a feeding of liquid fertilizer. Many times a spray of fish emulsion (a double whammy that not only foliar feeds the plant but also disguises its odor from predators that locate their chow by the smell) or a single dose of water-soluble chemical fertilizer will "cure" a plant within a day or so.

In spring, if slow-growing seedlings are being chewed down by slugs or flea beetles and fertilization doesn't solve the problem, most likely the seeds were sown too early or too sparsely. If you sow many more seeds than the final number of plants ultimately wanted, you can have a relatively benign attitude about insects: think of them as helping thin out the weakest seedlings. Sowing again a little later, when soils are warmer and more active and the sun is stronger, allows seedlings to grow faster from the start. As you know from Chapter 1, a late April sowing usually matures only a little after one made March 15.

Pesticides may be a short-term solution if fertilization doesn't help. When bad weather causes no-growth conditions at the beginning of the season, sprays can retard predation while plants wait for weather to moderate and growth to resume. But bad weather and decreasing light levels at season's end can also prompt troubles with diseases and insects on heat-loving crops; these are hardly worth fighting, since the plants' life cycle is virtually over anyway.

Certain vegetables are very fussy about the type of soil they will and won't grow in; these species may express their difficulty by *appearing* to be attacked by insect or disease, and there is little or nothing that can be done short of importing a bed of special soil or selling the property. This type of problem is especially common with weakly rooting species intolerant of clay soils, such as artichoke, celery, celeriac, melons (especially watermelons) and cauliflower.

The tai chi of gardening

I try to coexist peacefully with nature. Not having to battle insects for my food supply allows me to see pests as potential allies; they can help me grow a better garden. By following the lead of pests, I discover paths to even more natural gardening. One very important step along this road is abandoning austerity, or what some popular self-help psychologists and preachers call "poverty consciousness." Instead of planting a garden from which you'll only harvest exactly what you want if everything grows well, plant two or three times as much, so that pests and diseases could wipe out one-third of the garden without threatening your food supply or upsetting you. Plan to grow a garden that allows you to give away buckets of food most years.

Because in life, some years just *are* cabbage years. The sun doesn't shine much, the rains fall all summer, the tomatoes get late blight as soon as they start to ripen, melons and cucumbers fall helpless to powdery mildew, eggplants won't set, peppers don't mature, corn is very late, beans become covered with aphids. If the garden is big enough, at least you can eat a lot of salad greens, scallions and rutabagas. If the leek patch doesn't grow well one year but you planted twice what you needed, there will still be enough leeks.

The ramifications of this concept flow all the way from your back yard to the international scene. In agricultural societies where social justice prevails, farmers have enough land to grow many times their families' annual requirement and don't lose 70 percent of their effort to rents, crop shares and taxes. In healthy societies, when the inevitable drought or cabbage year comes, each family will wisely have enough stored food and surplus wealth to survive a poor harvest, and the social system as a whole will have enough savings to carry itself through. But in unjust agricultural societies such as El Salvador or Guatemala or Bangladesh, where only a few own virtually all the effective means of production while the suppressed many are forced to eke out a livelihood as best they can on wasteland or hillside—and then taxed heavily one way or another—the total social production is much lower, there is no margin of safety for the poor and the slightest mistake or misfortune spells catastrophe. The unjust society must then go begging.

Another way to avoid battling nature is to inspect and reject one of our cultural peculiarities—what I call the "American sanitary model." You know that in a supermarket, no one would buy spinach with a few holes in the leaves or a rutabaga with a few maggot scars on the skin. Should a consumer find a cooked cabbage worm in the frozen broccoli, the processor might be threatened with a lawsuit or a government investigation. Food is supposed to be *clean,* isn't it? Proponents of spraying commercial vegetables are absolutely right when they argue with organic growers: without sprays, one cannot raise most commercial vegetables to Grade A, #1 standards, such that all the plants in the field go to market absolutely free of insects or insect damage. Organic growers usually go broke when they try to compete in the regular commercial market using inefficient, short-lasting organic pesticides.

But why not change your attitude about what constitutes acceptable table fare and learn to coexist with insects? Remove as many of them as possible when the food is being prepared and ignore the one that may occasionally escape the cook's scrutiny. Better to eat a bug than a mouthful of pesticide. There's a big difference between a plant showing the effects of an occasional insect and one that has been severely damaged. As long as the plant is still growing vigorously, a few (even a few hundred) pinholes in the leaves or a scar on the cucumber's skin don't matter. As long as the cook can peel off the damage without wasting too much time, why

poison the soil or even bother to use organic strategies to handle the predation? Leave cosmetic spraying to the commercial farmers and their
unrealistic clientele. *The primary reason unsprayed vegetables are not
widely sold is that the public does not want imperfect-looking food.*

Pesty considerations

Your thinking also affects pest problems. The Judeo-Christian Bible
says man was put on Earth with dominion over the plants and animals.
I don't believe this statement means we are allowed to do exactly as we
please with our environment; we're finding out most painfully these days
that there are unavoidable consequences to pollution and other forms
of ecological mismanagement. I think what "dominion" really means is
that *Homo sapiens* has more spiritual or mental *force* than any other
life form on Earth, giving us the potential to control and shape Earth for
good or evil. I believe spiritual force is both collective and individual. On
the social level, it results in national and planetary consequences; on the
individual level, it strongly affects what goes on in *your* garden. Unfortunately, viewing the laws of nature as being influenced by ideas and
spiritual power runs contrary to what most of us have been taught for
the past century or two.

When you till up a piece of earth, fence it, change its pH, increase
its fertility, remove the native vegetation, sow and transplant and weed,
you assume a very active and powerful sort of ownership. Thenceforth,
a lot of what is going to happen in that garden will be the result of your
considerations. By considerations I mean a very special thing: the basic
assumptions each person has about reality, about what things signify and
about what is going to happen. The amazing thing about considerations
is that they're self-fulfilling. If you really consider you'll be successful, you
probably will be, unless you have other more basic considerations going
that contradict the first one. If people consider they'll become sick and
die young, that will probably happen, too. If marriage is considered a
happy state, it probably will be. Considerations can be either conscious
or unconscious—unsuccessful people possess numerous unknown
considerations.

You *have* basic considerations about that garden you have taken
ownership of, and because you own the space so strongly, your particular
considerations are going to be powerfully actualized there. Far out, you
say? Well, like all such ideas, the power of consideration can't really be
proved. If it agrees with what you already believe, you'll say it's right on.

If it doesn't, you won't understand the idea or will disagree if it seems to contradict some other opinion of yours. Though the above assertions can't be proved, they can be demonstrated by what scientists regularly dismiss as anecdotes that prove nothing. Here are a few anecdotes that "fail to prove" how people's considerations actualize in the garden.

Years ago, a fellow from southern Oregon wrote and asked why my garden book did not include his excellent remedy for root maggots in radishes. His method was amazingly simple, requiring no sprays, covers or other complexities. He mixed up a strong solution of table salt and water and sprinkled that along the rows of radishes just before they started bulbing. The result: no maggots in his radishes until they'd grown far beyond mild, tender, eating size.

Where did he get this method, I asked.

Figured it out himself, he told me.

So I thanked the man most kindly, told him I'd try his remedy and put it in the next edition. I did not bother to try it though, because I know I myself have an unshakable consideration that a little salt water will in no way prevent the cabbage fly from laying eggs around the radishes, nor will a trace of table salt in the ground keep those maggots from developing. But that man believes in his method, and consequently it really works—for him. I fulfilled part of the bargain: I did finally include his method in my book. You're welcome to try it.

Here's another: every year, with the aid of black plastic mulch and big transplants started early, Dr. Jim Baggett grew an eggplant trial on hot black loam near Corvallis, just about the most favorable place in the entire Willamette Valley to grow eggplant. Every year, a few very early hybrid varieties managed to set some medium-sized eggplants. And every year without fail, open-pollinated Black Beauty, the most popular and widely grown variety east of the Cascades, grew a nice bush that remained totally fruitless—because to set and mature fruit, most varieties of eggplant need much warmer nighttime temperatures than we have in the maritime Northwest.

One day some years back, a woman who resented expensive hybrids phoned me demanding to know why I did not recommend Black Beauty. She had moved to Seattle just that spring from Texas, where she had grown Black Beauty for years and years; having moved a bit of seed with her, she had confidently planted three Black Beauty seedlings alongside her new Seattle house. They did magnificently and at that very moment were covered with fruit, though it was a bit smaller than she got in Texas.

I made a regrettable mistake. Conjuring up all my Authority, I said,

"Madam, that's impossible. You absolutely *can't* grow Black Beauty here!" and told her about Jim Baggett's years of trying to grow the variety in a much warmer and more favorable spot than Seattle. I'm sure that if she believed me, she was never able to get a crop from Black Beauty again. I should have kept my mouth shut and let her continue to succeed.

Know your foes

Spirituality and Sir Albert Howard aside, there are occasions when insects must be fought or too much of the garden will be lost. What follows is a summary of the little I've learned about common garden pests in the maritime Northwest. Unfortunately, I am the wrong person to write an authoritative statement about insects and their control. I've always made healthy soil and had a positive mental attitude about how my garden was going to grow. So in my garden, only the most ubiquitous and prolific pests make their presence felt at all, although I am sure there are others lurking unnoticed. I do not know the whys and wherefores of the brown-spotted cucumber flower nibbler, the purple poppy plucker or the sneaky weed nabber. I *am* intimately acquainted with a few common insects, a couple of diseases, slugs and some other critters that burrow under my garden beds. (Specific plant diseases are discussed in Chapter 8.)

If this information does not describe your particular plague or how to lessen its effect on your garden (or on your attitude) or how to control it without artificial poisons, you might consider giving up on organic gardening and asking your friendly garden-center owner or extension agent for advice. The Extension Service people have a wide knowledge of many minor pests and diseases; however, they're not likely to recommend a solution any organic gardener would be happy with. And garden centers have a wide repertory of high-powered poisons that can kill almost anything living in or around the soil. The best I can say of these substances is that at least the ones permitted to be sold to the gardener are not the kinds that kill humans quickly in tiny doses; how they may affect your body over the years, I do not wish to speculate about here. I am fairly certain home-garden pesticide residues will be less damaging than those in the supermarket. Perhaps the effect of toxic residues also depends to some extent on what your considerations about them are.

Aphids (Aphididae family)

Often called plant lice, these are small, soft-bodied insects that cluster on leaves and stems, sucking sap from the plant. Their predation causes leaves to curl and cup; in large numbers, aphids can weaken or stunt a plant, reducing yields. Aphids can multiply with amazing rapidity, exploding from nothing to a serious threat in days. They also transport various plant diseases such as pea enation.

Aphids often have a close relationship with ants, which "farm" them much like humans graze cows on pasture. Ants place aphids on leaves and then milk a sweet secretion from their livestock. Aphid control often entails elimination of ant nests. Ants protecting aphid colonies may be killed safely by setting out ant poison stakes, which contain sugar and arsenic (arsenic is a natural mineral poison quite acceptable to me as an organic gardener as long as it's not broadcast about the environment or left where kids, pets or livestock can get at it). The ants carry the poisoned sugar back to feed their larvae and queen, thus neatly wiping out the nest.

Aphids can be sprayed off leaves with a hose and nozzle; once removed, the ones you sprayed will not find their way back, though others may. Safer's soap is a fine organic insecticide for aphids. Made from special saponins, Safer's also controls scales and several other pests. Safer's is virtually nontoxic to animals and most insects, though it can be harmful to the plants themselves (phytotoxic) if used in excessively strong concentrations.

Cabbage maggots (*Hylemya brassicae*)

These are the larvae of an innocent-looking little fly. The sly fly usually waits until the root system of a cabbage family member is extensive enough to support a brood of larvae (when the stem is about a quarter-inch in diameter) before laying its eggs on the soil's surface near the plant. After hatching, the larvae burrow down and begin to feed on the root system of the host plant.

The gardener suddenly discovers the maggot at work when the cabbage, broccoli, cauliflower and sometimes Brussels sprout plants wilt and collapse or become stunted and barely grow. The maggots are also found tunneling through turnips, radishes and the lower portions of Chinese cabbage leaves, though they tend to leave rutabagas alone or at most scar up the thick skin, which is peeled away before cooking. Unfortunately, in almost every case too much damage is already done before the maggots are noticed. An exception is kale, the most vigorous member of the brassica family, which develops such a large and fast-growing root system that it will accommodate large numbers of root maggots and still make a fine plant. (This last statement may not hold true where infestations are much higher than I am used to dealing with.)

Growing brassicas without pesticides requires encouraging rapid root development, which can mean paying attention to improving soil tilth as well as fertility. Vigorous root systems can tolerate a good deal more predation without the plant wilting or becoming noticeably stunted. In the case of radish and turnip crops, timely harvest can get them out of the ground before the maggots have invaded many roots. If maggot predation is totally eliminated, the plant size and ultimate yield of brassicas will be greater. Non-organic gardeners who wish to really Grow brassicas may want to repeatedly use chemical soil drenches available in garden centers.

Gardeners can avoid much trouble by planting between peaks in the root maggots' population cycle. Early spring brassicas are particularly susceptible to attack because there are usually high levels of maggots during April and May. By early June, cabbage fly numbers decrease rapidly as the spring maggot hatch pupates in the soil. So May through July is the time to sow main brassica plantings. Maggot levels increase again in late summer when the pupae hatch out, but by then non-root brassica crops are usually large enough to withstand considerable predation, while light intensity has dropped so much that even if plants do lose some root, they are not likely to wilt.

Using a sawdust collar to protect against cabbage root maggots

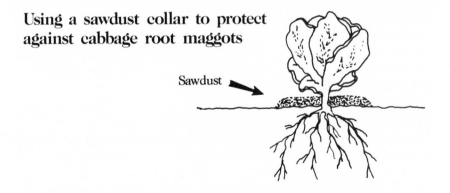

Sawdust

Until a few years ago, there were no organic pesticides effective in the soil against the root maggot. The late Blair Adams, research horticulturist at the Washington State University Extension Service in Puyallup, did extensive trials on a number of traditional organic remedies for root maggots. He found that dustings of wood ashes—once widely recommended—actually attracted cabbage flies; he speculated that in unlimed, acidic, calcium-deficient soils, the calcium-rich wood ashes might boost the growth of brassicas enough to compensate for the increased predation the ash caused. Diatomaceous earth, helpful against hard-shelled insects even in the soil, did not kill the soft-skinned maggots. Blair found that careful and persistent hilling of soil around the plants' stems provided a little protection and increased the survival rate of seedlings somewhat by burying the root system deeper.

The best control he could come up with was the collar. Gardeners had used tar-paper collars for a long time, but Blair felt that sawdust was better. A ring of sawdust about 1½ inches thick, six to eight inches in diameter, touching the stem and carefully maintained, will prevent the fly from laying its eggs on the soil's surface. Radish and turnip seed sown on the soil's surface and covered with a four- to six-inch-wide band of sawdust one inch deep will also be protected, but timely harvest is still essential because the swelling roots push aside the sawdust and expose themselves to the fly.

Since Blair did his work, another organic remedy has become available. Researchers in the field of integrated pest management discovered that certain species of parasitic nematodes effectively attack root maggots in the ground. If large numbers of these microscopic life forms are seeded into the soil surrounding brassica seedlings, they can live for months and actively knock off maggots as fast as they hatch out, even breeding and maintaining fairly effective population levels. Parasitic nematodes will also control numerous other pests that may or may not be a problem in the maritime Northwest, including wireworms, onion maggots, carrot weevils, cutworms, rhododendron root weevil larvae, strawberry root weevil larvae and cucumber beetle larvae.

There have been problems using these nematodes. Early promoters had difficulties with quality control and uniform vitality from lot to lot. The nematodes are easy and cheap to culture by the billions, but not so simple to transport or store out of the culture medium. They have been used most successfully when removed from their culture vats and shipped by overnight air freight while being held at low temperatures in special media, and then used immediately. This suits commercial growers, who can phone up and order a few hundred dollars' worth the day before transplanting brassica seedlings or when they notice trouble in the field. In the past, nematode cultures sold to home gardeners off the shelf have often been virtually dead and totally ineffective. In my eagerness to promote the use of this control when I first discovered it, I sold Territorial customers many hundreds of small packets of ineffective nematodes, along with many hundreds of packets that still retained good vigor. Needless to say, I received a lot of complaints and I gave up the product in disgust.

Nematodes are still not suitable for sale off the shelf in a garden center, but better storage technologies and culturing techniques have been developed. If the product is purchased fresh, the gardener can now hold it under refrigeration for several months before the nematodes lose viability. Obviously the order should not be placed too many months in advance of anticipated need.

See also the section below on carrot rust fly, which discusses using fabric screens to limit access by flying insects.

Carrot rust fly (*Psila rosae*)

As I mentioned before, this is a pest with which I have little personal experience. I know from the literature that the fly begins breeding rapidly in late summer and will go through a generation every month, often increasing to wildly high numbers by midwinter if the weather is not too severe. Carrots started in late May, after the spring hatch is through, may well finish their growth cycle relatively unharmed and be harvested by late summer. However, carrots left in the ground become increasingly infested by rust fly maggots as the winter progresses.

Nematodes will be of little use against this maggot because it is most active at a time of year that soil temperatures are low, which inactivates the nematodes. Covering the bed with well-anchored Reemay may give a gardener a maggot-free crop. Du Pont brought out Reemay not long ago. It's a very lightweight, semi-transparent, spun-polyester fabric much like mosquito netting. Similar materials from other manufacturers are rapidly appearing to compete with Reemay; the best of them may be Agrinet. The neatest thing about these fabrics is that they allow air and water to pass through and are held up by the plants as they grow. If *carefully anchored* with a sprinkling of soil all around a bed or row of plants, the fabric makes an effective insect barrier as well as a growth-enhancing cloche that doesn't require ventilation or special watering. To deter the rust fly, thin the carrots when the tops are three or four inches tall, to about 150 percent of their normal spacing (to allow for the slight loss of light Reemay causes) and then cover the bed. Gardeners have used homemade solutions similar to Reemay for years, building screened boxes to cover their growing carrot crop and prevent the fly from laying.

Storing carrots during winter by carefully laying sheets of plastic over the carrot tops and a few inches of straw over that for insulation might prevent the fly from gaining access, though it may also make a haven for field mice.

Flea beetles (*Phyllotreta striolata*)

These tiny, black, hopping insects chew pinholes in leaves and primarily affect members of the cabbage family but occasionally feed on other vegetables, including beets and tomato transplants. They particularly like sucking on thick, juicy brassica cotyledons (the first two leaves that emerge after germination), where the seedling stores its remaining food reserves until it develops a true leaf and really gets growing. In high numbers, flea beetles stunt and kill seedlings. Fast-growing, healthy plants will not be seriously stunted, though their leaves may be highly perforated.

Overwintering adult beetles migrate to the garden in spring from surrounding fields, where they naturally feed on wild plants, and begin to feed on newly sprouted or transplanted vegetables. Later in spring, the adults lay eggs in the soil, which quickly hatch out. Flea beetle larvae feed on potato tubers and various roots, usually without doing much damage, until they pupate. After maturing into adults, the beetles then continue to feed until they hibernate in fall.

Farmers who want the maximum yield per acre, and who make or lose money on the basis of a few percent one way or another, use sprays because the yield and cash return lost to flea beetle predation outweigh the expense of the pesticide. The gardener need not think that way. What difference does it make if you harvest a nine-pound cabbage instead of an 11-pound one, or an 18-ounce head of broccoli instead of one weighing 20 ounces?

Fairly severe flea beetle problems can usually be handled by raising husky, well-hardened transplants that don't go into shock and stop growing when set out (like cheaply raised commercial seedlings do), or by overseeding, which gives the beetles lots to chew on while leaving the gardener enough survivors to establish a stand. If plants are being too heavily damaged, they're probably not growing fast enough. In that case, the best strategy may be liquid fertilizer and improvement of soil tilth and fertility before the next planting.

Severe infestations can be sprayed with several types of pesticides, the safest being rotenone (an organic poison made from ground tropical plant roots), which is available as a dust or a powder to mix in water. Rotenone is very, very effective, but short-lasting; it must be sprayed every few days until the seedlings are growing well and producing much more new leaf than the beetles are chewing away. Another acceptable organic pesticide is Red Arrow, a liquid combination of rotenone and pyrethrum (obtained from a perennial daisy) with a "synergist" called piperonyl butoxide, an evil-sounding name for a substance actually derived from natural sources that increases the potency of both rotenone and pyrethrum. The pyrethrum probably has little effect on flea beetles. Red Arrow seems to knock down insects faster than straight rotenone and will handle a wider range of pests.

Commercial brassica growers in Europe use an effective organic seed treatment against the flea beetle. Called gamma beta toxin, it is a virus culture that is used to coat seed. The virus is rapidly fatal to flea beetles but nothing else. When seed is treated with gamma beta toxin the seedlings go unmolested for about six weeks after germination, by which time they have developed three or four true leaves and can easily outgrow normal flea beetle predation. The treatment costs a mere 50 cents per pound of seed or only a few dollars per acre, much less than it costs to spray chemical pesticides for flea beetle control; however, the material is not available for use in the United States because the Environmental Protection Agency has not approved it. To jump through all the hoops the EPA has erected to "protect" us would take many millions of dollars, and so far no chemical companies have bothered dealing with the federal bureaucracy. I don't know if their lack of interest is due to the small size of the potential market for gamma beta toxin or the much higher profitability of the pesticides now being used. In this case, the EPA is encouraging the use of expensive and highly profitable chemical sprays and discouraging the use of cheap but effective organic alternatives.

Imported cabbageworms (*Pieris rapae*)

These are the larvae of a white butterfly often seen fluttering about the garden. Their clusters of small, yellowish, bullet-shaped eggs are laid singly on cabbage family plants, usually on the undersides of the leaves. A similar pest is the cabbage looper (*Trichoplusia ni*), the larvae of a night-flying brown butterfly. Its round, greenish-white eggs are laid singly on the upper surface of leaves. The larvae of both pests hatch out quickly and grow rapidly, feeding on brassica leaves. They can do a great deal of damage in a short time, especially if they begin feeding at critical times such as during the early formation of cabbage heads or if their numbers are excessive. Once the larvae reach their full size (1¼ to 1½ inches), they pupate unnoticed.

In a small garden, handpicking the larvae and tossing them away from any cabbage family plant can be sufficient control. An extremely effective nontoxic pesticide called *Bacillus thuringiensis* is widely available, marketed as Bt, Dipel or Thuricide. Bt can be sprayed the day of harvest because it is a bacterial culture lethal only to the cabbageworm, cabbage looper and a few close relatives. The culture remains active on the leaves only for a few days, but even if sprayed only once, it seems to persist in the garden at a low level, as infection is transmitted from decaying infected worms to healthy worms, greatly reducing their numbers for the rest of the season. If sprayed every few weeks, Bt can offer control good enough for finicky growers who become grossly offended at the very idea of a cabbageworm appearing in their broccoli or cauliflower heads.

Leafminers (*Liriomyza* spp.)

Leafminers are the maggots of a small fly similar to the cabbage fly or carrot rust fly. These larvae most enjoy tunneling through leaves of beets, chard and spinach, although they'll also mine bean, blackberry, lettuce and other leaves. I have not had any trouble with leafminers, but many maritime Northwest gardeners to the north do. I know of no organic insecticide that will control leafminers effectively because they're protected from sprays by being inside the leaf itself.

I once sent a section of Reemay to a Washington State gardener who complained of leafminer problems completely ruining every beet crop he tried. The gardener carefully covered most of a beet bed with Reemay after the seedlings were large enough to thin and weed, and kept the cover in place undisturbed until harvest. His unprotected beets were thoroughly ruined—not one plant survived to make a beet root. Under the Reemay, there was a fine harvest, though the fabric did drop light levels somewhat so the beets were a bit toppy with smaller roots than he would have liked. As with carrots, this problem can be eliminated by thinning the beets to a slightly wider than normal spacing.

Slugs (Gastropoda)

More garden damage is done by the small gray slug than by its larger and more noticeable relatives. Slugs eat seedlings, nestle inside lettuce and cabbage heads, and can ruin new plantings in a few nights. They'll also damage fruit, especially ripening tomatoes and strawberries.

Slugs hide and lay eggs under garden debris, so keeping soil bare, putting garden trash carefully in a compost pile and eliminating daytime hiding places, such as boards lying on the soil, will *slightly* reduce populations. Slugs are the major reason that year-round mulching, so popular with eastern gardeners, is unworkable in the maritime Northwest. Gardeners who find slugs multiplying beyond the minor annoyance level can try switching to later sowings so seedlings grow faster, and sowing more seeds to give the slugs some extras to knock off. Banding a little fertilizer along seedling rows or below transplants might increase growth rates sufficiently that slugs are no longer a serious threat.

Large populations can easily be reduced organically by trapping. The simplest method is to lay boards on the garden paths. Each morning at sunrise, many slugs will hide under these boards. The gardener can then turn the boards over during the day, handpick the slugs and drop them into a jar of detergent solution, salt water or gasoline, or sprinkle a bit of salt on them. A friend of mine with a small garden likes to go out at night with a gasoline lantern and a pair of sharp scissors, snipping hundreds of slugs in half. He needs to do this only once or twice a month to keep slug populations manageable.

Though I am generally opposed to chemical pesticides, slug baits made *only* with metaldehyde are acceptable to me (though not to capital-O organic gardeners), but I won't use baits made with other more potent substances, like fluoride poisons. Metaldehyde is a simple organic substance similar to wood alcohol. It breaks down into harmless substances rapidly in soil, which is why other more potent baits use other more effective poisons. Slugs love to intoxicate themselves to death with metaldehyde in the same way they'll happily drown themselves in beer. Slug bait need not be used in the garden itself, but instead may be sprinkled in a 12-inch-wide band or "slug fence" around the perimeter of the garden. Since slugs do not know where they are located—beyond the knowledge shared by all life forms that wherever they are is "here"—they travel at random. A barrier of slug bait will prevent slugs from entering the garden for several weeks, while those already in the garden will die on the barrier when they leave. Reactivated every few weeks, a bait barrier can quickly reduce garden populations. One problem with slug bait is that it can be fatally attractive to pets. A more aggressive approach, which still avoids broadcasting slug bait among the vegetables you're going to eat or around the garden where pets might taste some, is to construct traps out of pie tins and sprinkle bait in the tins. To make a trap, sink a small pie tin in the soil, its rim flush with the surface; suspend a larger, inverted pie tin a few inches above to guard the lower one from rain or irrigation by inserting four long supporting nails through the rim. Capital-O gardeners can fill the lower pie tin with stale beer.

A few years ago, I was introduced to a fine Swiss organic slug control product. Called Fertosan Slug Destroyer, it consists of a natural gelatin containing herbal attractants and some alcohol. I managed to get a gallon in through customs for trial—it worked fine. A few ounces of gel poured into small holes in the earth resisted the effects of rain and did not degrade for several weeks; the little holes gradually filled up with dead slugs pickled in gel. However, the patented stuff couldn't be imported from Switzerland for resale nor be manufactured under license in the U.S. without the same level of EPA and U. S. Department of Agriculture approvals demanded for lethally poisonous pesticides. The Swiss company put me in touch with an American who had obtained a license to manufacture the slug gel on this side of the ocean. He confidently started the approval process, but he became bogged down in the bureaucracy and vanished, probably after losing a lot of money. Thus, we are protected by our benevolent government.

Symphylans (*Scutigerella immaculata*)

These pests are given little more than a casual mention in even the most extensive eastern garden pest guides, but these tiny critters cause more trouble in western Oregon and parts of Washington State than most of the other pests put together. *Unfortunately, gardeners rarely realize lurking symphylans are the cause of their difficulties.* The average gardener starts out with a few years of success, but unnoticed symphylan populations gradually build up to plague levels. Problems are often attributed to bad seed or mysterious diseases; many people with low failure tolerances give up gardening altogether.

Luckily, I was warned about symphylans from the beginning. Over the big hill east of Lorane was a pretty good garden store in Cottage Grove where I used to buy my supplies. The owner told this enthusiastic capital-O organic gardener who had just arrived in Oregon, "You'll have a great garden over there for a year or two. Then things will start to go wrong. There's a little soil pest we have here in Oregon called the symphylan, and you won't be able to handle it with anything you organic gardeners know about. The only thing that will kill symphylans is Dyfonate, a restricted-use pesticide."

He pointed out a sack of Dyfonate on a high shelf above the window. "All the farmers around here use it before growing most vegetable crops. They couldn't harvest any row crops at all without it. *You* can't legally buy Dyfonate—it takes a special license. But I can, and I'll be happy to supply you with some and explain how to use it."

"No, thanks!" I said emphatically, with all my capital-O certainty— which I still had in those innocent days. "I'm sure I'll find a way to deal with any pest that comes along without using something like that."

I was right, but not as right as I would have liked to have been. I did discover organic controls for symphylans, but for all that, I can't say I'm happy with what I've learned. I can manage them, but it costs. Does it ever cost.

Imagine a quarter-inch-long, flattened cylinder of white or pale brownish-pink flexible wire, jointed like a crawdad's tail and edged with 12 pairs of little legs coming out of each joint. The front joint is the head, with two long thin feelers attached. That's the symphylan. This shy little soil dweller moves fast and doesn't like light. It lives several years, breeds relatively slowly and can move as deep as five feet into the soil or lurk near the surface. A single individual will generally confine itself to an area with a radius of only 15 or 20 feet. Symphylans are so small, so fast and so well camouflaged that several dozen of them can be hiding in a shovelful of soil and yet only someone intently looking for them may ever realize their presence. The only way to be sure you've got symphylan problems is to carefully pick through a shovelful of soil laid on a sheet of cardboard or newspaper and do a count—entomologists consider 10 or more per shovelful the level at which symphylans become a pest.

The only predator known to control their population levels is the ground beetle, a common, inch-long, heavily armored black insect. It is not a very effective predator, but its ability to hunt for symphylans increases when the soil is light and airy, permitting the beetle to move more freely through the soil's surface layers. Symphylans eat two things: rotting organic matter and tender emerging root tips. A major natural control on their population is the fact that soils west of the Cascades dry out significantly every summer, forcing the symphylans to seek moisture deep in the earth where there is little food to support them.

Symphylans seem to prefer some vegetable species over others and do the most damage to plants with the least vigorous root systems. Symphylan problems first show up after the garden plot has been used for a few successful years: all of a sudden, spinach, beets, strawberries and cauliflower won't grow. Cauliflower is stunted, spinach and beets germinate but fail to grow and the stand disappears. With heavier infestations, spinach and beets don't even seem to germinate, because the symphylans consume the root tips as they emerge from sprouting seeds and kill the seedlings before they break into the light. Once I broadcast an entire pound of vigorous beet seed into a heavily infested raised bed, and not one seed "sprouted." Bad infestations begin to stunt more vigorous brassicas like broccoli and cabbage, and may affect peppers, beans, celery and a wide range of other species. Tomatoes, carrots, corn, parsnips, parsley, lettuce and members of the squash family seem relatively immune to all but the worst infestations.

When I first discovered them wrecking things in my trial grounds, I acquired much of the above information from books and experts at OSU and then spent a lot of time staring off into space meditating on the symphylan. I imagined that one hundred years ago, when virtually all of the maritime Northwest was forest, symphylans lived on the rotting forest duff and munched occasional root tips. When homesteaders cleared the forest, planted fields and made pastures, the organic matter content of the soil dropped markedly, reducing the symphylan population and somewhat increasing their appetite for root tips. However, judging from the crops farmers use Dyfonate on, most pasture grasses and weeds aren't particularly appealing to symphylans, and neither are the roots of most grains (which are also grasses). Nor are fava beans.

Common lore about the symphylan goes, "They weren't in this field until I brought them in with that load of manure. Now they're a plague." Well, that's not quite right: the symphylans weren't brought to the field with the manure, the manure fed them. It's when the farmer or gardener also begins to irrigate a piece of ground that the soil ecology is really thrown out of whack; then the symphylan is permitted to feed and breed much more effectively. Which brings me to the first handling for symphylans I worked out.

Clay soils must be heavily manured if most vegetable crops are to grow well enough to produce a decent garden. But manure and irrigation beget a plague of symphylans, which in a few years begin to cause havoc. One solution to this problem is to manure and manure and manure, building such a high level of fertility and tilth that most species of vegetables can outgrow symphylan predation, while increasing the effectiveness of the predator beetles. I've encountered many organic gardeners who have "built their soil" and grown a good enough garden for years without realizing they even had symphylans. However, most of them experience mysterious failures that they attribute to disease or poor seed. Because building higher and higher levels of organic matter is an imperfect solution, I've come to believe that in symphylan country, when it comes to manure or compost, less is better whenever possible.

Another way to manage symphylans is to feed them enough root tips that they're diverted from vegetable crops. Imagine a field from the symphylans' viewpoint: the gardener tills in all growing vegetation, and then plants a row of seeds or transplants, surrounded by much bare soil. Natural-

Know your foes

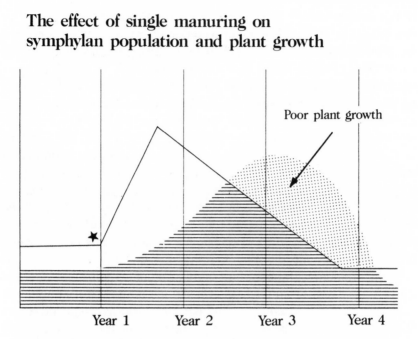

The effect of single manuring on symphylan population and plant growth

The effect of repeated manuring on symphylan population and plant growth

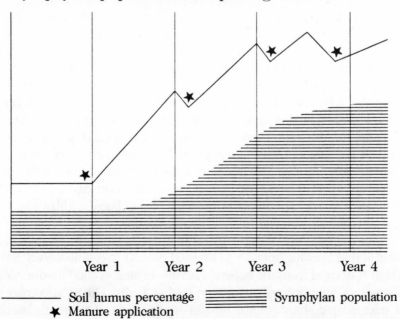

ly, the symphylans all flock to the few little growing plants and nibble away, wreaking havoc. Suppose instead that after tilling the gardener had first thickly broadcast and raked in buckwheat seed, creating a dense enough stand that the buckwheat seedlings stood only an inch or so apart. Since symphylans like buckwheat roots as well as most other fare, they'll have lots and lots to eat once the seedlings sprout. Buckwheat is a very easily removed "weed"—touch it with a hoe and it's gone. Once the bed is covered with little buckwheat plants, the gardener can hoe out four- or five-inch strips to plant seed in or make holes in the ground cover to set out transplants. As the vegetables grow, the buckwheat can gradually be hoed back as it begins to compete with them for light. A green manure trap crop is a workable and proven strategy, but it does require very patient and thorough hoeing to prevent swamping the vegetables. I've even resurrected stunted sowings of cauliflower by establishing belated stands of buckwheat around them.

One problem with buckwheat is that it's not at all frost-tolerant, and it won't grow well when daylengths begin to shorten, so it's only plantable from the last frost until mid-July. For spring sowings of ground covers, cheap radish seed purchased by the pound could be useful. The cheapest kind might be that sold for sprouting in health food stores. Radish is also easy to hoe out if it's caught before it bolts. To feed symphylans on sowings made after early July, field turnips or radish might work.

Perversely, dealing with symphylans is an area where the organic gardener has the edge over the one habituated to chemicals, because garden centers can't sell home gardeners any chemical that is effective against symphylans. Diazinon will not kill them, though it will make them unhappy enough to reduce predation a bit if used repeatedly in very high doses—but who would want to eat stuff that had been drenched in diazinon at levels far higher than recommended? The commercial growers' standby, Dyfonate (the trade name for fonophos), when tilled in will kill symphylans for many weeks, temporarily lowering their population, but Dyfonate is so toxic to humans that ingesting as little as two milligrams (a few granules) is sufficient to cause death in most cases. That's why Dyfonate is a restricted pesticide and can't be purchased without a special license requiring training in "safe" pesticide use.

One organic control that may work in the soil effectively enough to even permit growing spinach in infested ground is diatomaceous earth, which is derived from the skeletal remains of single-celled marine algae. The natural unprocessed type, often sold as Perma Guard, is composed of microscopic sharp-pointed diatom shells made of silica, a glass-like

Symphylan rotation

Year	Treatment
One	Manure, lime and broadcast phosphate rock in prior autumn. In spring, grow vegetables.
Two	Grow vegetables.
Three	Grow vegetables. Symphylan problems will begin appearing.
Four	Using a bit of fertilizer as needed, grow unirrigated dry crops like favas, grains, field beans, quinoa, carrots, potatoes, and peas, *or* green manure with favas, *or* merely dry fallow in weeds.
Five	Ditto.
Six	Ditto. Lime in fall, then spread manure, even over standing favas if in a fava rotation (see Green manure/favas in Chapter 8), and till.
Seven	Back to year one.

Note: This rotation is still somewhat tentative, as I have not yet had sufficient time to experience the entire rotation on more than one soil type. Currently, I am actively researching the dryland farming portion. At Lorane on clay, I have already seen the effect of three years of dry fallow, growing dense stands of fava beans. The result is totally rejuvenated soil ready again to produce vegetable species without any hint of symphylan problems for several years. I am sure that it would be much better to grow favas than to let the weeds take over, because the first year a weedy field is turned into a garden, the weeds have, as it were, a field day.

substance. When hard-shelled critters like the symphylan and other insects get these sharp particles caught in the folds of their joints, they are punctured, leak their vital fluids and die. There are two problems with working diatomaceous earth into the planting rows or around transplants. One is that the stuff is fairly spendy. It takes a big handful to protect a transplant and a thick dusting raked in along a seed row, so it must be purchased in at least 50-pound quantities to even begin to be cost-effective. The other is that the clay in the soil immediately begins to coat the sharp points, gradually ending their effectiveness. Perma Guard will work for several months, but that's it.

Rotations and dry gardening are the best organic controls for symphylans. After several years of irrigation have made symphylans a problem, the difficulty is easily cured by allowing the garden to return to a native condition for several years, if you can afford to do that. This means at least a two-step rotation lasting about six years. Unfortunately, rotational techniques are not workable for most urban gardeners working in very limited space.

Further reading

Plant pathology, any textbook.

This is a required subject in any agricultural college, dealing with the physiology of plants and the nature of disease organisms.

Invertebrate zoology, any textbook.

Another required subject for agriculture students. Basically a descriptive study, it outlines the nature and habits of many plant pests in a much more thorough manner than the typical pest guides directed at the gardener. I would not have been able to figure out how to handle the symphylan had I not first become acquainted with what science knew of its habits and then spent a long time leaning on my hoe handle, staring out into space musing on the critter, until I obnosed what lay beyond the obvious solution of poisoning it.

The Encyclopedia of Natural Insect and Disease Control, edited by Roger B. Yepsen, Jr. (Emmaus: Rodale Press, 1984).

Plant Diseases: The Yearbook of Agriculture, 1953. USDA.

Rodale's Garden Insect, Disease & Weed Identification Guide, Miranda Smith and Anna Carr (Emmaus: Rodale Press, 1988).

This illustrated guide is helpful for determining what you've got. However, its suggested handlings aren't always regionally useful. For example, it says that asparagus, cucumber, lettuce, radish and tomato are host plants for the symphylan, when actually cucumber, lettuce and tomato are plants least bothered. It also recommends handling symphylans by pouring a tobacco infusion into the soil. Even if the nicotine did not kill everything in the earth, the cost would be prohibitive in areas like ours where the entire garden would have to be treated, perhaps several times every year.

How to Grow It

Since I have given my attention to the cultivation of the soil, I find I have no competition to fear, have nothing to apprehend from the success of my neighbor, and owe no thanks for the purchase of my commodities. Possessing on my land all the necessaries of life, I am under no anxiety regarding my daily subsistence.
—John Sillett, *A New Practical System of Fork and Spade Husbandry,* 1850

This handy reference guide is organized in "cultural groups," or what I think of as "vegetable families." Scientifically trained readers may be mildly amused that I have not followed strict rules of botanical classification. But I believe a system of classification and definition is only useful if it permits a person to do something with it; understanding vegetables as members of larger families that grow similarly helps a gardener successfully grow unfamiliar members of the same family. I believe thinking this way also encourages the gardener to experiment with new vegetables, which is useful for anyone who wishes to become more self-reliant.

These are the groups I think in:
- *Solanums*: eggplants, peppers, tomatoes
- *Legumes*: beans, peas, green manures
- *Greens*: celery, celeriac, corn salad, endive, lettuce, mustard, parsley, spinach, Swiss chard, rocket, sorrel
- *Brassicas*: broccoli, Brussels sprouts, cabbage, Chinese cabbage, cauliflower, collards, kale, kohlrabi, rutabagas, turnips
- *Roots*: beets, carrots, chicory, Hamburg parsley, parsnips, potatoes, radish
- *Cucurbits*: cucumbers, melons, pumpkins, squashes
- *Alliums*: garlic, shallots, leeks, onions
- *Miscellaneous*: asparagus, sweet corn, herbs, sunflowers and other low-demand staple food crops.

How to use this chapter

Planting dates in this section are for the Willamette Valley gardener. Readers to the north or south, along the coast or at higher elevations must make adjustments.

Spring and summer come later to the north and at higher elevations; gardeners there should plant their spring and summer crops a week or two later than the dates I suggest. Spring starts earlier along the coast but "summer," if it ever comes, arrives later. Coastal gardeners might start their spring crops a bit earlier, their summer crops about the same time as in the Willamette, and hope for the best. Spring and summer arrive earlier south of Drain, Oregon. Gardeners along the southern Oregon coast, in the Yoncalla Valley, along the Umpqua and in southern Oregon should start their spring and summer plantings a week or two earlier than I suggest. Fortunate gardeners in northern California (in respect to climate only) might start their spring crops as much as three or four weeks earlier.

Fall comes sooner to the north and higher elevation gardens; growth rates there slow sooner than they do in the Willamette. Summers are cooler along the coast, which has the same effect. Gardeners there should start their fall/winter and overwintered crops a week or two sooner. Fall comes later to the south. Gardeners south of Drain should sow their later crops a week or two after I suggest for the Willamette. Gardeners in northern California might hold off starting for fall/winter/overwintering as much as three or four weeks later.

The plant spacings I recommend in this chapter are based on a garden

Local planting dates

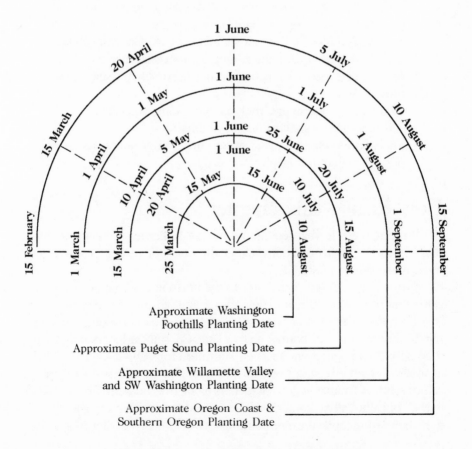

Approximate Washington Foothills Planting Date

Approximate Puget Sound Planting Date

Approximate Willamette Valley and SW Washington Planting Date

Approximate Oregon Coast & Southern Oregon Planting Date

laid out in semi-permanent raised beds, 3½ to 4½ feet wide and as long as you like. When the directions say to plant or sow seeds every so many inches in the row, with the rows x inches apart, it means in parallel rows that run across the width of the bed. For larger plants like tomatoes or cabbages, the directions will sometimes say to plant on 18- to 24-inch centers. In this case, what is envisioned is a regularly spaced pattern atop the bed.

Spacings suggested in this section are what I use in my garden. They grow well-developed vegetables in moderately well-fertilized soil enjoying abundant irrigation (except where otherwise specified). In southern Oregon or northern California, where heat-loving species grow faster and larger, gardeners might want to space out plantings a bit more. Those to the north could grow their heat-lovers a little closer together because they'll not get as large. Lovers of giant beets can increase my recommended spacings; those who like little beets can decrease them. The same is true for cabbage heads, which will vary a great deal in size according to soil fertility and the amount of space each plant has to grow in.

Of course, there are limits. Increasing plant spacing more than 33 percent beyond what this book recommends will probably make purposeless gaps in the bed. Decreasing spacings by more than one-third may be all right for some crops, but not at all for others. Lettuce, for example— especially heading types—will not develop properly when crowded. Competing carrots do not make good roots; radishes don't bulb. Densely grown bush beans, on the other hand, will make larger yields of slightly smaller pods. This may be acceptable in a postage-stamp back-yard garden if the gardener doesn't mind spending a lot more time harvesting.

If you're a novice gardener, try my recommendations and see what happens. You can always make adjustments next year.

I recommend only organic fertilizers, most frequently the complete organic fertilizer blend given in Chapter 2. It is more than adequate. Sometimes variations on the blend are suggested to raise or lower the amount and speed of release for different nutrients. Fertilizer is best applied twice: first broadcast and tilled into the growing bed, and then banded beside or below seeds or transplants. Occasionally, I recommend sidedressing (sprinkling fertilizer over the ground and raking it in shallowly). When I advise broadcasting fertilizer before sowing or transplanting, about one gallon of complete organic fertilizer per 100 square feet of growing bed will be sufficient unless otherwise stated.

For each vegetable in this chapter, I suggest specific varietal choices. Some varieties are widely sold and easily available, and for those no sources will be given. Other varieties are rarer. The following abbreviations are used to indicate seed sources:

ABL—Abundant Life Seed Foundation
BUR—W. Atlee Burpee Company
HAR—Harris Seed Company
JSS—Johnny's Selected Seeds
NIC—Nichols Garden Nursery
STK—Stokes
TSC—Territorial Seed Company
T&M—Thompson & Morgan

The seed business changes rapidly: new varieties are constantly being developed; old ones fall out of favor and disappear. Much of what is available in 1988, as this section is being written, may not be sold three years from now. For that reason I also explain how to select varieties.

Solanums

Solanums are semitropical or tropical plants that we in the Northwest grow as frost-sensitive annuals. Here, the Solanaceae family must be coddled and rushed into maturity before summer's end. In the tropics, some solanums are perennials, making a continuous yield as long as the grower continues to restore the soil exhausted by their heavy bearing. I knew a Fijian home gardener who had a five-year-old eggplant "tree" that was mulched with chicken manure several times a year, and I once saw a vigorous three-year-old tomato vine in Los Angeles that had been cut back each fall and nursed over two winters under a sheet of clear plastic.

Very intolerant to cool conditions, *especially in the seedling stage*, solanums must be raised under climate-controlled conditions until they have three or four true leaves. Were tomato seeds to be sown outdoors, germination might not be possible until mid- to late May; peppers might not sprout outside until mid-June. Though growth might be rapid after direct seeding, the first ripe peppers would not appear until the end of summer at best; direct-seeded early tomato varieties might begin to ripen fruit by late August. That's why maritime Northwest Solanaceae are given a six- to eight-week head start and then transplanted; this way, we can enjoy two to three months of harvest in a climate far to the north of this family's natural range.

Unless the weather is really warm and sunny and the nights stay above

55°F, peppers and eggplants grow very slowly and may even suffer permanent damage. In the Willamette, it doesn't warm up that much until mid-June. The key to success with peppers and eggplants (and melons and cucumbers, too) is to delay planting until the weather really suits the crop. Some cabbage years, "stable night temperatures above 55°F" does not describe the maritime Northwest summer at all.

One year I saw an amazing demonstration of how poorly these tropical species are adapted to our region. It was the first year I built a super-duper extra-large hot frame equipped with a fully adjustable, thermostatically controlled heating cable. I quickly discovered that solanaceous plants Grew at an amazing rate if I turned up the soil temperature to 78°F instead of the usual 70°F. My peppers responded by making huge, lush leaves such as I had not seen since I left California. I planted them out in mid-June as 18-inch-tall bushes in gallon pots, bearing half-sized fruit. The weather was warmer than average that summer, but the growth rate immediately dropped, and fruit-set and leaf-size declined to half what they had been in the hot frame! All that changed was that the nighttime lows were dropping into the 50s; in the bottom-heated frame, air temperature at night had never fallen below 65°F. If the summer had been a cool one, I'm sure those soft beauties would have gone into total shock and stopped growing, probably for the entire summer. In a heated greenhouse, peppers will readily Grow to a bushy four-foot height in one season!

Many gardeners don't fully appreciate this relationship between temperature and growth, thinking of growth as the effect of soil fertility, and thus doctor up reticent solanums with more fertilizer. This can be destructive. A slow-growing plant has little use for more nutrients. Since the plant can't build new leaf tissue with unneeded fertilizer, nutrients concentrate in the vascular system and can reach toxic concentrations, stunting the plant and preventing any further growth. A wiser response would be to first erect a cloche over solanums and then fertilize when they're growing fast.

Being tropical plants, solanum seedlings can be easily shocked by cold conditions. Minor shocks stop growth for a day or two. Severe, repeated shocks will stunt plants and prevent rapid growth from ever occurring even if temperatures become virtually ideal. Cold soil can be a shock to newly transplanted seedlings used to greenhouse conditions. Depending on the species, nighttime lows between 40°F and 50°F are shocking. Solanums can be hardened to become somewhat more tolerant to low temperatures—though not very much more tolerant. Raising quality transplants means walking a tightrope between hardening them off as fast as possible and not shocking them in the process. It is much better to delay transpanting solanums than to risk severe temperature shocks. Busy gardeners who buy transplants are advised to purchase pepper and egg- plant seedlings in mid-May, repot the seedlings in large (four- to six-inch) pots that will hold enough moisture to not need constant tending, harden them off in a crude cold frame for a few weeks and *wait until the nights warm up before transplanting.*

Solanums prefer soil with a pH of about 6.0, but they will grow fine between 5.5 and 7.0. All are fairly heavy feeders; however, overabundant nitrogen will promote too much vegetative growth while reducing fruit set. One moderate feeding of complete organic fertilizer below the trans- plants when they're set out will provide about six weeks of high fertility levels, perfect while the seedlings make rapid growth and begin flower- ing and fruit set. Additional fertilizer broadcast and tilled into the grow- ing bed before transplanting will provide a healthy background level through the entire summer.

Solanums are generally self-fertile. Some occasional crossing may occur in peppers and eggplants, but isolations of 20 feet are sufficient to pre- vent most unwanted crosses. Hybridization of solanums will markedly in- crease vigor and yield, though open-pollinated tomatoes and peppers will yield adequately in most of the maritime Northwest. In marginal areas where weather barely suits the species, that extra bit of hybrid vigor can make a considerable difference, particularly with eggplants and peppers.

Eggplants (*Solanum melongena*)

When in its seedling stage, this species is the most temperature- sensitive of the garden Solanaceae, requiring the warmest conditions to sprout and make initial vegetative growth. However, once eggplants have four or five true leaves and have hardened off a bit, they will produce more foliage than peppers under poor conditions. But cool nights are con- trary to fruiting, and in most areas of the maritime Northwest eggplant needs artificially warmed night temperatures to achieve good fruit-set and develop full-sized fruit. South of Longview, Washington, a black plastic mulch is sufficient, but along the coast and in the rest of Washington State, the use of large cloches or a greenhouse would probably quadruple the yield of even the earliest and most chill-tolerant variety.

Culture: Raise transplants like peppers (see Chapter 6, Buying and Raising Transplants). But be more cautious about hardening off eggplant seedlings. In the Willamette, eggplant seedlings may be set out on June

10 most years. A few weeks before transplanting, fertilize, till and then lay a sheet of black plastic over the entire bed. Anchor the sheet with soil along the edges, taking care to leave as much plastic exposed to the sun as possible. Cut small holes in the plastic on about 24-inch centers, then work from one-quarter to one-half cup complete organic fertilizer into the soil below each hole. The plastic soaks up solar energy, raising soil temperatures a few degrees and increasing the radiation of heat from soil below the plants at night, which creates a slightly warmer micro-climate—a little difference that makes all the difference. If growth slows during August while weather conditions are still sunny and warm, feed with liquid fertilizer to provoke renewed growth. New fruit will be set only while the plant is making vegetative growth.

Garden planning: A healthy European variety such as Dusky Hybrid will produce four to six large fruits in a season. It might yield three times that much in California. Japanese and other small-fruited types will produce 15 to 20 fruits each. I usually grow three to four plants each summer. Eggplants follow nicely in succession behind early peas or overwintered green-manure favas.

Insects and disease: Healthy eggplants are rarely bothered by anything but low temperatures and lack of nutrients. Problems after mid-September are probably symptoms of overall constitutional weakening caused by decreasing light intensity and cooler nights, and should be ignored.

Harvest: The fruits are best picked while slightly immature, before much seed development has occurred—when the fruit has stopped enlarging rapidly but the skin is still shiny and thin. About mid-September, the plants cease growth and fruit-set. At this time, harvest all well-developed fruit to take a burden off the weakening plant. The smallest fruits may be left on the bush in hopes that sunny warm temperatures will prevail into October, allowing further development of fruit already set.

Saving seed: Eggplants are almost completely self-pollinated, but an occasional extraordinarily energetic bee does effect crosses. Purity can be ensured by a 20-foot separation between varieties. Seeds mature after fruits reach full size and the skin has toughened. Harvest the overmature fruit, crush it into pulp and wash the heavier seeds free of the lighter pulp. Finally, dry the seeds thoroughly on a newspaper at room temperature. If open-pollinated varieties were productive in our gardens, saving seed would be that simple. However, with the exception of a very few Japanese types, only hybrid varieties are vigorous enough to set and ripen fruit west of the Cascades.

Varieties: Only a few early hybrid varieties consistently produce much fruit, the best of them being the widely available Dusky Hybrid. Early Bird (TSC) makes slightly smaller fruit than Dusky and ripens a week or two sooner. Johnny's varietal offerings change rapidly, but the company's eggplants are generally excellent here. Early Black Egg (TSC) is an extremely early open-pollinated type with smallish pear-shaped fruit (in fact, it's the only open-pollinated variety I know of that's adapted to our region). Short Tom (TSC, T&M) is a Japanese hybrid with very small but very early traditional Oriental cucumber-shaped fruit. Be quite wary of other varieties. If you want to experiment, make sure the variety matures at least as quickly as Dusky. Even if grown with black plastic mulch, old standards like Black Beauty may produce big, healthy-looking bushes in this climate, but they won't set fruit in our cool nights.

Peppers (*Capsicum annuum*)

Climatic variations make quite a difference in pepper varietal performance. South of Drain, Oregon, almost any variety will do all right. In the Willamette, the more tropical small-fruited types like Serrano and many familiar heat-demanding California market bells do not do well at all. North of Longview, Washington, and along the coast, peppers will not grow very well outside of cloches or greenhouses. Small-fruited pepper varieties are generally somewhat earlier and easier to grow than bell types.

Culture: See Chapter 6 for raising transplants. Nighttime lows under 50°F will shock seedling peppers, but hardening off can improve that only by a degree or two. Though slightly benefited by black plastic mulch, peppers will usually do all right without any forcing if transplanting is delayed until mid-June in the Willamette. In cool summers, I've had much better luck growing peppers under tunnel cloches or Reemay-like fabrics until they start ripening fruit. Transplant on 18- to 24-inch centers, depending on how warm the summers are where you garden. Work one-quarter to one-half cup complete organic fertilizer into the soil below each seedling. If growth slows before mid-September and the weather is still warm and sunny, dose the plants once with liquid fertilizer to see if it will provoke a growth response—if it does, side-dress with a sprinkling of complete organic fertilizer, shallowly raked or hoed into the soil around the plants.

Garden planning: In our cool climate, bell types usually produce six to 10 fruits per plant. Small-fruited varieties make dozens.

Insects and diseases: Rarely a problem. Heavy infestations of symphylans may stunt peppers.

Harvest: Many varieties change color from green to red or yellow as they ripen, acquiring thicker, juicier walls and a sweeter taste in the process. This is also true of thick-walled hot peppers such as Jalapeño and Hot Wax. If thin-walled hot varieties such as Cayenne and Red Chile, which are intended to be used dried, have not ripened by summer's end, harvest the entire plant before frost or excessive rains rot the fruit and hang upside-down in a cool, dim place. All the mature fruit will ripen and dry simultaneously.

Saving seed: Allow the fruit to color fully before harvest to obtain fully developed, high-germination seed. Spread the seed on a sheet of paper to dry fully at room temperature before storage. Peppers have a somewhat higher likelihood of crossing than eggplant. Varieties should be given 50 feet of isolation—especially if you're growing sweet and hot types in the garden at the same time.

Varieties: There are great differences in how varieties grow and make fruit under cool conditions. Very tropical types such as Serrano will hardly grow at all; standard California market varieties such as Cal Wonder, Keystone Resistant Giant and Yolo Wonder will produce plenty of vegetation but be very late to mature fruit and usually yield poorly, though these types would do better in southern Oregon. Staddons Select (TSC, STK) is the best open-pollinated bell type I know of. Golden Bell, Golden Summer and Gypsy are large-fruited sweet hybrids that do well. That extra bit of hybrid vigor shows to good advantage in the maritime Northwest. New hybrid pepper varieties come and go in a flash, and peppers fruit in all sorts of colors and flavors. Pepper lovers should experiment freely, but try only varieties as early as or earlier than the successful bell varieties mentioned above. Stokes has a large selection of early peppers of all sorts but also sells many late varieties that won't make it here. Johnny's and Territorial are safe sources to play around with—nothing in their catalogs will be too late. Generally the earlier small-fruited peppers mature well enough. My favorite hots for sauce are Surefire (TSC), which is a hybrid Hungarian Hot Wax, and Hot Portugal (TSC, HAR), a variety similar to Cayenne Long Thick.

Tomatoes (*Lycopersicon esculentum*)

Tomato seedlings, the most vigorous of the garden Solanaceae, can grow and set fruit even under fairly cool conditions. However, getting that fruit to ripen before summer's over is not always so certain. Careful varietal selection and proper handling are vital if you wish to harvest more than buckets of green tomatoes.

Culture: The earlier fruit set can occur, the sooner tomatoes ripen. The gardener can do two things to encourage early fruit set. One, choosing the correct variety, is discussed below. The other is to transplant a well-hardened seedling so no growth check occurs. See Chapter 6 for how to produce tomato seedlings or harden off ones from the garden center.

Tomato harvests increase geometrically over the summer. If the harvest were weighed each week, pickings might go: one pound the first week, two pounds the second, four pounds the third, eight the fourth, 16 pounds the fifth week, and so on. The really big harvests come at the end of the season—you get them by having the vines start ripening at the earliest possible moment. I get my earliest and largest harvest by growing eight- to 10-week-old hard seedlings in a cold frame. I have them ready to transplant into a large tunnel cloche about three weeks before the last usual frost date and grow them in the cloche until the entire bed is a green mass of tomatoes pushing against the walls. This usually occurs by July. Once I remove the cloche, ripe fruits start appearing almost immediately, giving me eight to 10 weeks of steadily increasing harvest. I think a little extra effort leading to ripe tomatoes in early July is worth it. If the harvest doesn't start until August, there are not many weeks left before the vines fall apart from weakening sun, cool nights and fall rains.

Determinate types usually ripen their first fruit very quickly and grow compact bushes that tend to bear heavily for a month or so and then taper off. With our short ripening season, tapering off doesn't matter much. Determinate varieties cannot be trellised or pruned and don't benefit much from staking, as they have been bred to hold most of their fruit up off the ground. Some tomatoes are lost to slugs and rot or are overlooked by the picker, but these losses are more than offset by earlier ripening and ease of growing. Most determinate types should be spaced on two-foot centers, though some smaller varieties may be more closely spaced.

Indeterminate types yield the highest quality tomatoes, are usually a little later to mature, and make ever-expanding vines that never stop setting new fruit. These sorts can make quite a tangle if allowed to sprawl on the ground, in which case they should be spaced out four feet apart in all directions. Indeterminate varieties are usually propped up in cages or grown on trellises of one sort or another. My favorite system for growing indeterminate varieties came from the English glasshouse trade. I plant seedlings out early under a large tunnel cloche in two parallel rows down a four-foot-wide raised bed, the rows 36 inches apart, the seedlings 18 inches apart in the row. When the bushes are about 18 inches tall, the cloche is removed. Seven feet above the two rows of seedlings I then erect two parallel horizontal beams (2x4s) supported by posts or "X" frameworks about eight feet apart. Every nine inches along the beams, I tie on and drop a length of stout bailing twine—two strings for each plant—and tie the twine loosely to the base of each seedling. Then the plant is pruned back to two leaders, the terminal one and a single vigorous one on the side. As each leader grows, it is guided round and round the twine; new leaders are pinched off as they appear. This management only takes a few minutes each week. If a vine reaches the top, it is allowed to drape over the beam and return toward earth (most years, six to seven feet of vine growth is all I get before the season ends). Trellising and training produce slightly earlier ripening, slightly tastier and much larger blemish-free fruit.

In addition to fertilizing the bed, I band complete organic fertilizer, one-quarter to one-half cup worked into the soil below each seedling when transplanting. If growth slows during August, I broadcast a little more fertilizer around the plants and rake or hoe it in shallowly, or feed with liquid fertilizer.

Garden planning: One well-grown 100-square-foot bed, half in early determinate varieties and half in trellised indeterminate varieties, keeps my family, many visitors and some of our friends eating bowls of fresh tomatoes during the season. If extensive canning is intended, another bed of the same size should produce about 250 pounds of ripe processing tomatoes from determinate vines.

Transplant tomatoes into a bed that grew overwintered green manure; when the vines begin to fall apart, sprinkle crimson clover or poppy seed on the bed to establish a winter ground cover.

Insects and diseases: Flea beetles are notorious for attacking newly transplanted seedlings, though well-hardened plants are never touched. Rotenone or Red Arrow sprayed every two or three days will protect soft seedlings until they harden off, come out of shock and begin growth. Tomato hornworms and fruitworms (rarely found west of the Cascades) can be easily killed with Bt.

Most of the diseases tomatoes have been bred to resist are found only in commercial tomato-growing areas such as Florida or California and are no cause for concern to the gardener. Tomato late blight, a fungus that killed virtually every maritime Northwest tomato plant in August 1983, comes about when the vines experience too many weeks of cool, damp conditions—which both weakens tomatoes and promotes the fungus. Though farmers have chemical fungicides in their *batterie de cuisine* to prevent the disease, there is no cure once late blight strikes. There is no known varietal resistance to the blight, though scattered plants did survive in 1983, mostly ones located in very favorable microclimates such as against a white-painted wall under a roof overhang that kept off most of the rains. I'm sure we'll see late blight again in some future cabbage year.

Two problems with tomatoes *appear* to be diseases but aren't. If large amounts of water are added to very dry soil, tomatoes often respond by curling their leaves, and the blossom ends of fruits may blacken and rot. Tomato leaf curl and blossom-end rot can be prevented with proper irrigation, maintaining a steady moisture supply and liming soil to make sufficient calcium available. End-rot occurs when moisture fluctuations interfere with calcium uptake. Adding lime to complete organic fertilizer blends will reduce or eliminate blossom-end rot.

Harvest: There are three cultural practices that enhance ripening. Determinate varieties tend to grossly overbear; thinning, by removing more than half the flower clusters from determinate tomatoes, lightens the fruit load. This permits the vines to ripen bigger, better-flavored, earlier fruit. (Overbearing varieties of apple trees are similarly thinned—if they weren't, the fruit would be tiny and tasteless.) The gardener can also encourage complete ripening of all the fruit by removing virtually *all* the flower clusters and immature tomatoes beginning about September 1, forcing the vines to ripen their remaining fruit load. A third trick is to attempt to kill the vines by withholding water, starting mid- to late August, depending on how water-retentive the soil is. If the vines can be put under severe moisture stress, they'll ripen their entire fruit load as they die. However, nature sometimes defeats this strategy by sending late-summer rains, which often cause the vines to fall apart and become diseased.

Green tomatoes, if harvested when full-sized but not yet ripe and brought in before being touched by frost, will ripen in the house. We usually bring in several buckets just before the first frost. These keep us in ripe tomatoes for six to eight more weeks. Though there are many involved systems promising more success with indoor ripening of green fruit and even a special Burpee variety that produces green tomatoes especially for ripening after the frost, we've found that if buckets of blemish-free, clean fruit of any slicing variety are kept fairly cool and are checked every few days for coloring fruit, most of the tomatoes ripen and very few rot.

Saving seed: Tomatoes are invariably self-pollinated, with no danger of unwanted crossing. To save seed from open-pollinated varieties, simply remove the pulp from a few fully ripe tomatoes (overripe, slug-eaten ones hiding under thick foliage are ideal) and place the pulp in a drinking glass or mason jar on the kitchen counter. Allow the mash to ferment. After three to five days, the solids rise to the top and the seeds settle to the bottom. Slowly run water into the glass to float off the pulp, leaving the seeds. Pour the seeds into a strainer, wash them thoroughly in cold water and dry on a sheet of paper. The only trick to obtaining high-germination seeds is to conduct the fermentation speedily at a temperature over 70°F. Cold fermentations lasting more than one week often result in dead seed.

Varieties: Any variety described in a seed catalog as needing over 72 days to maturity (or longer than Fantastic Hybrid) will not likely ripen heavily north of Drain, Oregon. Heat-loving beefsteak types and "main season" varieties especially do not do well in the maritime Northwest. This is because cool nights can prevent pollination, causing the fruit to abort; ripening is also retarded. There is a considerable varietal difference about what constitutes "too cool."

One very interesting group of open-pollinated varieties was developed for maritime conditions by Dr. Jim Baggett. Starting with a determinate parthenocarpic Russian tomato variety (one that sets seedless fruit when cool nights prevent pollination), Baggett bred a series of bushy little varieties that set and ripen in the Willamette *weeks earlier than any other early varieties*. These include Oregon 11, Santiam and Gold Nugget (TSC, NIC) and Oregon Spring (TSC, NIC, JSS). I consider the best-flavored firm-meated slicer we can grow to be Fantastic Hybrid (TSC, STK), though others including Ed Hume prefer Pic Red, bred and supplied by Harris. Pic Red probably is better for the Puget Sound area. Other reliable varieties include Early Cascade, Bonny Best, IPB (ABL), Kootenai (TSC) and Willamette (NIC). Popular "mid-season" hybrids such as Celebrity, Floramerica, Big Boy and Better Boy, though billed as only a few days later than Fantastic in the east, are much later west of the Cascades and tend to be disappointing. Old eastern standards with superior home-garden flavor, such as Marglobe and Rutgers, never ripened fruit for me at Lorane. Johnny's open-pollinated varieties sometimes don't set fruit very well here—I don't know why. Rob Johnston claims nights at Albion, Maine, are just as cool as those in the Willamette, but they can't be. ABL has several local heirloom open-pollinated types. The major catalogs present a bewildering assortment. Beware, especially of Burpee's—their tomatoes get rave reviews in national garden magazines but they're bred where nights are warm.

Gardeners who make tomato sauce or paste using anything but varieties bred for that purpose may be practicing false economy. Salad or slicing varieties have a very high water content: a potful of salad tomatoes cooks down to almost nothing; slicing varieties make watery whole-pack stewing tomatoes. Canning varieties, which have little juice and a high percentage of solids, cook down rapidly into thick sauce and hold up for whole-pack. Such standard varieties as Nova, Roma, Heinz 1350 and San

Marzano, which are carried by most major seed companies, don't ripen nearly as heavily as Chico III, Sprinter, Ropreco, Heinz 2653VF and Peto #95.

Most small-fruited varieties are fairly early, though Yellow Pear and Yellow Plum are almost as late as most of the old large-fruited yellow types. Though Golden Jubilee produces absolutely the most delicious, rich-flavored, big yellow tomatoes, many summers it fails to ripen much fruit. Golden Delight (TSC, STK) and Taxi (JSS) are much earlier and nearly as tasty. Most earlier red-cherry varieties are prolific here. If you like cherry tomatoes, try Jim Baggett's Gold Nugget (TSC, NIC) for a unique mild flavor and an abundance of early fruit. In fact, Gold Nugget is usually the first ripe fruit in my garden, year after year.

Legumes

Lustily growing legumes create their own nitrates and abundant organic matter when grown as green manures. Nitrogen fertilizer is not needed to provoke lush legume growth—in fact, high soil nitrate levels force legumes to become consumers, preventing nitrogen fixation. Legumes do feed heavily on potassium, phosphorus, calcium and magnesium. There's an old farmers' adage that goes, "Feed your phosphate to your clover, feed your clover to your corn (plow it in), and you can't go wrong." If the plot has been adequately limed and manured within the past two or three years, legumes will usually flourish; infertile soils will also require a phosphate-rich fertilizer. Bone meal is the best single fertilizer for legumes, because it contains large amounts of readily available phosphorus and a little nitrogen. The 4:1:1:1 complete organic fertilizer mix I recommend (see Chapter 2) contains too much high-nitrogen seed meal for optimum legume growth. It overstimulates vegetative growth, makes legumes get "leggy" and may actually reduce pod set. A better ratio for legumes would be 1:1:1:1.

Legumes do not actually make nitrates from air by themselves, but in cooperation with certain specialized soil bacteria, which form little pinkish nodules along legume roots visible to the naked eye. Without the bacteria, legumes become consumers rather than makers of nitrogen. If soil contains a reasonable amount of organic matter (most soils in the maritime Northwest not in commercial row crops do contain 4 to 5 percent organic matter), it will also support active populations of all sorts of soil organisms, including those that colonize legume roots. Dead soils, chemically farmed for years, may have had most of their organic matter burned out by nitrogen fertilizers. In that case, even though the gardener adds manure or compost, it may take several years to reestablish a healthy balanced soil microlife; legumes at first may not encounter the necessary bacteria and may require inoculation.

The first thing I do when investigating poorly growing legumes is to pull out a plant and carefully inspect its root system for nodules. Then, regardless of what I find, I usually side-dress with some fertilizer to save the existing crop, and seriously consider increasing the organic matter content before I grow any other crop. Fine clay soils, which tend to be airless even when organic matter has been increased somewhat, retard the development of nitrates around legume roots. In that case, a nitrogen-rich fertilizer may also be needed.

The amount of nitrogen fixed by legumes is not inconsequential. Garden beans and peas will fix 60 to 80 pounds of nitrogen per acre. That's enough to feed a succeeding crop of small winter grain, beets, carrots or other low-demand vegetables. Clovers fix more—up to 100 pounds per acre in the root system and stubble alone, with another 25 or 30 pounds in the aboveground vegetation. In many cases, that's enough nitrogen to grow a reasonable yield of sweet corn, lettuce or squash. The most amazing nitrogen-fixer of all is the fava bean. Overwintered favas will create over 200 pounds per acre, often enough to grow the more demanding brassicas. If tilled under before the seed is set, legume vegetation is so nitrogen-rich and tender that it will rot completely and allow sowing of the succeeding crop within two weeks. Non-legume green manures can take three or more weeks to thoroughly rot; if overly mature and woody when tilled in, they can retard sowing by a month.

Bush Beans (*Phaseolus vulgaris*)

Bush snap beans, which don't need trellising and can be mechanically harvested, were developed mostly for the convenience of canneries. Their taste (and probably their nutritional content) can't equal that of the pole bean because the crowded leaves on bush beans are layered on top of each other and compete for light; the leaves of pole beans are widely separated so almost every one can gather direct, unfiltered light. It is the effectiveness of the food manufacturing area (leaf) compared to the amount of pod production that determines how much nutrition (which we usually perceive as flavor) is available to be stored in each pod. In this respect, bush beans are like the Sub Arctic and certain other highly determinate, extra-early tomato varieties that have little leaf area, yet set a huge quantity of tomatoes that end up relatively tasteless. Some varieties of lower-yielding bush beans do have pretty rich flavor, but when I grow both kinds, the family rarely bothers with the bush varieties.

Culture: Like other species from the tropics, *P. vulgaris* beans only grow in warm soils; most varieties will not germinate at all if soil temperatures are below 60°F for long. In the Willamette, the first sowing can usually be made in early May, though on dark-colored, light-textured loams that heat up fast in spring it may be possible to sow a little earlier. At frosty Lorane, I had to wait until June 1. Fertilize each 100-square-foot bed with one-half to one gallon of bone meal or one gallon of low-nitrogen complete organic fertilizer. Sow bush beans 1½ inches deep, four to six seeds per foot, in rows 18 inches apart. After the seedlings are established and growing well, thin from six to eight inches apart in the row. Should a spell of chilly or rainy weather follow, that sowing may not germinate; if it does eventually sprout, the seedlings may be weakened and won't grow fast for a while, even if the sun returns. Standing there with only two puny leaves, waiting for warmth, shocked bean seedlings are defenseless against the Mexican bean beetle, which can rapidly nibble leaves down to nubbins. In good weather with decent nutrition, new bean seedlings will outgrow normal predation. When making early sowings, I try to outguess the weather and sow just before a dry sunny period. Sometimes the best thing to do when early bean sowings get into trouble is to immediately replant. The later planting may encounter nothing but clear sailing and end up maturing beans as early as the first sowing—outgrowing and outyielding the earlier attempt.

Garden planning: Bush beans are bred to produce intensely for a few weeks and then taper off. If a continuous harvest for the table is desired, make several sowings three or four weeks apart. The last one should be made in early July to begin yielding in early or mid-September. For earliest harvest, beans may be started under a cloche about three weeks earlier than normal and grown under protection for several weeks after the last usual frost date. Follow an early bed of beans with late brassicas (kale, rutabaga, Chinese cabbage, overwintered broccoli or cauliflower) or fall-garden salad greens (lettuce, spinach, corn salad or endive). The harvest from 50 square feet of raised bed provides our family with all the fresh beans we can eat, plus as many as we feel like picking to give away.

Insects and diseases: Mexican bean beetles can be controlled with rotenone or Red Arrow, sprayed every few days. If beetles are still doing too much damage once the plants have a few leaves, consider boosting growth with liquid fertilizer or with a little complete organic fertilizer broadcast around the bean plants and shallowly raked or hoed in. Beans are sensitive to several diseases that are spread by touching damp plants. Wait until the sun has evaporated the morning dew before handling beans. Most new varieties are disease-resistant.

Harvest: Bean bushes are delicate and easily damaged by handling, so remove the pods gently. And pick frequently—keeping the plants carefully picked will extend their production period. Pods about four-fifths of full size are more tender and flavorful.

Saving seed: Natural crosses between varieties are extremely rare, so isolation is unnecessary. Neither is there much variation in individual plants, though some varieties do throw frequent mutations. Select for plants with the best initial appearance that produce the most pods the soonest, or that seem to have the best raw flavor—and do not harvest these. Allow the pods to form seed, and permit it to mature and begin to dry down. If the seed dries completely on the bush, germination and vigor will be higher, but if the garden is watered frequently, it's better to pull the plants as soon as the first pods are fairly dry, then hang small bunches in the shade under cover to finish. If the pods are not dry by the time September's rains and heavy dews begin to lower seed germination, pull the plants, finish indoors and hope for the best. (Also consider growing an earlier variety next year.) Then thresh out the seed. (See "Saving seed" under Field Beans for an improved method.)

Varieties: Green, "blue," yellow, filet, flageolet, haricot vert, Dutch, English, Guatemalan, purple-mottled, longpod, fatpod—just about every one of the dozens of varieties of *P. vulgaris* bush snap beans I've grown has yielded well enough, though some are higher-yielding than others. Some pods get tough and fibrous quickly while others hold on the bush and retain good eating quality quite a bit longer. Feel free to experiment without much risk. There seems to be little difference in flavor between varieties, especially after cooking. There are much more noticeable differences in the flavors of raw pods. I prefer Blue Lake types. Blue Lake Bush OSU 1604B (TSC) has long been the variety grown for Willamette Valley canneries—and for good reason. The pod is very slow to develop seed or strings and remains tender even after it's quite large. Blue Lake Bush 274 makes a larger, more vigorous plant, but the pods form seed and strings and get tough quickly. Very slow seed-development lowers seed yields, so the wholesale price of BLB 274 seed is quite a bit less than BLB 1604B, which is probably why so many garden-seed companies sell 274. There are many other excellent proprietary Blue Lake strains; the seed catalog will probably say if the variety is similar to or derived from Blue Lake. Johnny's has a new one called Easy Pick that is becoming widely grown for Willamette Valley canneries.

Purple-podded types, which turn green when cooked, are slightly more vigorous sprouters in cool soil and make better growth under cool conditions, and should be considered seriously for early sowings and in coastal and cooler microclimates. I don't think Royalty Purple Pod is the equal of a new variety called Royal Burgundy. Bush wax beans don't become really waxy the way some old pole wax types did; they're only a different color—same flavor.

Horticultural Beans (*P. vulgaris*)

These are bush varieties bred not for tender pods, but for large, rapidly developing seeds, good to eat in the "green" stage. The pods are picked when the seeds are fully formed but not dried down. Horticultural beans are usually very early, and most varieties can be used first as snap beans (though because they're bred for seeds, the pods are on the tough side and rapidly develop strings as the seeds form), then as shell beans and finally as dry beans. Horticultural beans are grown just like bush beans.

Varieties: Taylor's or French Horticultural are virtually identical varieties. Taylor's is known regionally as Speckled Bays or Bayos or by any of 20 other names. Black Coco (TSC), a French Horticultural variety with pretty good snap bean pods, is currently my favorite dry bean. Johnny's offers a very wide selection.

Pole Snap Beans (*P. vulgaris*)

Pole beans take a week or so longer to start producing than bush types, but they go on producing all summer, ultimately yielding quite a bit more for the space occupied. In this respect, pole beans are to bush beans as indeterminate tomatoes are to determinate tomatoes. Their vining habit has not been civilized into a compact bush, and their spread-out leaves trap more light and create much more flavorful pods—and likely more nutrition, too.

Culture: Pole varieties must be grown on a trellis, fence or strings. Today, all cannery production uses bush varieties; the traditional Willamette Valley commercial trellising method for Blue Lake Pole beans was to zigzag a string every eight inches up and down between two stout parallel wires, one a few inches above the ground, the other about seven feet up. The pioneers used skinny fir poles with the bark left on, often set up as tripods lashed together at the top, and grew a few vines up each pole. Along a trellis, sow the seeds 1½ inches deep, one seed every four inches, and thin to one seedling per string when well established. Fertilize with about one gallon bone meal or low-nitrogen organic fertilizer blend per 100 feet of trellis.

Garden planning: Most pole varieties yield continuously to the end of summer, so only one sowing is required. Fifty row feet or two parallel rows on a four- by 25-foot raised bed produce more beans than my family can eat fresh. Serious bean fanciers might consider a single early sowing of bush beans to tide the kitchen over until the later pole varieties start bearing.

Insects and diseases: Same as bush beans.

Harvest: It is essential to keep pole varieties picked clean. Allowing even a few pods to form seed will reduce further pod set. If gently and completely harvested, most pole varieties will produce until the end of September. Like all snap beans, the pods are better-flavored and more tender if picked on the immature side, with the exception of Kentucky Wonder Wax, which gets waxier with age.

Saving seed: Same as bush beans. For highest vigor, pick off individual pods when the seeds within are nearly dried.

Varieties: Of the traditional varieties, Blue Lake Pole has the slowest seed and string development, with slightly longer pods than the bush varieties—this is the bean that made Willamette Valley canneries famous nationwide. Bush 1604B, though tasty for a bush variety, is insipid in comparison. Kentucky Wonder has a richer, beanier flavor. There are two Kentucky Wonder strains, brown- and white-seeded. The brown-seeded type has rapid seed and string development and is a good general-purpose variety for both snap and shell beans. The white-seeded type is slightly earlier to mature and has much slower seed and string development. I prefer the white. Kentucky Wonder Wax (TSC) is a unique variety with a tender, waxy texture and bland flavor. Burpee has two unique selections: Burpee's Golden, a yellow "wax" bean, and Romano, with an "Italian" flavor and rapidly developing, round shell beans used in traditional Italian soups. Lilly Miller, our regional seed-rack supplier, custom-produces Oregon Giant, an old, early maturing variety with huge, watery/tender, mild-flavored, mottled purplish-green pods and large, fast-developing seeds good for shell beans. Oregon Giant does tend to quit producing before the summer ends. Pole beans are still a commercial item in Europe, where gourmets discuss the finer points of vegetable quality. Dozens and dozens of specialty varieties exist there. I've grown many European sorts; though interesting, none are any better at this time than Blue Lake or Kentucky Wonder White Seeded. Thompson & Morgan has several in its catalog. Johnny's offers both improved and heirloom pole types.

Runner Beans
(*P. multifloris*, also known as *P. coccineus*)

This species is very popular in England, where people commonly think the snap beans (*P. vulgaris*) we like to eat do not have any flavor at all. And compared to runner beans, that's true. Runners produce thick, fuzzy pods with an intense beany flavor—too strong for pleasurable raw consumption. But cooked, they taste very rich and settle satisfyingly in my stomach like steak. I'd guess that the protein content of *P. multifloris* is much higher than ordinary snap beans. Like the Brits, I've come to relish runner beans.

Culture: Grow like pole beans. They tend to mature a bit later but grow well under cool conditions. The vines are a little more vigorous and run longer distances than *P. vulgaris* pole varieties.

Harvest: The better culinary varieties have very slow seed development, though the huge pods are much more tender if picked when three-quarters grown. Some varieties with very rapid seed development and huge seeds make better shell beans.

Saving seed: Unlike *P. vulgaris* pole beans, runner beans have some tendency to cross-pollinate, so seed savers should grow only one variety. Some have white flowers, some have red.

Varieties: Scarlet Runner is an old variety offered by many U.S. companies, but it tends toward fast seed development and tough, fibrous pods. It is often grown as an ornamental on trellises for its big sprays of showy red flowers. Scarlet Emperor (TSC) has much slower seed development, tender pods, a sweet full-bodied flavor and equally showy flowers. Thompson & Morgan offers many varieties, some bred to make extremely long fancy pods, both white- and red-flowered. Oregon Lima (ABL) is not a lima at all, but a white-flowered, white-seeded runner bean with rapid seed development, useful primarily as a shell bean.

Fava Beans (*Vicia faba*)

Large-seeded favas are faintly known to some Americans as "horse beans" and loved by the English as "broad beans." Their hardier small-seeded relatives are known to a few Americans as "bell beans," to the English as "tick beans" if spring-sown and as "winter beans" if fall-sown. Canadians, with their strong Commonwealth connection, are well acquainted with the species. Favas of all sorts should eventually become much better known to Americans west of the Cascades because the species is amazingly well adapted to our climate. All the major field crops of the maritime Northwest are grown over the winter, and favas are the only edible legume that has this potential.

Fava beans can taste pretty good. They are consumed in the green stage like peas or shell beans; dried favas are used for bean soups and *frijoles refritos*. But favas can also taste pretty bad. Favas tend toward bitterness, thick tough skins, bland mushy centers and a strong cooking odor. Unfortunately, Americans have had their opinion of the fava's worth poisoned; for many years the only readily available variety in the United States was Windsor—not bad eating during its short season as a shell bean, but awful when dried down and cooked like a dry bean. Windsor is also not winter-hardy this far north. There are much better varieties.

Culture: Favas freeze out anywhere from 6°F to 20°F, depending on the variety. The hardier ones may be overwintered and will mature dry seed without irrigation—a big advantage in the maritime Northwest. Overwintered varieties are sown between October 1 and November 15 after fall rains moisten the soil—the earlier the better. Less hardy sorts can only be spring-sown, during February and March. Very vigorous, favas generally don't need fertilizer when grown in built-up garden soil; as a field crop, their plot should be limed, treated with phosphate rock and perhaps a little fertilizer on poorer, heavy soils. *For spring-sown shell beans*, sow on raised garden beds, one seed every four inches, 1½ inches deep, in rows 18 inches apart. *For dry beans*, raise overwintered varieties if possible. Sow one seed every eight inches, rows 42 to 48 inches apart, and keep well weeded from spring until the seeds are drying down.

Garden planning: Shelling favas are finished in June, making their bed a good spot to grow salad greens or brassicas for fall harvest or overwintering. With small-seeded varieties, dry seed yields run as high as two tons per acre on fertile soil; without irrigation, as little as 200 row feet will fill a 50-pound sack. Large-seeded varieties don't yield nearly as well.

Insects and diseases: We don't have much experience with favas in North America yet. After growing dozens of fava varieties since 1979, I have noted no disease problems. I'm sure there are whole books about the diseases and pests of favas in England. Bean or pea weevils will chew chunks out of their leaves in spring, but this minor damage causes little loss of yield.

Harvest: Pods form in May and June, with shell beans ready by early June and the pods drying down by early July. Large-seeded varieties tend to fall over from the weight of the forming pods. It may be helpful to pinch the tops of large-seeded favas when they reach 18 to 24 inches tall, which encourages the plant to bush out from the base and produce a larger number of shorter stalks with less tendency to topple. Large-seeded varieties grown for dry seed are very forgiving about timely harvest: the seed is held tightly in hard, wrinkled-up pods that don't shatter; as well, July and early August are usually dry, so the seed may be harvested almost at one's leisure. Small-seeded varieties have more delicate pods. Once the seed has dried down, it will begin to shatter and fall on the ground. These sorts should be harvested as soon as possible. Spread the mostly dry stalks on a large tarp right in the fava patch, piled not more than 10 inches thick; allow the stalks to dry until they're crisp and black. If rain threatens before threshing, cover them with another large tarp. One sunny afternoon after the night's moisture has been baked out and the pods are really crisp, hold a "rain dance" on the stalks, breaking the seed free, or beat them with a flail or pair of thin sticks about the size of a policeman's baton. Winnow in a light breeze or in front of a window fan until the seed is clean. Two energetic adults can thresh and winnow 100 pounds of seed in about two hours.

Saving seed: See harvesting section. Favas do have some tendency to cross—about one in 2,000 seeds may be hybrid if more than one variety is grown. Different varieties should be separated by 100 feet or more.

Varieties: Almost all U.S. seed companies still offer Windsor, an old large-seeded, bitter-tasting, mealy-centered variety with a tough brown skin that's not hardy enough to overwinter (except perhaps in northern California or along the southern Oregon coast). Aquadulce Claudia (TSC) is a much hardier and better-flavored, light-colored, large-seeded type. Originally from Spain, where it is overwintered, it's hardy to about 12°F and will survive most Willamette winters. Another new variety has just been developed by Aprovecho, a non-profit foundation concerned with ecology in lesser developed countries, located near Cottage Grove, Oregon. Aprovecho Select Fava (ABL) is the best-tasting large-seeded variety I know of, though its absolute hardiness is uncertain because the variety was only discovered three or four years ago and we've had very mild winters since then.

Small-seeded Banner (TSC) is hardy to about 7°F and is used primarily as a green manure crop. Like Windsor, Banner is edible but far from choice—brown-seeded, bland-flavored, rather tough-skinned, somewhat strong-smelling (though that dissipates with cooking) and slightly bitter (the bitterness can be overcome with seasoning). Thompson & Morgan, typical of a British seed house, lists numerous fava varieties in its catalog. I have been growing and selecting from a broadly diversified Third World gene pool of overwintered small-seeded favas since 1982; in 1988, I finally isolated two delicious high-yielding individual plants. When I wrote this book I had three ounces of seed for each variety; half of it was planted in October 1988 for increase. Perhaps in a few years, our regional seed companies (TSC, ABL) will begin selling Umpqua, a fava bean I hope the entire maritime Northwest has been waiting for because it's a high-yielding, choicely edible culinary bean *and* green manure, all rolled up in one variety.

Field Beans (dry *P. vulgaris*)

Growing dry *P. vulgaris* beans is possible west of the Cascades, but dicey. September rarely comes with dry weather free of heavy dews, which means that in any area that must sow dry beans after early May harvest will be difficult. People living south of Drain, Oregon, will have a much easier time with field beans.

Culture: Grow like bush beans. *With irrigation,* sow seeds four inches apart in rows 24 inches apart. Thin when established to eight inches in the row. Stop watering when the first pods start drying down to force the rest of the seed load to ripen. *Without irrigation,* sow seeds as early as it's possible to get them to germinate, six inches apart in rows 42 to 48 inches apart. Thin when established to 12 inches in the row. *Keep extremely well-weeded.* Grown without irrigation, beans quickly come under moisture stress, which halts seed set and prompts earlier drying down.

Garden planning: Irrigated yields run around a ton per acre or 50 pounds per 1,000 square feet. Dryland yields are about 25 percent of that at best, unless we have a rainy summer (which may increase yield but can make harvesting difficult). That's why I've spent a lot of energy investigating the overwintered fava bean.

Insects and diseases: Same as bush beans.

Harvest: Harvest when 90 percent of the leaves have yellowed and the pods have dried, but before the pods begin to shatter. Pull the plants from dry earth, pile them on a large tarp and dry a few more days before threshing. That's how one harvests dry beans in Idaho or other areas where intense summer heat matures beans by September and where late summer remains dry and sunny. In most of the maritime Northwest, though, few varieties reach this stage of maturity before conditions deteriorate. Usually the plants have to be dried indoors, either bunched and hung or loosely stacked on a porch and carefully turned every few days. (Again, consider growing favas.) Threshing can be done with a flail or by banging the plants (held by the stems) against the inner wall of a 55-gallon drum. Winnow the seeds by slowly pouring them back and forth between two five-gallon buckets in a gentle breeze or in front of a window fan. If you've had problems with bean weevil larvae, freeze the seed for a week or two to kill the eggs or larvae. Don't freeze the seed you're saving to sow next year.

Saving seed: A certain degree of variation and mutation develops in all beans. Higher-quality seed stocks are maintained by selecting a few perfect plants each year, flagging them in the field, harvesting them separately and then increasing their seed for seed stock, carefully removing any off-type plants. For the highest possible quality, grow out the progeny of each selected plant in a separate row or section of row and then only save seed from those rows that appear perfectly uniform and have all the desirable traits selected for. This good seed may be "bulked" together and increased for stock seed. Careful purification like this is done each year by the highest-quality bean-seed growers. In the home garden, it might be done once in four or five years, if at all.

Varieties: Taylor's Horticultural is widely grown west of the Cascades because it is one of the earliest. Territorial sells a number of other very early varieties that I discovered while doing dry-bean trials at Lorane, including Red Beans, Soldier and Black Coco. These days, my dry bean of choice is Black Coco. Any variety from the supermarket will probably produce an acceptable yield, though it may not mature as early as one might like. Johnny's Selected Seeds and especially Abundant Life carry wide dry-bean assortments, concentrating on early maturity.

Lima Beans (*P. limensis*)

Despite trying almost every summer at Lorane since 1979, I have not yet succeeded with heat-loving limas, though I have been told numerous times that King of the Garden will succeed if started indoors and transplanted out. Even Geneva (JSS) with "cool soil tolerance" would not set seed at Lorane, though it did grow a better bush than any variety I've ever seen. Next year, I'll do a trial here at Elkton, where nights are warmer, and perhaps I'll say something more positive about limas when this book goes into its next edition.

Soybeans (*Glycine max*)

Soybeans are heat lovers. A few chill-tolerant varieties can make enough vegetative growth to yield modestly in the warmer parts of our region, though not likely north of Longview or along the cool coasts. Unlike other legume species, soybeans grow vegetatively for a while, and then cease growing when blooming and seed set begin. The larger the bush gets before flowering, the more seed will be set. Because we have to sow rather late and because vegetative growth is slow under our cool conditions, the bushes tend to be small when flowering starts, so yields are low. For this reason, soybeans aren't a good candidate for dry beans.

Culture: Sow a little later than snap beans because soybeans germinate poorly when soil temperature is below 65°F. Sow one inch deep, one seed per inch, in rows 12 to 18 inches apart. Thin to three or four inches apart in the row. Soybeans aren't vigorous sprouters and won't push through heavily crusted soil. Fertilize like *P. vulgaris*.

Garden planning: Triggered by photoperiod, soybeans mature all at once, usually in midsummer. Ten to 20 row feet will probably be plenty for eating fresh.

Insects and diseases: No known problems.

Harvest: The Japanese love to eat immature soybeans as we eat shell beans, clipping the entire bush at the base and steaming it for five to 10 minutes. Then they pick off the hot pods and pull them through their teeth, popping the green seeds out of the pod and into their mouths. It's much like eating popcorn. For dry beans, harvest promptly, as the seeds tend to shatter easily out of the pods.

Saving seed: Same as for bush beans, though maturity will be earlier.

Varieties: Soybean varieties are bred to match the photoperiod of a certain limited range of latitudes, flowering when daylength decreases to a certain point. I think there are seven daylength zones from the southern United States (zone one) to southern Canada (zone seven). The Willamette, at 45° latitude, is in zone six. Varieties bred for more southern latitudes flower much too late to mature. I've only had good results with Envy (JSS, ABL) and Fiskeby (ABL, STK). Prize (BUR) is much too late this far north.

Peas (*Pisum sativum*)

Almost any pea variety makes tasty and easy-to-grow maritime Northwest garden food *if planted early enough*. Unfortunately, when weather turns hot and sunny, an unavoidable regional pea disease called enation wipes out every traditional home-garden variety. Consequently, many of us think peas can't be planted early enough to beat the disease, and consider peas hard to grow. If that describes you, please think again. Raised beds permit very early sowing even on heavier soils, and there are now enation-resistant varieties that may be sown well after the earliest possible sowing date and harvested into summer. (See Chapter 3 for a thorough discussion of raised-bed gardening.)

Culture: Peas will sprout in very cold soils and grow under chilly conditions. But they are subject to numerous root diseases, especially when soils are wet and cold. So February sowings are usually successful only on coarse-textured, dark-colored soils. Even with raised beds, clayey soils should not be sown until March. Flat-ground-got-to-rototill-before-sowing gardeners cursed with clayey soils may not think they can plant anything until May, but with the new enation-resistant varieties, sowings as late as mid-May will still mature and taste good.

On raised beds, plant the seed thickly, several seeds per inch, about 1½ inches deep in rows 18 inches apart. Do not thin. Fertilize with a gallon of bone meal broadcast and worked into each 100 square feet of bed before sowing. Keep weeded until the peas fill in between rows and make a solid stand.

Older varieties needed trellises three to four feet high to enhance ease of harvest and prevent diseases caused by humidity trapped in a tangle of vines. Trellises can consist of strings, netting or chicken wire. I've had good luck getting very early sowings of climbing peas to grow when *thinly* interplanted with spring-sown green manure stands of small-seeded favas— the four-foot-tall favas support the peas, which climb up the bean stalks. The peas can be picked until they're done, and then the entire mass of vegetation is tilled in or composted. Most modern varieties are both disease-resistant and dwarf, and will not climb a trellis even if one is offered.

Garden planning: Dwarf varieties are *determinate,* meaning they yield for a short period and then quit. A single 100-square-foot bed supplies our family's fresh table needs for one to two weeks of intense harvesting. I sow a bed every few weeks from late February through mid-April. By the time the mid-April sowing has been harvested, the bush beans are coming on and we're tired of peas. *Indeterminate* climbing varieties keep on producing for a long time, but must be sown very early to mature before enation chops them down.

Peas leave the bed in particularly nice shape when they're pulled out. Any bed that has come over the winter bare, or that has held overwintered crops harvested by early April, is a good candidate for peas (or small-seeded favas). Even if the peas aren't needed for food, the vines make good green manures.

Dry soup peas should be grown in an area of the garden where irrigation can be avoided; plant less densely if irrigation is not available at all.

Insects and diseases: There are numerous pea diseases—wilts, yellows, mildews, streaks and enation, to name but a few. Most years they won't be a problem, but wet, damp, cloudy weather encourages disease. There's not much an organic gardener can do about pea diseases anyway, except to grow peas in raised beds to enhance soil drainage, fertilize well with bone meal to boost overall health and vigor and choose resistant varieties. West of the Cascades and south of Puget Sound, the worst trouble comes from enation. This disease is spread by the green peach aphid, which hatches out and begins travelling when the weather turns summery. Enation makes the pods look mottled and warty, ends flowering and pod set and then kills the vine. Many gardeners mistakenly think heat killed off the peas. None of the old home-garden standards is enation-resistant, though these may still be grown if sown early enough to mature before June's heat.

Harvest: Shelling peas are best picked on the small side, before the seeds have begun to get tough. Keeping the vines picked clean encourages somewhat longer production. Freezer types tend to form lots of pods that fill out all at once, for a single overall harvesting. Snow peas (edible-pod peas, or *mange-tout*) are usually picked small, before string and seed form, but many varieties don't toughen too rapidly and if allowed to develop a little string, they'll also become much sweeter (the strings are easy to strip out right in the field as the pods are picked). Snap peas are much sweeter if allowed to develop seeds and strings.

Saving seed: Let some vines mature seed, harvest the vines, fully dry on a tarp, thresh and store. It's that simple! To simplify drying down, you may want to plant peas intended for seed in an area that won't be irrigated.

Varieties: Such old standards as Little Marvel, Lincoln (small, delicious peas), Dark Skinned Perfection, Early Frosty, Freezonian and the like need no trellising and will mature if sown early enough to beat enation. Enation is not a serious problem north of Puget Sound; thousands of acres of Dark Skinned Perfection (probably the highest-yielding variety known) are still grown for freezing in the Skagit. Abundant Life Seed Foundation, located on the Sound, makes no effort to sell enation-resistant varieties. Alderman and Tall Telephone, the very best-tasting of the classic old garden peas still available, require a trellis, the earliest possible sowing and fast growth to mature before being wiped out by enation. Enation-resistant types like Maestro, Corvallis, Knight, Olympia, Grenadier and Mayfair are much better adapted south of the Sound.

Oregon Sugar Pod, a highly enation-resistant snow pea developed by Jim Baggett at OSU, is the basis of a new snow-pea farming business in the Willamette that supplies the entire nation during summer when California production falters. Rembrandt and Dwarf White Sugar (TSC) are climbing snow peas that seem to have some enation resistance and can be picked a lot longer than Oregon Sugar Pod. I consider Rembrandt a gourmet variety. Dwarf Grey Sugar, an old snow pea variety, has tough, tasteless pods and rapid seed and string development; Mammoth Melting Sugar, grown during cool weather on poles along the California coast, makes the largest and finest-quality snow peas on vigorous climbing vines, but is not enation-resistant and matures too late to beat the disease.

Snap peas are the newest thing and I like them very much. To date, none are enation-resistant. Sugar Snap is an indeterminate trellised type with the best flavor (for the same reasons that pole beans and indeterminate tomatoes taste best), but is often a bit too late to produce a good yield before enation takes it out. Sugar Ann is an earlier maturing bush variety with a flavor nearly as good as Sugar Snap. Though the stringless Sugar Daddy is touted as being the wonder snap pea, it's relatively flavorless. It will probably catch on with the supermarket trade. I think there will be many new snap varieties in coming years, and I hope that some of them will be enation-resistant.

Alaska is the traditional dry pea for soup. Johnny's also sells Capucijners, a traditional Dutch field pea with a unique flattened seed. It cooks quickly into a delicious, rich brown gravy.

Garbanzo Beans (*Cicer arietinum*)
Lentils (*Lens culinaris*)

These species are not quite as frost-hardy nor as tolerant of cold soil as the garden pea. Grown for dry seed that matures in July when the soil naturally dries out, they are best planted in an area of the garden where irrigation may be withheld without harming other crops. Garbanzos are also known as chickpeas, Egyptian peas, and Bengal gram.

Culture: Sow early March to early April—earlier is better because more soil moisture will remain to support the crop, but the sowing date will depend on when your soil becomes warm enough to sprout the seed. Plant about one inch deep, three to four seeds per foot in rows 36 to 48 inches apart. Lime and phosphate rock worked into the plot may provide adequate nutrition; the best fertilizer is bone meal at about five to 10 pounds per 100 row feet, tilled into the row before sowing. Thin seedlings when established: garbanzos to about eight inches apart in the row; lentils about four inches apart. Keep well weeded, as the seed crop will need all available soil moisture.

Harvest: Like dry beans, but harvest will occur in midsummer.

Saving seed: When you grow them to eat, you've also saved seed to replant.

Varieties: Abundant Life offers three varieties of garbanzos. I find the small black ones particularly tasty and tender—300 percent better than the big, tough, yellow ones. Any bag of lentils or garbanzos from the grocery store will probably sprout and grow fine. There are a number of different varieties, though there is no way to know what you're getting when you buy "seed" in the grocery store.

Green Manures and Field Crops

The best sources of seed for common green manures are local feed and grain dealers and better garden centers. Territorial Seed Company sells regionally adapted green manures by mail, but shipping costs for inexpensive species often double the price. When considering garden green manures, ease of tilling in the mature vegetation is the crucial consideration; gardeners usually don't have heavy tractors.

Crimson Clover (*Trifolium incarnatum*): This is the most widely available legume cover crop for our region. Though it grows rather badly on poorly drained soils and will be disappointing on very acid or infertile ones, crimson clover is easy to sow, reliably winter-hardy and easily eliminated in spring. Plant late September through October. One pound of seed sows about 500 square feet (15 to 25 pounds per acre when precision-planted). Broadcast the seed evenly and rake or till in shallowly—about one inch deep. In September, crimson clover may be sprinkled into deteriorating beds of melons, cucumbers, or solanums, to sprout and take over by October. Once the fall rains begin in earnest, crimson clover may be scattered in beds of tall-growing winter crops like kale and Brussels sprouts and allowed to sprout on the soil's surface (but this method uses two or three times as much seed to establish a thick stand). Low-growing and non-competitive until spring, it will take over the beds in March, swallowing the stumps and remains of winter crops. If it's destined for very early tilling, sow a much denser stand.

Regardless of when it is sown, crimson clover flowers in April. Once in bloom, it should be tilled in as soon as possible; when seed formation starts, the stems rapidly become tough and woody, take longer to break down and become harder to handle. On raised beds and small plots, blooming clover may be scythed down, the vegetation raked up and composted and the root stubble hoed in. The stubble will be rotted and gone within 10 days, rapidly leaving the bed ready for a new crop. The clover may also be cut with a powerful lawn mower. Early in spring, beds of crimson clover may be shallowly and gently hoed in, tops and all. The very succulent small greens rot within days, permitting easy sowings of spring mustard, spinach and other very early crops without rototilling.

Crimson clover seed should cost between 65 cents and a dollar per pound. This clover has intense crimson flowers, is an *annual* variety and is very succulent—easily killed with a hoe or tiller. Beware of other types of clover. Perennials such as red, sub, Dutch and white clover form strong root clumps and underground runners that resist tillage and re-establish themselves. Red clover (pink flowers) can become one of the most difficult weeds to eliminate. I know, because years ago an ignorant or unscrupulous garden store merchant sold me some "crimson clover" that was really red clover. I had clumps of red clover coming up in my trial plots for three years despite persistent hoeing.

Austrian Field Peas (*Pisum arvense*): This green manure is a very small-seeded, winter-hardy pea. Austrian field peas may be grown alone or in combination with a grain such as winter wheat or barley. When field peas are interplanted with grain, the nitrogen fixed by the peas improves the grain's growth, while the grain physically supports the pea vines. A pea/grain combination produces an enormous amount of biomass, but the combination is hard to handle with light equipment; it takes a tractor to turn under. It also takes at least three weeks before grains break down enough to allow easy planting. Field peas tend to tangle small tillers when the vines have become long; instead of tilling, the vines can easily be pulled out of raised beds by hand and composted in piles. Like other peas, they leave the beds in fine condition for the next crop.

Field peas may or may not grow in soils that aren't fertile enough or well-drained enough for a lush stand of clover—it's worth a try. They also mature somewhat later than crimson clover, which allows heavier, slower-draining soil more time to dry before the maturing green manure demands tillage. Field peas are broadcast at a rate of about one pound per 100 square feet (200 pounds per acre sown with a grain drill). The seed costs about 25 cents per pound. Sow as early as possible in October; hoe or till in about 1½ inches deep.

Favas (*Vicia faba*): As a *green manure*, sow only small-seeded varieties; these grow much taller than large-seeded types, producing a lot more biomass. Small-seeded favas also have a much higher seed-count per pound, requiring fewer pounds of seed to establish a stand on a given area. In late September through October (and even into early November in southern Oregon or northern California), sow one to two inches deep, one seed every four inches in rows 12 inches apart; or broadcast five to 10 pounds per 1,000 square feet (150 to 250 pounds per acre from a pea seeder) and till in shallowly. Favas also make excellent green manure sown in early spring—if you can get on the ground. Before the seeds start forming (mid- to late May), the stalks are brittle and can be turned under rapidly with a walk-behind garden tiller (without tangling), even when the stand is thick and four to five feet tall. Like clover, the stalks may also be scythed down, raked up and composted, the stubble hoed in by hand. In one respect, favas are like field peas on heavy soils—seed formation begins much later, which gives the crop more time to grow without becoming tough and woody, while allowing the soil time to dry down.

In the east, spring-sown favas are becoming increasingly popular with farmers, but these varieties aren't suitable for fall sowing. The only winter-hardy small-seeded variety available at this time is Banner (TSC). A few years ago, Territorial was the only supplier of Banner, importing the seed from England. Since then, a few local farmers have begun growing Banner, so winter-hardy seed is beginning to appear in farm supply and feed stores. Watch out for "bell beans," spring-sown varieties that will disappoint you. Small-seeded favas should cost about the same as Austrian field peas—about 25 to 30 cents per pound from bulk bags. When purchasing by mail order, the buyer will pay again as much for shipping and handling as for the seed itself.

Because there is apparently some undesirable organism that may be transmitted by the seed, Canadian authorities impose prohibitive precautions concerning the importation of favas, though I'm sure some few pounds of Banner have made it across the border without inspection or declaration and will eventually be offered for sale from local farm productions in the province's lower mainland.

For symphylan control, or to eliminate mysterious diseases or to generally rejuvenate an old garden, plan a three-year fava bean dry fallow/green manure, while moving the vegetable garden to another plot. In autumn of the first year, sow as though raising dry seed without irrigation, but do not harvest the seed. Planting for seed production takes only a few pounds per 1,000 square feet. Keep the plot very free of weeds through summer so the soil won't be weedy several years later when it goes back into vegetables. Most of the dry seeds will hold on the tall bushes all summer, protected from sprouting by the pods even if there are a few light rains. There may be as much as 100 pounds of dry seed standing on every 1,000 square feet. As soon as the fall rains start, even if it is as early as September, knock down the plants as you till the plot shallowly but thoroughly, setting most of the beans an inch or two down and eliminating any germinating weeds. An amazingly dense stand of favas will appear!

Allow the favas to grow, overwinter, set seed and mature the next summer. Weed growth will be strongly suppressed by the dense stand. Though highly overcrowded, enough seed will still set to permit yet another very dense stand of favas to be established in fall (the beginning of year three) by again tilling in the bean stalks. The next spring, till in the favas as a green manure and put the plot back into irrigated vegetables. Symphylan populations should be quite low after three years of favas and no irrigation, while organic matter content will have been maintained and soil nitrogen levels will be quite high.

For symphylan control, it's essential not to irrigate or manure the field. I don't think it is necessary to grow only favas for three years to eliminate the pest, but I suspect symphylans don't like eating fava roots. Growing edible field crops, such as various cereals, quinoa, lentils or garbanzos, during a three-year dry rotation will also eliminate most symphylan problems, while keeping the plot very free of weeds, ultimately saving a lot of work when the plot is rotated back into vegetables.

Tyfon: There's nothing better than a green-manure crop people can eat; Tyfon, a turnip and Chinese cabbage cross, is one. It is hardy to about 10°F, forms deep taproots that break up the soil and grows mild, edible greens similar to mustard spinach. Sown in late summer, some plants will form tasty turnips during midwinter. Tyfon can be sown from May through September at rates of about one ounce per 100 square feet or 10 pounds per acre; broadcast the fine seed and rake or hoe it in shallowly. Tyfon sprouts and grows amazingly fast and doesn't flower until late March after overwintering. The unopened flowers make an acceptable sort of "broccoli." I like fall-sowing Tyfon on beds I'm going to plant early in spring because its long taproots pull out easily by hand from a raised bed, leaving no stubble and a ready-to-plant seed bed. Commercially, the very palatable leaves are used as animal feed; spring sowings may be cut several times in a single season. Tyfon produces more biomass per unit of time than any other green-manure crop known. Seed is available from Territorial and Nichols.

Corn Salad (*Valerianella locusta olitoria* **):** Discussed later as a salad green, this very hardy plant may also be densely sown on raised beds, harvested through the winter for salads and then allowed to go through rapid spring growth, flowering by April. Even in bloom, the vegetation is very tender and may be easily chopped into the bed with a hoe, creating a very fine seed bed. Allowed to mature seed, corn salad may naturalize as an edible weed, along with sheep sorrel and purslane. To use corn salad as a green manure, broadcast and shallowly rake in about one ounce of seed per 100 square feet of bed during September after the heat of summer is over. I like to grow one bed each winter. Seed is widely available. For more details, see "Corn Salad" further on in this chapter under Greens.

Grains (Gramineae spp.): Any winter cereal—wheat, barley, oats, rye— may be used as a green manure. Grains grow fairly well on wet, poor soils as long as the soil pore space doesn't completely fill with water for days at a time during heavy winter rains. But they have liabilities as garden green manures. They're physically tough, requiring powerful equipment to till in. Cereals also rot slowly, resulting in a late garden if the spring is a wet one. The grain that "yields to the disc" most easily is winter wheat; soft white winter wheat varieties well-adapted to maritime conditions can be purchased in feed and seed stores and health-food stores. One pound of seed densely covers 100 to 200 square feet. Broadcast seed and till in shallowly mid-September to mid-October. Be sure to process the vegetation early in spring before the seed heads form or the plants will become very woody and tough.

Buckwheat (*Fagopyrum esculentum*): Buckwheat is the unexcelled summer green manure! It grows fast on moderately acid soil of low fertility, matures seed without irrigation and rapidly forms such a dense cover that it shades out competing weeds and grasses. Buckwheat is not frost-hardy and will only make rapid growth from May through July. By August, decreasing daylength forces buckwheat to flower almost as soon as it sprouts. Buckwheat is also one of the best weeds you can have in your garden, being so tender and delicate it is very easily hoed out or tilled in. I've even tilled in hip-high stands of thick buckwheat with a front-end tiller without tangling (a supposed impossibility according to the companies touting rear-end tillers).

Buckwheat goes from sprout to full bloom in five to six weeks. Once in full bloom, vegetative growth slows and the stalks get woody. I'd suggest using buckwheat as a short-term green manure on bare spots where something will be planted in a month or so. One pound of seed covers 300 to 500 square feet and should be broadcast and tilled or hoed in about one inch deep.

I've not yet grown buckwheat for seed, though I know of one organic farmer north of Eugene who tried a crop and harvested it successfully— though not profitably. If you'd like to experiment with saving seed, sow as early as possible to preserve as much soil moisture for the crop as possible, let the crop mature seed, thresh it out and winnow it.

Greens

There is no proper botanical classification called "greens." I include many different species with similar characteristics in this one group: they all rush into vegetative growth after germination, are harvested before they have begun to flower and are consumed for their top growth. Greens have been bred to produce thick, succulent and usually sweet leaves and sometimes juicy, tender stalks—but only in fertile, moist soil.

Nutrient requirements change as vegetables go through periods of seedling establishment, vegetative growth and reproduction. During the seedling stage, plants do best with abundant potassium and phosphorus but only a little nitrogen. Once established and growing rapidly, most species benefit from much more nitrogen relative to other nutrients. When flowering, fruiting and seed formation occur, leafy growth usually stops or slows, and the plant's need for nitrogen again declines. Often, a plant that is fruiting or making seed will transport nitrogen from leaf cells to the fruit or seed; too much nitrogen in the soil during reproduction can interfere with fruit development. (Some species have different strategies; cucurbits and solanums, for example, simultaneously grow vegetatively and make fruit, and continue doing this as long as weather conditions permit.)

As a group, greens require high levels of soil moisture, moderate amounts of phosphorus and potassium and fairly high amounts of nitrogen. If I were a chemical-fertilizer user, I'd brew up something like 20–10–15 for growing them. Breeders frequently select greens for abundant top growth at the expense of root development, so it's essential to maintain soil moisture and apply fertilizer close to the seedlings' roots. Once the soil has warmed up well, organic matter breakdown in "built up" soils may provide sufficient nitrogen, but in spring, fertilizer is especially important. Unless the soil is especially rich, fertilizing will result in much sweeter and more succulent greens. However, greens sown for fall harvest will be more resistant to cold if they grow less lushly, so fertility should be reduced for crops sown after mid-July.

Celery (*Apium dulce*)
Celeriac (*A. rapaceum*)

Celery is the most demanding crop I know. The seedlings are delicate, slow-growing and hard to get established. This species requires more fertilization than any other garden vegetable, and amazing amounts of water if it is to make fast, succulent growth. Celery grows best under mild nights and cool days with intense sunlight, which is why commercial crops are produced along the southern California coast close to the sea, where the maritime influence moderates temperatures yet light levels are intense and dependable. Starting celery too early is dangerous, for the species has a tendency to bolt prematurely (and, considering how much work must go into the crop, most disappointingly) if given too many hours of exposure to temperatures below 50°F. I've found it more dependable to consider garden celery as a crop for late summer, fall and winter harvest.

Celery has a very small lateral root system. If direct-seeded, its carrot-like taproot will extend down four feet or more, drawing on subsoil moisture. Feeder roots nearer the surface are few and close to the plant. This affects optimum watering and fertilizer placement. Transplanted celery has its taproot broken and forms a more fibrous, shallower root system that extends a little further laterally and needs to be watered more frequently. The weak and inefficient root system is poorly adapted to airless conditions, so clayey soils must be well and deeply amended with organic matter for this crop. Despite heavy additions of manure or compost, celery will grow to supermarket standards only in coarse loams or sands, and then only with skillful handling and some good luck.

Culture: Slow-growing at all stages, celery transplants can take 10 to 12 weeks of patient care. Chapter 6 details how to produce celery seedlings. Direct-seeding is much less work. From mid-April through the first of June, form deep furrows about 24 inches apart across a raised bed and sprinkle in one-half cup complete organic fertilizer for each four or five row feet. Fill in each furrow and make a second, shallow furrow above it, about a quarter-inch deep. Celery seed should be sown thinly; however, the seed is so tiny that it is impossible to accomplish. That's okay, because when it's direct-seeded the germination percentage will not be high. Cover the seed with finely sifted compost or aged barnyard manure, or a mixture of sifted sphagnum moss and soil. Slow-sprouting celery seed germinates best when on the cool side, taking two weeks or so depending on the temperature. April and early May sowings are usually kept naturally moist by weather conditions; if the soil dries down, gently sprinkle the seeds as needed to keep them moist. After germination, gradually thin the seedlings as they establish themselves. When the plants are three to four inches high, they should stand 12 to 16 inches apart in the row. *Keep the plants well watered during summer's heat.* It might be a good idea to locate the celery patch close to a sprinkler or other reliable water source so the celery patch can be hand-watered every few days in addition to regular overall garden irrigation. If growth slows, water with liquid fertilizer every two weeks or side-dress with complete organic fertilizer raked or hoed shallowly into the soil *close to the plants.* One side-dressing may last four to eight weeks. *It is essential that the plants grow rapidly without check* or the stalks will become pithy, stringy and tough. Stop fertilizing about September 1 so the plants harden off a bit as fall approaches.

Grow celeriac exactly like celery.

Garden planning: A dozen celery plants will provide enough to spruce up your salads without picking the plants bare. With good management, celery is going to occupy the bed for nearly a year. Mature plants can be protected under tall cloches over the winter, where they'll make more winter growth and have a better chance of surviving frosts.

Celeriac is different. Our family can go through five or six dozen roots in the course of a winter. Hilling up a little soil over the root when fall weather checks it will protect celeriac from freezing in frostier areas.

Sprinkling a bit of crimson clover seed in the celery or celeriac bed in fall will establish a non-competitive green manure that will take over in spring.

Insects and diseases: Though there's a whole shelf's worth of books and journal articles about celery diseases found in commercial growing areas, I've had no problems.

Harvest: Celery will certainly be harvestable by late summer from direct-seeded plants; earlier sowings can be picked by midsummer. Do not cut the entire plant as market gardeners do. Instead, pick the outer largest stalks as needed. If the winter is mild, celery tolerates continuous light pickings until it bolts and begins seed formation in spring. Even while bolting, the unopened flowers and tender stalks below them are good salad greens.

Saving seed: Celery is a biennial, flowering in its second year unless it freezes out. Too much cold weather in the seedling stages can make celery "think" it has overwintered, so it bolts in summer before it's full-grown. This is also a "bad" trait, so occasional early bolters should be culled by the seed saver, though plants that start flowering in summer are not likely to mature seed in any case. Celery is pollinated by insects and freely crosses with other varieties and with celeriac, so to prevent most crossing, isolate varieties by at least 200 feet. There's no need to grow celery and celeriac seed in the same year, since the species makes very long-lived seed (seven to 10 years with decent storage). Even if the crop freezes out two winters in three, home gardeners should be able to produce their own seed. Before bolting occurs, dig up six to 12 surviving plants (even more would be better) and transplant them where water can be withheld once the seed starts drying down. Because of the species' weak root systems, it might not be a bad idea to mulch plants intended for seed. Celery flowers are small, white umbels, similar to wild carrot. The seed is easily detached from the drying flowers, so take care when harvesting. Finish drying the seed heads under cover on newspapers to catch shattering seeds.

Varieties: All seed companies offer Utah 52-70 in one variant or another. Avoid the "Florida" selections, which are bred to mature in winter at southern latitudes and daylengths. Harris calls its commercial-grade Utah variety Clean-Cut. Pascal types are more resistant to early bolting. Golden or Golden Self-Blanching types have shorter stalks and usually less-vigorous growth. I've had bad luck with the golden varieties.

Celeriac is grown for its rough, bulbous root, which is peeled and then steamed, fried or used in soups. It tastes much like celery stalks and is not starchy. We love celeriac slowly butter-fried to a crispy golden-brown atop the woodstove. Celeriac doesn't absorb fat like parsnips or potatoes, so a tiny pat of butter is enough to prevent sticking and flavor a whole skilletful. All mail-order seed companies sell some sort of celeriac. Quality selections are free of big lateral roots and are smoother, cutting down waste. The best variety I've ever grown is Arvi (TSC). To get commercial European market-grower quality, I'd buy my celeriac seed from Johnny's, Harris or Territorial.

Chicory (*Cichorium intybus*)

Even though most forms of chicory are eaten like endive, its culture more closely resembles that of root crops. See Roots.

Corn Salad (*Valerianella locusta olitoria*)

In Europe, small grains like wheat, barley and oats are called corn; what we call corn in North America, Europeans call maize. Corn salad was once a winter-hardy, wild, edible salad weed that came up in the stubble of harvested "corn" fields. In recent centuries, the species was bred for increased leaf-size and flavor. Still pretty wild, if corn salad is allowed to go to seed in the garden, it will naturalize into an edible weed.

Culture: Corn salad has not lost its ability to grow well in soils of only moderate fertility. Fertilizer remaining in the bed following summer crops is usually enough for it. The low-germination seeds will not sprout until soil temperatures have dropped well below their August peak, but they should be planted before late September. Sow three seeds per inch, one-half inch deep in rows at least 12 inches apart. Do not thin much. (See the section on Green Manures for another slant on growing corn salad.)

Garden planning: Sow following any crop that finishes up in September—for example, bush beans or lettuce. Fifty row feet is enough to supply a large bowlful every week for winter salads. My family finds the flavor too strong to eat corn salad alone, but it does spice up other greens. Corn salad goes to seed in April; the flowering stalks remain tender for several weeks but get spicier and spicier. The bed can be replanted in late April.

Insects and diseases: None known.

Harvest: Grip the small leaves with your fingertips in small clumps and cut with a sharp knife an inch or two above the ground; this allows the plants to regrow. Then wash the leaves thoroughly and drain.

Saving seed: The light, irregularly shaped seeds form in late April and drop to earth or travel a goodly distance in strong winds. Spread a sheet of cardboard under the plants to catch falling seeds and collect them daily. At best, corn salad seed lives only a year or two; be sure to dry it thoroughly before storage.

Varieties: Several strains are available, some with larger leaves than others, different bolting dates and slight variations in hardiness. The differences are mostly insignificant. All varieties are much hardier than our maritime Northwest winters seem to require.

Endive (*Cichorium endivia*)

Many people think endive is a sort of lettuce, but it is not. Lettuce is an annual, only slightly frost-hardy (occasionally it behaves as a biennial, overwintering when we have a mild, rainy year and bolting in spring). Endive, also known as escarole, is a biennial relative of chicory and very hardy compared to lettuce. Freeze-out for most lettuce varieties is about 21°F; some exceptional strains of lettuce will survive brief exposures to 19°F. Endive has overwintered in my garden protected from rain by only a very drafty cold frame, and survived temperatures below 7°F with no sign of damage. The bitterness of endive decreases noticeably after hard frosts have worked the plant over a few times, which is why California supermarket endive is not comparable to our home-garden stuff.

Culture: Though endive can be grown as a summer vegetable from sowings in spring or early summer, I sow it only for fall and winter harvest. To grow unprotected endive, sow in early August to early September. To fill a cold frame, sowings may be as late as October 1. Rich garden soil will provide enough nutrients for a fall or winter crop, but first broad-casting and tilling in complete organic fertilizer with a higher-than-normal kelp content will make a great difference on poor soils. Sow seeds one-half inch deep, two to four seeds per inch, in rows 18 inches apart. Massed layers of overlapping leaves tend to rot more easily, so thin gradually and *carefully*—the rosettes should develop fully, but the plants shouldn't become overcrowded. The later the seeds are sown, the closer the seedlings may be spaced. Early sowings in fertile soil will grow huge heads if thinned to about 18 inches apart in the row; thin later sowings to about 12 inches.

Garden planning: Good salad greens are scarce in some winters. Unprotected August sowings often remain in good condition all winter if the weather is on the dry and mild side; endive may last only till January if the winter is harsh and humid. Usually it's not the cold that does endive in, but rain and damp-induced mildews and molds, which gradually rot the beautiful rosette back to a stump. Later sowings, which don't head until midwinter, have less tendency to rot and may withstand weather that would destroy bigger plants.

A drafty cold frame, even one that will hardly increase nighttime temperatures, will keep off the damaging rains and increase daytime temperatures enough to encourage more growth. I suggest that you plant much more endive than you think will be needed and put a roof of some kind over as much of it as possible. Late-sown, endive-filled frames can be started in beds that grew melons, cucumbers, corn, tomatoes or other hot-weather crops.

Insects and diseases: Not a problem if kept dry in winter.

Harvest: When harvesting most types of winter salad greens it is best to cut individual leaves, which permits the plants to continue production. Though in Europe endive is sometimes blanched by tying up the leaves into a tight head for a few weeks before cutting, the maritime Northwest's rainy, frosty weather may not permit blanching. Besides, winter's cold makes the species quite tasty without doing this.

Saving seed: Endive is a self-pollinated biennial. Plants that survive the winter may be dug in March and transplanted to a dry area of the garden. The plants will regrow in spring and bolt by summer, looking a lot like wild chicory. I've had good luck growing seed without any irrigation, by spacing the plants two feet apart in rows four feet apart and mulching by May. The gnarled stalks will grow three feet high or more, covered with small chicory-blue flowers that leave behind little rock-hard knobs full of seed. When the stalks are partly dry, cut and finish under cover; *dry until brittle*. Milling the seeds out can take a lot of sweat. The best home system I know of is to spread the stalks out on a concrete walkway or slab and pound them with a flat-bottomed, three-inch-thick, five-foot-long wooden staff (or something similar) until the seeds separate. Then sieve the remains through a large-mesh food strainer to remove the big stuff; the seed will pass through. Winnow the seed from the dust and chaff by pouring it from bucket to bucket in a mild breeze. Endive seed is long-lived. One plant will produce about a half-ounce of seed.

Varieties: Two basic types are grown. One sort has frilly leaves like Salad Bowl lettuce; the other, usually called Batavian endive or escarole, has broad plain leaves. Large heads of both tend to have semi-blanched inner leaves. Most endive varieties sold in the United States are intended to be commercially grown in California or Florida, and are not necessarily as cold-hardy or rain-resistant as the species can be. These U.S.-produced varieties include Salad King, Green Curled and Broad Leaved Batavian. Northern European selections may be more resistant to winter stresses. To intelligently buy seed, look for descriptions like "handles bad weather" or "tolerates low temperatures" and Dutch-sounding names. Johnny's concentrates on fancy European selections for summer or early fall harvest, rather than the varieties we need for winter. Why should they sell winter varieties when Maine conditions don't permit endive to last long once the snows fly? I'd grow Frisian (STK) and anything from Territorial or Thompson & Morgan.

Lettuce (*Lactuca sativa*)

A slightly frost-hardy annual leafy green, lettuce can be easily harvested from late spring through late fall. It is a common misconception among health-conscious people that lettuce is devoid of nutrients. This is only true of crisphead or iceberg types. Full of high-protein chlorophyll, looseleaf varieties are nutritionally the equal of any other salad green. The popular crispheads are also the most difficult to grow, as they demand ideal soil and weather conditions to head properly.

Lettuce needs a fair degree of fertility, abundant soil moisture if it is to grow fast and be sweetly succulent, and weather on the cool side. The main trick to producing good lettuce is *early and careful thinning*. Given ample room to expand rapidly, with enough water and nutrients to support rapid growth, the rosettes develop beautifully in any soil type and most maritime weather conditions. A well-grown legume cover crop or soil built up with ordinary manures and composts may provide sufficient nutrients to grow decent summer lettuce, but moderate amounts of fertilizer will really Grow it. However, iceberg and butterhead types given too much nitrogen tend to blow up (loose, poorly shaped heads) or suffer tipburn (thin, blackened edges on interior leaves). Growing head lettuce well takes a bit of experimentation to discover what the most compatible kind and amount of fertilizer is for the crop and your soil.

Lettuce has a very dense root system that breaks down rapidly after harvest, leaving the soil in nice condition. Lettuce stores up a lot of water in its core and so can survive drought handily, but if it is to Grow into something highly edible, it needs a lot of moisture. Careful attention must be paid to irrigating this shallow-rooted species, or rapid growth will cease and bitterness will result.

Culture: Use of cold frames can extend sowing dates by about one month, both earlier and later; without protection, sow outdoors from April through mid-August. Iceberg types won't head if sown after mid-July. To Grow lettuce, broadcast one gallon of complete organic fertilizer *or* five gallons of chicken manure compost *or* five gallons of fresh chicken manure per 100 square feet of bed and work into soil. In spring, a little fertilizer may also be banded along or beneath the furrow to kick the seedlings into rapid growth. Sprinkle the seeds thinly in the furrows, one-half inch deep, in rows 16 to 18 inches apart. *Thin gradually without permitting any crowding* so looseleafs stand about 10 inches apart; icebergs, bibbs and romaines should stand 12 to 16 inches apart, depending on the variety.

Garden planning: Our family (except my 16-year-old daughter, Sayle) prefers anything to iceberg types. Because we like huge fresh salads daily (each one of us makes a daily meal of salad so large that our personal portion would normally grace an entire average American table of six), I grow continuous productions of lettuce during its season, sowing about 100 square feet every three to four weeks. That is all the time an assortment of varieties will remain in good eating condition.

Sometimes I interplant new sowings of lettuce between older rows, making one continuously harvested bed that lasts all summer. I start by sowing the rows about 24 inches apart. When the plants in the first sowing are two to three inches in diameter, new rows are seeded between the old. The maturing heads are far enough apart that they do not shade out the rows of tiny new seedlings coming up between them. As the big heads are cut, the new ones are thinned gradually. By the time the first sowing is all cut, the fastest varieties in the second one are being harvested. Then the cycle may be repeated, by hoeing in the stumps of the first sowing with a bit of fertilizer and compost and planting new seeds for a third lettuce crop, and so forth. This way, one bed produces lettuce from the first sowing in April through the last harvests of winter. I start another bed of the hardiest sorts for fall harvest about mid-August, because growth rates slow as summer fades and I want to have large pickings as long as possible into winter.

Protected by crude cloches (described in detail in Chapter 3, Planning the Garden), lettuce may be started about March 1 and as late as October 1. Some varieties are hardy to 19°F and may last out a mild winter, especially if under cloches.

Insects and diseases: I've never had any problems except for having to pick slugs out carefully enough to satisfy my daughter.

Harvest: Cut heads as needed. Many varieties become bitter or bolt very quickly after maturity, so it's wise to grow several different varieties at a time and make successive sowings every three or four weeks.

Saving seed: Lettuce rarely cross-pollinates, so little or no isolation is needed. Lettuce is an annual; commercial seed is produced in California, where a long, mild growing season permits the slowly developing seed to mature. It is difficult to mature seed in most of the maritime Northwest from spring sowings. But we can grow lettuce seed by sowing it late in summer and overwintering the plants. Some mild winters that will happen naturally; sometimes a frame is needed to get the seedlings over the worst of winter; sometimes they freeze out. But lettuce seed lives many years, and it should be possible for this region's gardeners to keep their own seed going by trying every year or so. Another approach is to start plants for seeds indoors very early—say mid-January—and transplant them out about mid-March. This way, seed may mature by September.

Dig up several overwintered plants and transplant to a part of the garden that won't have to be watered with the other vegetable crops, or sow a row in that part of the garden during September and hope it overwinters. Lettuce is so drought-tolerant that it may make seed (though not sweet, tender leaves) without irrigation if mulched. By midsummer, overwintered plants will have bolted, flowered and be forming seed. With lettuce, the trait of holding in the bed after heading up without bolting or becoming bitter is a good one, so if enough plants are being grown to do some crop improvement, rogue out the first individuals to bolt.

Lettuce seeds are held in small "cups" left after the fuzz blows away (like dandelions) and tend to shatter quickly and fall to the ground. When most of the flowers have finished blooming and some seed has shattered, cut the stalks and carefully lay them on sheets of newspaper under cover to finish ripening. Thresh the seed by shaking the thoroughly dry stalks in a drum, or rub the heads between your palms over the newspaper.

Winnow the seed by pouring between two buckets in a mild breeze.

Varieties: Just about any type of looseleaf will grow fine, though in my trials work I've discovered a few varieties bred for southern latitudes that become confused by our daylengths and bolt prematurely (fortunately, rare in U.S. garden-seed catalogs). My personal favorites among the common American varieties are Prizehead, Red Sails, Slowbolt (a hardy Grand Rapids strain that I find best for winter cold frames and low light levels) and Buttercrunch. For Boston or bibb types, I prefer the fancy European market selections sold by Territorial, Johnny's and Stokes. Of the romaines, I find Valmaine the best grower with excellent flavor.

Most varieties have a bad trait from the gardener's viewpoint—they mature uniformly and don't hold long without becoming bitter or bolting. Buttercrunch and Slobolt hold the longest in highly edible but overmature condition. On my continuous-harvest bed, I mix seed for all the abovementioned varieties and thin so that the bed grows a more or less equal percentage of all the varieties, located at random. This spreads out the time of harvest from only 10 days or so (for any one variety) to about four weeks.

Ithaca or Salinas seem to grow the best iceberg lettuce.

Mustard (*Brassica* spp.)

Brassica chinensis, B. pekinensis, B. juncea and *B. japonica* are used for their edible leaves and stalks; *B. alba* and *B. nigra* are usually grown for their seed, from which we make the condiment mustard. Mustards are less prone to damaging infestations by the cabbage maggot and most grow more like lettuce than cabbage, which is why they're included in this section. I consider mustards an essential part of any year-round maritime Northwest food production system. If not cooked to death, they are much more delicious than most North Americans realize. Small quantities of certain milder sorts are good in salads.

Culture: Most gardeners have a hard time growing spring mustards. The plants grow slowly and then bolt before they get large enough to reward the gardener for all that effort. Mustards actually are easy to grow, but only when some basics about the species are understood. Highly photoperiodic, all mustard varieties but one rapidly go to seed under the influence of lengthening days, and so must be sown very early in spring if they are to grow big before mid-May's long days make them bolt. Mustards may also be grown for fall and winter harvest, sown after mid-July when days shorten again. Fall mustards are easiest to grow; success with spring mustards may require a brief science lesson.

"Specific heat" is the change in the temperature of a substance resulting from absorption or radiation of a certain fixed amount of heat energy. Simply put, it takes many more calories of heat-energy to raise the temperature of a given amount of water one degree than it takes to raise the temperature of the same amount of iron one degree. In other words, water has a higher specific heat than iron—in fact, water has just about the highest specific heat of any substance. That's why when solar designers want to store heat energy, they frequently use barrels or tanks of water—and water has the added advantage of being cheap.

This principle applies to gardening. Light soils have one-third the water-holding capacity that clay soils have. Thus, loams have a much lower specific heat and warm up quickly in spring. Heavy soils hold much more water; clay must absorb many more calories to heat up the same amount. So clay soils warm up much more slowly in spring and may easily be five or more degrees colder than a sandy loam in April or May. This makes huge differences in the growth of many early crops. I found out to my deep sorrow at Lorane that no matter what you do to improve clay, with respect to spring soil warm-up, you can't turn a sow's ear into a silk purse.

Spring mustard must be sown very early, sprout successfully and grow fast if it is to make any size at all before bolting. It's easy to grow spring-sown mustard in warm, loamy soils. But since biological activity, nutrient release, seed sprouting and root development go slowly when it's cold, and since heavy soils are cold in spring, growing spring mustard on clays is not so easy. Raised beds dry out heavy soil faster and additions of organic matter lighten clay soil a little, helping it to warm up slightly faster and grow mustard—to a degree. On heavy soils, it's best to sow spring mustard in cloches or cold frames.

Sow in early March in furrows about half an inch deep, two or three seeds per inch, the rows about 18 inches apart. To grow fast, mustards also need high levels of available nitrogen in spring. So in addition to broad-casting and working in complete organic fertilizer before sowing, sprinkle about two tablespoonfuls of blood meal immediately after germination beside each four or five feet of row, very close to newly emerging seed-lings (but not touching them, as blood meal will burn plants). Thin gradually so plants stand about six inches apart when six to eight inches high. Do not thin too rapidly, as some seedlings will succumb to flea beetles, slugs and generally harsh weather. For fall and winter harvest, sow mid-July through mid-August, and separate the rows by 24 inches because the plants will grow much larger. Gradually thin late sowings to 12 inches in the row. Fertilization suitable for other greens will produce excellent fall and winter mustard harvests.

Garden planning: Eight to 10 row feet is usually enough in spring; for winter, twice that might not be excessive, and real mustard lovers will want even more. Spring mustard will be done before June, leaving the bed for summer solanums, beans or other heat-lovers. With luck, fall crops will overwinter and last until April, ideally followed by peas, other greens or root crops.

Insects and diseases: Flea beetles are hard on slow-growing seedlings. The best solutions are lots of extra seedlings, high fertility, cloches and frames to enhance growth and, if all else fails, sprays of rotenone or Red Arrow.

Harvest: In spring, after thinning small seedlings to about six inches apart in the row, harvest every other plant by cutting it off at the base, increasing the in-the-row spacing to 12 inches. Then cut mature plants or pick off large outer leaves as needed. In fall, snip individual leaves through the winter. If garden food is scarce in April, unopened mustard flowers make passable "broccoli," very sweet and tender.

Saving seed: Mustards are pollinated by bees and freely cross with each other (also with turnips and Chinese cabbage), producing many interesting but often not-too-edible progeny, so do not permit more than one variety to form flowers in spring. Mustard seeds often last seven years with good vigor, so the seed saver could keep several varieties going. The clusters of small yellow flowers form pods containing several seeds each. When half of the pods are dry, cut the stalks, finish drying on a tarp, thresh out the seed by walking on it and winnow by pouring the seed and chaff between two buckets in a mild breeze. Allowing the flower stalks to fall on the ground will probably result in a self-perpetuating mustard patch that needs only an occasional covering with compost or manure to maintain fertility.

Varieties: I believe all mustards originated in the Orient; many varieties are amazingly beautiful examples of the plant breeder's art, with frilly leaves on long, graceful stalks. Others are rather plain. Only a few have become part of the conventional American assortment. Green Wave and Southern Giant Curled are hot and mustardy. Green Wave is slightly slower to bolt in spring, which makes it a better candidate for growth in our spring weather. A much finer mustardy variety is Miike (Red) Giant (TSC, ABL) with reddish-purple leaves and broad, thick stalks. It's not merely hot, but also sweet and flavorful. Miike is also hardier than Green Wave— much more likely to overwinter. Tendergreen (or Mustard Spinach) is a plain-looking, broad-leaved sort, with virtually no pungency or flavor, and American selections have deteriorated into much variability and earlier bolting. Late Komatsuna (TSC, ABL) is the original slower-bolting Japanese variety that, while still mild, has good flavor and retains uniformity. Tendergreen II is a much more vigorous hybrid Komatsuna. Tai Sai (TSC), a pac choi variety, has long, white, celery-like stalks, broad green spoon-shaped leaves and a very pleasant, mild flavor. Pac choi is essential to Oriental cookery. Chinese Pac Choi (TSC, JSS, ABL) is *the only mustard I know of that can be sown later in spring, grown summer, fall or winter, and will not bolt immediately.* Like Tai Sai, it has long stems, though they're not as white or as refined. Where Tai Sai might suit the Oriental restaurant trade, Chinese Pac Choi is home-garden delicious and much more versatile. Green-in-Snow (TSC) is a newly available variety from China that is, as its name implies, the hardiest known mustard, suitable only for fall and winter. Mizuna (TSC, ABL, JSS) is another sort only suitable for winter because it bolts too fast in spring. Mizuna makes a dense rosette like frilly endive and has a mild flavor. Territorial offers a very fancy hybrid Mizuna.

Though mustards aren't much of a commercial crop in North America, they are still a big item in the Oriental diet. Japanese and Chinese seed companies have many interesting varieties that are sometimes available from specialty mail-order companies. Improved hybrid varieties are rapidly being developed for Japanese and Chinese domestic markets; compared to open-pollinated sorts, they offer perfect uniformity and amazingly increased vigor.

Some other greens that are cultured just like mustard but are not the same species include Santoh (TSC), edible chrysanthemum (TSC, JSS), Tyfon and raab. Santoh is a type of Chinese cabbage that doesn't head and is slower to bolt in spring or fall than heading sorts.

Raab (also known as rapa) is a type of turnip grown for its edible greens. The most rapid grower of all greens when spring-sown, raab fills the pot before any other new crop can be harvested, but it bolts quickly. The unopened flowers are also very good. Raab is not nearly as choice eating as mustard greens.

Tyfon, mentioned earlier as animal fodder and green manure, has palatable leaves as good as Tendergreen mustard. Being biennial, it won't bolt right away; it may be spring-sown and then cut and recut from May through February. Occasional plants make nice turnips, too.

Edible chrysanthemum is actually a small-flowered member of the chrysanthemum family, used as a stir-fry green in Japanese cookery. It is easy to grow, cultures like mustard and may be sown from April through August. It should be harvested before the flowers begin to open, at which time it becomes very spicy. For a continuous supply make successive sow-ings about three weeks apart.

Parsley

See Roots.

Spinach (*Spinacia oleracea*)

Spinach is a natural for the maritime Northwest. Our long, cool springs and mild autumns grow large, tasty plants. In fact, the species is so well adapted that much of the world's spinach seed is grown in the Skagit Valley. Spring spinach is much like mustard; all the caveats in the mustard sec-tion concerning cold soil and daylength apply here, too. Remarkably cold-hardy, spinach almost always overwinters successfully, though it won't make as much growth as mustard or endive under low winter light levels. Spinach also demands plenty of nitrogen; in spring, strong fertilizers are essential.

Culture: For *spring harvest,* sow early in March for harvest in May. For *early summer harvest,* sow bolt-resistant varieties before mid-May for harvest before the end of July. A window of opportunity opens for *late summer, fall and winter harvest,* sown from mid- to late July through mid-August. Spinach seed germinates well under cool conditions; in fact, hot soils reduce germination. Though a few varieties resist bolting well enough to grow in midsummer, it's difficult to get June and July sowings to sprout very far inland south of Longview, Washington.

Broadcast and work in complete organic fertilizer before planting. Sow seed one-half inch deep, three to four seeds per inch, in rows 14 to 18 inches apart. In spring, band a little additional fertilizer immediately below or beside the seeds, or side-dress with two tablespoons of blood meal per four or five row feet immediately after germination to enhance rapid growth.

It's a good idea to delay the initial thinning until the seedlings have one true leaf and are growing fast, because there will be many losses. Spinach grows fairly well when crowded a bit. Gradually thin seedlings to three inches apart in the row by the time the plants are three inches in diameter.

Garden planning: In spring and summer, the harvest from 50 square feet of fast-growing bed will make all the salads and cooked spinach our family can use. Grow spinach in spring following a legume green manure. Follow an early March sowing with another in mid-April of a late-bolting variety for harvest into the summer. For fall, grow a lot more because once the plants size up, they stop growing, and will, at best, hold all winter to be gradually picked down. Keep spinach beds well weeded in winter. I realize it is hard to weed in winter, but if the plants aren't swallowed by weeds, and if the fall beds manage to overwinter in good condition, a side-dressing with blood meal in early February will provide a "kick in the pants" that may well result in much more abundant pickings during March and early April.

Insects and diseases: Symphylans seem to prefer spinach over most other species. When they're chewing below, even thickly sown stands gradually (and mysteriously) disappear before the seedlings really get established. Organic gardeners can try dealing with symphylans by banding a big handful (per four or five row feet) of Perma Guard (insecticidal diatomaceous earth) in a deep furrow below the seeds. This will set the symphylans back enough to permit a decent harvest. When your spinach starts to have problems, it's time to consider a rotation into dry fallow if you're a country gardener (or to consider trying diazinon granules if you're not an organic gardener).

How can I, a self-proclaimed organic gardener, even parenthetically recommend diazinon, you ask. Well, I figure that gardeners are better off growing their own food in naturally enriched soil with the help of a mild chemical pesticide like diazinon than becoming demoralized, giving up on a crop or on gardening altogether, and buying devitalized vegetables from the supermarket that have been sprayed with even more-poisonous stuff.

Spinach is more frost-hardy than the maritime Northwest generally requires to survive our winters. But constant moisture, heavy rains, frosts and low light levels combine to weaken plants, making them susceptible to various molds and other diseases. Newer varieties that are resistant to many of these diseases will produce a lot more new growth during winter than the older sorts, and may survive the winter when old standards gradually succumb to mold and rot. For winter harvest, try growing huge individual plants, thinning them much farther apart—eight to 12 inches—so air can move freely around leaves and molds don't form so readily. Simply giving spinach the protection of a leaky cloche or cold frame will keep it drier and raise daytime temperatures enough to let it reliably overwinter.

Saving seed: Spring and overwintered sowings bolt and form huge quantities of seed. Plants intended for seed should be located where general garden irrigation won't wet them down. Spinach is wind-pollinated and readily outcrosses; varieties must have at least one mile of isolation to maintain purity. Since varieties are so similar, purity may not matter too much except when you wish to produce bolt-resistant types for summer growing. The species makes male, female and hermaphroditic plants. The first bolters will be an undesirable type called "dwarf males" and should be rogued before they can contribute pollen. The male plants open small pollen sacks; only the females form seed. Males generally bolt first, so, early bolting being a bad trait, breeders have developed hybrid varieties consisting of only females. I wouldn't hesitate to grow my own seed from hybrid varieties and gradually develop a reasonably uniform open-pollinated gene pool. The seed stalks ripen unevenly, so delay harvest until the stalks are brown. Cut the stalks, dry fully under cover and thresh out seed between your palms.

Varieties: Bloomsdale is the classic open-pollinated home garden sort. Its thick, savoyed (crinkly) leaves have the sweetest and richest flavor. There are many Bloomsdale strains—Winter, Wisconsin, Virginia, etc; the gardener usually has no idea which is being sold. The strains vary somewhat as to disease-resistance, bolting date and cold-hardiness. Winter Bloomsdale, sometimes called Cold Resistant Savoy, is the best all-around choice for spring or fall. Nobel, an old standard with thick, flat, fine-flavored leaves, is usually later to bolt than Bloomsdale types. A new savoy hybrid, Tyee, is quite a bit slower-bolting than the Bloomsdales, just about as tasty, and disease-resistant enough to overwinter and make some regrowth during winter. Giant Winter (ABL) is an open-pollinated variety for winter gardens; the catalog says the seed is produced only from overwintered plants grown on the Olympic Peninsula. However, Abundant Life is in the rain shadow of the Olympics, right on temperature-moderating Puget Sound, and enjoys unusually dry winters. How well Giant Winter would stand up to heavy rains and a cold Willamette winter compared to Tyee, I don't yet know. For late spring sowings, try these slow-bolt hybrids—Indian Summer (JSS) or Mazurka (TSC).

Swiss Chard (*Beta vulgaris cicla*)

Chard is a beet, and as easy to grow as beets, but it's bred for large, succulent greens instead of root development. It is frost-hardy and stands through most winters without freezing out. Chard will produce a lot more leaf if fertilized like other greens.

Culture: Sow between April and June, eight seeds per foot, seeds three-quarters of an inch deep, in rows at least 18 inches apart. Thin gradually to 10 inches apart in the row. Earlier sowings (made before spring rains taper off too much) sprout more easily. Periodically banding organic fertilizer along the rows will greatly increase the rate of leaf regrowth.

Garden planning: Ten row feet sown early will result in a nine-month supply, enough for most families who like chard.

Insects and diseases: I've had no problems. Symphylans and leaf-miners could cause difficulties. See Chapter 7, Diseases and Pests, if you do have trouble.

Harvest: Cut individual leaves as needed. If regrowth is too slow, fertilize.

Saving seed: Just a variety of beet, chard will cross with other beets. The seed-saving procedure is identical. See "Beets" under Roots.

Varieties: Fordhook seems the hardiest, but most commonly available chard varieties, which are produced in the Skagit Valley by overwintering, should survive normal maritime Northwest winters. Some fancy European varieties don't handle summer heat very well. Ruby or Rhubarb chard tends to bolt prematurely if sown early.

Miscellaneous Salad Greens

There are numerous minor species that will spice up a salad—especially important during winter when repetitious garden meals can become as confining as the perpetual rains. These greens are basically weeds bred for slightly larger, more succulent leaves. They require little or no fertilizer or special care.

Sorrel (*Rumex* spp.): A perennial bred from sheep sorrel (a native weed that will appear throughout the garden, especially during winter). French sorrel (*R. scutatus*) is much larger and more flavorful than plain sorrel (*R. acetosa*). Used in moderation, the sour leaves make bland cabbage salads more interesting. Sow the fine seed thinly and shallowly during April, when moist conditions facilitate germination and the long growing season ahead permits the plants to be enjoyed to their fullest. The rows should be about 18 inches apart. Ten row feet will provide all the cuttings a family could use. Thin to a few inches apart in the row when established. Cut leaves as wanted; be sure to pull out occasional seed stalks as they appear—try to get them "from the roots." The plant will continue to make new leaves, more if not permitted to form seed.

The plants may disappear in a harsh winter, but will resprout early in spring. Many varieties bolt incessantly after overwintering, so it is better to start a new patch every April. There are differences among varieties as to leaf size, shape, sourness and frequency of bolting. The market for this green is so small in North America that there's little certainty of getting the same strain even from the same seed company two years in a row.

Garden Purslane (*Portulaca oleracea*): A larger, upright version of the low-growing weed, garden purslane grows much like its ancestor. But unlike the undistinguished source plant, it is a tall, handsome specimen that resembles a jade plant. It is frost-sensitive; sow at the same time as beans. Purslane makes rapid regrowth; pinch off stalks as wanted and use in salads.

Rocket (*Eruca vesicaria sativa*): Also called roquette, rugola and arugola, rocket is an almost-wild brassica that looks more like wild cabbage than a garden vegetable. Rocket bolts quickly unless sown late. Grown in heat, it gets much too spicy to eat agreeably; grown under cool conditions, the leaves are uniquely and moderately peppery. A few in a salad is enough. Sow mid- to late August, plant the seed about half an inch deep; cover with sifted compost or rotted manure to enhance germination in that dry, hot season. Ten row feet will be more than enough. Picking off seed stalks at the base during winter encourages more leaf production. Eventually, you'll lose patience with the bolting flowers and permit the plant to make seed. Smaller leaves on the seed stalks may still be used in salad. Save the seed if you wish. Rocket will not cross with other garden brassicas, as far as I know.

Brassicas

Of all vegetable species, perhaps this family is best adapted to our climate. Brassicas thrive in cool weather, are frost-hardy—some extremely so—and are dependable producers even during those damp, cloudy summers that I call cabbage years. Brassicas are also very nutritious food; it has been said that the labor that built the Great Wall of China was fueled not by rice, but by cabbage.

Included in the family are all the coles—kale, rutabagas, cabbage, cauliflower, broccoli, Brussels sprouts, collards and Chinese cabbage, as well as some species I discuss in other parts of this chapter, such as radishes, turnips, mustards and rocket. Probably derived from only a few closely related wild species, the brassicas have a unique genetic potential to be "grotesqued" by the breeder: terminal buds have been wildly exaggerated into cabbages; axial buds have swollen into Brussels sprouts; small flower clumps are now giant broccoli and cauliflower; petiols have elongated into celerylike stalks; stems have thickened into rutabaga and kohlrabi; roots have fattened into turnips and radishes. Unfortunately, the more a single aspect of the species' genetic potential is emphasized, the more vigor the variety loses. Coarse brassicas such as kale, collards and Purple Sprouting broccoli will grow lustily in soil of only moderate fertility. More refined rutabagas and Brussels sprouts need higher fertility levels, while the intensely inbred cabbage, cauliflower, kohlrabi and broccoli demand the finest soils and lots of fertilizer—though less-refined types of "field cabbage," traditionally grown as animal fodder, are more vigorous than the others and can almost be considered in the same league as kale.

Brassicas demand little phosphorus compared to vegetables that make edible seeds, but they do require high levels of nitrogen and potassium. *Heavy feeders on calcium,* brassicas grow much better when the soil pH is above 6.0. Even in fairly neutral soils, additional lime in the beds can markedly improve growth. Not only will a calcium deficiency stunt plants, but in cabbage and Brussels sprouts it will also cause internal browning of the leaf margins or a sort of "tip burn."

The cabbage fly seems to prefer some types of brassicas: Chinese cabbage and turnips are the most attractive, rutabagas the least interesting. The fly's preferences and the variety's inherent root system vigor determine how damaging the fly's larvae will be. Cauliflower is usually the most poorly rooted; a little root loss can be fatal. Brussels sprouts have much more vigorous root systems that can better tolerate predation. Kale is almost never noticeably damaged by the maggot, at least not at the predation levels I have experienced in my gardening. Neither is the cabbage fly uniformly troublesome throughout the maritime Northwest. Washington State has a higher level of infestation than Oregon, and the Skagit Valley probably has the worst cabbage-fly trouble in the United States. Chapter 7, Diseases and Pests, explains how to handle the cabbage root maggot as well as a few other brassica pests.

The family is also troubled by a brassica-specific, soil-borne disease called clubroot. Each type of brassica is affected somewhat differently. The infected roots swell grotesquely and efficiency is inhibited. Mysterious wilting and stunted plants with swollen, knobby roots are indications of clubroot. Healthy soil can become infected by soil transported on purchased bedding plants, by compost made from infected plants, and even by the gardener's shoes and tools. If clubroot is present, one should take care not to spread the disease by composting infected plants; instead, burn them. Clubroot is not easy to eliminate completely; the garden must be kept clear of all brassicas as well as certain host weeds for a period of seven years. Liming soil to a pH of 7.2 to 7.5 will greatly inhibit the disease, though overliming must be done with an awareness of maintaining a proper ratio of calcium to magnesium. However, even three or four years without brassicas will greatly reduce the fungus's effect. The Extension Service (U.S.) prints a fact sheet about clubroot (EM 4205) that is free for the asking. A few brassica varieties carry resistance to one or more strains of the disease (the seed catalog will proudly let you know about that), but resistance to one strain does not necessarily mean resistance to the strain infecting your particular plot.

Back-yard gardeners with infected plots might consider instituting a three-year rotation with half the garden out of brassicas and perhaps two sets of tools (and shoes?) to avoid transferring infected soil from plot to plot—much like a kosher kitchen. Rural gardeners should think again about the wisdom of a three-year dry fallow that also reduces symphylan levels. In fact, the longer I garden, the more an organic heresy becomes real to me: *continuously growing vegetables (even Organically) inevitably creates unhealthy soil.*

Brand-new gardens started from pasture or lawn always grow much better for the first few years. Heavy fertilization, building up organic matter, maintaining high levels of soil moisture all year—these practices seem to inevitably result in highly unbalanced conditions, gradually sapping the garden's health and causing numerous mysterious difficulties. Commercial vegetable farmers, who may not be able to fallow their fields or rotate into low-value unirrigated crops without going bankrupt, frequently feel forced to fumigate their fields—killing every living thing in the soil with methyl bromide or other violent toxins in an effort to control runaway diseases and pests. The natural cure probably demands returning the plot to field crops or unirrigated unfertilized weeds and grasses for a time.

Early sowings of most leafy crops, including brassicas, benefit greatly from a little blood meal. At any time of year, most types are fairly demanding and need abundant fertilization, though brassicas for fall and winter harvest should not be forced into rapid growth after the end of August— they need to harden off, toughen up and develop maximum frost-resistance. For all brassicas, a gallon of complete organic fertilizer worked into each 100 square feet of bed before planting would be minimum nutrition; the more demanding types need additional fertilizer banded below the seedlings and perhaps even more side-dressed as the seedlings grow. Varieties to be overwintered should not be side-dressed or encouraged with banded fertilizer until spring regrowth begins (February), when they can be side-dressed to produce the maximum yield.

Italian broccoli, ordinary cauliflower and cabbage have this genetic program: grow a fixed number of leaves, and then flower or head. They will make their pre-programmed number of leaves at more or less the same rate of speed, in good or bad soil, under high or low fertility. But under good conditions, the plant will have waxed large when the task is done—and the head will match. Under poor conditions, the plant will be stunted and the head tiny. Because brassicas usually become larger overall as they make each additional set of leaves, later-maturing varieties produce much larger heads.

Northern European wild cabbage plants are much hardier than Italian strains, but lack the traits that lead to massive flower heads. Overwintered broccoli and cauliflower were engineered to tolerate northern winters by crossing Italian strains with brassicas derived from English wild cabbage. They are programmed differently—flowering is triggered by increasing photoperiod after exposure to a certain amount of chilling during winter. Still, the larger the plant has grown when flowering commences, the larger the head will be.

Brassicas generally adapt well to transplanting. Most gardeners think that transplants must be raised or purchased to grow cabbage, cauliflower, broccoli or Brussels sprouts, but this is not so. If vigorous, fresh seed is sown outdoors when weather conditions are favorable and if the soil is welcoming to brassica seedlings, direct-seeded plants will grow faster than transplants and will mature only 10 days to two weeks later than six-week-old seedlings transplanted at the same time the seeds are sown. Direct-seeding successfully demands two basic strategies: following the native habit of the species regarding its establishment by seed in the wild, and putting the potting soil outdoors rather than in the pot.

Brassicas form seed in pods containing five or six seeds each. The pod protects the seeds within; all the seeds in the pod sprout as a group in a cluster. It is very easy for a disease or pest to knock over an individual brassica seedling, easy for the tiny plants to be swallowed in weeds and lost, easy for one weak seedling to fail to push past a clod or through a thin crust—they survive all these threats much better when in a little cluster. If the gardener imitates nature in this respect—sowing a little pinch of seed wherever a plant will be wanted and gradually thinning the seedlings as they become established—success is almost assured.

The more refined brassicas have greatly weakened root systems that demand airy, fertile soil—especially when in the seedling stage. The transplant raiser can easily accommodate this limitation by mixing up a special soil mix. Though it's nearly impossible to turn the entire garden into potting soil, it is not too much trouble to make raised beds, incorporate organic matter only in the surface two inches and thus create a growing medium very favorable to the growth of all delicate seedlings. The gardener also has the option of putting small quantities of potting soil under each clump of brassica seedlings. This is easier than you might think—in fact, it's the easiest of all methods of starting even the most delicate brassica seedlings. Simply mix up a few buckets of potting mix (see Chapter 6, Buying and Raising Transplants) and prepare the growing beds: broadcast complete organic fertilizer, work it in and rake the bed reasonably smooth. Then pour complete organic fertilizer in numerous little piles on top of the bed, one-quarter to one-half cup per pile, spaced out on 18- to 24-inch centers (depending on the variety being planted). With a small shovel or your bare hands, work each bit of fertilizer into about a gallon of soil, creating a little zone of very high fertility for the seedlings to grow into. Then scoop out a one-cup-sized hole in the middle of each fertilized spot and fill the hole with one cup of potting soil. Plant a pinch of seeds in that. All the cultural directions that follow suggest direct-seeding brassica crops.

Saving seed from fancy, open-pollinated brassicas does not adapt itself easily to most gardening situations. Except for Chinese cabbage and radish, brassicas are biennials that must overwinter without freezing out or rotting before blooming. Wild brassicas usually sprout with the fall rains and overwinter as tiny seedlings. Fully developed brassicas may have a much harder time surviving winter.

Seed for brassicas of many sorts is produced in the Skagit Valley. Stock seed of very high purity is sown late in summer, and the resulting six- to 10-inch plants overwinter and then bolt in spring without ever having developed into mature specimens. The fields are not rogued. This sort of inexpensive production is called "seed to seed." But after a few generations of seed from unrogued fields, brassicas rapidly degenerate into a useless hodgepodge of undesirable variation; at best, they become suitable only for the garden-seed trade.

Seed-to-seed methods yield reasonably pure seed *only* when the stock seed is extremely uniform. To obtain high-purity stock seed, mature plants must be carefully selected for trueness to type, dug and overwintered in cellars or pits. The stock seed may also be grown in a southern location where the mature plants are very likely to overwinter; occasionally mature specimens are protected by covering them with soil or plastic. Stock-seed fields are grown under extreme isolation to prevent random crossing because any outcrossed individual present in a seed-to-seed field will multiply itself many thousandfold.

Broccoli, cauliflower, cabbage, Brussels sprouts, collards, kohlrabi and Scotch kale (the type that grows a tall central stalk) all cross with each other. Rutabagas and Siberian kale cross with each other. Seed for Italian broccoli and cauliflower—not very hardy compared to other brassicas—

is produced in California. We *can* easily grow overwintered broccoli and overwintered cauliflower for seed in the maritime Northwest. Kale, winter-hardy Brussels sprouts, winter savoy cabbage and rutabaga are also fairly easy. More difficult but possible are kohlrabi and the sorts of market cabbage that head in late summer. To prevent most crossing with other flowering brassicas, isolation of half a mile is required.

To preserve a brassica variety, the home gardener must grow it as though it were stock seed. In early spring, dig carefully chosen overwintered mature plants and move them to a part of the garden that won't need to be watered with the rest of the vegetables. Take at least six plants— better several dozen to avoid loss of vigor due to excessive inbreeding. By April, overwintered plants put out seed stalks covered with yellow flowers that mature into small pods, each containing four to six seeds. When the pods first start drying down, irrigation should cease. (I've grown highly vigorous seed without any irrigation, though the yields were lower.) As summer progresses, flowering tapers off and eventually the majority of the pods contain mature, dried seed. At this stage, the huge masses of pods are cut, windrowed to dry in the field on tarps or dried under cover, threshed, cleaned and stored. The seed will last four to 10 years, depending on its initial vigor and on storage conditions. Each plant will produce over an ounce of seed.

Hybridization of brassica varieties has become a seed-industry standard. Consequently, many of the older, open-pollinated types are no longer quality selections. Hybrid varieties are usually perfectly uniform and much more vigorous. Tim Peters at Territorial says that to develop an open-pollinated variety from hybrids, it's best to start with two or more different but closely similar hybrid varieties and permit them to freely cross. Then, with each succeeding generation, select rigorously for the desired traits.

Broccoli (*Brassica oleracea italica*)

This is one of the easier brassicas to grow. Broccoli has large, vigorously sprouting seeds that take to direct-seeding. It will produce in clayey soils and those of only moderate fertility, but to get big supermarket-sized heads, high nitrogen levels and airy soils are required from sprouting to the initiation of flowering.

Culture: Plant broccoli in little clumps, a pinch of seed one-half inch deep, over a spot where organic fertilizer has been worked into about a gallon of soil. Space early varieties on 18-inch centers; late varieties, on 24-inch centers. Thin gradually to the best single plant without permitting light competition. Thinning should be completed by the time the seedlings have two true leaves. If growth slows, side-dress the plants with a highly available nitrogen fertilizer. If side-dressing is done just when the central flower first begins to form, the main head will be only slightly larger, but side-shoot development will be much faster and heavier. To obtain the hardiest overwintered broccoli in very frosty areas, adjust the sowing date and soil fertility so the plants grow about 12 inches high before November's chill checks further growth. I sow mid- to late July without banding extra fertilizer under seedling clumps. Do not side-dress Purple Sprouting until after it has overwintered and begun its rapid spring growth (early February). You do want to provoke the most rapid possible spring growth. Use blood meal or another readily released nitrogen source.

Garden planning: Maritime northwest gardens will supply broccoli most of the year. Earliest harvests come from overwintering Purple and White Sprouting broccoli, which is sown in midsummer and harvested in March, April and early May. Next in succession are spring-sown transplants of Italian types. Seeds may be started indoors as early as February for setting out mid-March under small paper hot caps or in cold frames. These will flower by June. Outdoor conditions permit direct-seeding or unprotected transplantings in mid-March or April, depending on the spring weather patterns that year. These sowings mature in July. The last sowing of Italian broccoli should be made before mid-July (in more northern areas, perhaps by July). The latest sowings mature in October or early November.

Hybrid Italian varieties head all at once. To lengthen the harvest, I sow two or three hybrids at one time; a single multiple-variety sowing heads-out for three or four weeks, followed by pickings of side shoots for another three or four weeks. Sowing about a dozen plants of mixed varieties every six weeks from February through July 15 keeps us in broccoli all summer and fall. (Sowing mixed cauliflower and mixed early cabbage varieties at the same time in the same patch fills up an entire bed and also keeps the kitchen continuously supplied with these vegetables.) Overwintering broccoli comes on in a season when there is little else to eat; at that time we make whole meals of broccoli stir-fries mixed with scallions or leeks. So I plant two 100-square-foot beds each summer to supply us during spring.

Insects and diseases: Italian broccoli has a more vigorous root system than cabbage or cauliflower, and is better able to handle predation from symphylans or maggots. Overwintered broccoli seems as vigorous as kale (and by the look of it, Italian broccoli was probably crossed with kale to create Purple Sprouting broccoli). Direct-seeding, using lots of fertilizer and sowing many more seeds than are ultimately wanted handles most insect problems.

Harvest: The central head should be cut when the "beads" begin to fatten, but before they open into yellow flowers. With all broccoli, side shoots develop after the central head is cut. These smaller flowers may result in quite a substantial harvest from slower-maturing, taller varieties that make more leaf axials before flowering. Short, early varieties are bred for once-over mechanical harvest, and usually produce few side shoots. If the side shoots are carefully cut where they emerge from the main stalk, the plant will make fewer but larger and tastier shoots. If any leaf axials are left growing on the harvested side shoot, each one will put out even smaller side shoots, diverting plant energy from the main axials still unsprouted lower on the stem and resulting in a much larger harvest of much smaller, tougher, less tasty side shoots.

Purple Sprouting broccoli has been bred to delay opening its flowerettes, which permits them to fatten up and sweeten as they swell—harvest should be delayed as long as possible.

Saving seed: The earliest sowings of Italian broccoli won't mature seed until very late summer at best, making production dicey. Besides, such old, open-pollinated sorts as Waltham 29, DeCicco, Italian Sprouting and Spartan Early aren't much good any longer; they produce smallish variable heads with side shoots often larger than the central head. If plants do survive an unusually mild winter, they may be dug, transplanted to an area where irrigation won't affect them and permitted to make seed. Territorial's Umpqua is the only decent open-pollinated Italian variety I know of.

Purple Sprouting and White Sprouting are very easy to produce seed from. They're usually in full bloom by May and mature seed nicely in midsummer. These varieties vary considerably in head quality. I'd wait until after the main flowers appear and then select the best plants for seed production, transplanting them to a dry area of the garden.

Varieties: Umpqua (TSC), bred and produced by our local Burbank, Tim Peters, is the only quality open-pollinated Italian type on the market today. Johnny's Selected Seeds has expressed interest in carrying Umpqua, and it may appear in the catalog. Thompson & Morgan's Romanesco is a very late open-pollinated variety that produces gigantic, knobby, cauliflower-like heads. The version of Romanesco from Abundant Life is very poorly rogued with many off-type, relatively useless heads. Except for the earliest spring harvest, avoid rapidly maturing hybrids intended for mechanical harvesting or "close spacing" (Green Duke, Premium Crop, Emperor)—these produce fewer side shoots. The later the variety matures, the taller it will become, yielding more side shoots and a larger central head. Some of the better hybrid varieties include Southern Comet, Septal, Octal, Green Valiant and Shogun.

Purple Sprouting (TSC, ABL) and Territorial's White Sprouting (a variety that looks like a cauliflower-kale cross) came originally from England. The flower is not as fancy as Italian broccoli, but it tastes as good and is very much appreciated in spring when there's not much else to eat. Purple Sprouting is pretty much a home-garden variety in England, with all that that implies about the low quality of seed available. Territorial has found a reliable British supplier with reasonably uniform selections featuring plants where most of the heads are of high quality.

Brussels Sprouts (*B. oleracea gemmifera*)

This very hardy vegetable has been bred to emphasize the natural brassica tendency to form cabbage-like axial buds. (Cabbages sometimes make axial sprouts along their stems when overmature; Brussels sprouts sometimes loosely "head" at the top.) Early-maturing varieties tend to be short, with the sprouts close together. Later ones are bred to be taller, with separations between sprouts that prevent trapped water from rotting them. Early varieties seem to initiate bud formation after reaching sufficient height or growing for a certain period; sow them earlier and they'll mature earlier. Bud formation in late varieties is triggered by decreasing photoperiod. Sown too soon, late varieties may grow very tall and fall over in winter; sown too late, they will be short, with fewer leaf axials and so fewer sprouts. Either way, they form sprouts at much the same time.

Most people do not realize how delicious Brussels sprouts are because they've only tasted California supermarket sprouts. With many brassicas, sharp frosts enhance sugar content and increase tenderness, so local sprouts are much better eating—though our frosty, rainy winters are not conducive to producing the pretty-looking sprouts that come from California. There's some special life-energy located in a bud—similar to a seed, it's the place where new life starts growing. To me, it seems as though a little Brussels sprout has nearly the same amount of life force as is contained in a big cabbage, so even a small serving of them is very filling.

Sprouts have lower nutrient requirements and are somewhat less fussy about soil quality than cabbages, broccoli or cauliflower. In England, this crop was traditionally grown in heavier soils not suitable for the more lucrative brassicas.

Culture: Sprouts need a steady supply of nutrients and water to make continuous growth during summer. But too much nitrogen makes plants too tall, and worse, it makes the sprouts "blow up" (produce loose sprouts) and less resistant to winter weather. Sprouts support themselves better on heavier soils; gardeners on lighter loams and sands might consider staking their plants or starting them a few weeks later than normal to keep them shorter. I sow Brussels sprouts about June 1 and don't grow early varieties. Who wants Brussels sprouts in August when there are tomatoes? Sprouts are easier to grow from seed than broccoli. Space plants on 24-inch centers and grow like broccoli.

Garden planning: I want to begin eating sprouts about November and continue through the winter until they bolt. Twenty-four to 30 mid-season plants and the same number of later ones supply my family adequately. Grown on 24-inch centers, our sprouts occupy about 200 square feet of bed. Sprouts allow a fair amount of light to filter through to hit the bed; a sprinkling of crimson clover in October will take over the bed by March.

Insects and diseases: If sprouts are direct-seeded in June, the worst of the cabbage maggot infestation can be avoided. In my garden, by the time the fall maggots return, the large, vigorously rooted plants don't seem bothered. Aphids can be troublesome, wrecking the crop by covering and penetrating half-formed sprouts. Colonies can be hosed off or sprayed with Safer's soap, but the easiest solution is to concentrate on later varieties that don't form sprouts until both summer and the aphids are gone.

Harvest: Sprouts enlarge first at the base of the stem and can be snapped off a few at a time, starting at the bottom and working up over a period of several months. Commercial growers pinch off the growing tip about a month before harvest, encouraging all the sprouts to fill out simultaneously—not a good idea in the garden. Some gardeners break off the lower leaves a few at a time as they harvest up the stalk, thinking this fattens the sprouts by letting more light in. Doing this also lets enough light strike the ground to grow some clover. Others point out that the leaves form an umbrella that keeps rain off the sprouts, protecting them and enhancing their appearance. Both views are right.

In mid-March, the unopened bolting flowers make a delicious sort of "broccoli," with a milder flavor than cabbage, rutabaga or kale flowers.

Saving seed: Sprouts are among the hardiest of brassicas and usually overwinter successfully. Grow seed as for broccoli. Select seed-making plants for large, clean, compact sprouts with nice green color. Open-pollinated varieties exhibit considerable variation and could be selected

for better taste, later maturity, wider sprout spacing and the ability to retain good harvest quality late in the season. Unfortunately, hybrid varieties
are so superior that no open-pollinated varieties of commercial quality
remain in existence—late ones have especially deteriorated. Seed savers
may have to start with hybrids and develop their own open-pollinated
strain from there.

Varieties: Open-pollinated varieties such as Catskill or Long Island
have gone the way of Waltham 29 and DeCicco broccoli; besides, these
varieties are too early for the maritime Northwest, with poor field-holding
qualities. Roodnerf Late Supreme (TSC) is only a little better as far as
uniformity of selection—at least it has the redeeming virtue of being late-
maturing, harvestable from November through March. Thompson &
Morgan still offers a few midseason and late open-pollinated sprout varieties,
but judging by trials I've done on other European open-pollinated late
varieties, they are going to be as poor as Roodnerf—and much more
expensive.

Magnificent hybrid varieties are available from Dutch, English and
Japanese seed companies. The Japanese varieties aren't particularly cold-
hardy but are more "reasonably" priced—wholesale seed costs less than
$200 per pound! Jade Cross has very good flavor but is too early. Prince
Marvel is perhaps a better Japanese selection, but it's also on the early
side. Captain Marvel is a little later in my trials (though some catalogs
list it as earlier than Prince Marvel); it squeaks past the worst of the aphids,
to start yielding about October. I think it also tastes a lot better than Prince
Marvel or Jade Cross. The really primo hybrids are Dutch. Don't believe
it when Stokes or Johnny's says one of their varieties is "late." Buy hybrids
from Territorial or Thompson & Morgan.

Dutch and English hybrid seed costs around $400 per pound (that's
just about a buck a gram) *wholesale*, but fortunately, nearly every hybrid
seed makes an equally good plant and a gram contains several hundred
seeds. Even if direct-seeded as I suggest, one gram can start 50 plants
for a few dollars. Because of the seed cost, this is one brassica the gardener
might want to start with transplants.

Cabbage (*B. oleracea capitata*)

Salad cabbage is one of the most important vegetables I grow. Harvests
can be had from May until March, yielding more food per square foot
than just about any other vegetable except root crops. Cabbages are
nutritious—one can just about live on them, especially when the weather-
man gives us a cabbage year.

How to Grow It

Culture: There are three basic types of cabbage: early (and "midsea-son," a slightly slower-maturing early); late; and overwintered (or spring cabbage, as the English call this type). Each is grown slightly differently.

Early cabbages are fast-growing, smaller types grown on tight spac-ings. They don't have much cold-tolerance compared to the really sturdy late varieties. The varieties found in supermarkets are universally early types. Earlies can be set out as transplants mid-March, the same time the earliest broccoli goes out; they do better during this chilly month when hot caps or cloches are used. From April through the end of June they may be direct-seeded. Most earlies are grown on about 18-inch centers and cultured like broccoli, though there is rarely any need to side-dress cabbage. (Midseason varieties, being later and larger, are best spaced on 24-inch centers.) Earlies tend to be the most delicate of the cabbages, demanding the best soil and the most insect protection. Direct-seeded early types take about three months to mature. The cabbages that appear in American supermarkets from November through July are all early varieties, grown in the south. Small red and small savoy cabbages are also early types.

Late cabbages are slower to mature. The standard lates offered in eastern U.S. seed catalogs usually take 120 days or so to mature, and are grown either for making kraut or for root-cellar storage. They are intended to be sown in June and harvested about the end of September. Late varieties often grow poorly if sown in spring—the increasing daylengths make their heads become pointy instead of round, and they burst. Late cabbages are usually grown on 24-inch centers—and for big heads or a few "giant" varieties, 30 inches might be more appropriate. Lates bred for eastern North America usually won't hold in the field too long after heading. The English and Dutch have developed *very late varieties* suited to their climate—and ours. These "very lates" must be sown about June 15 to head up from October through December. The latest ones will hold in the garden until March and withstand all the frost and rain our climate can usually dish out; they'll even tolerate being frozen solid for days at a time and begin growing again after thawing. Late types are also grown like broccoli, though usually without side-dressing. In fact, it is important for their growth rate to decline so they can harden off by the end of sum-mer, if they're to develop maximum hardiness. Late savoy cabbages are the most vigorous and freeze-hardy, the type most tolerant to poor soil conditions and the best salad cabbage—the ideal garden cabbage.

Overwintered cabbages are a gambler's crop, grown in the same way that seed-to-seed brassica production is carried out in the Skagit Valley.

Seeds are sown in early September without much fertilization (none is usually needed in decent garden soil). The idea is to get the seedlings to grow to their hardiest size—six or seven true leaves each and six to eight inches in diameter—before winter's chill and low light levels check their growth. In spring, they're side-dressed, go into a growth spurt and will usually make good heads during April or May without bolting first. Unpredictable variations in fall weather can make big differences in their growth rate—that's why they're a gamble. If they're too small when winter comes, they'll freeze out; if too big, they'll bolt in spring without heading. Generally, overwintered cabbages make small heads, so final spacing may be 18 by 18 inches. I've had good luck with spring cabbage at frosty Lorane by starting them later (in October), growing them in cold frames over the winter and transplanting eight-inch seedlings about the end of February. Gardeners in northwestern Washington State, where winter freeze-outs are common, might profitably try this type of culture. It can also work with overwintered European Alpha-type cauliflowers bred specifically for this type of growing.

Garden planning: I depend on cabbage, so I usually start a dozen overwintered plants in September. That supplies us with spring cabbage—if they don't bolt or freeze-out. A dozen early transplants go outside, mid-March. In warm springs these do fine; other years, they've been chewed to death or hopelessly stunted and were a waste of effort. Early in April, I sow another dozen earlies directly in the bed, including a few reds to spice up summer lettuce salads. These always do fine; by June, I'm in cabbage for sure. I'm also in new lettuce by then, so a cabbage supply is not as vital until fall. To avoid wasting cabbage when there's lettuce, I only start a half-dozen earlies about mid-June along with my main sowing of late varieties for fall and winter harvest. It takes about 200 square feet of bed sown with very late varieties to keep my family in salad from November through mid-March.

Even vigorous late savoys appreciate good ground, so the crucial main sowing always goes into a bed that was composted and put into green manure the previous fall.

Insects and diseases: Flea beetles can make hash of direct-seeded cabbage seedlings. Sowing five to 10 seeds for every plant wanted prevents the need to spray flea beetles most years. Root maggots especially trouble early varieties sown before June, though they do less damage to direct-seeded plants. Cabbageworms are easily controlled with a spraying of Bt. Chapter 7, Diseases and Pests, covers all these pests and how to effectively handle them.

Harvest: Early green varieties tend to burst quickly after heading up. If very late types head up late in the season when lower light levels and chilly conditions prevent rapid growth, they'll hold through the winter; if they head up during September or early October, they may burst. Thus, late varieties should be sown on the late side—but if sown too late, the heads will be small. Gardeners will have to experiment a bit, seeking the ideal sowing date that matches their microclimate and soil. Sometimes winter cabbage heads will appear to rot; often there's a good head underneath the slimy outer layers.

Saving seed: To grow seed for late-maturing winter-hardy varieties, handle like Brussels sprouts. Some tight-headed varieties may need to have their heads scored with a two-inch deep X in early March to permit the seed stalks to emerge. Often even the stumps in the field will put up seed stalks. Seed saving from early varieties (which will rarely overwinter outdoors) can only be accomplished by having them head up in early fall, protecting the plants over winter and setting them out again in spring. In Denmark, where winters are too frosty for reliable overwintering, mature plants are sometimes buried under a few inches of soil in October and then exposed in spring, to make seed. Before virtually all the world's cabbage seed was grown in the Skagit Valley, local eastern varieties were produced by digging whole plants, roots and all, carrying them over the winter in root cellars and transplanting them out when the soil thawed.

Varieties: Like other sorts of brassicas, hybrid cabbage varieties have virtually replaced the old standard open-pollinated sorts, which now are grown cheaply only for the garden-seed trade. The remaining early open-pollinated varieties are such pointed-head sorts as Jersey Wakefield or its variants (not popular in the U.S.) and Golden Acre types, which are small, green, round-headed cabbages, usually with pale yellow-white centers. If buying open-pollinated cabbage, I'd deal with Johnny's or Stokes. Hybrid early varieties change fashion so rapidly there's not much point in listing and rating those currently available. When buying early hybrids, look for types that promise to hold in the field without bursting. Beware of the many market earlies selected primarily for density (Stonehead: does it ever look good—heavy as a rock, round and as uniform as peas in a pod —and tough as cardboard) and those bred for high yield per acre (which are likely to be watery and bland).

Of the entire world's plant breeders, only the Japanese seem never to forget that the end user of food is the human mouth, not the eye. I've always loved Japanese-bred vegetables such as Princess (TSC), a Golden Acre hybrid and my personal standard of excellence when it comes to an early variety. I hope it continues to be available for a long time. The savoy cabbage, with thin, crinkly leaves, makes superior salads and slaws and doesn't do badly when cooked—it's far better suited to garden use than the typical market sort. Salarite, Savoy Prince, Savoy King and Savoy Ace are all excellent-flavored, thin-leaved, tender, sweet early savoy types from Japanese breeders. All these and Princess also have good field-holding ability (for earlies). Ruby Ball is the best-eating hybrid early red—naturally of Japanese lineage—with the ability to hold a long time without bursting.

If you like green supermarket cabbage, for late maturities, grow Danish Ballhead selections—hybrid or open-pollinated. These are sure-growing, all-purpose late sorts that mature in September or October and will stand in the field until Christmas and sometimes longer. As with the earlies, hybrids now completely dominate the commercial market. Custodian (JSS, STK) is an excellent Japanese hybrid of this sort, tenderer and sweeter than most, with good field-holding ability. The English and Dutch have bred smaller, very late market-sized hybrids such as Winterstar (TSC) that are well-protected by wrapper leaves so the interior heads retain good appearance when cut for market after holding in the field for several months. Thompson & Morgan offers several fine varieties in this class, though its catalog suggests sowing dates that are far too early for us. All Danish Ballheads tend to be a bit tough and fibrous—as they must be to withstand frost and contrary conditions. These varieties, called "storage cabbage" or "wintergreen" by the Dutch, are intended for overwintered storage under climate-controlled conditions similar to those used to keep apples. They also tolerate our winter weather outdoors pretty well. When making choices among these sorts, buy the latest maturities available and look for long holding ability. Johnny's, Territorial and Stokes are the best sources. There are many late-maturing reds; like Danish Ballheads, they tend to be tough and fibrous, as they must be to hold a long time.

Many seed companies sell special varieties for making sauerkraut. Some are poor for home use because they've been bred for the American taste—to be tough enough to withstand canning after being sliced very thin—something not necessary when making kraut at home. The Dutch have bred better sorts for this purpose, like Hitstar (TSC). Decent kraut can be made from any sort of cabbage. In our home, we prefer it made from savoys. Freshly made kraut eaten before it gets completely sour is far superior; in our region, we can make fresh sour cabbage in small quantities most of the year. Few people realize that sauerkraut is an extremely healthy food when made without salt. All salt does is conveniently wilt the leaves and release the water they contain. If the cabbage is pounded thoroughly with a baseball bat in a five-gallon bucket before it is crocked and weighted, its juice is rapidly released and the cabbage ferments well. Please try salt-free sauerkraut! Those addicted to salt can add a tiny amount when it is eaten.

For late salads, we grow June-sown savoys, not Danish Ballhead supermarket types. European savoys are tough and hardier; Japanese savoys are tender, sweeter and slightly less hardy. Chieftain Savoy (Japanese), once the open-pollinated standard in this country, is now badly deteriorated. It matures in September and holds until Christmas. Savonarch (TSC) is a late, very vigorous hybrid in the same class as Chieftain, but it's much more uniform, equally tasty, and has superior field-holding ability. Savonarch matures in October and holds past New Year's. This variety is so crucial to my food supply that I'm working on developing an open-pollinated variety out of Savonarch, a project that will take many years if it is ever successful. The "late" hybrid savoys from Stokes and Johnny's are actually midseason types in the European market and will be tough compared to Savonarch, though not much hardier. For very late savoy cabbage, only Territorial and Thompson & Morgan offer the same slow-growing, superhardy selections used in England for cutting after New Year's. Try January King and Wivoy.

Territorial and Thompson & Morgan are sources for overwintered spring cabbage.

Chinese Cabbage (*B. rapa pekinensis, B. rapa chinensis*)

Chinese cabbage is not an easy garden crop at any time of year. Like its close relative mustard, Chinese cabbage is an annual with a strong tendency to bolt if it experiences increasing daylengths. Getting it to head in spring is impossible. Chinese cabbage also bolts readily in summer and fall; it must be grown very rapidly without growth checks or serious predation if a quality head is to form before seed stalks begin emerging.

Culture: Chinese cabbage requires airy soil that provides very high nutrient levels and lots of moisture. Unless compost is used, heavy soils must be well amended with organic matter far in advance so that preliminary decomposition will have occurred before Chinese cabbage is sown. Light soils aren't so fussy. In addition to broadcasting fertilizer, band one-quarter to one-half cup complete organic fertilizer below each four to five feet of furrow. Sow the strongly germinating seeds about one per inch, one-half inch deep, in rows 24 inches apart. Thin gradually *without permitting any crowding* so the plants stand 18 inches apart in the row by the time they're five or six inches in diameter. Do not try transplanting; Chinese cabbage does much better if its taproot remains intact. Keep the plants well watered; they have very shallow feeder roots and must make very rapid growth to head successfully.

Garden planning: Early varieties, bred for summer harvest, barely head before bolting. If they grow very rapidly, late heads may stand a month in cooler weather before putting up a seed stalk. Four to six good-sized heads will make a gallon of *kim chee,* a Korean-style sauerkraut made with hot peppers, garlic and Chinese cabbage.

Insects and diseases: Small gray slugs don't damage the heads, though they do like living in them. Root maggots attack in an unusual way: instead of invading the roots, they tunnel through the bases of the leaves, frequently cutting through the vascular system, which collapses the leaves and causes the head to rot. Some varieties seem to handle maggot infestations better than others; you can always trim off the bottoms of the outer leaves. During the last three weeks of growth while the heads are forming fast, spraying frequently with Red Arrow, making an attempt to get the spray into the head itself, will greatly reduce maggot problems, as may heavy innoculation with predatory nematodes when the seeds are sown. Flea beetles also chew the leaves badly, slowing the overall increase of the plant. Since the "bolting clock" is ticking away and the plant must be forced to grow as fast as possible, this is one species for which it makes sense to spray flea beetles. Instead of constantly dosing the crop with Red Arrow, the organic gardener who is serious about growing Chinese cabbage might consider putting the crop under a spun polyester cloche (Reemay) as soon as the seedlings are thinned to their final spacing, solving both the flea beetle and root maggot problems with one treatment.

Harvest: Heads must be cut promptly before they bolt or are overly damaged by root maggots. Bolted heads put up *delicious* flower stalks; if cut before the flowers open, they are excellent in stir-fries and winter salads.

Saving seed: As far as I know, there are no longer any reliable open-pollinated strains available, and the seed-making process starts too late in the North to grow seed from plants that have already headed, unless they overwinter and continue making seed the next spring. If fully headed late plants do overwinter in your garden, several similar commercial hybrid varieties might be worked back into a decent open-pollinated one. Chinese cabbage is insect-pollinated, will cross with mustards and turnips, and requires a mile of isolation for reasonable purity.

Varieties: There are no longer any uniform open-pollinated varieties that make a high percentage of decent heads. High-quality commercial

hybrid varieties sold in North America originate from Japanese seed companies. The hybrids offered change fashion so rapidly that, as with early
ballhead market cabbage, there's little point in describing the varieties
being sold in 1988. Stokes, Johnny's and Territorial are all reputable sources
that keep up with changes in the Japanese market. They all divide their
offerings into early and late types. The earlies can be sown after May but
tend to make small heads; the lates make big yields but must not be sown
before mid-July. However, sow too late and the plant will not head by fall.
I've found August 1 to be about the last workable sowing date.

Cauliflower (*B. oleracea botrytis*)

It took me many years to learn how to grow cauliflower reliably. I
made the effort with this difficult vegetable because I love to eat it. Really
fresh garden cauliflower is much sweeter than that from a supermarket
cooler.

Growing cauliflower is a lot like growing Chinese cabbage. Except for
very late and overwintered varieties, it must be propelled into the most
rapid possible growth from the start and nothing should slow it down.
If a cauliflower has its growth stopped or checked, the plant will not form
a decent curd later on. If you use garden-store transplants, make sure they
aren't potbound; set out homegrown ones promptly. Because transplants
are frequently shocked when set out, I've come to feel it is much easier
to direct-seed cauliflower—in fact, directly seeded, it becomes a fairly easy-
to-grow vegetable if the correct varieties are used.

Culture: Cauliflower is more delicate than cabbage or broccoli, though
it is grown just like them. I reserve my more fertile beds for cauliflower.
Delay sowing or transplanting of earlies a few weeks longer than you would
for more hardy brassicas. Set out the spring's first transplants in early
April; make the earliest outdoor sowing about April 1; the last sowing
must go in by July 15 and will head in fall. Space cauliflower 18 to 24
inches apart. It may be helpful to side-dress the plants when they're about
eight inches tall with a bit of blood meal or liquid fertilizer; like broccoli,
the size of the curd depends on how large the plant is when it has grown
the requisite number of leaves and starts flowering. If the plant is big and
husky at that time, the curd will be, too. If the plant is smallish, the curd
will be small and often bitter. If growth was significantly checked, the plant
may "button" and produce a tiny curd no matter how big the plant.

Overwintered cauliflower is easiest to grow. Sow about August 1 and
grow as for Purple Sprouting broccoli. It is not as vigorous as overwintered
broccoli, though, and demands slightly more fertilizer. The eight- to 12-inch

plants overwinter and can survive temperatures below 10°F (sometimes below 6°F if they're healthy and tough when summer ends and are then hardened off by increasingly severe fall weather). In spring as soon as growth resumes (probably mid-February), side-dress overwintered cauliflower with a tablespoonful of blood meal sprinkled around each plant or work complete organic fertilizer into the soil around the plants as you eliminate the weeds.

Garden planning: The maritime Northwest has a good climate for a long supply of cauliflower. The harvest begins with overwintered curds in April and May; the earliest spring transplants can be cut in June; direct-seeded varieties are harvested from late June through November. Cauliflower has been bred to mature uniformly, so (as with broccoli) sow and grow several varieties with different maturities to permit weeks of cutting from a single sowing date. I've found that if I sow 12 to 24 plants of mixed varieties every four to six weeks from mid-April through mid-July, I cut cauliflower every few days from late June through November. I do pretty much the same with broccoli, and start both at the same time in the same bed. Overwintered cauliflower is cut at a time when there's not much else going in the garden, so I start about 50 plants each August.

Insects and diseases: Cauliflowers tend to have delicate root systems, easily ruined by the root maggot—especially Snowball varieties and their derivatives. Snowball types are bred primarily for the Salinas Valley, where most of the cauliflower eaten in the U.S. is grown. In the Salinas area, most fields are irrigated, many soils are light and loamy, and the plants are protected by powerful soil pesticides—so the varieties have been bred to grow big tops (and thus be higher-yielding) but pay for it with skimpy root systems that don't withstand predation. Commercially, that trait appears to be of no consequence; in a maritime Northwest home garden, weak roots can be disastrous. Varieties bred for the northern European market are intended to be grown without irrigation, but the crop buttons rapidly if subjected to moisture stress; in Europe, heavier, moisture-retentive soils are used to grow cauliflower. All these factors combine to make European cauliflower varieties more strongly rooted—especially compared to Salinas-bound varieties. Early sowings of Dutch and English varieties can be adequately protected from the cabbage root maggot by sawdust collars or parasitic nematodes; in my garden, later sowings of European sorts usually grow adequately without protection.

Pinkish or purplish discoloration of the head is a natural response to stress and does not affect the edibility of the plant. "Pinking" is common to certain varieties, like Snow Crown.

Harvest: Cut the flower when the curds are beginning to become "ricey" or separate a bit. This is a trifle later than when commercial crops are cut, but it results in much larger yields.

Saving seed: Regular types are derived from southern European wild cabbages and aren't hardy enough to overwinter this far north. Seed from overwintered cauliflower is easily produced here—in fact, it is being grown in the Skagit for Dutch seed companies. Simply permit the finest plants to form seed like any other overwintered brassica. When I owned Territorial Seed Company, I found it slightly amusing to buy Dutch-cauliflower seed that had originated as stock seed in Holland, been shipped to Mt. Vernon by the pound for increase, shipped back to Holland by the ton, then imported back into the United States by the pound—through all the various customs and Department of Agriculture hassles.

Varieties: This is one brassica where hybrids have not yet become the industry standard, so open-pollinated sorts are carefully selected; however, hybrids are beginning to appear, and the inevitable switch to hybrids is probably going to occur. As with other commercial brassicas, varieties fall in and out of favor so rapidly that there's not much point in suggesting specific ones. Instead, I recommend dealing with quality suppliers and avoiding snowball types.

Commercial-quality overwintered cauliflower is available only from Territorial and Thompson & Morgan. Abundant Life has a strain it grows itself that is almost certainly "home garden" quality. For regular cauliflower, grow only Dutch or English varieties; some of 1988's most popular European imports are White Summer, White Fox, Andes, Taipan, Dominant, White Rock, White Top, Cervina and Vernon. Stokes has the widest assortment of top-quality commercial grade varieties available in North America, most of them imports from Europe. When dealing with Stokes, avoid any variety named "snow" or derived from a snowball type except Snow Crown, which is a Japanese snowball hybrid that is so vigorous and early it should be considered for the first cutting of spring. I'd buy my cauliflower seed from Territorial because it offers the longest maturity range available and sells only premium Dutch types. Territorial is the only North American supplier that sells a commercial-grade, very late, slow-growing variety for harvest in late fall. Called Jura, it heads mid-November if sown mid-July. If the weather is good in mid-November, you get fine curds to finish out the year; if the weather is very frosty or rainy during the 10 to 20 days that the curds form, their quality will be poor. I think a variety like Jura is well worth the gamble.

"Purple cauliflower" is actually a cauliflower/broccoli cross; it tastes more like broccoli but looks like cauliflower.

Collards (*B. oleracea capitata*)

Collard greens, called cabbage greens or coleworts in England, are a non-heading sort of cooking cabbage, best grown like kale for winter harvest. Vates is hardier than Georgia. Johnny's has a new Vates selection called Champion, produced and bred in the Skagit Valley. The Japanese primary growers are now selling hybrid collards, but they're probably not hardy enough to overwinter here.

Kale (*B. oleracea acephala*)

About the most vigorous, easiest-to-grow garden brassica, kale (sometimes called borecole) is very similar to the wild cabbage from which the entire family was bred. The leaves and petiols of most varieties are salad-quality greens, especially if cut finely. Kale develops more sweetness after some hard frosts, but may quickly become tough if not used shortly after cutting. Consequently, the supermarket product from California is doubly inferior to garden kale.

Culture: Grow like Purple Sprouting broccoli, sowing midsummer, one-half inch deep in rows 18 to 24 inches apart. Thin gradually so the plants stand 12 to 18 inches apart in the row. Broadcasting some fertilizer into the bed before sowing and keeping the plants watered is more than adequate pampering.

Garden planning: Kale is more nutritious by far than cabbage; its green leaves are full of high-protein chlorophyll. Perhaps I am being refined by the garden, but each year I come to like more chewy, strong-flavored kale in my salads and less tender, mild-tasting cabbage. So each year I find myself growing more kale. It is also a lot easier to grow than cabbage. New gardeners might start with about 50 square feet of bed in this crop. I grow several hundred.

Insects and diseases: No problems at all in my garden.

Harvest: Cut individual leaves as needed. Plants don't grow much after mid-November, but spring regrowth starts early. A light side-dressing of blood meal in mid-February will produce a lot more spring leaf. The flower stalks make good "broccoli," though they don't have a broccoli flavor; they appear at the same time Purple Sprouting broccoli is in bloom.

Saving seed: Like any other biennial brassica. However, Siberian kales only cross with rutabaga; Scotch varieties, which grow a tall central stalk, cross freely with other members of the cabbage family.

Varieties: Since there's virtually no North American commercial market for kale, all domestic kale seed produced for North American seed companies is strictly for the home-garden trade—usually called Blue or Green Curled Scotch. There's nothing wrong with these varieties; in fact, they're locally well adapted, having been produced in the Skagit Valley through overwintering. More refined varieties come from Holland and England, where kale (there called *boerkool* or farmer's cabbage) is a popular market crop. I prefer Westland Winter (TSC) and hybrid Winterbor (TSC, JSS), along with Siberian and Red Russian—a red Siberian (TSC, ABL).

Kohlrabi (*B. oleracea caulorapa*)

This peculiar brassica has been grotesqued into making a bulbous stem, a sweet-flavored, turnip-like vegetable without the characteristic harshness or pungency of the turnip. The bulb is held above the soil, where the edible part (at least) is impervious to the root maggot.

Culture: In hot weather, kohlrabi makes tough, pungent, woody bulbs, so avoid growing for harvest after mid-June or before October. Sow in April for June harvest and again mid-July through mid-August for fall harvest. Sow seeds two to four per inch, one-half inch deep, in rows 18 inches apart. Thin very carefully as the seedlings become established, so the bulbs stand three inches apart in the row; *crowded kohlrabi fails to bulb well.* In spring sowings, banding a little fertilizer in addition to broadcasting it into the beds makes faster growth and sweeter, more tender bulbs.

Garden planning: Because spring sowings mature quickly and won't hold long without losing their good culinary qualities, small sowings are appropriate at that time. If you're a real admirer of the vegetable, consider making the first sowing in a frame in March and subsequent small sowings every two weeks through April. Fall crops can stand in the field for some time and retain good eating quality, especially if first-class varieties are grown. I sow about 50 square feet for fall harvest.

Insects and diseases: Kohlrabi tends to have a weak root system, and if maggots are thick in spring, it may have trouble. Fortunately, mild infestations only affect the root system, leaving the bulbs untouched—a big advantage over turnips or radishes.

Saving seed: The vegetable is not as hardy as other biennial brassicas, though it will overwinter in milder years. Hilling up soil over the bulbs (but not the leaves) in November will get them over the worst of winter. A very refined brassica, kohlrabi takes careful selection to prevent a good percentage of the plants from being worthless.

Varieties: Cheap U.S.-grown varieties are produced strictly for the home-garden trade and contain a high percentage of plants that fail to make decent bulbs. They're usually called Purple Vienna or "White" Vienna. The popular Japanese hybrid, Grand Duke, is not well adapted to our northern latitudes; Winner F1 (TSC) is much better. There's no significant eating difference between purple- and green-skinned types. I'd buy my seed from Johnny's or Territorial to be sure of getting the best European selections. In the case of kohlrabi, Stokes seems to be selling garden seed.

Rutabagas (*B. napus rapifera*)

There's a multitude of reasons to find a big rutabaga patch in a self-sufficient garden. Rutabagas simply left out in the garden all winter keep well enough to suit me. They're also very easy to grow—almost as vigorous as kale. Rutabagas produce amazing yields of flavorful roots that make a non-starchy potato substitute; they're also less susceptible to damage by brassica pests than are turnips. And certain home-garden varieties have a wonderful sweet flavor far superior to supermarket fare or turnips. Read on!

Culture: Highly vigorous, rutabagas will usually grow well enough in soils that have had recent additions of manure or compost: however, broadcasting fertilizer into the bed before sowing will ensure a big crop. So fertilize—why not get gigantic roots for only slightly more effort than it takes to grow smaller ones? Sow the seed during July, before mid-month. Sprinkle it thinly in half-inch-deep furrows, rows 24 inches apart. Thin gradually to eight inches apart in the row. *Careful thinning is essential* because crowded rutabagas don't form big roots.

Garden planning: Rutabagas yield abundantly. A true fancier or someone really trying for winter self-sufficiency might try a 100-square-foot bed for starters. When the crop is done, the bed is a good place for spring peas or lettuce; rutabagas grow very well when they follow a pea crop or fava bean green manure.

Insects and diseases: In my garden, the root maggot seems relatively uninterested in rutabagas, though it sometimes tunnels through the skin—rarely into the bulb. Slugs like to dig cavities; so do mice. Then the bulbs rot. Those with less pleasant experiences might consider digging the crop and storing it in the garage or root cellar, as they traditionally did in the north.

Harvest: In my garden, the roots hold in decent condition and can be dug until March, when they start going to seed. Most damage from insects and other critters is minor and can be peeled away. If winter turns freezing cold for only a short spell, the roots, which sit mostly on top of the ground, may freeze solid and then rot afterward if not protected. So during November, consider covering the bed with flakes of straw, burying the roots three inches or so deep. This is enough protection to get past a three- to five-day cold snap of 10°F weather.

Saving seed: After overwintering, rutabagas go to seed like other biennial brassicas. Rutabagas cross only with Siberian kales.

Varieties: Most Purple Top or Laurentian selections available in American seed catalogs will produce decent roots. There are some especially tasty selections like Altasweet (STK, TSC), with a really sweet flavor you can't get in a supermarket. You'll find the widest selection of quality varieties from Stokes, which supplies the Canadian market, where rutabagas are a popular winter vegetable. Also check out Thompson & Morgan, a company primarily supplying the British home gardener, where rutabagas are a major winter crop and are called Swedes or Swedish turnips.

Turnips (*B. rapa rapifera*)

Turnips are biennial brassicas that grow like radishes (an annual) but require more fertile soil. In the maritime Northwest, organic turnips are much easier to grow for greens than for roots, though sometimes the root maggots leave the gardener a few turnips that have not been completely ruined. See also "Radishes" in the Roots section.

Culture: Turnips need fertile, airy soil and plenty of moisture to grow fast enough to "outrun" the cabbage root maggot. They will grow amazingly fast if supplied with all the necessaries. If they mature quickly enough, the maggots will have barely hatched out before the roots are plucked from their grasp. Turnips may be started from April through August. In fertilized soil, below each five feet of furrow, band an additional one-quarter to one-half cup of complete organic fertilizer. Sow the tiny seed thinly, one-half inch deep, in rows 24 inches apart. When the seedlings are established, thin *carefully* to three inches apart in the row.

Garden planning: Because turnips must be harvested promptly, frequent small sowings are in order. Turnips grow quickly, and their space may be followed by other crops.

Insects and diseases: Chapter 7, Diseases and Pests, discusses systems for managing root maggots, including nematodes, sawdust mulches and protective row covers. Flea beetles can slow down growth and give the maggots time to invade; spraying them may be in order if the leaves are becoming very ragged.

Harvest: Turnips will grow six to eight inches in diameter (like huge rutabagas) if given the space, but they are much better picked on the small side, both for milder flavor and to avoid the root maggot.

Saving seed: Like rutabagas, most turnips are biennial, though less hardy than rutabagas, and may require careful mulching to get over the winter. Some varieties are annual (Crawford and Shogoin) and are spring-sown for seed production. Turnips may cross freely with mustards and Chinese cabbage.

Varieties: Purple Top White Globe and such variants as Milan, Strap Leaf and some new hybrids of this type from Japanese seed companies are less attractive to the maggot than the many tasty, milder-flavored, all-white hybrid varieties that originate in Japan. For greens, any variety is edible, but Shogoin was specially bred for this purpose.

Roots

Several vegetable species produce edible roots; most are biennials. Their common growth habit is to thrust a taproot farther down than competing annuals can reach—deep into subsoil moisture and nutrient reserves—and then to fill a portion of this root with stored food. Root-crop species are adapted to relatively infertile soils. For example, wild carrot (Queen Anne's Lace) is a nuisance weed in poor pastures; it is smothered out by grasses in rich soil. The basic survival strategy of most root crops is to bank a large supply of food using one year's subsoil moisture supply. Then, instead of having to use the current supply of light, water and nutrients more efficiently than their shallow-rooted competition, biennials can use their "bank" to outgrow annuals or can wait until their competition can barely make any food, choosing this auspicious moment to make seed.

However, this adaptation doesn't necessarily mean vegetable biennials will make succulent food for a lazy gardener. If the soil is soft and friable, and abundant moisture supplies remain available, the storage area will swell up uniformly, producing shapely and tasty carrots, beets, parsnips, Hamburg parsley, burdock roots or chicory. If the soil becomes hard and compacted or the moisture supply fluctuates radically, the roots will develop irregularly and may be tough and bitter. Potatoes and radishes (annual species) are equally sensitive to soil compaction and moisture levels. On heavier soils, this sensitivity demands the use of uncompacted raised beds. Obviously, commercial root crops can be produced efficiently only on deep, coarse loams and sands. Grown in extremely rich soil, biennials may not store as much food, so the gardener should not encourage these species with too much fertilizer. Instead, maintain moderate nutrient levels and concentrate on creating loose, moist soil. Softening up clay soils by incorporating massive amounts of manure or compost can create the dilemma of also providing too much nitrogen for proper root development. The solution on clay is to prepare the root beds a year in advance, growing highly demanding species the first year and then using next year's remnants of fertility for root crops.

Thinning is vital for root crops; when crowded, few individuals develop to their potential. Only very poorly selected home-gardener-only varieties with extreme variations in vigor from plant to plant will produce some decent roots when overcrowded; those highly vigorous individuals will totally overwhelm their competitors and develop reasonably well.

Hybrid beet and carrot seed are available these days. Though hybridization doesn't make as much difference in vigor as can be found with some species, it does produce more uniform beets and carrots. This is particularly true of carrot varieties, where hybrids are becoming commercial market standards and the old standards are deteriorating as garden selections.

To grow biennials (beet, carrot, parsley root, parsnip) like "field crops" without irrigation, sow as early as the seed will sprout; it may be that only loam soils will permit satisfactory enough early tillage. Work over the rows with a garden fork or long spade in a narrow strip 10 to 12 inches deep to enhance the rapid penetration of tap roots; while doing this, work in one gallon of complete organic fertilizer per 100 row feet. Make rows 42 to 48 inches apart. Thin carefully; by the time the seedlings are four or five inches tall, they should stand two or three times as far apart as the mature roots will be in diameter. This is much wider spacing than irrigated crops need. Keep well weeded through the summer. Start harvesting from mid-July. The roots will grow amazingly large and may hold in the soil until next spring. In frosty areas, hill up a little soil over the crowns in late October to prevent freezing (and then rotting) should winter turn harsh.

Beets (*Beta vulgaris*)

Beets are native to Mediterranean climates, where soils are usually alkaline. The finest beets come off well-limed loam soils. Because most of the food storage area is located on or above the surface, nearly any soil type that isn't too acid will grow beets—even clays, as long as they are deep and made permeable with additions of organic matter. Beets grow best when temperatures are moderate and soils warm, though some early varieties can be started in April. Spells of cold weather or periods of heat-induced moisture stress result in "zoning," white rings that don't affect the flavor much.

Culture: Since beets form roots on the surface, it is not usually necessary to work the bed deeply when growing them on permanent raised beds. Beets have a low to moderate nutrient requirement; broadcasting and tilling in about one-half to two-thirds of a gallon of complete organic fertilizer per 100 square feet of bed, or last year's significant addition of organic matter and half that much fertilizer tilled in before sowing, is sufficient for a good crop. Sow from April through June. Make early sowings one-half inch deep; make later ones three-quarters of an inch deep and sow a little more seed. Each beet seed is actually a fruit containing several embryos, but because germination rate is often low, it's best to sow two to three seeds per inch, in rows 18 inches apart. When the seedlings stand about three inches tall, thin carefully so the plants stand as far apart as you'll want mature roots. For baby beets, that's about one inch apart; canners (uniform selections for once-over harvest) should be thinned three to four inches apart; winter-storage varieties can grow six inches around. For table use, grow a home-garden variety such as Early Wonder, which varies considerably in vigor from seedling to seedling— thin seedlings casually, eliminating any dense clumps, then harvest roots as they enlarge. Smaller, weaker ones will fill in the row spaces as the large beets are pulled.

Garden planning: Crudely thinned home-garden table beet selections can yield tender young beets for a long time. I've found that a few rows across a raised bed keep our family in all the table beets we want all summer. For winter use, I sow about 50 square feet of bed about July 1. Borscht lovers might want to plant four times as much.

Insects and diseases: Bean beetles may chew on slow-growing seedlings in spring. The non-spray solution is to plant lots of seed or wait until the soil warms up a bit before starting the beet patch. Leafminers may attack beets; for organic handling, see Chapter 7, Diseases and Pests.

Harvest: Mature beets can stand a long time awaiting harvest, though in very hot weather they may become woody. Winterkeepers and some Detroit selections develop thick, protective skins and hold outdoors from October to March, retaining good eating quality throughout the winter. Protect overwintering beets with a two- or three-inch-thick straw mulch. If they freeze, they'll rot immediately. In those areas where winters are too severe, or mice, slugs and rain combine to ruin beets left in the garden, they may be dug and kept in a cellar, shed or pumphouse like potatoes.

Saving seed: Beets are wind-pollinated biennials. Their light pollen can carry a mile or more downwind. Beets also freely cross with chard. Since beet seed can easily last four or five years and since this region produces the world's most vigorous beet seed, you can grow seed from different varieties in alternate years. Harvest seed-roots in early November. Select for narrow crowns, fine tap-roots, uniform shape and deep red color. Transplant selected roots to a part of the garden that won't be irrigated. Set each root deeply enough that the crown will be at the soil line, 12 inches apart in rows about four feet apart. Then hill several inches of soil over the crown to protect it during winter. When the worst of winter is past, uncover the crown and wait. The roots will put forth new leaves, then seed stalks, which bloom and make seed. All the gardener must do is keep the patch clean of weeds, reserving all available soil moisture for the beets. When half the seed is dry, cut the stalks and finish drying under cover on a tarp or sheets of newspaper. Strip the seed from the stalks by hand; clean the dusty seed by pouring it between two buckets in a mild breeze. Six plants will produce over a pound of seed. If harsh conditions make outdoor survival of overwintered roots unlikely, root-cellar them like potatoes and plant out again about March 1.

Varieties: Early Wonder is the single best variety for the garden. Most selections have tall, tasty tops and variable maturity and don't require perfect thinning. Early Wonder types also make better growth in cool weather than most canners. Detroit types (including Ruby Queen) are widely available and grow better when sown after spring has settled a bit. The new hybrid varieties are mainly Detroit types. Little Ball (TSC) and Little Miniball (STK) are bred for dense plantings of small, perfectly round roots for canning whole as "baby beets." Usually they are very tender and sweet. Cylindrical beets such as Formanova, Cylindra and Forono are bred for canneries, which need a shape that can be conveniently sliced into uniform rings. They are also fast-cooking, a trait that saves canneries time and money. Growing deep into the ground more like carrots than beets, cylindrical varieties develop better in light soils. Winterkeepers (often called Lutz) grow very large roots that tend to be irregularly shaped, thick-skinned, very sweet and bred especially to hold through the winter. They are best sown about July 1 to mature in October. The gardener should feel free to experiment with any beet variety, including white, yellow, sugar beet crosses and monogerm. I've never had a variety-linked failure with beets.

Carrots (*Daucus carota sativus*)

Poorer pastures throughout the maritime Northwest are covered with Queen Anne's Lace (wild carrot). This should convince anyone that carrots are well adapted to our region. Wild carrot being so abundant on our side of the mountains, culinary carrot seed (which freely crosses with wild carrot) must be grown east of the Cascades, where wild carrot's lacy white flowers can't be found. If the carrot rust fly maggot can be deterred and wireworm damage is minimal, carrots can be one of the easiest crops to grow, producing amazingly high yields per square foot.

Carrot seed germinates slowly, often taking 12 to 14 days to sprout, yet the small seeds must be shallowly sown. The shoots are weak and cannot force their way through crusts, compacted clay or puddled soil. Plantings started before the heat of summer usually germinate well enough because the soil stays moist and crust-free naturally. However, sowings made after May are dicier. I've found that mixing a bit of sphagnum moss into the soil covering the carrot seed or filling the furrow with sifted compost will retain moisture and prevent crusting, resulting in very good germination. This technique is also useful for parsnip seed; in fact, it is a good practice for any shallow midsummer sowing.

Culture: What the carrot seedling encounters during its first six to eight weeks of life determines the quality of the root it will produce. Immediately after sprouting, the carrot puts down a taproot. If that root does not encounter compacted soil, impenetrable clods or zones of high nitrogen concentration (such as might come from pieces of undecomposed fresh manure or chemical fertilizer granules), it will grow straight down without forking or crooking. If the soil then remains soft and moist and the roots don't overly compete with each other or with weeds, the upper four to 12 inches of the root will swell with stored food. To grow good carrots in heavy soil, manure should be spread and worked in the previous year. If organic matter content must be increased immediately before sowing, well-ripened compost should be used.

In all but very sandy soil, the bed must be well-cultivated immediately before sowing carrots. But tilled soil tends to slump back into its native level of compaction within two months of tilling, so it's essential to make the seedlings grow very fast—to "outrace" the hardening earth. Once they've started storing food, carrots are able to push against gradually compacting soil much more strongly. To make sure my carrots do not lack any usable nutrition, I first broadcast about two-thirds of a gallon of complete organic fertilizer over each 100 square feet of bed. Then I deeply break up the soil, using a 12-inch spading fork. I push the fork into the soil to the hilt every three or four inches, then pull back on the handle to pop the soil loose a foot down. If I could find a 14- or 16-inch spading fork, I'd use that. Then I run a rototiller over the bed several times until it is *thoroughly pulverized eight inches deep.* If I did not have a tiller,

I'd break up the soil by repetitively turning it over with and chopping it with the fork. This may seem like a lot of work, but in finely tilled soil, the carrot yield may be two or three times higher. Besides all this tilling, growing carrots takes a lot of picky, time-consuming thinning. It's actually less trouble and more rewarding to Grow an intensive plot well than to "sort of grow" a larger area. Why start off in a way that won't ensure success?

In early April, I usually start a small patch in roughly worked soil. But I wait until the soil has dried down to exactly the ideal tilling point before making serious sowings—usually about the same time I start beans, unless we're gifted with a sunny spring. A last sowing before July 10 yields big roots before autumn checks their development. In furrows one-half inch deep, sprinkle the seed thinly, two to four seeds per inch, the rows about 18 inches apart. In hot weather, cover with sifted compost or aged sifted manure. Thin gradually but *carefully and thoroughly* so that by the time the seedlings stand two inches tall, they're as far apart in the row as the mature roots will be in diameter—generally about 1½ inches apart. Keep the bed weeded carefully. Sudden increases in soil moisture after periods of dryness can cause many varieties to split and then rot.

When carrot seed is sprinkled into the furrow by hand, the almost inevitable result is a tangle of crowded seedlings. This makes for unnecessarily time-consuming and painstaking work; it can easily take over an hour to correctly thin an overseeded 100-square-foot raised bed. No matter how long it takes, thinning carrots is well worth the trouble, but let me suggest a thinning short-cut. Depending on the size of the seed and its germination percentage, a heaping quarter-teaspoon of carrot seed will sow 25 to 50 row feet. Instead of trying to distribute that tiny pinch of seed by hand equally into five to 10 rows across a raised bed, thoroughly mix the seed into exactly one gallon of finely sifted compost and try to distribute the mix equally along the bottom of the furrow. To help you achieve exactly that, keep in mind that one gallon contains eight pints. Then cover the seed with a little more sifted compost. The result will be a very high germination percentage and *uniformly spaced seedlings that require very little thinning*.

Garden planning: One well-grown, 100-square-foot bed of carrots sown in spring (about 50 row feet) keeps my family supplied during summer and fall. One more sown about July 1 finishes sizing-up in October and is consumed during winter, after the first bed runs out. If I wanted to juice carrots, I'd grow five times that amount.

Insects and diseases: Rust fly maggots and wireworms burrow into carrots, causing rot and leaving a bad flavor around the track they make. Handling maggots is discussed in Chapter 7, Diseases and Pests. I cannot offer any remedy for wireworm damage, except to comment that it is minor in my garden (though it does increase, the longer the roots are in the soil). The occasional "trail" can be cut away before the carrot is eaten. If damage is too severe, consider digging your carrots in late October and storing them in a root cellar. The traditional method is to fill a barrel with layers of carrots and damp coarse sand.

Harvest: Carrots hold all winter in the ground without serious damage in my garden. At frosty Lorane, I covered the carrots with a few inches of straw in November to protect the crowns from freezing in the event of a severe cold snap. (If they freeze, they'll rot.) Covering the mulch with a sheet of plastic increases the protection by keeping the bed dry, but may make a haven for field mice, which eat the roots.

Saving seed: Carrots are bee-pollinated and need isolation of one mile to grow fairly pure seed. It would be easy to grow seed in our climate, but for the presence of wild carrots everywhere. Wild-carrot crosses result in whitish, dry, fibrous roots with little sweetness. Tim Peters, a serious plant breeder and trial grounds master at Territorial Seed Company, says he has grown carrot seed around Myrtle Creek by transplanting the roots 12 inches by 24 inches apart in March, covering the seed plants with a five-foot-tall screened tent to keep out all insects, and locating the carrot bed where there is an active ant hill. The ants pollinate enough flowers to set a decent seed yield. One could also introduce a small bee hive for a few weeks during the main flowering. To preserve uniformity, grow carrot seed only from painstakingly hand-selected perfect roots.

Varieties: Almost any variety will grow in our climate. The long Imperator types preferred by the supermarket trade require very coarse-textured deep soils to develop well-shaped roots. Cylindrical Nantes varieties with the highest sugar content are best for earlier sowings and summer eating; they have the lowest fiber content and so are tender, but without strong fiber, the Nantes tend to split easily when large and don't stand up to winter too well. Danvers (or Flakkee types, as the Europeans call them) make pointed roots six to seven inches long with higher fiber contents that hold well in the ground during winter. These are what I sow in July. The short, broad Chantenay varieties develop better in clayey soils than any other sort. Thompson & Morgan also offers an Autumn King variety—huge carrots bred expressly for in-the-ground winter storage. I don't like the coarse flavor of Autumn King types. Flavor and tenderness vary greatly with variety, so the gardener should experiment.

On the Continent, the old names like Flakkee and Nantes are disappearing, as quality European companies increasingly compete with proprietary patented varieties whose appellations do not evoke anything reminiscent of "Nantes" or "Amsterdam forcing"; the old open-pollinated commercial varieties are rapidly being replaced with hybrids. Buying from Thompson & Morgan can be very confusing for this reason. Johnny's takes pity on the poor gardener, and buys the finest available seed, often hybrids from Dutch companies, but then labels them "Nantes" or what have you. Buy winter carrots from Territorial.

Chicory or Belgian Endive (*Cichorium intybus*)

The various forms of chicory are biennial root crops that form edible tops. They grow in relatively infertile soils. There are great differences between varieties: some are eaten out of hand like bitter forms of endive; some must go dormant and regrow in spring before the leaves lose enough bitterness to be edible; the most refined types are dug in fall when the tops die back and then forced to resprout under controlled conditions, making Belgian endive, a very pricey gourmet specialty.

Culture: *Non-forcing types* are sown in June or early July for fall and winter harvest and are very easy to grow. Plant seeds one-half inch deep in rows 18 inches apart; thin gradually to eight to 12 inches apart in the row. Fertilizer is not usually needed in garden soil. *Forcing types* must be carefully grown with all the formalities required for premium carrots, to produce uniform roots. Thin carefully to six to eight inches apart. Overly dense stands produce too-small roots. Too loosely spaced stands produce overly thick, coarse roots. Excessive nitrogen makes plants too leafy, with thick crowns, undesirable for forcing. Ideally, roots should be six to eight inches long when mature. The roots are dug from September to December and may be kept in cold storage until spring. If the tops are still green, the roots are dug and laid in rows outside for several days, then the tops are cut off, leaving about a half-inch of stalk above the shoulder to avoid damaging the growing point.

Commercially, the roots are taken from cold storage and tightly packed into a wooden box about 16 inches deep; the roots are trimmed at the bottom so the upright crowns are all on one level; the spaces between them are filled with fine, slightly moist light soil. Then the crowns are covered with eight more inches of fine soil. To retain moisture, the soil is covered with straw. The box is then heated to 65°F (precisely) to force "chicons" to sprout. In about three weeks, Belgian endive is ready for harvest. Lower sprouting temperatures make the process too slow for the profit-conscious; higher temperatures make tough, bitter heads. At home, a big wooden box in an unheated room in the low sixties would probably be adequate.

Garden planning: This is not a vegetable the average gardener is going to want to devote much space to. A very small quantity of some leafy varieties spices up salads.

Insects and diseases: None known yet.

Harvest: *Non-forcing types:* Sugarhat will stand for weeks in autumn like endive. Treviso is best overwintered with a little soil hilled up over the crowns to prevent freezing. It becomes edible when it resprouts in early spring. Round-heading types are best sown on the late side (early August) to mature when things cool down, or they'll be extremely bitter.

Saving seed: Same as endive.

Varieties: As North Americans become increasingly interested in this vegetable, more and more European selections appear in our seed catalogs. However, Thompson & Morgan is best for ones that overwinter outdoors. Johnny's and Stokes carry an assortment for fall harvest and for forcing. There are huge differences in the uniformity of selections. Sugarhat (Zuckerhut) forms a big green head like a romaine lettuce and is the only leaf chicory I find sweet enough to eat willingly in fall. Catalogna is like a wild dandelion, an annual whose flowers are picked before they open. Perhaps the Italians know what to do with Catalogna—cooked or raw, it seems inedibly bitter to me. But then, so does the tropical bitter melon so loved in the Orient.

Parsley (*Petroselinum crispum*)

Most people buy transplants unnecessarily. This salad garnish is easy to direct-seed if it's started early. And most people do not know that the best aspect of parsley may not be the leaf, but its delicious edible root.

Culture: Parsley seed germinates slowly, best under cooler conditions. If seed is sown in April, naturally cool damp soils enhance germination without attention from the gardener, but if sown in May, parsley must be guarded against drying out for nearly three weeks. Once sprouted, parsley is a vigorous grower. *To grow leaf parsley:* in April, sow seed thinly, one-half inch deep, in rows 18 inches apart. Thin gradually to two or three inches apart in the row. If leaf production falters, side-dress with fertilizer. *To grow root parsley:* culture like carrots, taking extra pains to work the soil deeply, and thin to three inches in the row. Parsley root is less tolerant of heavy soil than most types of carrot but more tolerant than parsnip.

Garden planning: One four-foot row of leaf parsley across a raised bed sown in April produces all the garnishes and seasonings we can use from July through to next spring. Root parsley is similar in flavor to parsnips, though it grows somewhat better in heavier or shallower soil than parsnips will tolerate. Root parsley also holds in the ground all winter.

Insects and diseases: None known.

Harvest: Snip leaves as needed. In mild winters, the leaves are available all winter; in colder areas, they die back. If mulched so the crowns don't freeze, leaf parsley will resprout in spring for a second short round of cutting. Dig root parsley from September to March. Cover the roots with a little straw to prevent freezing.

Saving seed: Parsley is an insect-pollinated biennial, grown like beets for a seed crop. Leaf varieties do not require digging, selection and replanting, because there is no concern about root shape. Overwinter the plants and allow to make seed. Seed for root varieties should be grown only from carefully hand-selected roots, dug in October and replanted like carrots.

Varieties: There are subtle flavor differences among curly-leaf varieties; some have longer stems; some are more or less curled. Be a gourmet if you wish. Flat-leaf types are strongly flavored, good for drying into parsley flakes. Buyer beware: the root varieties offered in North American seed catalogs might be high-quality, uniform European selections (where parsley root is a commercial crop) or cheap stuff grown for the domestic garden-seed trade without careful selection. Most root varieties are fairly long and need deeply worked soil. One variety, Toso (TSC) develops a shorter root that may do better in heavier soils.

Parsnip (*Pastinaca sativa*)

Very similar to carrots in habit, parsnips are much more prone to hairiness in strong soils and demand deep, loose beds if well-formed, straight roots are to be produced. It's much easier to grow parsnips on loam soils.

Culture: Work the bed deeply and finely with a spading fork—to 12 inches at least. Fertilize the bed only if the soil is very poor, and then use only half as much as you would for any other crop. Sow the seeds from May through mid-July. Early sowings sprout more easily but produce overly large roots; July sowings produce supermarket-sized, slightly better keepers but germination is touchy in hot weather. Sow seeds three-quarters of an inch deep, three or four seeds per inch, in rows 18 inches apart. In hot weather, cover the seeds with sifted organic matter and keep moist until sprouted. *Thin the seedlings carefully.* Thin early sowings to at least four inches apart; thin July sowings to about two inches.

Garden planning: Early sowings mature in summer; July sowings mature in fall. Either way, the roots will probably hold in the soil all winter.

Insects and diseases: Parsnips seem invulnerable to everything except field mice, which prefer its sweet roots to carrots.

Harvest: Protect the crowns from freezing by hilling up a little soil over them or layering some straw over the bed. Dig as wanted until spring, when they resprout. Parsnip leaves taste like tough celery and in *small* quantities will round out winter salads.

Saving seed: Like carrots. The seed tends to shatter easily when ripe, something like dill, so harvest promptly and dry fully under cover. Parsnip seed tends to be short-lived, lasting at best two years with high vigor. It also tends to be low-germ.

Varieties: There's not much commercial market for parsnips, but for uniform crops, the seed must be grown from painstakingly hand-selected roots that take considerable effort to dig, inspect and replant. Stokes's Hollow Crown Improved is probably garden-seed quality, while their Harris Model is "grown from hand-selected roots," though the company sells both varieties for the same price. Johnny's says its Harris Model is "uniform" but prices it like the cheapest of seed, and also sells an expensive English variety—parsnip is a big commercial crop in Europe and high-quality seed stocks are common there. So naturally, Thompson & Morgan sells three well-bred varieties, including one it says is the first hybrid parsnip. The original Harris Model was bred by Jos. Harris Seed Company—so Harris/ Moran still has a proprietary interest in maintaining this variety to the highest possible standards. Harris's price for Harris Model is more than double that of Stokes's! Territorial confidently buys the finest available commercial-grade Harris Model direct from the originator—Harris. *Caveat emptor.*

Potatoes (*Solanum tuberosum*)

Potatoes are solanums like tomatoes; however, they make root-like tubers that need soft soil and demand fertility levels similar to other root crops. Nor are potatoes heat-demanding like other solanums. For these reasons, potatoes find their home in this section.

You might not think that potatoes, being so inexpensive, are worth the trouble they'll take and the space they'll occupy. If you grow the same #2 varieties in the garden that are sold cheaply in the supermarket, you might be right. However, not only are home-grown varieties free of sprays and sprout-inhibiting chemicals, but there are home-garden varieties that make supermarket potatoes taste like a sad excuse for food. Commercial varieties are commercial because they are the highest yielding, not because they possess the best flavor. These two aspects, yield and flavor, are necessarily opposed. The fewer tubers set, the more nutrition the vine can pack into them. Home-garden potato varieties are delicious all by themselves—a health food that doesn't need to be deep-fried or slathered in butter, sour cream, vinegar, salt, pepper or ketchup.

Culture: The single most important cultural aspect of potato growing is having light-textured soil so the tubers can swell easily and prolifically. Commercially, the best potatoes are raised on sandy loams. In heavier soils, the bed should first be well amended with manure or compost. If the organic matter is rich in nitrogen, additional fertilization may not be needed; in fact, it may be harmful. Feeding too much nitrogen to potatoes results in lanky vines that set few tubers.

Seed potatoes are obtained by cutting whole potatoes into chunks, each containing several eyes. Do this about a month before planting. The chunks are placed on a tray in bright light while the cuts "skin over" (form a callus) and the eyes begin to sprout. Then it's time to plant. Some gardeners who save their own "seed" potatoes set aside the smaller tubers for this purpose. These don't need cutting, but they do need to be greened-up, initiating sprouting exactly like cut-up "seed." For luck, set out the earliest potatoes on St. Patrick's Day (March 17). Make the last sowing by mid-June.

On raised beds, broadcast about one gallon of complete organic fertilizer per 100 square feet and till. Suppose the bed is four feet by 25 feet. Down the length of the bed, dig two 25-foot-long, shallow, parallel trenches, 10 inches wide and perhaps six inches deep. Locate each trench about eight inches in from the paths on each side of the bed. Carefully pile the soil taken from the trenches in a long mound between them. In the trenches, drop one seed potato per foot and cover shallowly by raking a little soil down from the bed's center. As the vines grow, gradually pull more soil down over the stalks, not quite covering their growing tips. This can also be done while hoeing the weeds. If frost should hit, the vines will burn back only to the soil line and immediately resprout. Keep raking soil over the growing vines until the center of the bed becomes a long, shallow depression and the rows of potatoes are hilled up somewhat.

Without irrigation: It is possible to grow potatoes without irrigation, though yields will be lower. On soils that permit early tillage, plant out seed potatoes as early as possible—certainly before April 1. Prepare the planting rows as deeply as a rototiller will go and work in one gallon of complete organic fertilizer per 100 row feet. Make rows about 48 inches apart. The soil may be wet and end up kind of rough. That's okay. Push the seed potatoes into the earth about an inch deep; plant one seed potato per foot. As the potatoes grow, hill up soil over the row with the hoe as you *keep the patch totally weed-free* so the potatoes get all the soil moisture.

Heavy ground usually can't be tilled very early. Rather than wait until the soil had lost too much moisture to produce an irrigationless crop, I'd till the previous autumn, mulch the row to prevent winter rains from compacting the soil, remove the mulch in spring, sprinkle fertilizer over the row and, without tilling, drop the seed potatoes right on the surface and begin scratching up a little soil to hill over them.

If you've hoed the weeds thoroughly, by July the rows should look like long mounds about eight inches high and about 16 inches wide (full of potatoes) and the vines will be drying down. At this point, hill up a little extra soil to make sure any potatoes near the surface are thoroughly buried. (Potatoes exposed to light turn green and develop toxic amounts of solanin.) Start digging as needed for the table through the summer. From late September until mid-October, dig the remaining potatoes and put them in storage. Try to dig them before the skins become completely wetted again. Cured all summer, the skins will be unusually tough but otherwise the eating quality will be fine. Yields will be lower than in irrigated plots.

Garden planning: A 100-square-foot bed containing about 50 feet of trench yields about 100 pounds; 100 row feet of dryland potatoes yields about 100 pounds.

Insects and diseases: Flea beetles do like to chew on potato leaves and their larvae are supposed to damage the tuber's skins, though I've had no noticeable trouble in this respect. Scab is a disease that attacks the potato's skin. Scab decreases storage life, making tough, scabby patches which have to be cut away before cooking. This disease is said to be promoted by higher soil pH, and liming is supposed to be *verboten* in the potato bed. But I've never considered this warning to be significant, and have grown potatoes in well-limed beds without scab.

Harvest: Begin digging early potatoes once blossoms form, taking a plant or two as needed. When the vines begin to deteriorate, withhold further water to dry the soil and toughen the skins, enhancing storage potential. When the vines are completely dead and the soil dried out, dig the tubers. (Obviously, this idealized harvest schedule rarely works.) Keep stored potatoes dark, damp and cold but protected from freezing. I store my potatoes in buckets in the pumphouse where they last until March, when they naturally resprout, just in time for St. Pat's Day.

How to Grow It

Saving seed: Certified seed potatoes from the garden center are guaranteed free of viral diseases that reduce yields. However, if the potatoes in your garden grow all right, there's no reason to assume they have any diseases or will "catch" them. I'd sort out the smaller potatoes at harvest to use as seed next spring. Some people believe in using the largest, finest specimens for seed, thinking they'll grow the finest, largest potatoes. Usually I make my June sowing with sprouting, shriveled-up roots, but even if the sprouts are several inches long, everything works out fine.

Varieties: I'm expected to provide something better than a tasteless ball of starch. Of the commonly available varieties, our family prefers tasty Yellow Finns. Isabelle, my health-conscious wife, complains when she finds herself wanting to season her potatoes. I used to keep her happy in this respect, but after I sold Territorial Seed Company, we travelled for two years; I had no garden and lost my potato collection. Once it included several British home-garden delicacies and Belle du Fontenay, a yellow-fleshed finger potato with a creamy-rich flavor. Now that I'm resettled, I plan to resume collecting.

Isabelle doesn't like Nooksack Cascadian, a typical supermarket Idaho type bred for Whatcom County and a prolific yielder. Garden centers usually offer three varieties: a red-skinned type and a tasteless baking (Idaho) type she won't eat, and a white, thin-skinned poor keeper (usually White Rose) that she will. Any potato from the supermarket that has begun sprouting (most are treated with chemicals to prevent this) will probably yield acceptably. Eventually, the "anti-sprouting" chemical is overcome by the tuber's imperative to sprout.

Some traditional varieties are still being grown by more experienced gardeners. Ask around. You might also investigate what's available in the better health-food stores, co-op markets, farmers' markets and places like Seattle's Pike Street Market or Vancouver's Granville Island Market. If you travel to Europe, remember that the people there are more discriminating about the flavor of food, that the Europeans eat a lot more potatoes than we do, and that farmers' markets are common. We never travel without a small saucepan and an immersion coil or small Primus stove and pan set to evaluate the local produce. I can't legally suggest you break the law, and I have to warn you that it's not legal to import living plants—even a few small tubers in your purse or pocket—without first going through a complex USDA Plant Protection and Quarantine drill. If you do break the law in this respect, the living plants may be taken from you at the border if you declare them or if your person is carefully searched. You've been officially warned.

Radishes (*Raphanus sativus*)

Technically, radishes are an annual brassica, but I classify them as roots because they have a very high water requirement, need soft, humusy soil to grow properly and have little use for the high nutrient levels other brassica crops demand.

Culture: Rapid growth is the single most important aspect of producing quality radishes. The plants' shallow root systems are poorly adapted to heavy soil. Though the species stores a lot of water and can survive and go to seed in droughty soil, radishes make sweet and tender bulbs only with adequate moisture. But the lighter soils radishes prefer don't hold a lot of moisture reserves. Where most crops will not suffer when soil moisture drops to 60 percent of capacity, radishes need soil held well above 70 percent of capacity at all times; for really succulent radishes, 80 percent of capacity would be ideal. So commercial radish growers water every few days and invest in extensive irrigation systems. Another way to help light soils retain moisture, or to help heavy, moisture-retentive soils loosen up, is to incorporate goodly quantities of organic matter. Usually, manures that are not mostly sawdust and reasonably well-made composts also provide sufficient nutrients for the crop as well. Or broadcast and till in about two-thirds of a gallon of complete organic fertilizer per 100 square feet of bed and be prepared to water the radish bed every other day in hot weather.

Sow from March through August; spring radishes stay naturally moist and may prove most successful *if they escape the maggot;* summer crops may prove disappointing in very hot weather no matter how much you water. Radish seed usually germinates at high percentages. Carefully placing one seed per inch, one-half inch deep in rows 12 inches apart, is easier than thinning a lot of crowded seedlings later. *Radishes will not bulb when crowded.* By the time the seedlings are developing a true leaf, they should stand one to two inches apart.

Garden planning: Bulbs are generally mature within a month of sowing and must be harvested promptly. A single sowing may be picked for 10 days at most. Radishes are a good crop to sow between rows of other crops; they'll be harvested and gone before the other species begins to need the room. I've found that spring interplantings in beds of overwintered onions tend to deter flea beetles.

Insects and diseases: Two insects make radishes hard to produce. Flea beetles seem to prefer radishes to most other chow, and chew so many holes in radish leaves that growth is slowed and root formation is retarded. But slowly grown bulbs are hot and woody. Worse, the slower they grow, the longer the bulbs remain in the soil and the more likely they are to become the prey of the root maggot. When flea beetles are thick, they should be sprayed every few days with Red Arrow or rotenone. Another approach is to choose tall-topped varieties that produce enough leaf area to tolerate some predation; commercial growers often prefer short tops, which permit closer plant spacing, higher yields and more profits. Of course, the market gardeners' arsenal includes more-potent and longer-lasting pesticides than Red Arrow.

Maggot infestations can be reduced by harvesting promptly before the fly larvae have a chance to invade, and with a number of other techniques discussed in Chapter 7, Diseases and Pests. Radish crops are a natural candidate for protection under Reemay-like spun fabrics, which handle both flea beetles and cabbage flies simultaneously. The fabrics should be carefully laid down about 10 days after sowing, after the seedlings have been carefully thinned and weeded.

Harvest: Promptly! Even if effectively protected from root maggots, the small varieties popular with North Americans rapidly become pithy, split or get hot when allowed to grow too large. There are two other edible parts of the radish most people are not familiar with. The tops make acceptable stir-fry or soup greens, especially in spring after one of those rare Arctic winters have wrecked the entire winter garden. The seed pods that form after bolting are tender, with a mild, radishy flavor if picked before seed formation gets too far along. The pods are excellent in salads.

Saving seed: An annual; seed production is easy. Allow early sowings to bolt and make seed! Harvest the stalks when most of the seed has dried out, thresh and clean. But seed produced this simply is best used for sprouting like alfalfa seed. Quality seed production is not so easy if you want your home-grown seed to yield a good percentage of decent bulbs. When you're picking the radishes for the table, select the most ideal roots for seed production. Choose only perfectly red, round, thin-skinned roots with single, fine, hairlike taproots and tight, small crowns. Pinch off half the (larger) leaves to reduce moisture stress and transplant the bulbs about 12 inches apart in rows about 24 inches apart. If I started with a commercial quality variety, for making seed I'd only select that one absolutely perfect bulb from a dozen acceptable ones. If I started with home-garden quality radish seed, I'd be lucky if one plant in five or six even bulbed, much less made a perfectly shaped bulb! Situate the radish seed patch in a section of the garden where water may be withheld when seeds are drying down. Radish varieties cross freely with each other;

varieties must be isolated by half a mile. Radish seed remains vigorous for up to seven years.

Varieties: Most small-bulbed varieties grow well when sown spring through summer, unless temperatures are very high during bulb formation. Champion is the best for early spring and late summer sowing, but will not bulb under long summer days. The novel multicolored Easter Egg is derived from Champion. Avoid short-top varieties unless you're prepared to spray flea beetles frequently. Marabelle, from a Dutch seed company (JSS) is absolutely the most perfectly uniform commercial variety I've ever grown—but if the flea beetles get at its small leaves, you get nothing. The Dutch company that produces Marabelle especially recommends it for greenhouse culture where space is expensive and everything can be controlled. Stokes does a big business supplying commercial radish growers—if in doubt, I'd buy taller-topped varieties from Stokes and stick to commercial varieties (these will be offered in "sized seed") and believe what the catalog says about planting seasons. I've had difficulties with white Icicles. Also avoid the larger white Oriental radishes that the Japanese call *daikon* and Koreans call *mu,* and the big winter radishes like Black Spanish. Slow to form, these inevitably are riddled with maggots unless screened or heavily dosed with pesticides.

Cucurbits

Cucurbits are annual fruiting vines. Included in the Cucurbitaceae family are cucumbers, melons, pumpkins and squashes. All are sensitive to frost and poorly adapted to cool, damp weather. Apparently the family originated from desert plants growing along stream banks or where there was subsoil moisture—many cucurbits still develop deep taproots. When exposed to high humidity, especially combined with cool weather, cucurbits fall prey to powdery mildew, a disease that covers their leaves with a whitish "dust," preventing photosynthesis and rapidly killing the plant.

In descending order of hardiness, cucurbits go: squash, cucumber, cantaloupe, watermelon. Squash will grow vigorously in the maritime Northwest, except in foggy areas directly adjacent to the windward coast, where conditions are very cool and damp all summer. Cucumbers are almost as hardy, but are more touchy about germinating and need to be sown a little later than squash if they are to avoid being stunted by seedling diseases. Fortunately, cucumbers are also very fast-maturing and will form plenty of fruit, even when sown late. Cantaloupe can be grown throughout the Willamette and along the Columbia to Longview, Washington; if mollycoddled, they can be raised at higher elevations in western Oregon such as Lorane. Watermelon will produce only scantily in the warmer parts of the Willamette most years but is fairly reliable in southern Oregon.

Getting cucurbit seed to sprout outdoors requires an understanding of their family—and a little persistence. Cucurbit seedlings are even more sensitive than adult vines to powdery mildew when exposed to damp, cool conditions. They are especially vulnerable while germinating. Cucurbit seeds also need warmer soil than most species. Ideally, after the soil gets warm enough, the large seeds are planted deeply and *not watered after sowing.* This way, the roots find adequate moisture deep in the bed, while the sprout comes up through relatively dry soil and the new leaves don't succumb to mildew before they even open to the sun. So the gardener must hope it won't rain after sowing. Rain not only increases soil moisture, but also drops soil temperature, slowing the rate of sprouting, further weakening the seedling and making it even more vulnerable to disease. Gardeners who try to help cucurbit seed sprout by watering it frequently experience poor germination. Only sandy soils—which dry out very rapidly—may have to be watered during sprouting. But after being watered, sandy soils dry out and heat back up very rapidly.

It's a sound practice when sprouting cucurbit seed outdoors to immediately resow adjacent to the first sowing if it rains or becomes chilly before emergence. In the event both sowings sprout, the one that was rained on may have been stunted and will not grow well; it can be hoed out if the second sowing grows better. When the year is wet and unsettled, I like to sprout cucurbit seeds indoors in small pots so I can control soil moisture and temperature. (See Chapter 6, Buying and Raising Transplants.) Once sprouted, the small pots are sent out to the cold frame for only a few days while the containers fill sufficiently with roots, and then the seedlings are carefully transplanted.

All cucurbits make separate male and female flowers. Male blooms appear as a simple flower containing only stamens. The female is easily recognized because it forms at the end of a large ovary resembling a miniature fruit. As the young vine grows, its genetic program requires the formation of a certain number of leaves before flowers begin to form— often as many as 10. The first flowers to form are males, and the vine sets five or more male blooms before the first ovary is produced. I call this period of the plant's cycle "early vine growth." Once female flowers are produced and pollinated, the vine begins growing more rapidly and alternates male and female flowers throughout the rest of its life. In the cooler districts of the maritime Northwest, obtaining ripe melons and fully mature winter squashes demands the earliest possible fruit-set, or the fruit forms too late to mature properly. So early vine growth must be hastened. This is not always simply accomplished, because early vine growth is greatly retarded by the kind of cool, damp conditions we frequently have in June. In cooler areas, the gardener should seriously consider raising transplants and using black plastic mulches or cloches to create a more optimum environment.

Cucurbits make vegetative growth as long as weather conditions permit; fruit is ripened concurrently. So the vines have a continuous need for fertilization. The sprawling vines are hard to side-dress, so are best fertilized by tilling slow-release organic fertilizers into the bed before planting.

Pollination is done by bees and other insects. If seed is to be produced on a large scale, intercrossable varieties must be separated by a mile or more. Since most of the squashes, all cucumbers and some of the melons will cross with each other, gardeners who want to produce their own seed could be limited to only one variety in each type. Fortunately, it is easy to hand-pollinate cucurbits. Early in the morning before the bees become active, remove a freshly opened male flower from one plant, locate a newly opened female bloom on another plant, insert the male stamen into the female flower and brush it against the pollen receptors in the time-honored manner used by many of Earth's species. This effects pollination. Then, to prevent further unintentional pollination, the female bloom must be protected from insects for a few days. Squash, with their huge blossoms, are simple to protect: shut the flower by twisting the tip and secure it with a thin string or wire twist-tie. Eventually, the squash flower will fall off naturally. The tiny blooms on cucumber and melons must be slipped inside a small paper bag, with the bag tied firmly against the ovary. The bag must be removed in a few days to let the fruit develop. Mark the intentionally pollinated ovary by loosely tying a brightly colored piece of yarn or strip of cloth on the stem, and permit this individual fruit to become part of your seed supply. Be sure to do this with at least several different plants to prevent depression of vigor from inbreeding.

Cucumbers (*Cucumis sativus*)

Cucumbers are almost as intolerant of cool, damp conditions as cantaloupes, but they mature so quickly that they can be grown successfully almost anywhere in the maritime Northwest. Patience is the key to success with this species; wait until conditions outdoors are favorable before sowing seeds. In the Willamette, summer comes "for real" after June 1 most years; cucumber seed rarely germinates well before this date, nor will transplants grow. In fact, seedlings set out before nights stay warm usually die rapidly from mildews. (Planting on dark-colored light loams that heat up faster, or starting seeds under cloches, may permit *slightly* earlier sowing and transplanting.) However, once seeds are up and growing, the vines develop rapidly. I can usually harvest cukes from late July until the end of September, when the vines break down as the weather cools and becomes wetter. That's a long enough season to become thoroughly tired of eating cukes every day.

Culture: Try a tentative first sowing of cucumber seeds about the same time tomato seedlings are set out. Broadcast and work in complete organic fertilizer on a raised bed. Every two feet down the center of the bed, pour one-half cup of additional fertilizer in a little pile and, with a shovel, work it into a few gallons of soil, making a little "hill." Push a clump of five or six seeds into the hill, 1½ inches deep. If all goes well, they'll sprout quickly. If the weather turns cool or it rains—which is what usually happens—resow immediately. Be prepared to make additional sowings in the same hills weekly until one sprouts fast and takes off. Once the seedlings are up, water the bed as needed. When the seedlings have their first true leaf and are growing rapidly, thin each hill to two plants.

Garden planning: I usually grow about 80 square feet of cucumbers. This requires about eight hills down a 20-foot-long raised bed. During August we pick a bucketful every other day. The vines will be falling apart by late September, making the bed available for an overwintered green manure.

Insects and diseases: Other than powdery mildews, I've had no troubles. The vines will succumb to mildew as soon as summer weather begins to fall apart. Though some varieties are "resistant," all this means is that they'll grow a few days longer under bad conditions before breaking down.

Harvest: If seeds are allowed to develop, fruit-set slows; if enough fruits on a plant are forming mature seed, additional fruit-set stops until that seed is mature. Keeping the vines picked makes them more productive. Large cukes make good chicken food or compost; they're not prime table fare.

Saving seed: Cucumbers do not cross with other cucurbits, but they do cross with all other cucumbers. Different varieties must be hand-pollinated or isolated by at least 1,000 feet for fair purity. The seeds are mature when the fruit is over-mature and has turned yellow. Remove the seeds and pulp around them and ferment them in a bowl at room temperature, stirring daily. After three to six days, the pulp will liquify. Pour it off, wash the seeds and dry completely at room temperature on a newspaper. The "Giant Armenian" or "Serpent" cucumber is actually a melon of some sort.

Varieties: The best open-pollinated types for our region are Marketmore (slicer) and SMR 58 (pickler). Unfortunately for the seed saver, any burpless variety early enough to mature here is a hybrid. Burpless types originated in the Orient, tend to mature later and are intolerant of cool weather—choose the earliest hybrid burpless varieties for success. Hybrids, both slicers and picklers, grow slightly better and yield sooner than open-pollinated varieties. Because not all varieties adapt to marginal maritime conditions, I'd buy hybrid seeds from Johnny's, Stokes or Territorial, and choose hybrid varieties that are earlier than Marketmore.

Some hybrids are gynoecious, meaning they make only female flowers; pollination is accomplished by having a small percentage of the seed in the packet produce another similar variety that does make male flowers. Since the first five or so flowers on normal varieties are male, all-female flowers means earlier harvesting. Tiny gardens growing only one or two vines of a single variety should not risk gynoecious hybrids—there may be no male flowers available and then no fruit will set. Another sort of cucumber is the "greenhouse" type; it also produces only female flowers. However, these must not be pollinated, or the fruit becomes an inedible gourd. That works in a bee-free greenhouse, not outdoors. Apple or Lemon are old home-garden varieties that make lemon-sized fruit with deep green or white flesh and a remarkably sweet, crisp texture like some exotic tropical fruit. The latest thing is the Middle Eastern cucumber—a smaller, thin-skinned, better-flavored fruit popular in Lebanon, Syria and Israel. It tends to be late and heat-loving; only a few of the earliest hybrids will produce here.

Melons (*C. melo*)

Muskmelons and cantaloupes are so poorly adapted to cool humid conditions that they won't produce outside of cloches north of Longview or on the coast. Watermelons are even dicier—they'll grow only in the hotter parts of the Willamette on the lightest, warmest soils, and in the banana belts of southern Oregon. *One must also be very selective about choosing varieties.*

Culture: Melons strongly prefer light soils that warm up quickly and encourage their delicate root systems. Heavy soils may grow the crop if amended with organic matter, but they may require black plastic mulches (as for eggplant) or cloches to attain sufficient heat by sowing time. Even on dark-colored loams, a black plastic mulch might not be a bad idea. Sugar production in melons is closely related to the amount of magnesium available; using dolomitic lime in their complete organic fertilizer is wise.

About May 25, start seedlings indoors (See Chapter 6, Buying and Raising Transplants). At more or less the same time, prepare a bed as though for cucumbers, with fertilized hills every two feet up the center of the bed. Lay a sheet of black plastic over all and anchor the edges with soil, leaving as much plastic exposed to the sun as possible. Cut out a six-inch hole over each hill to receive the seedlings. By the time seedlings are set into the bed, the plastic will have heated the soil up considerably. Transplant the seedlings about mid-June. In southern Oregon, melons may be direct-seeded like cucumbers, though a black plastic mulch might still be useful.

Garden planning: I never ripened a watermelon at Lorane, nor did the sparsely set unripe fruit ever get bigger than a grapefruit. I grew fine cantaloupes about 10 to the vine in a good summer. At Elkton, though, it's melon paradise! In this banana belt, a 100-square-foot bed of mixed melons overwhelms us with the sugary fruit for about a month. When the beds fall apart in mid-September, I scatter clover seed in them; it sprouts and takes over during autumn.

Insects and diseases: Even disease-resistant varieties *might* come down with powdery mildew during a short spell of really unsettled weather during summer, but by September, the weakening light, cooler nights and heavier dews combine to weaken all varieties. Once September weather turns rainy, the season's over—the leaves mildew, all ripening ceases and the immature fruit rots.

Harvest: Cantaloupes and muskmelons slip the vine (detach) easily when ripe. They do not ripen after harvest! They'll only ripen when the leaves put sugars into the fruit. Supermarket cantaloupes are brilliantly bred to imitate the flavor of a ripe melon when picked unripe. But they're never the equal of a real ripe cantaloupe. If left to "ripen" on the counter, supermarket stuff softens up but it cannot become sweeter or tastier. I have not been pleased by a supermarket cantaloupe since I learned what a truly ripe one tasted like. Occasionally, honeydews from the market are good. Ripe ones can be selected only by persons armed with sensitive non-smoker's noses, who don't mind making a spectacle of themselves as they poke through the pile sniffing out a rare ball of perfume. The ones that slosh when you shake them aren't ripe, only old and beginning to fall apart inside; and they don't really smell like ripe melons—more like rotting ones. But you can sniff at the stem-scars on dozens and dozens of cantaloupes without ever finding one that smells really fragrant. That's because truly ripe cantaloupe are too soft to ship and go bad too quickly. Watermelons do not improve after harvest either and must be knowledgeably thumped by the gardener to judge ripeness.

Saving seed: Generally the procedure is like that for cucumbers. Cantaloupes, which have netted skins, don't cross with such muskmelons as honeydew, which have smooth skins; neither crosses with watermelons. When the fruit is dead ripe, the seeds are mature. If I lived in California, I'd certainly know in which pollination group to assign all the exotic heat-demanding melons like Crenshaw and Santa Claus.

Varieties: A few locally well-adapted, open-pollinated cantaloupe varieties, like the famous Spear Melon, are still preserved by home gardeners, though the seed is not readily available. Try Abundant Life for what remains. One good open-pollinated variety, Iroquois, is still sold commercially (STK, TSC). Hybrids, with their increased vigor, are much more successful, outyielding open-pollinated varieties by double, but even so, only a few of the earliest hybrids do well. I'd stick to Harper Hybrid, which makes fruit of excellent quality and is as reliable as a melon can be in a region where melons can hardly grow at all. Of the honeydews, Earlidew Hybrid doesn't have quite the flavor or yield of Honey Drip when summer is on the cool side. I'd advise caution when experimenting with melon varieties. During cool summers, I've seen dozens of hybrid early cantaloupe varieties fail to ripen anything, even on dark-colored, light loam soils at the OSU Vegetable Crops Research Farm outside Corvallis.

Some watermelon varieties that will produce (as well as watermelons *can* produce) are Crimson Sweet, Sugar Baby, Sweet Meat Hybrid and Yellow Doll.

Squashes and Pumpkins (*Cucurbita* spp.)

Of all the cucurbits, squash is most tolerant of cool conditions. Almost any maritime Northwest garden can produce summer squash; however, in cooler microclimates some care is required to get winter squash fully ripe—squash develops fruit only on sunny days when the temperature is above 70°F. Though our frost-free growing season may be long, it may not include as many warm, sunny days as we'd like.

Culture: The only hard part of growing squash is getting the seed to sprout. Like other cucurbits, squash will not germinate in cold wet soil. But once they're up and growing, squash will tolerate harsh conditions that would immediately ruin the more delicate cucurbits. Where cucumber seeds need soils that remain at temperatures above 65°F and melons need soil above 70°F to sprout, squash will sprout at 60°F if only the soil is not too wet (but it does much better when soil is well above 60°F). If at all possible, "psychically" sow the seed at the beginning of a long spell of sunny weather. To avoid lowering soil temperature, don't water after sowing. And if weather conditions worsen, resow weekly until one sowing sprouts and begins growing strongly. Winter squash needs every available day to fully ripen its fruit. In cooler areas, a second sowing might fail to mature: there I would seriously consider starting winter varieties indoors, transplanting the seedlings a few days after sprouting.

For growing winter squash, prepare the beds as though for cucumbers. Winter squash are highly vigorous vining types; space their hills three feet apart down the center of the bed and be prepared to find the vines crossing the paths and getting into neighboring beds a bit. I locate my winter varieties on an edge of the garden where the vines can go harmlessly through the fence. Summer squash don't need nutrient-enriched hills; they may be sown two feet apart in two long parallel rows about 30 inches apart down a four-foot-wide raised bed. For both summer and winter varieties, sow four to six seeds per spot, 1½ inches deep; thin winter squash to two seedlings per hill, summer squash to one plant per spot.

Garden planning: Five or six summer squash plants provide most families with all they want to eat. Mine really loves summer varieties, so I grow about 20 plants on a 100-square-foot bed. Winter squash vines usually produce 50 pounds or more per hill—large-fruited varieties yield three to five squash of 10 to 15 pounds each; small-fruited varieties yield 10 to 15 squash of three to five pounds each.

Insects and diseases: Like other cucurbits, squash gets powdery mildew when the weather becomes too cool and humid to suit it. When mildew ends the ripening process on winter varieties, it's time to harvest. Squash seedlings get powdery mildew if the weather is not warm and sunny. They can become diseased even before emergence. Mildewed seedlings rarely recover to resume proper growth.

Harvest: Summer squashes are best harvested on the small side, while they still have the tenderest skins and most delicate flavor. Permitting large squashes to remain on the bush initiates seed formation and reduces set of new fruit.

Winter squashes usually need every possible day to fully ripen. Unripe squash have light-colored, flavorless meat and thin, light seeds. When fully mature the meat is usually deep orange and the seeds are fat and dense after drying down. A fully mature winter squash will also have a shriveled, brown stem that no longer transports nutrients into the fruit. Allowing winter squash to remain in the field long after powdery mildew has killed off the leaves, or very many days after the first light frost has burned back the leaf cover, only lowers storage potential. To enjoy the longest possible shelf life, sponge off the skin of winter varieties with a disinfecting bleach solution or fill the kitchen sink with it and roll the squash around in disinfectant for a few moments. This kills mold spores that may later rot the squash. Then cure the skins by drying them at room temperature for a week or so. Squashes store best at 55°F and low humidity, with air freely moving around them. I've successfully kept ours in a cool back bedroom closet and also under far less ideal conditions—under the sink in the kitchen where temperatures were warmer. Some varieties will last until late April without rotting.

Saving seed: There are four basic squash species: *C. pepo*, *C. maxima*, *C. mixta* and *C. moschata*. Each family will cross freely with other members of the same family as well as outcross with other families in most cases. Fortunately for the seed saver, *C. pepo*, the most ubiquitous group, will not cross with *C. maxima*, the other main garden group. *C. moschata* will cross with both *C. pepo* and *C. maxima*. *C. mixta* is a tropical sort primarily containing the cushaw squashes and pumpkins, not usually grown in the North.

C. pepo includes all the summer squashes, most pumpkins and certain winter squashes such as Acorn, Delicata, Vegetable Gourd (Johnny's calls this Japanese variety Sweet Dumpling), Vegetable Spaghetti and Gem (or Rolêt). *C. pepo* varieties can usually be recognized by their small seeds. These are also the fastest to mature, usually requiring about 90 warm sunny days. Gardeners in cooler areas can pretty much count on getting fat, vigorous seed from *C. pepo* types, and in fact should concentrate on these for their winter squash supply.

C. maxima varieties include the large, hard-shelled winter squash such as Sweet Meat, Buttercup, Delicious and numerous Hubbards. Their seeds are much bigger than *C. pepo* varieties, require slightly more heat to sprout and taste better—making the best edible "pumpkin seeds." I particularly like munching seeds from Sweet Meat. *C. maxima* needs about 120 warm sunny days after emergence to fully mature seed and flesh. Most summers in the Willamette Valley 120 warm sunny growing days is all we get: seed from immature fruit will be low germ and low vigor, and the flavor of the flesh will be less than ideal.

C. moschata varieties consist of butternut types. They too are longer-growing, requiring 120 to 130 days for full maturity of fruit and seed, and may need a little more heat to equal the growth of *C. pepo* or *C. maxima*. Except in southern banana belts, gardeners will have trouble getting fully ripe butternuts.

The laziest route for the seed-saving gardener rural is to choose only one type of *C. pepo* and one *C. maxima*, or to hand-pollinate selected flowers. For the first, I'd take Early Prolific Straightneck (summer squash) or Gem (summer and winter from the same short vine) for my *C. pepo* and Buttercup or one of the Japanese Kuris for my *C. maxima* variety. Isolation is very important when growing cucurbit seed; for urban gardeners who can't control what grows in neighboring gardens, hand-pollination may be the only workable system. The seed is removed from the mature fruit, washed free of pulp by rubbing it in water, and then fully dried. With dry, cool storage, the storage life of fat, well-filled seed is over seven years.

Varieties: Hybrid varieties are beginning to appear for all types of squash in all families. Hybrids, being more uniform and vigorous, are rapidly becoming dominant among summer squash varieties because that's where the big commercial activity is. Many old standard open-pollinated summer varieties are becoming disappointingly ragged, with plants producing irregular fruit. Most summer squash varieties taste much the same when cooked, though we've noticed that yellow-skinned ones tend to cook down into a thicker, starchier, richer-flavored mash than green-skinned ones. For winter squash, most varieties grow well enough; the main choice is size, the length of your growing season and your family's taste preferences. Full-sized butternuts do well only in warmer areas. Cool-area gardeners should try Ponca, which is a much earlier, smaller-fruited butternut variety. In my opinion, Delicata and Vegetable Gourd have the richest flavor of all the winter varieties with the added advantage of small size and quick *C. pepo* maturity. They're also better keepers than the popular acorn types.

Alliums

Included in this group are leeks, shallots, scallions, onions and garlic. All are frost-hardy; some, to our great good fortune, are remarkably hardy. By careful planning, we can produce a superior year-round supply of fresh, sweet, salad-quality alliums (though not necessarily bulb onions all year); the poor eastern gardener (and supermarket consumer) must depend on sacks of hot, pungent, keeping onions to get through winter and spring.

Like mustards and spinach, alliums are highly photoperiodic. Regardless of sowing date, the species or variety will bulb or bolt when daylength dictates. However, unlike mustards, alliums are biennial: many respond to decreasing days; others only bulb after experiencing winter and then increasing daylengths. In another respect, bulbing alliums are much like cauliflower, broccoli and cabbage: the size the plant has already attained when bulbing starts determines the ultimate size of the onion or garlic head. This means that bulbing varieties have to be Grown as fast as possible before vegetative growth stops. Alliums need abundant nutrients while making vegetative growth, but once bulbing starts, they have no further use for fertilizer; in fact, any further nutrients the plant needs are drawn down from the leaves, which gradually wither as the bulb matures.

Alliums have small, coarsely textured, shallow root systems, poorly adapted to clayey or droughty soils. On the light soils they prefer, careful attention must be paid to keeping soil moisture levels up (without leaching). Banding slow-release organic fertilizer or side-dressing close to the plants will provide nearly ideal nutrient supplies and provoke the fastest possible growth. Growing husky plants on clayey soil can be difficult because incorporating sufficient organic matter to lighten soil enough to suit alliums unbalances the soil's nutrient levels, to the detriment of plant growth. At Lorane, if I had any really well-ripened compost, I'd save it for the onion patch. And no matter how painstaking my efforts, I could never grow onions on clay half as large as they grow easily on light loam soils.

Getting seeds of the allium family to sprout and initially grow has discouraged many gardeners. Consequently, growing bulb onions from easy-to-plant sets has become popular, even though set-grown onions are of very poor quality compared to these started from seed. It is easiest to sow alliums in spring when weather is usually mild and the soil stays naturally moist. Allium seed sprouts well in cool, damp soil, taking up to two weeks to germinate. Because it is small and sown shallowly, the seed must be kept moist during spells of hot weather; because the shoots are weak, the soil must be kept free of crusts. Since the root systems are small, fertilizer must be banded close to the seedlings. Later sowings of scallions and overwintered bulb onions, if made on raised beds with high surface-humus contents or covered with sifted compost and watered daily during sunny weather, usually germinate well.

Alliums transplant very easily, even when the roots are completely bare. This makes it easy to avoid the hazards of direct-seeding by starting alliums in a nursery. For some species, I've found it ideal to create the allium nursery bed right in the garden: a few row feet sown in highly humusy ground near a handy sprinkler can be coaxed into life, grown until pencil-sized, then dug, shaken apart, their tops trimmed back to prevent transpiration shock and transplanted.

Some alliums have been propagated from bulbs for so long that their seed has become infertile or non-existent. Included in this group are garlics, some shallots and certain non-bulbing onions that don't set seed but create top bulblets. Allium flowers are insect-pollinated; varieties have to be isolated by at least several hundred feet for fair purity (commercial seed fields are separated by a mile or so). Allium seed is lightweight and short-lived—two to three years at best. Getting high-vigor seed with long storage potential is also dicey. High temperatures during seed formation can kill the embryo, as can molds and various diseases of the seed head. Crop failures or seed that is too weak to sell are typical setbacks in the onion seed business. But seed prices are high, making this high-risk venture a bonanza affair.

I generally avoid the common garden-book topic of companion planting, because I believe that it is better to say nothing than to say something negative. I also remember my Russian grandfather's saying: "If you like it, it's good for you." And I remember my own views about the power of consideration—if you believe in it, it works. Well, I never much believed in companion planting, though I did read about it and spent a number of years trying to observe its effects. And I did notice just one—a powerful one. Any legume interplanted with alliums, or sown in soil that was just in alliums, is somehow stunted by a substance left in the soil by the allium. But alliums are unaffected by legumes.

Garlic (*A. sativum*)
Shallots (*A. cepa ascalonicum*)

Garlic and shallots are admirably adapted to our climate and make big yields here. Our harvests can keep excellently, because these species form bulbs during midsummer when the dry weather cures their skins well. The delicious aroma of fresh drying garlic in the kitchen is a treat we anticipate each July.

Culture: For good garlic bulb formation the soil cannot be compacted. But the crop must overwinter; bulbs form underground the next summer. So amend clayey soils with plenty of compost before planting. Shallots form on the soil's surface and aren't so fussy. Break a head of garlic into separate cloves; with shallots, plant the entire clove. Sow them from September through mid-October, root-side down, three to four inches apart, one inch deep, in rows at least 18 inches apart. In rich garden soil use no fertilizer at sowing; in poor ground, close to the cloves band about two-thirds of a gallon of complete organic fertilizer per 100 row feet before planting. To harvest large bulbs or cloves, side-dress the overwintered plants when the crocuses begin to come up (in February) with three or four tablespoonfuls of blood meal per five row feet. To harvest the largest bulbs, side-dress again about April 1 with complete organic fertilizer, hoed in shallowly, close to the plants. (The root system's effective lateral spread will not exceed one foot from the plant.)

Garden planning: Remember that bulbs won't be mature until mid-summer. This is one crop very suitable to growing without irrigation: for dryland garlic, plant cloves six or eight inches apart and on the late side after late-summer rains moisten the ground, in rows spaced about three feet apart. With careful weeding and a little mulching late in April, the crop will mature on field moisture.

Insects and diseases: I've had no problems.

Harvest: Some types of garlic put up a seed stalk. When the seed is mature, so are the cloves—though the seed is almost never viable. Some varieties brown off at the top like bulb onions. One variety, locally called Italian Silverskin (or Rocambole), makes miniature bulblets on top, each of which will grow a separate garlic. I've found it optimal to remove this bulblet cluster before much development occurs, to redirect the plant's energies toward making a larger below-ground bulb. The cleanest garlic is dug before the outer skins dry out. The dirty outer layers are peeled away and the head is allowed to dry indoors in a braid, or clumps of stalks are tied together and hung. If allowed to remain in the ground too long, the bulbs split and soil enters between the cloves. Shallots usually brown off like onion tops and are ready to harvest when fully dried out. A single shallot clove yields five or six.

Saving seed: To harvest the largest cloves, plant only the largest cloves. Varieties of garlic do not cross, nor do they make viable seed. Some types of shallots do make good seed, though these are still best propagated from cloves—from seed, the cloves will be fewer in number the first year and much smaller.

Varieties: The best varieties are often not found in seed catalogs, but in ethnic specialty stores or gourmet groceries. One unusual kind is called Elephant garlic because each of its cloves is as large as a normal head of garlic. Many local gardeners grow it, and a few mail-order seed companies sell it. In June, Elephant garlic may be spotted from a distance by the huge bluish seed balls it forms five feet in the air. What gardener growing it could refuse you a clove or two to start with if you asked nicely? I think (and so do many gourmets) that Elephant garlic has poor flavor and culinary qualities; it's more like a leek than garlic.

There are many types of shallots with various flavors and skin colors. Some Authorities classify certain types as "multiplier onions" and others as "true" shallots. Other Authorities state that all these are in the same family and none are "truer" than any others. Johnny's catalog says it sells true French shallots, not multiplier onions. Two varieties are available from Thompson & Morgan. I can only state that any shallot or multiplier onion is tasty eating and almost certain to be very well adapted to our climate and to trouble-free home-garden culture.

Leeks (*A. porrum*)

This section is not only about how to grow leeks; in it, I also attempt to suggest why a maritime Northwest gardener seeking a year-round onion supply might replace storage onions—those pungent things that keep in the pantry from the end of summer until next spring (and sometimes longer)—with leeks.

To supply the kitchen part of the year, overwintered bulb onions *are* very easy to grow, even in clayey soils. They have the finest culinary qualities of any bulb onion and mature in June, rounding out all that sweet summer garden food with sweet, tender bulb onions. Unfortunately, even when they're cured to the max, I've never had any overwintered onions left past Thanksgiving. What to do from November to May?

Pungent bulb onions that keep from late summer until late spring are commonly grown in the east. They can be raised here, especially on the light soils that spring-sown bulb onions strongly prefer. But the storage onions we grow rarely store very well; our late-summer conditions are not conducive to curing bulb onions. Leeks eliminate all problems of curing and storage—they can be harvested fresh from October until April. On heavy soil where an onion would barely bulb at all, leeks grow fine. Leeks are much milder than storage onions and far better in salads, and, as any gourmet can tell you, superior for cooking. Doubt this? Check out the price of even old, over-sized leeks in the market! For all these reasons, I no longer struggle to produce storage onions, but have come to depend on easy-to-grow leeks instead.

Culture: When grown on clayey soils, leeks do better if the soil has been well amended with organic matter. Not only do they have the same limited root system vigor of the other alliums, but loose soil permits their shafts to enlarge readily. It also makes them much easier to dig. To get

Autumn leeks transplant May

Winter Leeks Sow May

really big, leeks also need a goodly amount of nutrition.

The planting date is determined by when the leeks are to be first harvested. *Autumn leeks* are sown indoors very early in spring and transplanted outside in May. They will be big by September and may become absolutely gigantic during fall. Chapter 6, Buying and Raising Transplants, explains the initial production stages for autumn leeks. *Winter leeks* are sown outdoors mid-April through May. This is an easy time to germinate allium seed outside. Though winter leeks are direct-seeded and could be grown like big scallions, for better culinary quality they are sown in a special nursery bed and transplanted a few months later.

All the following directions assume the gardener wants to grow enough winter leeks to replace several sacks of storage onions. Prepare the nursery bed by spading about an inch of well-aged compost and a pint to a quart of complete organic fertilizer into a four-foot-long section of raised bed. If you've got any, work in an additional inch of sphagnum moss. Hoe and rake the nursery bed until it is virtually clodless. In other words, make a four-foot square of four- or five-inch-deep potting soil outdoors. Sow about 10 seeds per inch, one-half inch deep, in three rows about 12 inches apart. If the sowing date is closer to the end of May than to the middle of April, cover the seed with finely sifted compost or aged manure to prevent it from drying out before sprouting. Thin the seedlings only if grossly over-crowded; try to end up with about four seedlings per inch—after all, you're raising transplants. Three short rows like this, only 12 row feet, will make enough seedlings to fill well over 100 linear feet of trench in a few months.

Whether sown for autumn or winter harvest, leek seedlings are usually transplanted into the bottom of deep trenches, because the most edible portion of the plant is the blanched stem. The deeper the seedling is buried, the longer the white part of the stalk will be. When transplanted, though, the seedlings should not be covered deeper than the first leaf joint or soil will get into the stem itself and may be there when the leek is cooked. This means the trench should be gradually filled in as the newly trans-planted seedlings grow. It also implies that tall, leggy transplants with a lot of distance between their roots and the first leaf joint are desirable. When raised in transplant trays, it's hard to get autumn leeks more than three-sixteenths of an inch in diameter or very tall before they must be transplanted. Winter leeks raised in crowded nursery beds under a fair degree of competition will be pencil-thick and quite leggy in a few months —a big advantage for raising a fancy product.

When transplanting alliums, if the ratio of leaf area to root is altered to reduce the demand for water placed on the damaged root system, the seedlings are almost sure to survive and resume growing rapidly. To prepare leeks for transplanting, dig the seedlings or pull them out of the tray and separate them by shaking the soil from the roots. Holding the seedlings in a bundle with the bases of the plants at a uniform level, cut off the top half of the leaves with sharp scissors. Then put the clipped seedlings in a small bucket, pot or plastic bag to keep the roots moist. Do not let them dry out before transplanting. For winter leeks, it's wise to wait until midsummer when the seedlings have become quite crowded and over-competition is beginning to slow their growth. At this stage, they will be the tallest they can rapidly grow and will be quite husky. It's better to transplant winter leeks during a spell of cloudy weather (if there is one in midsummer).

The steps needed to prepare the bed for transplanting sound more difficult than they actually are. Once you've done it the first time, you'll realize it's a snap. (Flat-ground long-row gardeners can easily translate the following directions into "tillerese.") First work a raised bed deeply, incorporating about a gallon of complete organic fertilizer into each 100 square feet. Starting at one end of the bed, make a deep furrow across the bed with a hoe or trenching tool, up to eight inches deep and as narrow as possible. I've got a special furrower shaped like a small plow on a wooden handle that will quickly make a narrow trench. Trenching will temporarily shift some soil into the path—that's okay.

Take a handful of transplants, kneel in the path, lean over the bed and set the leeks in the trench about two inches apart, roots on the bottom of the trench, all leeks straight up, leaning against one wall of the trench. Then, by hand, push enough soil back into the trench to cover the roots about an inch deep; stand each seedling perfectly upright by gently tugging on it; pat the soil down around the roots to hold them in place; sprinkle a side-dressing of complete organic fertilizer in the trench (about one cup per four trench feet) and then, using the loose soil deposited in the path by the trenching, carefully and gently fill in the trench. Remember, for clean leeks, do not fill the trench deeper than the first leaf joint of the seedlings. You're finished with that row. If you've done it right the leeks will be buried as deeply as possible, the trench will not be completely filled up, the leeks will be two inches apart in a straight row and the first leaf joint of the seedlings will be just above the soil filling the trench.

Move about 18 inches up the bed, make a second trench and fill it with leek seedlings. Repeat this until the entire bed has been transplanted. Then hand-water the trenches thoroughly. If the weather turns particularly hot during the next week, water every few days. Then let the bed grow.

Sound like a lot of work? It takes me about two hours to dig transplants, trench and replant about 16 four-foot rows across a four-by-25-foot raised bed. Such a bed keeps our kitchen in organic leeks all winter. I think that is easily worth two hours! What do 200 pounds of storage onions cost? Keep in mind that commercially raised onions are sprayed with assorted pesticides, frequently a chemical to wither the stalks and enhance curing, and inevitably many doses of herbicide.

In such a fertile environment, the leeks quickly resume rapid growth and as they do, the weeds will also reappear. Hoe the weeds in such a way that each time you do, a little soil is pulled down into the trench. Take care not to get soil into the leaf notches. As the leeks grow, completely fill in the trenches and then begin to hoe soil from between the rows and hill it up against the leeks. By October there will be shallow trenches between the rows of leeks and the soil will be piled several inches higher around the stems; the leeks will also be so thick you won't be able to hoe very well again. If you've dug good deep trenches to start with, the leeks will be deeply buried. When they're dug, there will be long white stalks to enjoy.

Garden planning: I rarely grow autumn leeks. The bother of raising slow-growing seedlings in trays and transplanting such delicate seedlings is not worth an allium crop that matures when I've still got a supply of overwintered bulb onions and quality fresh scallions left. Winter leeks are easy to start, transplant rapidly and effectively and come on as the sweet overwintered bulb onions run out. I usually grow at least 100 square feet of them. I try to transplant winter leeks into a bed that grew early salad greens or my last harvest of peas.

Insects and diseases: I've had no insect problems. There are winter allium diseases that cause trouble when there is inadequate air circulation. Harvesting every other row of leeks during winter gradually opens up the bed and increases air circulation. In areas with very wet or very frosty winters, overall spacing might be increased if winter diseases appear.

Harvest: As mentioned above, first dig every second or third row to ventilate the bed. Leeks will grow slowly during winter warm spells, going dormant when the weather gets really frosty or it rains for long periods. Certain very late varieties are bred to be slow-bolting; if they have not grown large enough to suit you by the end of February, consider a side-dressing of blood meal to spur additional spring growth before seed stalks emerge in April.

Saving seed: Leeks bolt in spring, sending up a seed head that does not cross with other alliums. In early spring, select vigorous plants with long shafts between the roots and the first leaf-joint that do not have bulbous bottoms (an undesirable trait); dig them and transplant to a section of the garden where the leeks will not have to be watered with the rest of the garden. The root systems on mature plants don't develop very well after transplanting, demanding a fair amount of summer irrigation; however, sprinkling the seed heads induces molds that destroy the seed. Mulching the plants is wise. Around September, the balloon-shaped flowers will show the black seeds they contain. Cut off the flowers with about a foot of stem, and dry them under cover with the seed heads laid out on sheets of newspaper to catch the shattering seed. When they're fully dry, rub the heads between your hands to thresh out the rest of the seed.

Varieties: Autumn leeks are bred to be fast-growing, tender and mild-tasting. However, they aren't extremely hardy and won't survive freezing very well. In Europe, where leeks are very popular, they're intended for commercial harvests late in summer or early in autumn; some autumn varieties are bred for market gardeners who dig their fall harvest all at once and hold it in refrigerated storage, like apples. This sort of leek is popular in North American seed catalogs because overwinter survival of leeks is not possible in the north (except west of the Cascades). Winter leeks are bred for ultimate hardiness, so they're more fibrous, tougher and a little more pungent. Johnny's sensibly sells no winter leeks. Alaska (STK) is a commercial Dutch winter variety very popular with European market gardeners; Stokes says it is hardy to sub-zero temperatures, though I doubt it would survive rock-hard frozen soil for months. Thompson & Morgan sells several winter leek varieties.

Then there are "spring" leeks. These are winter-hardy varieties intended for commercial sale not during winter, but in spring. What makes them "spring" varieties is that they're very late bolting—and have the ability to hold in the field a month or more after winter varieties have put up seedstalks and become inedible. I prefer this sort myself, and grow Durabel (TSC).

Onions and Scallions (*A. cepa*)

It is said of knowledgeable people that they "know their onions." This old saw has a lot of truth in it, for growing bulb onions is tricky. Only overwintered onions are fairly easy to raise and tolerant of less than optimum soils. Fortunately, scallions and leeks make excellent, easy-to-grow onion substitutes.

Bulb onions may be grown from seed or sets. I have always encouraged people to use seeds because set-started onions are rarely long-keeping varieties, and the percentage of bolters and doubles harvested from sets is usually high. Sets do solve one problem many gardeners find overwhelming: getting onion seed to sprout and become established. Yet I've never experienced a field germination failure when I planted onion (or scallion) seed that would sprout well in a laboratory. Sowing it in fertile raised beds and covering the seed with pure, sifted humus (if sowing after the spring sprinkles stop) ensures good germination.

I really want you to know your onions. In North America, we grow three types of bulb onions and three sorts of scallions. Each requires different handling.

Sweet Spanish onions are large, long-growing types best adapted to daylengths at latitudes slightly south of the maritime Northwest; they're grown commercially in Utah, northern New Mexico and central California. The bulbs tend to be sweet and soft, with thick tender rings and little pungency. In our latitudes, sweet Spanish starts to bulb late in August. In that season, bulbing is limited by rapidly weakening sunlight; and the humid, cool conditions of late September complicate curing. Even the earliest of the sweet Spanish varieties won't be tops-down before mid-September at 45°F latitude. If sweet Spanish bulbs don't get very large, they'll be as pungent as any storage onion, so these sorts are best started indoors and set out in the garden late in spring as sizeable seedlings. At best, they have a limited storage potential; sweet Spanish bulbs won't hold in the pantry much past New Year's.

Storage onions grow faster, bred for northern latitudes like ours. To enhance their storage potential, breeders have selected for considerable pungency; hard, tough, thin rings; and thick, strong skins. I've had early storage varieties that "topped down" by late August and went into storage in early September. Heavier-yielding late varieties can be as difficult to cure as sweet Spanish onions, though it is precisely these late varieties that especially have the potential to keep from fall until late spring—if properly cured. Storage onions may be started indoors like sweet Spanish and transplanted out if the largest bulbs are wanted; sown later in spring and grown on tighter spacing, the yield from a bed of the same size can be just about as high but the bulbs will be smaller. Direct-seeded storage onions rarely grow large enough on heavy soils to make big bulbs.

Overwintered bulb onions have been commercially raised for a long time in southern California and the most southerly parts of New Mexico and Texas. These delicious, usually flat-topped summer onions show up in the supermarket starting late May and disappear from commercial trade by August when the first storage onions begin to appear. Northern Europeans were not fortunate enough to have winter growing regions like the Rio Grande Valley, so they developed varieties hardy enough to overwinter reliably in Holland and England—and places like western Oregon and Washington. Varieties for the north are sown in late summer, overwinter and mature in June. (Those for the south are sown in October or early November and are harvested in May.) Overwintered bulb onions are the easiest to grow of all bulbing types, though care has to be taken to obtain good germination when sowing onion seed in the heat of August. Overwintered varieties are not long keepers because they're very tender, soft and extremely sweet with hardly a hint of pungency—the best possible eating. Occasionally, I've had well-cured overwintered onions keep until mid-November.

Scallions come in three distinct types. Sweet Spanish derivatives are very late-bulbing Spanish varieties that are harvested before bulbing begins. These have been bred for a thin, translucent outer skin, sweetness and tenderness (though they tend to be rather pungent); rarely do they make good bulbs. If sown in spring, they'll reach useful size by midsummer and can be harvested until October, when they "bulb" and go dormant. This sort is most useful to the commercial grower who is going to harvest the crop and be done with it. The other two groups are overwintering sorts that share a common trait—they don't bulb under the decreasing daylength of summer. This is an advantage for the gardener, because a single sowing can be picked for months and months. Lisbons are tender, sweet, nonpungent scallions that go dormant in late spring after overwintering. They may be sown any time from spring through midsummer and last until next spring. Welsh onions (*A. fistulosum*) are pungent, kind of tough and far hardier than Lisbons (hardy enough, in fact, to survive a freezing winter in the east). Welsh onions bolt in March or April. Both Lisbon and Welsh onions may multiply during a Maritime northwest winter if sown early enough to achieve a good size.

Culture: *Sow sweet Spanish onions* in early spring indoors and transplant out late April to early May (see Chapter 6, Buying and Raising Transplants). Broadcast fertilizer and till the bed. Set out transplants three or four inches apart in rows at least 18 inches apart. Band one-quarter to one-half cup complete organic fertilizer beside or below each four or five row-feet of seedlings.

Sow storage onions during April. Earliest sowings make the largest bulbs, but sown too early the seedlings may be stunted by harsh spring weather. Very early conditions may also make the careful tilling needed for proper development of the onion's puny root system impossible. May sowings produce small bulbs and should be thinned accordingly; gardeners with heavy, late-tilling soil should seriously consider raising transplants. Broadcast fertilizer and till the bed. Sow the seed one-half inch deep, three or four seeds per inch, in rows 18 inches apart. Band additional fertilizer beside or below the seeds. Thin gradually so the seedlings stand two to four inches apart; the final spacing depends on how large the bulbs will grow and can only be judged from prior experience. Yields will be larger if the bulbs are crowded, but bulb size will be smaller. I suggest that you thin to four inches the first time you try storage onions.

Sow overwintered onions in mid-August. These seedlings must be as tough and hardy as possible to survive winter. They should not grow too fast, but should reach pencil size before winter's cold checks their development. Do not plant too early! If overwintered bulb onions get too big before spring, they'll likely go to seed rather than form bulbs. So do not use much fertilizer. Gardeners will have to experiment to find the sowing date and degree of fertilization that best suits their own soil and microclimate. At Lorane, I preferred August 1; at Elkton, I've found September 1 to be best.

Do not completely thin until early spring, because there will be some losses during winter; in February when regrowth begins (usually the crocus comes up at the same time), the bed should be carefully weeded, thinned to four inches apart in the row and side-dressed with blood meal and/or complete organic fertilizer. Thinnings may be transplanted at that time into any gaps, used to establish new beds, given to grateful gardening friends to teach them the wonders of overwintered onions or replanted densely for spring scallions. Side-dress again late in March with complete organic fertilizer, shallowly hoed into the soil between the rows; should March be especially rainy and leach-out your bed, consider another scanty side-dressing in April. Bulbing begins mid-May, and once that occurs, there's little point in additional fertilization.

Sow scallions like storage onions from April through July, depending on the variety. When well established, thin to about half an inch apart in the row. Late sowings intended for overwintering should not be as heavily fertilized as spring sowings and should be spaced out a little farther to enhance air circulation, which helps avoid molds and other diseases.

Garden planning: A row-foot of well-grown onions yields a pound or two. I can rarely cure storage onions well and prefer the flavor of leeks in any case, so I grow only overwintered bulb onions. Because bulb onions cure better in dry soil, it's wise to locate their bed where irrigation may be withheld during the month that bulbs are forming. I sow a small bed of scallions in April for summer, but scallions can rarely compete for our favor with the flavor of overwintered bulb onions. I make my major scallion sowing in July for winter salads. Scallions are also delicious in winter stir-fries. If unusually heavy winter rains wreck the scallion bed, I eat leeks without complaint.

Insects and diseases: I've had no insect problems. Onion diseases can be a nuisance during harsh winters when the beds are overcrowded. If this happens, see "Leeks" for a deeper discussion.

Harvest: If bulbing types divide into two separate parts (called "doubles" by onion growers), they will not keep long before rotting. Eat these first. Onions that put up a seed stalk (bolters) will not bulb proper-ly. When the flower stalk first appears, the plant should be pulled and may be eaten as a scallion. With overwintered onions, even under the best of circumstances, a small percentage will bolt and double; sown too early, the majority may bolt. Use these to round out the spring scallion supply as they appear. Once the bulbs are well developed, the tops dry out as the nutrients they contain are translocated down into the bulb. It is helpful if the soil dries out at this time, promoting the formation of a tough, hard skin. Overwintered onions naturally cure well in mid-June's dryness. The earliest storage varieties have a better chance of avoiding late summer rains. When half the stalks have naturally fallen over, break over the remaining tops, wait a week or so, and then dig the onions and shake all soil from their roots. Lay them out in the sun to dry; cover storage varieties at night to protect them from late summer dews. If it should rain, gather them up and finish drying under cover. After the bulbs are thoroughly dry, keep them in onion sacks. If not well ventilated, they may rot, so hang the sacks to allow free air circulation. Bulb onions store best in *dry* and cool conditions.

Harvest scallions by gradually thinning out the bed, permitting the remaining onions to grow bigger. Some varieties will multiply when large, refilling the bed.

Saving seed: The general procedure is similar to that described for leeks. With overwintered onions, the primary difference between a seed crop and a bulb crop is how large the plant has become when it ex-periences a period of cold weather. Seedlings will tolerate frost and chill, and still bulb; if the plant is larger than pencil-size, it will probably bolt from the same stimuli. Commercial-quality sweet Spanish and storage onion seed increases are grown from carefully selected mature bulbs that are overwintered in storage and planted back out very early in spring to resprout, bolt and make seed the next summer. Overwintered onion bulbs are planted back out in late fall, resprout, overwinter again and make seed the next summer. In either case, for seed production I'd select only perfect bulbs with narrow necks (better keepers, usually) that were the last to sprout in the sack. (Garden-seed-quality seed-to-seed productions for northern storage and Spanish onions can be cheaply grown by overwintering these varieties in the South, where they survive the winter handily as seedlings and bolt in spring without ever making roguable bulbs.) Incidentally, the sweetest onions also tend to be the flattest ones; round bulbs tend to be the most pungent. Remember that when selecting onions for seed-making; it's also a helpful guide for selecting sweeter onions in the supermarket. Onions that double or bolt before bulbing should not be allowed to make seed; if you use their seed, soon all your onions will have the same bad traits.

Varieties: Open-pollinated sweet Spanish types are out of commercial vogue, so the selections are getting pretty ragged. The same is true of storage onions. To stand a chance of getting decent seed, buy open-pollinated onion seed only from quality companies. Hybrid varieties are almost always of good commercial quality no matter who the final retailer is. There are also hybrid sweet Spanish/storage crosses that combine the milder flavor of the Spanish onion with the earlier maturity and longer storage potential of the storage type. For all these, varieties are so numerous and change so rapidly there is little point in listing them by name. *Always choose the earliest maturities.* Red onions are pungent storage types with red skins. Pickling onions are early maturing Spanish types bred for thin, tender, translucent skins that don't require peeling, and are planted on very dense spacings so they don't grow large. Because they're used small, picklers or "pearl onions" can be direct-seeded. One warning: many commercial onions bred for peat bog soils have root systems poorly adapted to "upland" or "mineral" soils, which is what gardeners have. Stokes has the widest assortment of quality onion varieties of any catalog, but watch out for the company's "muck" varieties.

Overwintered varieties include Sweet Winter (TSC, STK) and Walla Walla Sweet (JSS). Though people around here all know Walla Walla, Sweet Winter is every bit as fine. Territorial is very interested in overwintered bulb onions and now sells several overwintered red varieties, including Stockton Early Red, that flat, super-sweet, very mild purple onion that appears late in May in the supermarkets. Avoid overwintered varieties for southern latitudes, often called Grano or Granex, found in the Park Seed Company catalog and others. They bulb too soon in spring to make big bulbs and aren't hardy enough to overwinter reliably. Incidentally, overwintered onions can also be started in early spring and transplanted out like sweet Spanish types. They'll start bulbing in June, several weeks later than if they overwintered, be tops down in July and end up somewhat smaller than if they'd overwintered but will still be quite sweet.

Scallions with Japanese names are probably Welsh onions. Johnny's sells only these. Stokes and Harris offer them too, along with sweet Spanish types and Lisbons. Welsh onions are too pungent to suit me. Lisbon onions aren't hardy enough to handle eastern winters but are sweet and mild. They come in many variations. Some bulb in summer and immediately resprout; some bulb in spring only after overwintering; all tend to multiply. I prefer strains that don't form summer bulbs. Either way, I've always had good luck with mid-July sowings for fall, winter and spring.

Miscellaneous Vegetables and Field Crops

Asparagus (*Asparagus officinalis*)

Asparagus is a perennial that, like biennial root crops, stores food reserves in its root system. Early in spring, it rapidly converts those reserves into succulent shoots that grow several inches a day. However, unlike root vegetables, asparagus demands very rich soil if its spears are to be fat, tender and abundant. Commercial production is done on very well-drained deep soils that *stay dry in winter.* On our side of the mountains, keeping an asparagus patch alive over the winter can be dicey—it's virtually impossible on heavy, slow-draining soils. In dryer microclimates *and* on deep, light loam soils, asparagus may not be too difficult. Perhaps.

Culture: Asparagus can be started from seed, but this adds two years to the time one has to wait until the first harvest. Most gardeners buy two-year-old roots from a garden center. In early spring before the asparagus roots sprout, make trenches about 12 inches wide and at least eight inches deep, four feet apart or more. Pile the soil from each trench carefully along one side. Put a couple of inches of well-aged manure or compost into the bottom of the trench. Sprinkle five pounds dolomite lime, five pounds phosphate rock (or bone meal) and a gallon of complete organic fertilizer into each 100 trench feet. Stand in the trench with a shovel or spading fork and work the organic matter and rock flours in as deeply as possible, trying to break up the soil an additional 10 inches down. Then spread the same amount of organic matter, lime and phosphate rock (no more fertilizer) over the mound of soil removed from the trench. It will blend in when the trench is filled.

Carefully spread each root back out into a circle (as it originally grew) and lay it on the soil in the trench, crown up. Plant one root per foot; cover the roots about one inch deep by pulling some soil back down into the trench. The roots sprout in March. As they emerge, gradually fill in the trench, leaving only the tip of the shoot exposed. The trench will be completely filled by May.

In fall, when the tops turn brown, cut them down and compost them, then mulch the bed with an inch of manure or compost. Every few years, add 10 pounds of lime per 100 feet of row. Every spring after the crop has been harvested, sprinkle a gallon of complete organic fertilizer over each 100 row feet of bed. Keep the bed very well-weeded and deeply irrigated in summer. The root system naturally goes down more than four feet. "Weeds" include any little asparagus plants that start from seed—if not pulled out, these will gradually crowd out the big roots and reduce the size of your spears.

Garden planning: The bed may last indefinitely if fertility is maintained, if weeds are carefully controlled, if little seedlings are weeded out and, most importantly, if drainage is good enough that the roots don't die from various soil diseases occasioned by wetness. All the hassle of establishing a bed may seem a lot of trouble, but unless heavy freezing or canning is intended, only 25 row feet of healthy bed will supply an average family.

One sure solution for shallow or slow-draining soil is to build a four-foot-high, four-foot-wide, treated (Cuprinol is the only non-phytotoxic preservative) wooden box to sit atop your native dirt, fill it with highly enriched *sandy loam* and grow your crop in that. If necessary, you can cover the box with a plastic sheet in winter to keep the rains out.

Another solution currently being tested at my house is to plant the crowns right on the soil's surface after tilling, and to gradually hill up soil over the root crowns *with imported soil* so the paths don't become water-filled canals during winter. Drainage should be better this way. I'm not yet sure how asparagus crowns will grow when covered only a few inches deep. In my mild microclimate, they're very unlikely to freeze out.

Insects and diseases: Well-drained soil will prevent most losses from moisture-related diseases.

Harvest: There should be no harvest the year that two-year-old roots are transplanted. Only a few thin shoots per crown will emerge. If these grow well and the bed survives the winter, next year there will be many more of larger size; harvest the spears for only one week, to allow the roots to feed an abundance of strong foliage and develop big food reserves. The next year the bed should be thick with spears, and these may be cut for up to three weeks or until the size of the shoots begins to decrease, at which time the bed should be allowed to develop ferns and recharge its underground food reserves. Old, really fertile beds not overcrowded with small, weak crowns can be cut for a month or longer every spring.

Saving seed: Asparagus is wind-pollinated and sexual like spinach or hemp—there are male and female plants. Female plants develop red seed balls; because they do, less energy can be directed into food storage, so females produce fewer, smaller spears. Male plants release pollen from small sacks and then, without the burden of seed-making, store more food and produce larger, more abundant spears. Seeds should be gathered when the pods are dry but before they shatter. These may be sown in fertile soil in spring, one-half inch deep, in rows 18 inches apart and thinned to about 10 inches. After two years, the roots may be dug in winter and transplanted as given above.

To establish the highest-yielding bed that won't become overcrowded with seedlings, one trick may be attempted after the bed has proved to you that it will survive the winter. Dig and remove all female crowns when their sex can be determined and replace them with new crowns, or let the surrounding males gradually spread out and take over the area. The goal is a non-seed-producing bed containing only high-yielding male plants.

Varieties: Well-drained fertile soil is more important than varietal choices. Mary Washington and California 500 are recommended by Oregon State University. When you buy crowns, there may be little choice, or no clues to variety. European seed companies have recently developed hybrid *all-male* varieties similar to all-female types of spinach. These combine highest yield with hybrid vigor. The seed is quite expensive. Thompson & Morgan carries seed for one of these hybrids.

Sweet Corn (*Zea mays*)

Corn is easy to grow if properly fertilized and will adapt to almost any soil type. However, it won't always mature. Do you recall the story about Trucker's Favorite White from Chapter 5, Seeds? Corn maturation is not controlled by how large the plant has grown, nor by daylength (though there are some photoperiod-sensitive corn varieties). The change from vegetative growth to seed-making is determined primarily by how much heat the corn registers on an internal "temperature recorder." When the plant has experienced enough heat, then and only then will it cease vegetative growth, put up a tassle and begin making seed. Plant breeders understand this phenomenon and have developed a measurement called the "heat unit" to accurately quantify the conditions leading to maturity. After the last killing frost of spring, heat units are computed by adding up the number of hours during each 24-hour period that the temperature is above 50°F, and multiplying by the number of degrees the temperature is above 50°F.

In some wholesale vegetable seed catalogs intended primarily for other companies in the seed trade, varieties of corn are not described as taking any specific number of days to maturity, but are listed according to the number of heat units (HU) they require. The earliest maturing sweet corn varieties need about 1,300 HU to ripen; later types can require over 2,200 HU. A very early variety like Earlivee is listed by Stokes at 55 days and by Johnny's at 69. What they're really saying is that at their particular trial grounds, that number of days is, on the average, how long it takes to accumulate 1,350 HU—the number Earlivee needs. A later variety like Jubilee, which takes 84 days at Stokes and 87 days at Johnny's, needs about 1,750 HU. I tentatively conclude from the information in Stokes's and Johnny's catalogs that early summer is quite a bit warmer in Ontario than in Maine.

The Willamette Valley usually receives about 2,000 HU over the entire summer, with microclimates varying by 100 HU or so. At higher elevations in Oregon (like Lorane), average accumulation might be 1,800 HU; north, around Puget Sound, there might be only 1,500 HU. Southern Oregon banana belts might receive about 2,400; Umatilla, along the Columbia River in eastern Oregon, might get 3,000. So a Umatilla garden might grow two successive crops of early corn on the same plot in one summer, while a northwestern Washington foothills gardener might be lucky to ripen any early corn at all in a cool year.

Culture: Corn is wind-pollinated; if the silks are not thoroughly pollinated, the ears do not fill. To achieve thorough pollination, corn must be planted in blocks at least four rows wide by 10 feet long. For this reason, corn does not lend itself to raised-bed culture. Rain when the pollen is flying will also reduce pollination, so avoid overhead watering when the tassles are dropping pollen. The seed does not germinate in soil much below 60°F, though it is slightly more tolerant of cold, damp conditions than bean seed is. Corn is also sensitive to frost, so it should be sown no earlier than a few days before the last anticipated frost date. In the Willamette, corn is sown about May 1; at frosty Lorane, I planted it June 1, though it would have sprouted earlier most years. Broadcast and till in one gallon of complete organic fertilizer per 100 row feet. Then make at least four adjoining deep furrows about 30 inches apart with a hoe or furrower. Sprinkle about a half-gallon of complete organic fertilizer into each 100 feet of furrow and mix it in slightly by gently running the hoe or furrower down the furrow one more time. In the same furrow, drop about four seeds per foot and cover them 1½ to 2 inches deep. To avoid lowering soil temperature, do not water after sowing if at all possible. Hope for warm weather and quick sprouting. Within a couple of weeks of germination, thin the rows so the seedlings stand eight inches apart in the row. Keep the weeds thoroughly hoed until the corn is knee-high and then stay out of the patch to avoid compacting the soil.

Garden planning: Though truly fresh sweet corn is a wonderful treat, it takes up more garden space and time than it is worth to me personally. Since I stopped growing variety trials for Territorial Seed Co., I've had none in my garden. (I continue to grow a little unirrigated open-pollinated field corn that we grind for breakfast mush.) Hybrids mature very uniformly and remain in good eating condition for 10 days at best. Simultaneously sowing three hybrid varieties that mature at 10-day intervals can create a five- to six-week harvest. The corn patch is a good spot to grow a fine stand of favas or clover when the crop's done; scatter the seed late in September and till it and the standing corn stalks in shallowly.

Insects and diseases: Earworms can be handled with Bt, sprayed when the tassles first drop pollen and again about 10 days later. This pest is rarely seen in our region.

Harvest: Each variety has slightly different indicators. The ears may be ripe when the wrappers are browning off slightly; sometimes the ears will lean out when ready for picking.

Saving seed (and growing field corn): Five hundred feet of isolation will prevent most crossing, especially if the seed crop is upwind of any other corn. The appearance and flavor of the seed is partially determined by the genes of the seed, not only of the parent plant; so if, for example, you grow mulitcolored "Indian" corn near a patch of yellow corn, every ear in the corn patch will have occasional kernels of different colors, textures and flavors.

Open-pollinated sweet corn varieties will produce *at best* half the yield obtained from much more vigorous hybrids, so only a few open-pollinated varieties survive today. To rogue open-pollinated sweet corn, shuck the ear and examine its quality when picking it; if it is highly desirable, do not knock over the plant with your foot. Seeds may then be saved from the smaller second ears on selected plants that have been allowed to remain standing.

Miscellaneous Vegetables and Field Crops

To grow field corn without irrigation, sow as early as possible. Space the stand two plants per clump, with the clumps three feet apart, in rows at least three feet apart. Keep thoroughly weeded throughout the summer.

Harvest seed corn when the shucks have browned off completely and the seed is dry and shriveled. If it has not reached that point by the time late summer rains or dews stop the drying process, harvest the ears and finish drying them under cover. *Only the earliest varieties will mature corn seed in the maritime Northwest,* except in the southern parts of our region. Save seed for planting next year from many of the best ears.

Varieties: Open-pollinated sweet corn is hardly worth growing unless you're against hybrids on principle. The few open-pollinated varieties left in existence are poorly selected, low-yielding and far from the best eating. Since corn is not well-adapted to subsistence agriculture in our region, I don't see why even a self-sufficient gardener would put much energy into preserving open-pollinated sweet corn. Johnny's has the best of what's left and is the only company I know of still developing improved open-pollinated varieties.

Jubilee, the most popular main-season hybrid in the Willamette (and the entire U.S.), will just barely mature in warmer microclimates around the Sound; it's a very unlikely variety for Whatcom County or B.C. *The* standard of premium quality, Jubilee is found in virtually every seed catalog—though the talk of the trade is that a "better," new sugar-enhanced variety called Miracle will replace it. Harris only sells proprietary sweet corn varieties developed by its own breeders, including Wonderful, which is in the same quality class as Jubilee and takes about the same number of HU. Wonderful is listed in Harris's catalog at 82 days. Except in southern Oregon or northern California, I would not attempt any variety listed in a seed catalog as taking longer than Jubilee.

In western Washington and B.C., I'd choose an earlier variety to be my main crop. But early corns can't be both as high-yielding as Jubilee and simultaneously as fine-tasting. Earlies don't have much growing time to store up massive food reserves in the stalk before making seed. When corn pollinates, it rapidly begins translocating its food reserves into the fast-developing ear. (For a demonstration of this, chew on the pith in a corn stalk before the tassle drops pollen. If you wanted to make corn syrup, you'd boil down the juice squeezed from the pith. But after the ear has filled, the pith is no longer sweet.) That's why late varieties like Jubilee can make big, full-flavored ears. Many early varieties have been bred with profit in mind—the biggest possible ears that occupy a valuable field for the shortest period of time. But there ain't no free lunch on Earth.

I prefer smaller ears that have rich flavor. I've found the sweet corn varieties in the Seneca series are generally bred for taste. Territorial and Johnny's offer varieties primarily with the gardener in mind; Stokes and Harris are largely concerned with big-dollar farmer sales and carry a mix of commercial and garden types in their catalogs—but you can't always tell which is which unless you can read between the lines, and even then a person can be fooled by a sharp catalog writer.

Variations in corn are interesting, and have the advantage of seldom being intended for the commercial trade. I like bicolor varieties; they're no more difficult to produce than yellows. White corn tends to be too late; Silver Queen, the standard of white corn quality much in the same way Jubilee is the standard of yellow sweet corn, barely matures in the Willamette. Some of the supersweets are not worth the bother; they're very late, require isolation from regular corn (or else those kernels pollinated by regular corn taste like field corn), and the very shrunken seeds germinate poorly under less-than-perfect conditions. How do you wait until the soil is really warm before sowing and then mature a very late variety in our climate? I also don't like how they taste—it's more like eating sugar than eating corn. However, "SE" (sugar-enhanced) supersweets are only a little sweeter than normal, retain a rich, corny flavor, and are as easy to grow as regular corn.

For field corn, Abundant Life has a broad gene pool of early maturing, regionally well-adapted varieties. Johnny's has some of the best selections available in terms of uniformity.

Poppies, annual (*Papaver* spp.)

Well adapted to infertile soils, these relatives of the thistle and wild lettuce overwinter to produce extremely large, deep but very tender and easily rotted taproots that break up soil. Aboveground, the lush, frilly-leaved vegetation is tender and easily hoed or tilled into raised beds. Grown as a grain crop, seed yields approach 1,500 pounds per acre from infertile, unirrigated soils. The seed is easily hand-harvested and, like sunflower seed, contains about 50 percent delicious vegetable oil easily extracted by hand-pressing. The seed can also be soaked overnight and then ground in a blender to make a natural, spicy-tasting "mayonnaise salad dressing." As an oilseed it has no equal for adaptation to a climate that invites overwintering of other staple food crops. The sunflower is much lower-yielding when grown without irrigation, difficult to protect from birds and requires painstaking shelling before oil can be extracted; species like sesame and safflower don't adjust to our lack of summer heat; rapeseed oil (canola) doesn't lend itself to hand extraction with homestead technology, and rape requires high levels of soil fertility. Cultures that depend on the poppy are generally farming soil so infertile and droughty that no other cereal crop can be produced. So poppies contend strongly for a place in the gene pool of any maritime Northwest self-sufficiency buff.

Unfortunately, growing annual poppies may attract visits from the Authorities—particularly during and shortly after the time the colorful flowers are in bloom—and possibly some legal expenses. In Europe, opium poppies are a common garden flower and seed for them can be found in English, Dutch and Danish flower seed catalogs. Rodale's *Encyclopedia of Organic Gardening* treats *P. somniferum* as an ordinary garden flower with no special comments beyond a brief outline of its growing preferences. The legality of growing annual poppies is confusing. Local police have arrested people for growing them; however, if there is no attempt being made to extract drug substances from the flowering plants, I don't see how a prosecuting attorney could make a case for manufacture of a controlled substance. Nor is it clear how to distinguish *P. somniferum* from other look-alike annual species, which do not contain morphine in their plant sap but may contain numerous other alkaloids, some with unpleasant or toxic effects.

As a green manure, the very fine seed should be broadcast on a recently tilled raised bed or among growing vegetables any time during September, at a rate of one-half to one ounce of seed per 100 square feet. Sometimes poppies will establish themselves if sown in October. A half-pint mason jar with a few dozen small holes punched in the lid makes a good seed shaker for fairly even coverage. Irrigation or the fall rains will sprout the seed. In spring, till or hoe in the vegetation any time from March through May, but before seed stalks start emerging from the bolting plants. Once seed stalks form, the plants begin to get woody and harder to till in. The vegetation is very tender and rots fast; the multitude of taproots break up soil deeply and leave a very nice seedbed. I suspect there may be some substance left in the soil by the roots that inhibits certain soil pests such as symphylans.

As an oilseed, sow early—in September if possible. Till as soon as the soil has been moistened by fall rains; sprinkle the fine seed very thinly in shallow furrows, rows 42 to 48 inches apart; do not cover seed. A little fertilizer worked into the row before sowing will make a much larger harvest but is not necessary. Thin the seedlings gradually as the plants become established and go over the winter until early March, when they should stand eight to 12 inches apart in the row. Careful thinning makes big plants with big, easy-to-harvest pods; when crowded, pods are more numerous but smaller, and plants become too leggy and have a tendency to fall over. Keep well weeded to direct all moisture reserves to the seed crop. After blooming, the pods rapidly fill with seed. When the pods are dryish, cut the stalks, bundle them up and hang upside-down in the shade to finish drying, or let them dry in the field. Snip the pods off the stalks, fill a bucket with them and pound the pods with a baseball bat or something similar until the seed separates from the crushed pods. Sieve the seed from the dried husks in a big food strainer, and then, if necessary, winnow by pouring the seed gently from bucket to bucket in a mild breeze. Discard the dried husks, as these will contain various poisonous and intoxicating substances from the sap that dried in them.

"Wild" varieties have a bad trait—little holes open around the top of the drying pod, releasing the seed and making it hard to harvest. Grain varieties have this trait bred out of them, and often have lighter-colored seed with a milder flavor. The alkaloid mix of *P. somniferum* consists primarily of morphine, with traces of codeine and numerous other very toxic substances that can cause severe hangovers. Some drug varieties were selected for their alkaloid ratios. Poppies are almost invariably self-pollinated by the time the blooms open; collections of annual poppies contain a whole range of traits and possibly several annual species; individual plants with tastier seed and tight pods may be selected and will likely breed true thenceforth. Sources for seed include Abundant Life (though being an American company, its catalog, perhaps wisely, fails to note the exact botanical species of its "annual" poppies), Thompson & Morgan and many relatively unknown European flower-seed companies.

Quinoa (*Chenopodium quinoa*)

Here's an unexcelled cereal for the maritime Northwest homesteader. Recently "discovered," quinoa is the staple cereal of Altoplano native Americans in Peru and Bolivia. Of more interest to us, quinoa is also grown in southern Chile, where the climate virtually matches our own. Strains from Chile seem best adapted.

A domesticated lamb's-quarters, quinoa is extremely drought-resistant, tolerates chilly conditions and grows like a weed at high elevations and in infertile droughty soils. The seedcoat contains a bitter, somewhat poisonous soap or saponin that prevents insect damage and bird predation, but also must be removed before we can eat the grain. Fortunately, the saponin can, with patience, be soaked out at home; commercially grown quinoa, which is beginning to appear in health-food stores, conveniently has the saponins and seedcoat mechanically removed.

Quinoa must be sown early while there remains adequate soil moisture. Well adapted to our climatic limitations, its seeds sprout in chilly soil, and its frost-hardy seedlings may tolerate night temperatures in the low 20s. One organic farmer in the dry highlands of eastern Washington's Cascade foothills grows quinoa like wheat, because when crowded and under competition, the plants don't branch, but instead concentrate the harvest into a single seed head that can be harvested with a combine like wheat. I think the gardener will do better planting in rows about four feet apart, the seed sprinkled thinly in the row and gradually thinned to about eight inches in the row. Keep quinoa well-weeded to allocate all soil moisture to the crop. With only a little fertilizer, quinoa grows fast to a magnificent six or seven feet tall, with numerous bushy side shoots; the seed heads look a little like marijuana flowers and the seeds are dry in midsummer.

The main hazard is rain. Should the drying seed be moistened, it will sprout right in the head; so if rain threatens once the seed is drying, the plants should be cut, bundled and hung to finish under cover. For the same reason, early sowing—leading to the earliest possible harvest when weather is most likely to be dry—is essential. When the heads are dry, thresh the seed by walking on the stalks, spread on a tarp. Clean by pouring the seed back and forth between two buckets in a mild breeze.

To cook quinoa, soak a pint of dry seed overnight in a half-gallon mason jar with a screen lid such as is used to sprout alfalfa, then drain and refill. Continue soaking the seed and rinsing with cold water two to four times a day. Some varieties have harder seed coats containing more saponin than others, and the hardness of your water will regulate the effectiveness of soaking. The foaming saponins may be removed in 36 hours at best; when the water stops foaming when rinsed, the seed is ready for cooking. If 72 hours of rinsing and soaking pass with no end to the foaming, bring the seed to a boil for only a moment, pour off the hot soapy water, cover again, boil rapidly again for only a moment and pour off the water a second time. Now the seed is ready to cook.

Cook soaked quinoa like millet or oats. Add enough water to just about cover the soaked grain; simmer for 20 minutes or so. The cereal is good any time of day. Nutritionally it is oil-rich, and leaves you feeling satisfyingly full for a long time, much like oats. Far less than an ounce of seed will sow 100 row feet, yielding 25 to 50 pounds of seed. Quinoa from the health-food store won't sprout, because it's scarified to remove most of the saponins and eliminate the need for long soaking. Buy seed to plant from Abundant Life or Territorial Seed Company.

Sunflowers (*Helianthus annuus*)

The seed will sprout in cool soil and seedlings are slightly frost-hardy. In the Willamette, try sowing April 1 and again April 15; get them started as early as possible to make maximum use of remaining soil moisture. Sunflowers grow like field corn. Incorporate and till in one gallon of complete organic fertilizer for each 100 row feet. In rows four feet apart, sow two seeds per foot about an inch deep. Thin gradually to four feet apart in the row, and keep well weeded. Irrigation should be unnecessary on deep open soil that permits maximum root development. When you get to know the water-holding capacity of your land, higher plant densities may prove workable. Harvest when the seeds are mature (when the birds begin to eat them); cut the seed heads with a few feet of stalk and hang the flowers in bundles under cover to finish drying. Use as a culinary seed for munching. Higher-yielding hybrid varieties are used for market fields in the midwest. Good open-pollinated varieties are available from Johnny's and Abundant Life.

Grains (Gramineae spp.)

Home gardeners can produce their own wheat (*Triticum aestivum*), oats (*Avena sativa*), barley (*Hordeum sativum*) and rye (*Secale cereale*) in the maritime Northwest. Sow six to eight seeds per foot in rows about 12 inches apart. Every four or five rows, leave a 24-inch gap for a walkway. A little complete organic fertilizer at sowing time will produce a much larger harvest. Because of weeds, I wouldn't attempt small grains until the field had been in row crops for several years. Keep weeds hoed between rows during winter and pull as many as possible by hand in spring. Do not irrigate. When the seed heads have dried enough that the seeds are getting "chewy" (raw grains are delicious at this stage), cut with a scythe or sickle, tie the stalks into bundles or "shocks" about eight inches in diameter, and stand in the field to finish drying. Do you remember seeing old pictures with self-supporting tripods of shocks drying in the field? Lay fully dry shocks on a tarp and walk on them or beat with a flail or sticks until the seed separates from the head. One thousand square feet of fertilized grainfield will produce about 50 pounds of seed. It's a ridiculous amount of work to grow your own cereals in an era when we can buy a 50-pound sack of organically grown wheat for less than $20, and the ordinary stuff costs less than $3 a bushel by the ton! But I think it is fun.

Obtain adapted seeds from a local feed/grain store, co-op or farm supply outlet. After the first year, you can save your own. It takes about one pound of seed grain to grow 50 of eating grain. Wheat and rye are ready to use, though the soft white varieties adapted to our climate don't make particularly fine breads; I don't know how to pearl barley by hand; whole oats make excellent breakfast cereal if I could only find out how to efficiently remove the hulls by hand.

Index

Index

Index

About the author

Steve Solomon grew up in the Midwest, where he grew his first garden—all radishes—at the age of nine. He moved to California and then to Oregon, where he started the Territorial Seed Company and became recognized as an expert on organic vegetable gardening. Now retired from the seed-selling business, Steve is homesteading on the Umpqua River in Oregon and growing a year-round food supply, including grains, cereals, and legumes. He teaches master gardener classes and gives lectures around the Pacific Northwest.

SPECIAL OFFER
GET GROWING!

Sasquatch Books has arranged with Territorial Seed Company of Lorane, Oregon, to provide you with a sample packet of seed for your Northwest garden.

Choose one of the three vegetables listed below; then fill out and send the form at the bottom of the page. Your sample seeds will be sent with a full catalog from Territorial Seed Co., offering dozens of vegetable varieties ideally suited for home gardens west of the Cascades.

Buttercrunch lettuce
Similar to bibb types, but with thick, juicy, sweet leaves and tight, small heads. When the weather turns hot, Buttercrunch doesn't become bitter. It stands well into fall and makes good growth when used in spring cold frames.

Santiam tomatoes
A delicious determinate variety remarkably adapted to our summer's cool nights. Developed by Dr. Baggett at OSU, Santiam produces fruit especially early because blossoms don't drop when nights fall below 50 degrees. Later, when nights warm up, the tomatoes have seed. Determinate habitat; parthenocarpic fruit; very good flavor.

Sweet Meat winter squash
Extra-hard, thick, slate-gray skin protects round, 10-15 lb. squash all winter. Its excellent keeping quality and flavor have made it a favorite west of the Cascades, though it is virtually unknown in the rest of the United States.

ORDER FORM

☐ Please send me a sample packet of:

_____
(choose one of the vegetables listed above)

Name_____

Address_____

City/State/Zip_____

☐ Please send me a complete catalog of Sasquatch Books.

Return this coupon to:

Territorial Seed Company
P.O. Box 27 • 80030 Territorial Road • Lorane, Oregon 97451 • (503) 942-9547

GARDENING BOOKS FOR THE PACIFIC NORTHWEST
from Sasquatch Books

Our gardening books are available at bookstores and selected garden centers throughout the Pacifc Northwest. If you wish to order copies by mail, fill out the order form below and return it to us with your payment.

Growing Vegetables West of the Cascades
Steve Solomon's Complete Guide to Natural Gardening
by Steve Solomon

$14.95 × quantity _____ = _____

Winter Gardening in the Maritime Northwest
Cool Season Crops for the Year-Round Gardener
by Binda Colebrook

$10.95 × quantity _____ = _____

The Year in Bloom
Gardening for All Seasons in the Pacific Northwest
by Ann Lovejoy

$11.95 × quantity _____ = _____

Three Years in Bloom
A Garden-Keeper's Journal
by Ann Lovejoy

$14.95 × quantity _____ = _____

Subtotal _____

Washington state residents add 8.1% sales tax . . . . ._____
Postage and handling—add $1.00 per book . . . . ._____

Total order = $ _____

☐ I have enclosed payment of $_____.
   (Please make check or money order payable to Sasquatch Books.)

☐ Please charge this order to my credit card.
     MasterCard #_____ Expiration date_____
     VISA #_____ Expiration date_____

Name_____
Address_____
City_____ State_____ Zip_____

Payment must accompany order.

All orders are sent fourth-class book rate. Please allow three to six weeks for delivery.

☐ Please send me a free catalog of Sasquatch Book titles.

☐ I would like to use the *Best Places* guidebooks as a fundraiser for my club or organization. Please send me a discount schedule for bulk orders.

SASQUATCH BOOKS 1931 Second Avenue, Seattle, WA 98101 (206) 441-5555